AF471030

CONFRONTING
RELIGIOUS VIOLENCE

CONFRONTING RELIGIOUS VIOLENCE

A Counternarrative

Richard A. Burridge
Jonathan Sacks
Editors

with
Megan Warner

BAYLOR UNIVERSITY PRESS

scm press

Published in 2018 by SCM Press
Editorial office
3rd Floor, Invicta House,
108–114 Golden Lane,
London EC1Y 0TG, UK
www.scmpress.co.uk

SCM Press is an imprint of Hymns Ancient & Modern Ltd
(a registered charity)

Hymns Ancient & Modern® is a registered trademark of
Hymns Ancient & Modern Ltd
13A Hellesdon Park Road, Norwich,
Norfolk NR6 5DR, UK

Published in the United States in 2018 by Baylor University Press

British Library Cataloguing in Publication data

A catalogue record for this book is available
from the British Library

978 0 334 05713 0

Printed and bound by
CPI Group (UK) Ltd

CONTENTS

Foreword   ix
HEATHER TEMPLETON DILL

Acknowledgments   xiii

Contributors   xv

Introduction   1
RICHARD A. BURRIDGE AND JONATHAN SACKS

Setting the Scene

1   The Stories We Tell   19
JONATHAN SACKS

Part I
Biblical and Classical Background

2   (Re-)Reading the New Testament
in the Light of Sibling Rivalry   39
Some Hermeneutical Implications for Today
RICHARD A. BURRIDGE

3   Open Religion and Its Enemies   59
GUY G. STROUMSA

Part II
Reflections from the Front Line

4   Radical Encounters   77
Climate Change and Religious Conflict in Africa
ELIZA GRISWOLD

5   Empathy as Policy in the Age of Hatred   93
AMINEH A. HOTI

6   Devoted Actors in an Age of Rage   103
Social Science on the ISIS Front Line and Elsewhere
SCOTT ATRAN

Part III
Moral, Philosophical, and Scientific Reflections

7   Religious Freedom and Human Flourishing   133
ROBERT P. GEORGE

8   Compassionate Reason   147
*The Most Important Cultural and Religious Capacity
for a Peaceful Future*
MARC GOPIN

9   The Superorganism Concept and Human Groups   167
Implications for Confronting Religious Violence
DAVID SLOAN WILSON

Part IV
Theological Reflections

10   Monotheism, Nationalism, Violence   185
Twenty-Five Theses
MIROSLAV VOLF

11   Countering Religious, Moral, and Political
Hate-Preaching   195
*A Culture of Mercy and Freedom
against the Barbarism of Hate*
MICHAEL WELKER

12   Between Urgency and Understanding   205
     Practical Imperatives in Theological Education
     WILLIAM STORRAR

Concluding Reflections   219
     JONATHAN SACKS

Notes   223
Bibliography   255
Index   279

FOREWORD

HEATHER TEMPLETON DILL

In 2016 the judges for the Templeton Prize selected Rabbi Lord Jonathan Sacks as the 2016 Templeton Prize Laureate. Rabbi Sacks was honored for his effective engagement with faith leaders outside of the Jewish tradition, for his pioneering leadership of the Jewish community in the British Commonwealth, and for his ability to communicate what Rabbi Sacks called the dignity of difference, a recognition that the differences between faith traditions are a source of strength and not something to be deemphasized in the search for peaceful coexistence.

Sir John Templeton created the Templeton Prize in 1972 because he worried that his friends and colleagues had come to see religion and religious belief as boring, old fashioned, and even obsolete. Sir John's concerns may have been justified. As Rabbi Sacks explains in his opening essay, the secularization thesis seemed to capture the cultural zeitgeist that prevailed during the last third of the twentieth century, even as the tenets of that thesis were beginning to unravel.

Today, there is room to question the secularization thesis, as many authors in this volume make clear. But while religion has the capacity to impact the world for good through its moral teachings and its ethical standards, religion has and continues to be a source of great conflict and division. Rabbi Sacks has pointed out on numerous occasions that religion is a source of many geopolitical problems and social tensions. But he has also said that religion must be part of the solution. This insight is another reason the judges for the Templeton Prize chose Rabbi Sacks as the 2016 Templeton Laureate.

At the root of Rabbi Sacks' work is a deep commitment to scholarship and spiritual reflection. When Rabbi Sacks delivered the Templeton Prize lecture entitled "Faith in the Future: The Promise and Perils of Religion in the 21st Century" at the 2016 meeting of the Academy of American Religion and Society of Biblical Literature, he challenged theologians and professors of religious studies to pursue academic study for the sake of breaking down barriers between religious traditions. "Every one of us knows," Rabbi Sacks said, "that every religion has hard texts, texts which if taken literally and applied directly lead to hatred and violence and terror and war." Because these so-called hard texts can be condemnatory in nature, Rabbi Sacks says they must be reconsidered and reinterpreted. "The interpretation of religious texts has suddenly become incredibly important in the twenty-first century," Rabbi Sacks argued in his lecture. "I believe the only response adequate to the challenge of violent religious extremism in the twenty-first century is to begin a long process of rereading those hard texts in the context of the twenty-first century."[1]

But rereading "hard texts" also requires spiritual reflection. In his book *The Dignity of Difference*, Rabbi Sacks writes about the significance of diversity, "the glory of the created world," as manifested in part through the great variety of religious institutions and the distinct beliefs and practices that characterize the world's great religious traditions. "If we listen carefully," he writes, "we will hear the voice of wisdom telling us something we need to know." This is not, however, a straightforward claim. "This is a large and difficult idea," says Rabbi Sacks, "and I came to understand it only after wrestling with the place of religion in the modern and postmodern world."[2]

This book builds on Rabbi Sacks' interest in examining the paradoxes and complexities that often keep us from seeing the true nature of reality, and responds to the directive he issued to the theologians, philosophers, and biblical scholars at the 2016 AAR/SBL Conference. At that lecture, Rabbi Sacks encouraged religion scholars, theologians, and biblical scholars to work on the hard texts found in the Torah, the Bible, and the Qur'an. In this present volume, Rabbi Sacks seeks new insights and calls for further reflection on the stories that define our religious commitments and our spiritual identities. The scholarship we pursue to understand and reassess religious teachings and religious narratives can sow the seeds of mutual respect and a generosity of spirit between faith traditions. Because religion isn't going away, as Rabbi Sacks has said, it must therefore be a source of reconciliation. "Inter-religious theological enquiry," an idea William Storrar discusses in his contribution to this book,[3] will play an important role.

Sir John Templeton was not a steadfast adherent to a particular faith tradition. But he valued religious commitments and religious teachings and religious scholarship undertaken in a spirit of humility. In his 2001 book *Possibilities for Over One-Hundred Fold More Spiritual Information*, Sir John wrote:

> It can be a religious virtue reverently to cherish scriptural beliefs and to study them with the utmost seriousness. But of course a reverse side of this virtue can be a vice of intolerance. Is it easy to become intolerant if we are not diligent to guard our minds actively to be humble and to remember that despite differences in religious traditions we all have profoundly limited concepts with respect to the vast divine realities? Can love and the vastness of divinity reduce our differences as we seek to understand by a variety of different ways and through many various traditions? Can diligence in humility help heal conflict between many communities holding different religious points of view?[4]

This spirit of humility is what undergirds the Humble Approach Initiative, a program of the John Templeton Foundation responsible for the symposium that gave rise to this book. This spirit of humility is what characterized Rabbi Sacks' life and work as he led the Orthodox Jewish Community in the British Commonwealth and engaged in serious-minded scholarship. And this spirit of humility is what binds the essays in this volume together. It is my hope that the reflections herein will spark further questions, inspire additional research, and lead to productive collaborations between people of different faiths, traditions, and academic disciplines.

Heather Templeton Dill
President, John Templeton Foundation

ACKNOWLEDGMENTS

We would like to acknowledge our great debt of gratitude to everyone who has made this volume possible. First, of course, we must thank the John Templeton Foundation for choosing Rabbi Lord Jonathan Sacks as the Templeton Prize Laureate for 2016, without which none of this project would have started. We are grateful to Heather Templeton Dill for her generous hosting of the prize ceremonies in London and San Antonio and for kindly contributing the foreword to this volume. Particular mention must be made of Dr. Mary Ann Meyers and the John Templeton Foundation's Humble Approach Initiative for organizing the symposium on "Redeeming the Past and Building the Future: Confronting Religious Violence with a Counter Narrative" in London, January 28–30, 2017. Dr. Meyers' hard work and careful attention to detail was evident at every point during the symposium, and throughout her support during the process of getting the participants to contribute to this volume of the collected papers.

It was a privilege to share the symposium with ten other international scholars from very different fields—theology, philosophy, religious studies, anthropology, law, conflict resolution, journalism, education, and several branches of science—who responded to the John Templeton Foundation's invitation. Having read each other's papers in advance, we learned much over the course of the three days from our discussions, debates, and conversations, especially through listening to each other's contrasting experiences. We are grateful to everyone without exception for revising their papers for publication in this volume, especially in managing to keep to a very demanding schedule for the editing and publication process.

We are also very grateful to King's College London for hosting the symposium, especially to the Principal and President, Professor Ed Byrne, for presiding over the opening reception and dinner in the historic Council Room of King's and for granting permission to use his other rooms for the private conversations of the next two days, and to the professional services staff, including the catering and security teams who ensured that everything went so smoothly. We were honored by the presence of several observers throughout the colloquium—Jonathan Hellewell from 10 Downing Street; Dr. Grahame Davies, Assistant Private Secretary to His Royal Highness The Prince of Wales; and Canon David Porter, Chief of Staff for the Archbishop of Canterbury at Lambeth Palace—and we hope that our deliberations may assist them in their important work of preserving the world from violence.

We were delighted that Dr. Carey Newman, the Director of Baylor University Press, agreed to publish this volume, and we wish to express our thanks to his staff, particularly Cade Jarrell and Madeline Wieters, for all their assistance throughout the process of editing, production, and publication.

We are indebted, as always, to our own colleagues and staff, especially Joanna Benarroch and Dan Sacker in the Office of Rabbi Sacks, and Dr. Clare Dowding, manager of the Dean's Office, King's College London, without whom neither of us would be able to do all things which we do!

Finally, we want to pay tribute to Dr. Megan Warner, who was then teaching Hebrew Bible/Old Testament in the Department of Theology and Religious Studies in King's College London, not only for attending throughout the symposium, but also for assembling the various and disparate papers from all the contributors and for editing them into this coherent whole; without her enormously hard work, it simply would never have been completed.

Rabbi Lord Jonathan Sacks

The Revd Canon Professor Richard A. Burridge

CONTRIBUTORS

Jonathan Sacks. A philosopher and a scholar of Judaism, Jonathan Sacks served as Chief Rabbi of the United Hebrew Congregations of the Commonwealth for twenty-two years. After stepping down in 2013, he was named Ingeborg and Ira Rennert Global Professor at New York University, Kressel and Efrat Family University Professor at Yeshiva University, and Professor of Law, Ethics, and the Bible at King's College London. For more than three decades, he has played a leading role in advancing dialogue between religious minorities and dominant cultures. He graduated from Gonville & Caius College, Cambridge, with first-class honors in philosophy, followed by earning a master's degree in moral philosophy at New College, Oxford. He was appointed lecturer in Jewish philosophy at Jews' College (now the London School of Jewish Studies) in 1973, and he received rabbinic ordination in 1976. Two years later, he became the rabbi of Golders Green Synagogue in London. Rabbi Sacks was awarded a Ph.D. in collective responsibility in Jewish law from King's in 1981. He was appointed to the chair in modern Jewish thought at Jews' College in 1982 and became principal of the college two years later. After serving as rabbi of Marble Arch Synagogue in London from 1983 to 1990, he was named Chief Rabbi, and inducted in 1991.

During his service as the leader of British Jewry, he promoted the renewal of this Anglo-Jewish community in the face of dwindling congregations and growing secularization across Europe. Even as he emphasized the ethical dimensions of Judaism and the need for his coreligionists to share them with the broader community, he also stressed rabbinic teachings that proclaim wisdom, righteousness, and the possibility that true relationships with God are available to all cultures and religions. Rabbi Sacks was knighted by Queen Elizabeth II in 2005 and awarded a Life Peerage in the British House of Lords in 2009. He has been awarded seventeen honorary degrees and numerous prestigious international prizes in addition to the Templeton Prize. A frequent contributor to radio, television, and the press, Rabbi Sacks is the author of some thirty books, including *The Dignity of Difference* (2002) and *The Great Partnership: God, Science, and the Search for Meaning* (2011/2012) as well as *Not in God's Name: Confronting Religious Violence* (2015), which inspired this symposium.

Scott Atran. Currently tenured as research director in anthropology at France's National Center for Scientific Research (CNRS) at the Institut Jean Nicod–École Normale Supérieure in Paris, Scott Atran investigates the character of revolutionary violence, including transnational terrorism, in the making of human history and in the present geopolitical landscape. He also holds research positions at the Gerald Ford School of Public Policy and the Department of Psychology of the University of Michigan. He is cofounder of Artis International and founding fellow of the Centre for the Resolution of Intractable Conflict at Harris Manchester College and the Department of Politics and International Relations, Oxford University. A graduate of Columbia College, he received a Ph.D. in anthropology from Columbia University in 1984. He conducted research under Margaret Mead at the American Museum of Natural History, the University of Cambridge, Hebrew University in Jerusalem, and Birzeit University on the West Bank, as well as in the Muséum national d'Histoire naturelle and the École polytechnique in Paris.

In addition to his fieldwork on terrorism, Dr. Atran conducts research related to the cognitive and emotional foundations of religious belief and practice, and on universal and culturally specific aspects of biological categorization and environmental reasoning and decision making. He has often briefed the White House, Congress, the UK Parliament, and other governments on issues related to terrorism across national boundaries, and he has been personally engaged in conflict negotiations in the Middle East. He was appointed by the United Nations Secretary General to help prepare ways to implement UN Resolution 2250 on Youth, Peace and Security, following his speech to the Security Council in April 2015. Dr. Atran has published in English and in French, including three edited volumes and nine other books, some 130 papers in academic journals, and numerous articles for the media, including the *New York Times*, the *New York Review of Books*, the *Guardian*, *Libération*, *Foreign Policy*, and *Psychology Today*. His work and life have been spotlighted in the popular and scientific press, including feature and cover stories of the *New York Times Magazine*, the *Chronicles of Higher Education*, and *Science and Nature*.

Richard A. Burridge. Richard Burridge was appointed Dean of King's College London in 1993, where he also holds a personal chair in biblical interpretation. He is responsible for ensuring that the purposes of King's religious foundation are fulfilled, overseeing the chapels, prayer rooms, and Chaplaincy team, caring for the spiritual development and welfare of all students and staff, and fostering vocations to the ministry. He graduated from University College, Oxford, with first-class honors in classics, philosophy, and ancient history before teaching classics at Sevenoaks School in Kent. He combined training for the Anglican priesthood at St. John's College, Nottingham, with doctoral research at the University of Nottingham. Dr. Burridge was ordained to Bromley Parish Church in 1985, becoming Lazenby Chaplain and lecturer in Theology and Classics at the University of Exeter two years later. He was elected a Fellow of King's College (FKC) in 2002 and Sarum Canon Theologian at Salisbury Cathedral in 2013. He has been a visiting professor at many colleges and universities across Europe, the United States, South Africa, Mexico, Russia, Hong Kong, Australia, and New Zealand. He served on the Church of England's General Synod for over twenty years and has been a trustee and chair of numerous bodies and societies.

The revision of his doctoral thesis, *What Are the Gospels? A Comparison with Graeco-Roman Biography*, has significantly influenced gospel scholarship by drawing on insights from literary theory to demonstrate that the previous consensus of the gospels as unique was false, replacing it with what a biographical perspective means for gospel interpretation. It has gone through various updated editions (1992, 1995, 2004, 2018) and it contributed to Dr. Burridge becoming the first non-Catholic to receive the Ratzinger Prize for Theology, which Pope Francis awarded him in 2013. The author of numerous papers in academic journals and volumes of collective works, three of which Dr. Burridge has (co)edited, he has also written ten other books, including *Four Gospels, One Jesus? A Symbolic Reading* (1994, 2005, and 2014) and *Imitating Jesus: An Inclusive Approach to New Testament Ethics Today* (shortlisted for the

2009 Michael Ramsey Prize), applying the experiences of churches in South Africa to an exploration of the New Testament's ethical vision of inclusion for today.

Robert P. George. McCormick Professor of Jurisprudence and founding director of the James Madison Program in American Ideals and Institutions at Princeton University, Robert P. George works at the intersection of academia, religion, and politics, arguing the conservative case in contemporary culture-war battles on a range of moral-social issues, particularly with regard to natural-law arguments. He graduated from Swarthmore College with high honors and received both a law degree and a master of theological studies degree from Harvard University. Dr. George received a D.Phil. in philosophy of law in 1986 from Oxford University, which also conferred on him the degrees of Bachelor of Civil Law and Doctor of Civil Law in 2016. Dr. George joined the Princeton faculty in 1985 and assumed the McCormick chair as a full professor in 1999. He has been a visiting professor at Harvard Law School and has given endowed honorific lectures at Harvard, Yale, the University of St. Andrews, Cornell University, and other distinguished institutions. In addition to nineteen honorary degrees, Dr. George is the recipient of numerous awards, including the Canterbury Medal of the Becket Fund for Religious Liberty and the (U.S.) Presidential Citizens Medal.

The former chairman of the U.S. Commission on International Religious Freedom, he has served as a Judicial Fellow at the Supreme Court, as a member of the UNESCO World Commission on the Ethics of Science and Technology, and on the U.S. Commission on Civil Rights, the U.S. President's Council on Bioethics, the Ethics and Public Policy Center, the American Enterprise Institute, and many other boards of directors of academic and policy institutions. He is the editor of various series for several publishers and the author of some one hundred papers published in scholarly journals; in addition, Dr. George is the editor of eleven books, and the author of eight other books, including *Making Men Moral: Civil Liberties and Public Morality* (1993 and 1995), *Conscience and Its Enemies* (2013), and (with Patrick Lee) *Conjugal Union: What Marriage Is and Why It Matters* (2014).

Marc Gopin. James H. Laue Professor and director of the Center for World Religions, Diplomacy, and Conflict Resolution at George Mason University, Marc Gopin has led interventions for resolving interreligious and intercultural disputes for three decades, particularly in Israel,

Palestine, and Syria, but also in Afghanistan, Iran, Ireland, Switzerland, and Italy. A graduate of Columbia College, he studied at the Rabbi Issac Elchanan Theological Seminary of Yeshiva University and was ordained in 1983. He earned a Ph.D. with honors in religious ethics from Brandeis University in 1992. Dr. Gopin served congregations in Berkeley, California, and Cambridge, Massachusetts, before teaching, first at the University of Massachusetts at Amherst and then at American University. He joined George Mason in 1991 as a visiting assistant professor of religion and conflict resolution; in 1999 he became an adjunct professor of international diplomacy at the Fletcher School of Law and Diplomacy at Tufts University and an associate at the Institute for Peace Building at Eastern Mennonite University. He accepted his present position in 2003.

Dr. Gopin has trained thousands of people in peacebuilding strategies, and he has engaged personally in back-channel diplomacy with religious, political, and military figures on both sides of entrenched conflicts, especially the ongoing Arab-Israeli struggles over land, political status, refugees, and rights. He is widely respected for his ability to network across enemy lines without losing essential trust. The cofounder and, from 1989 to 1999, president of Hesed International, Inc., an organization based in Boston dedicated to development and relief in villages, he was also cofounder of the American Friends of Oz Ve'Shalom, supporting the religious Zionist peace organization advocating equality for Israel's Arab minority and the political rights of Palestinians. His work has been recognized by many awards including, most recently, the 2016 Peacemaker Award of the Association of Conflict Resolution. The author of numerous articles published in the scholarly and popular press, Dr. Gopin is also the author of seven books, most recently *Healing the Heart of Conflict: Eight Crucial Steps to Making Peace with Yourself and with Others* (2016) and *Compassionate Judaism: The Life and Thought of Samuel David Luzzatto* (2017).

Eliza Griswold. An investigative journalist and poet, Eliza Griswold has written extensively about the war on terror. Having graduated from Princeton University with honors in English (and the Bain-Swiggett Poetry Prize), Ms. Griswold earned an M.A. in English at Johns Hopkins University in 1997. She has studied at Harvard University as a Nieman Fellow and, most recently, as a Berggruen Fellow. She also has been a Woodrow Wilson Center Scholar, a New America Foundation Senior Fellow, a Guggenheim Fellow, and a Rockefeller Foundation Fellow. In 2010, she won the Rome Prize in literature from the American

Academy in Rome. A Ferris Visiting Professor of Journalism at Princeton in 2014–2015, she was an adjunct professor in the writing program at Columbia University in 2016.

Beginning in 2003, she traveled between the equator and the tenth parallel, the line of latitude seven hundred miles to its north that is the geographical and ideological line where Christianity and Islam intersect and often clash. Her journey from Nigeria, the Sudan, and Somalia in Africa to Indonesia, Malaysia, and the Philippines resulted in stories for leading newspapers and magazines and the book *The Tenth Parallel: Dispatches from the Fault Line between Christianity and Islam* (2010), which was awarded the 2011 J. Anthony Lukas Book Prize. She has published three cover stories during the past several years in the *New York Times Magazine*, and her work has frequently appeared in the *New Yorker*, the *Atlantic*, the *New Republic, Harper's*, the *Nation, Vogue, Vanity Fair*, and the *Financial Times*, among other publications; she won the 2004 Robert I. Friedman Prize in Investigative Journalism. Her first book, *Wideawake Field* (2007), was a collection of her poetry, while her latest book, a translation from Pashto of a collection of traditionally secret folk poems by Afghan women entitled *I Am the Beggar of the World* (2014), won the PEN Award for Poetry in Translation. Forthcoming in 2018 is *Burden of Proof: American Energy in Amity PA*, based on her reporting on fracking in western Pennsylvania, and *Everyone Is an Immigrant: Poems*.

Amineh A. Hoti. Since 2013, Amineh Ahmed Hoti has been the founder and executive director of Markaz-e-Ilm (the Centre for Dialogue and Action, CD&A), in Islamabad, Pakistan, a small, private educational and service organization that aims at reviving a culture of tolerance and acceptance, drawing on the indigenous tradition of *adab* (social decorum and mutual regard), which fosters respect and understanding among different religions, ethnic groups, and genders. She introduced the first interdisciplinary course for undergraduate and graduate students to sow seeds of peace by turning discord into accord and enmities into friendships. Educated at the Convent of Jesus and Mary in Murree, Pakistan, she earned a baccalaureate degree at the London School of Economics and took a Ph.D. in social anthropology at Cambridge University in 2004. As a visiting scholar at Lucy Cavendish College (LCC) in 2005, she headed the Society for Dialogue and Action and cofounded the Centre for the Study of Muslim-Jewish Relations (CMJR; offering peacebuilding courses to young people of different faiths and nationalities and to women of all ages, as well as to imams, priests, and rabbis). Dr. Hoti directed CMJR from 2006 to 2010, and she was a Fellow Commoner of LCC for seven years, during which time she taught Islam to Anglican ordinands at Ridley Hall, Cambridge.

In 2015 she became a member of the Global Advisory Council of the Alliance for Peacebuilding in Washington, D.C., and she also serves on the steering committee of the International Abrahamic Forum in Heppenheim, Germany. In addition to contributing to volumes of collected works, Dr. Hoti edited *Valuing Diversity: Towards Mutual Respect and Understanding* (2006) and led a CD&A team that produced two textbooks, *Accepting Difference: Uncovering A Culture of Diversity* (2015) and *Teaching Acceptance* (2015), Pakistan's first peacebuilding manual. Her book *Sorrow and Joy among Muslim Women: The Pukhtuns of Northern Pakistan* (2006) offers sensitive insight into Pukhtun and Pakistani society in South Asia.

William Storrar. Director of the Center of Theological Inquiry (CTI) in Princeton, New Jersey, since 2005, William Storrar—who has fostered the practice of collaboration in the church, the academy, and society for more than three decades—now leads his independent institute's mission of interdisciplinary research on global concerns. His work as a practical theologian focuses on public theology (the ways in which theology can contribute to civil discourse on public issues in the public sphere) and on the interdisciplinary dialogue between theology and the sciences and humanities on questions of common concern. Educated at the University of Edinburgh, he earned a Ph.D. in practical theology in 1993. Ordained a minister in the Church of Scotland in 1984, he served for eight years as a parish minister in Glasgow and Carluke. He was appointed lecturer in practical theology at the University of Aberdeen in 1992 and senior lecturer at the University of Glasgow in 1998. He returned to Edinburgh as professor of Christian ethics and practical theology in 2000, where he also directed the university's Centre for Theology and Public Issues and initiated the Global Network for Public Theology. He has served as an extraordinary professor of the University of Stellenbosch and as a member of the selection advisory committee for the Blumberg Chair in Astrobiology at the Library of Congress, and he is an elected member of the International Academy of Practical Theology and the American Theological Society.

Dr. Storrar has chaired the editorial board of the *International Journal of Public Theology* since its launch in 2007 and serves on other editorial advisory boards, including *Neue Zeitschrift für Systematische Theologie und Religionsphilosophie*. In addition to publishing papers in scholarly journals and volumes of collected works, he has coedited four books on public theology, including *A World for All?* on global civil society (2011) and most recently *Yours the Power: Faith-Based Organizing in the USA* (2013), which examines the role of congregations and faith-based organizations in training local leaders to mobilize communities for the common good.

Guy G. Stroumsa. Martin Buber Professor of Comparative Religion Emeritus at the Hebrew University of Jerusalem and professor emeritus of the study of Abrahamic religions at Oxford University, Guy Stroumsa focuses on cultural memory to understand the dynamics of encounters between religious traditions in the Mediterranean world from the mid-first through the mid-seventh centuries, demonstrating that transformations within one Abrahamic religion impact the other communities within "the Abrahamic eco-system." He also has examined the birth of the study of religion in the modern period. Dr. Stroumsa studied at the École Normale Israélite Orientale and the Faculté de Droit et des Sciences Economiques of the University of Paris before graduating cum laude from Hebrew University. He earned an M.A. at Harvard University, did further graduate work at the École Pratique des Hautes Études, Paris, and received a Ph.D. with distinction in comparative religion from Harvard in 1978. Returning as a lecturer to Hebrew University, he served for six years as the founding director of the Center for the Study of Christianity and was the Martin Buber Professor from 1991 until 2009. He was then the first professor of the study of Abrahamic religions at Oxford and a professional fellow of Lady Margaret Hall until he retired in 2013.

Dr. Stroumsa has been a visiting professor at many institutions, including the universities of Montreal, Geneva, Madrid, Frankfurt, Pennsylvania, Princeton, Bologna, Chicago, and Berlin, the École Biblique et Archéologique Française and the Dormition Abbey in Jerusalem, the Fondazione Collegio San Carlo in Modena, Penn's Center for Judaic Studies in Washington, D.C., the Annenberg Institute in Philadelphia, and the Einstein Forum in Potsdam, Germany. His many honors include the Médaille d'Or de la Ville de Toulouse (2011) and the Chevalier dans l'Ordre du Mérite (2011). Dr. Stroumsa is a member of various advisory boards, including the Center for Hellenic Traditions at the Central European University and two book series for Brill and Oxford University Press. In addition to publishing more than 130 papers in scholarly journals, he has edited twenty-one volumes and authored fourteen books in French, English, and German, most recently *The*

Making of the Abrahamic Religions in Late Antiquity and *The Oxford Handbook of the Abrahamic Religions* (both 2015).

Miroslav Volf. Henry B. Wright Professor of Systematic Theology at the Yale Divinity School, Miroslav Volf is the founding director of the Yale Center for Faith and Culture. He is concerned with the relation of Christian theology to public life, economics, and politics, and with dialogue between different groups, especially Christians and Muslims. Born in Croatia when it was part of communist Yugoslavia, and having grown up in a small Pentecostal community in Serbia, Dr. Volf studied philosophy and Greek at the University of Zagreb and theology at Zagreb's Evangelical-Theological Seminary where he received a baccalaureate degree summa cum laude. After earning an M.A. at Fuller Theological Seminary, he received both his Ph.D. in theology and his postdoctoral *habilitation* with highest honors from the University of Tübingen in 1986 and 1994, respectively. He taught as a lecturer and then as a professor of systematic theology at the Evangelical-Theological Seminary in Croatia, until moving to Fuller in 1991, becoming full professor in 1997, before being named to the Wright chair at Yale in 1998.

Dr. Volf has been a fellow at the Center of Theological Inquiry in Princeton, and he has received a Pew Evangelical Research Fellowship and received a grant from the Lilly Endowment for Sustaining Pastoral Excellence. He has participated in the Building Bridges Seminar at Georgetown University and the Global Agenda Council on Faith and Values of the World Economic Forum, and he has delivered numerous invited lectures, including at Stockholm, Duke Divinity School, Calvin College, Harvard Divinity School, Wake Forest University, and the University of Edinburgh. In addition to authoring some one hundred papers published in academic journals or in collected volumes, he is the editor of eight books, most recently (with Justin Crisp) *Joy and Human Flourishing: Essays on Theology, Culture, and the Good Life* (2015). He has also written fourteen other books, notably *Exclusion and Embrace: A Theological Exploration of Identity, Otherness, and Reconciliation* (1996) and *Allah: A Christian Response* (2011). His *Free of Charge: Giving and Forgiving in a Culture Stripped of Grace* (2005) was chosen as the Archbishop of Canterbury's 2006 Lent Book, while his most recent book is *Flourishing: Why We Need Religion in a Globalized World* (2016).

Michael Welker. Professor Michael Welker of the Theological Faculty of the University of Heidelberg is also director of its Research Center for International and Interdisciplinary Theology. He is a systematic theologian and an ordained minister in the Evangelische Kirche der Pfalz (Protestant Church of the Palatinate). Dr. Welker utilizes biblical traditions and philosophical and sociological theories to address the interplay among religious, legal, moral, scientific, and other cultural codes shaping the postmodern world's ethos. A graduate of the University of Tübingen, he earned a doctorate in theology under Jürgen Moltmann in 1973; Dr. Welker also received a Ph.D. in philosophy from Heidelberg in 1978. He was professor of systematic theology at Tübingen (1983–1987) and then held the chair in Reformed theology at Münster (1987–1991) before returning to Heidelberg as chair of systematic theology until his retirement in 2013. He was director of Heidelberg's Internationales Wissenschaftsforum and has held research fellowships and visiting or honorary professorships at Chicago Divinity School, McMaster University, Princeton Theological Seminary, Harvard Divinity School, Cambridge University, Emory University, the Finnish Academy of Science and Letters, and Seoul Theological University. He was awarded the Karl Barth Prize by Germany's Evangelische Kirche der Union in 2015 and will deliver the 2019–2020 Gifford Lectures at the University of Edinburgh.

Formerly on the board of advisors of the John Templeton Foundation, he serves on the advisory or editorial boards of the Chinese Academic Library of Christian Thought, *Evangelische Theologie, Jahrbuch für Biblische Theologie, Journal of Law and Religion, Verkündigung und Forschung, Journal for the Study of Christian Culture, Sino-Christian Studies,* and *International Journal of Orthodox Theology.* He is the author of some 350 papers in scholarly journals and in volumes of collected works, and he has written or edited fifty books, including *God the Spirit* (1994), *Creation and Reality* (1999), *Theologische Profile: Schleiermacher—Barth—Bonhoeffer—Moltmann* (2009), *The Theology and Science Dialogue: What Can Theology Contribute?* (2012), and *God the Revealed: Christology* (2013). *Quests for Freedom: Biblical—Historical—Contemporary* and *Images of the Divine and Cultural Orientations: Jewish, Christian, and Islamic Voices* were published in 2015, while Dr. Welker's latest book, *Europa Reformata: 1517/2017,* edited with Michael Beintker and Albert de Lange, marks the five hundredth anniversary of the Protestant Reformation.

David Sloan Wilson. SUNY Distinguished Professor of Biology and Anthropology at Binghamton University, David Sloan Wilson uses evolution as a conceptual framework for studying a broad diversity of subjects—from foraging behavior to altruism to individual differences—among organisms ranging from microbes, to insects, to fish and fowl to humankind. Best known for his work on multilevel or group selection, in which the fundamental ingredients of evolution—variation, heritability, and fitness differences—can exist at all levels of the biological hierarchy from genes to ecosystems, he believes that while the Darwinian revolution is complete for the biological sciences, it is still in progress for the study of the human species. A magna cum laude graduate of the University of Rochester, Dr. Wilson earned his Ph.D. in zoology at Michigan State University in 1975. He undertook research at Harvard, the University of Washington, and the University of the Witwatersrand before joining South Africa's National Research Institute for Mathematical Sciences as a senior research officer in 1976. He taught at the University of California, Davis, and Michigan State before becoming faculty professor of biological sciences at Binghamton in 1988. He was named to his present position in 2001, and in 2007 he helped to create the Evolution Institute.

Dr. Wilson is a former Guggenheim Fellow and the recipient of the SUNY Chancellor's Award for Excellence in Scholarship and Creative Activities. A former vice president of the American Society of Naturalists and a former member of the board of advisors of the John Templeton Foundation, he manages a number of programs to expand the influence of evolutionary theory in higher education, public policy, community-based research, and religion. He has published some two hundred papers in scientific journals and is the coeditor and author of many volumes, including his first book (with Eliot Sober), *Unto Others: The Evolution and Psychology of Unselfish Behavior* (1998), as well as *Darwin's Cathedral* (2002), *Evolution for Everyone: How Darwin's Theory Can Change the Way We Think about Our Lives* (2007), *The Neighborhood Project: Using Evolution to Improve My City, One Block at a Time* (2011), and, most recently, *Does Altruism Exist? Culture, Genes, and the Welfare of Others* (2015).

INTRODUCTION

On March 2, 2016, it was announced that Lord Jonathan Sacks, who had retired as Chief Rabbi of the United Hebrew Congregations of the Commonwealth in September 2013, had been awarded the Templeton Prize for that year. The prize was instituted in 1972 by Sir John Templeton to be given annually to "a living person who has made an exceptional contribution to affirming life's spiritual dimension, whether through insight, discovery or practical works." Often quoted at Templeton Prize ceremonies are Sir John's words: "No person may even know one percent of the infinite creative spirit. To learn anything, we must first become humble and rid ourselves of the egotistical idea that we already know everything about God."

Rabbi Sacks received the Templeton Prize pyramid at a private reception hosted by His Royal Highness The Prince of Wales at Clarence House later that spring, while the prize ceremony itself was held on May 26 at Central Hall, Westminster, during which Sir John's granddaughter Heather Templeton Dill presented Rabbi Sacks with the prize itself. In connection with the award, Rabbi Sacks gave the annual Templeton Prize Lecture at the American Academy of Religion/Society of Biblical Literature Conference in San Antonio, Texas, on November 20, followed by a special lunch debate with invited scholars from the major world faiths.

1. Rabbi Sacks and King's College London

As Dean of King's College London, I was privileged to attend both the prize ceremony in London and the events in Texas. Rabbi Sacks completed his Ph.D. through the philosophy and theology departments at King's in 1981, and we are proud to have him as one of our most distinguished alumni. He was awarded the Fellowship of King's College (FKC), our highest honor, in 1993, the year I became Dean, when I had the delight of first meeting him. But he has always been very keen to be involved with our theological education, and his regular seminars as a visiting professor in Theology are a treat, which I have eagerly anticipated each year. In 2004 as part of the 175th celebrations of King's, I invited him to participate in a term's lectures for the Associateship of King's College (AKC), our original award dating back to 1831, now taken by some two thousand students every year. The topic was "Forgiveness and Reconciliation," and it also featured lectures from Archbishop Desmond Tutu FKC, who also studied at King's back in the 1960s and who was spending a term at his alma mater as another visiting professor. Suffice to say that the whole term was very exciting and a great experience to share it with these two Fellows—but I particularly remember the lectures in which Rabbi Sacks was exploring his initial ideas about sibling rivalry in the Genesis narratives of Isaac and Ishmael, Jacob and Esau, and others.

We were delighted that Rabbi Sacks, after stepping down as Chief Rabbi in September 2013, joined King's as Professor of Law, Ethics, and the Hebrew Bible—and it enabled us to continue our conversations about not just biblical ethics but especially this topic of sibling rivalry, as he began to compose the book which eventually became *Not in God's Name: Confronting Religious Violence*, later published in 2015. It was immediately apparent that this was going to become a major work in the field of religion and theology—with enormous implications for how human beings should treat each other, especially in these difficult days of international conflict and tension, not least among and between the religious traditions. It is therefore no surprise that it led to his being awarded the Templeton Prize the following year.

2. The Templeton Humble Approach Initiative Symposium

I was therefore extremely pleased when the John Templeton Foundation approached us at King's to inquire about holding a symposium as part of their Humble Approach Initiative, which seeks to bring together scientists, philosophers, and theologians to debate and learn from one another in humility. We had worked together with the Templeton Foundation on a similar symposium when Rabbi Sacks' fellow King's alumnus, Archbishop Desmond Tutu, was himself awarded the Templeton Prize a few years earlier in 2013—and it was a delight to do so again. I continue to be particularly grateful to Mary Ann Meyers, the John Templeton Foundation's senior fellow who directs the Humble Approach Initiative, for all her hard work in organizing and directing the symposium, which was held at King's College London in January 2017.

In addition to Rabbi Sacks and myself, ten other scholars from a wide variety of theological, philosophical, and scientific fields were invited to participate in a couple of days of discussion under strictly confidential guidelines to enable and facilitate frank and honest debate and even disagreement. Each of us was asked to prepare a paper arising out of our own area of research and scholarship, and these papers were circulated in advance to enable us to have the maximum time for discussion. Rabbi Sacks presided over the whole symposium, assisted by the ever-watchful eye of Dr. Meyers, as the various papers were briefly introduced leading to questions and debate. After each section, there was a roundtable discussion, chaired by different participants, and the robust conversations continued through our various meals and coffee breaks. In addition, we were honored to have several nonparticipating observers from Clarence House, Lambeth Palace, and 10 Downing Street, as well as from King's Department of Theology and Religious Studies—an indication that these conversations were intended to have a wider impact than just our own discussion.

3. The Questions and Topics under Debate

All the participants had received the same guidance in the invitation, setting out the main concern to consider how a rereading of the hallowed texts of Judaism, Christianity, and Islam might mitigate the militancy whereby group identity can lead to deadly conflict. Particular questions were posed, including: Can a reexamination of biblical stories about sibling rivalry that appear to be at the heart of the problem of "them vs. us" enmity point to a solution? Is it possible to apply scriptural reasoning (in which members of different religious traditions discuss their sacred literatures in ways that engender trust) to social issues on a large scale? Can shared acknowledgments of and connections to God as creator, sustainer, and judge of the universe, discovered through such a process, be used to resist religious persecution and foster tolerance, justice, and peace? How do such deeply theoretical issues as changing views of supersessionism and differing approaches to hermeneutics impact our search for answers? Are there practical imperatives related to theological education and public policy stemming from a commitment to using theology to combat religiously motivated violence?

From a psychological perspective, we also considered whether empathy can inspire altruism. If so, how can it best be fostered? Or is "fellow feeling," as Adam Smith argued in *The Theory of Moral Sentiments*, a limited emotion? If so, can reason succeed in overriding selfish instinct? Specifically, as we face collapsed states in parts of the Middle East and the rise of violent extremist non-state actors that have led to vast migrations of people fleeing war and seeking sanctuary, how can we facilitate the extension of care beyond the boundaries of family, tribe, ethnicity, and nation? What research questions do we need most urgently to pursue in understanding cultural adaptation for prosociality and cooperation amongst groups?

4. The Structure of This Volume

It quickly became apparent that while our papers and conversations were extremely stimulating to those of us privileged to participate, the questions and our considerations of them deserved a much wider audience than even that of our observers. Therefore we were all invited to edit and rewrite our papers at slightly greater length with the intention of publishing a collected volume—and we are extremely grateful to Carey Newman and Baylor University Press for their willingness to publish this book and for all their assistance in its production. It is a mark of how important the conversation at the symposium was that all the participants quickly agreed to undertake this extra work. I am grateful to them for all their cooperation in producing these essays over a tight timescale.

The volume begins with an expanded version of Rabbi Sacks' opening paper, which set the scene for the symposium. The rest of the book consists of four sets of reflections from the different backgrounds and perspectives represented among the scholars participating. We begin with the biblical and classical background to consider the New Testament and the rise of supersessionism and anti-Semitism in the later Roman Empire. Then we move to reflections from the front line today, examining the impact of climate change and conflict in the poorer parts of the world of the Global South below the tenth parallel, attempting to deal with xenophobia, anti-Semitism, and Islamophobia in Britain and Pakistan, and analyzing the conflicts in the Middle East, especially around Syria and ISIS. This leads into moral, philosophical, and scientific reflections, including religious freedom, neuroscience, and the implications of evolutionary theory for considering human groups as a superorganism. Finally, we turn to theological reflections about monotheism, nationalism, and violence, as well as the role of mercy laws and freedom in combating hate, before concluding with a consideration of some practical approaches to dealing with all of this in theological education.

Setting the Scene

In his introductory essay, **Rabbi Sacks** explains the story behind his book *Not in God's Name* and draws attention to the intellectual and spiritual crisis we are facing today. His basic proposition is that "we are the story we tell ourselves," that how we tell our stories explains who we are and why we do the things we do—this storytelling approach became central to the whole symposium. He then outlines four master narratives which have dominated Western civilization from the seventeenth century: the secularization thesis, the accommodation thesis, the end-of-history thesis, and the Westernization thesis. After a consideration of the problems in our understanding of time as linear—which automatically assumes human progress—he argues that Europe since the Enlightenment has been engaged in an attempt to escape from identity in order to avoid the violence that arises from our groups, "us" and "them." He discusses three substitutes for religion as a basis for identity—the nation-state, class, and race—and the rise of Western individualism, before coming back to the renewed prominence of religion in the world today, together with the much less welcome development of religiously motivated violence. There follows a brief summary of the arguments in *Not in God's Name* about the roles played by dualism, displacement, and sibling rivalry in producing violence arising out of our identity in groups. Finally, Rabbi Sacks returns to his basic point about storytelling to challenge us to find new ways of telling our stories, especially about identity and the relationships of the three Abrahamic faiths that will provide an antidote to dualism, sibling rivalry, and violence as we discover that "even one who is not in my image—whose color, culture, or creed is not mine—is still in God's image."

Part I: Biblical and Classical Background

Rabbi Sacks' book *Not in God's Name* provides a masterful rereading of various foundational stories of sibling rivalry in the Hebrew scriptures.

Therefore, it is right that our first section takes the story on from the Old Testament into the New Testament and beyond into the first few centuries as the Roman Empire became Christianized.

Richard Burridge's essay is an attempt to apply Rabbi Sacks' rereading of the Hebrew scriptures to the New Testament to consider whether an assessment of sibling rivalry might help with the thorny issue of supersessionism and whether the New Testament sets out to replace Judaism in an anti-Semitic manner. It begins with a brief survey of how Christianity is sometimes seen as a "descendant" of Judaism that turns on its parents and replaces them. This is sometimes considered to begin with the so-called conversion of the rabbinically educated Jew, Saul of Tarsus, into Saint Paul, the founder of the new Christian— and Gentile—church. Instead, Burridge proposes a rereading in which careful attention to Paul's own writings suggest that he would not have recognized this description of his experience on the Damascus road, suggesting instead that it was more like a call, reminiscent of that of the Hebrew prophets, to take the good news of God's love to the Gentiles. Paul continues to speak very positively of his Jewish heritage and identity and his concern for his fellow Jews, particularly in later, more reflective letters like Romans and Philippians. The complex and variegated nature of all the different parties in Second Temple Judaism suggests that Judaism and Christianity do not fall into a "mother-child" matrix but are rather more like siblings, particularly after the destruction of Jerusalem and the Temple in 70 CE, from which emerged the two related groups of rabbinic Judaism (centered on the synagogue) and messianic Judaism (centered on the church). While Luke's two-volume work—his gospel and Acts—does concentrate on the growing Gentile mission, both Matthew's and John's gospels are essentially very Jewish in their character and assumptions, written in the dialectic style that characterized the internal debates between Jewish groups in the first century. In fact, compared to other contemporary literature, such as the Dead Sea Scrolls, the gospels' invective can be argued to be less harsh. However, the problem comes in the following centuries when these two gospels emerge from their original setting within *internal* Jewish debate and become the sacred scriptures of a separate religion, the early Christian church. Read in the context of the later *external* conflict between Jews and Christians, they can be read as anti-Semitic and have been used to justify discrimination and persecution from the early centuries through to the Nazi Holocaust. Therefore, we need to follow Rabbi Sacks' example of a rereading in which God's choice of one sibling does not necessitate the rejection of the other.

Drawing on his work in Paris, Jerusalem, and Oxford, **Guy Stroumsa** develops this argument beyond the New Testament into the first centuries, tracing in his essay the growth of the early church leading to Constantine and the proclamation of the Edict of Thessalonica in 380 making Christian Nicene orthodoxy the Roman state religion, together with the rise of anti-Semitism and persecution of the Jewish minority. He considers Assman's comparison of the monotheistic intolerance of ancient Israel with Graeco-Roman polytheistic tolerance, and he traces the apocalyptic roots in Judaism that led to both the Essenes and the early Christians. However, unlike those at Qumran, early Christians did not remain within Jewish sectarianism for long; rather, they soon evolved a distinct identity, rejecting the Mosaic law, ethnicity, and various boundary markers of Judaism. As rabbinic Judaism also developed its talmudic culture, it preserved Jewish habits of polemical debate between opposing views, while Christianity became increasingly concerned for orthodoxy, leading to intolerance of other views. With the success of Christianity under Constantine and the waning of pagan opposition, the stage was set for the demonization of Judaism. Furthermore, social identity now came to be seen in religious terms, rather than ethnic or cultural-linguistic ones, reinforcing growing intolerance. Stroumsa then contrasts eristic and irenic approaches to love, which, together with Christian activism and conviction, led to increasing violence in the name of God. To avoid this today, modern societies need to practice *open religion*, embracing pluralism.

Part II: Reflections from the Front Line

From these considerations of the ancient world, we turn to reflections arising from experiences in the places of conflict and religious violence in today's world. Poet and journalist **Eliza Griswold** draws on her work in the Global South to demonstrate how, contrary to Western secularist assumptions, religion has become a more important form of identity than any other, including ethnicity and nation. She illustrates this both from the case of sub-Saharan Africa, especially Nigeria, and from that of the Arab Spring in the Middle East. Attention to history reveals that for most of the last fourteen centuries Christians and Muslims have lived side by side peacefully. However, recently the growing religious revivals in both Christianity and Islam have led to increasing conflict, especially over dwindling resources, such as water, grasslands, electricity, and other aspects of basic survival. This is especially the case in the fraught band between the equator and the tenth parallel some seven hundred miles to the north—the area where the dry north of Africa, traditionally Muslim, meets the more fertile south, historically Christian, as Griswold demonstrates from both Nigeria and the Central African Republic. Furthermore, this is all exacerbated by the shifting weather patterns of global warming, with the consequent effects on things like migration. Increasingly, this means that religious identity becomes key to basic survival, giving rise to what appears to be religious violence—even though the main driver in our postcolonial world is the manmade environmental crisis. To address all of this will require dialogue within, as well as between, our faith traditions.

Next, **Amineh Hoti**, from Islamabad, directs our attention to the Muslim world, especially Pakistan, and the rise of Islamophobia alongside anti-Semitism in the growing refugee crisis. In contrast to those who argue that we have entered the "Age of Empathy," Hoti argues that it is more like the "Age of Hatred" with the rise of terrorism, anti-Semitism, and increasing Islamophobia, especially within America and Europe. She therefore considers recent initiatives to develop dialogue and empathy—as distinct from sympathy—in which she has participated. Particularly significant is the 2009 UNESCO report *Investing in Cultural Diversity and Intercultural Dialogue*. She illustrates such educational initiatives with the interdisciplinary courses at the Centre for Dialogue and Action, which she helped to set up in Cambridge, and later in Pakistan itself. If such initiatives are going to succeed, they must focus on religious leaders, the media, and the youth to develop courses on coexistence to combat increasing anti-Semitism and Islamophobia.

Thirdly, **Scott Atran** reports from the front line of the so-called war on terror, especially the conflict with ISIS. He begins with a comparison of today's situation and the wave of transnational terror at the end of the nineteenth and early twentieth centuries which led to the unravelling of the European order and the start of World War I. Common elements such as globalization and displacements have led to increasing nationalism, challenging the liberal consensus. When connected to morality and virtue, violence against other groups becomes a requirement. The specter of transnational terrorism has led the U.S. government and others to expend vast sums of money, yet the fear of relatively small terrorist groups dominates Europe and the United States, not least through our own media coverage. In contrast to our assumption of rational actors, the devotion to sacred values gives these groups a much greater will to fight. Atran demonstrates this from the results of interviews and psychological experiments conducted with pro- and anti-ISIS fighters, which reveal that these values and commitments arise from a fusion of self-identity with the group. The fierce devotion of such fighters is also examined in interviews from anti-ISIS groups such as the Peshmerga, Kurds, and Sunni Arab militias. Although such fighters and groups may recognize their physical weakness relative to the might of the United States, they make up for it with "spiritual formidability." This is reinforced by the importance of social networks, as is illustrated from the pattern of the Paris-Brussels attacks in 2015–2016. From this, Atran concludes that the idea of the "Clash of Civilizations" is a woefully inadequate explanation of the current situation, while the counternarratives developed by Western governments are ineffective. In contrast, recruiters for groups like ISIS turn young people's passion and empathy into moral outrage, for which any sacrifice will be made. Only a resurgence of the social vitality of our transcendental values and cultural ideals—not material assets alone—can resist this strategy, and this is the key existential issue for our future.

Part III: Moral, Philosophical, and Scientific Reflections

From these considerations of the ancient and modern worlds, we turn to reflections from moral philosophy and science. First, the distinguished lawyer **Robert George** discusses religious freedom and human flourishing. He begins by considering whether religious freedom is best understood as a social contract—that is, "I respect and tolerate your beliefs in the hope you will similarly accept mine." However, this approach does not do justice to the human search for meaning and value. This suggests that these ultimate questions are constitutive of our humanity and therefore must be protected as a human right, free from compulsion, including the right to change one's religion or, indeed, to hold none at all. Abuses of religious freedom not only violate the core of our humanity but also cause political, economic, moral, and social harm, so we must all protect and promote religious freedom within the human family. This requires mutual understanding between different faiths, which is not the same as theological agreement. That which is fundamental to human fulfillment is termed *basic human goods*—which means that laws that honor these rights are viewed as just, while those that violate them are unjust. This is true both at the individual, personal level and at the institutional and political level. George argues that basic human goods are prior to rights, so that human life is never a mere instrumental means to an end but an intrinsic good; the right to religious freedom is similarly an irreducible human good. However, religion is more than a merely human thing—it includes a right relationship with God or the divine, since humans are intrinsically religious beings. Paradoxically, religious authorities have sometimes denied religious freedom on the grounds that "only the truth has rights"; however, it is actually people who have rights, even when these people are in error. One must recognize the possibility of the religious good being advanced outside one's own context of faith. Therefore, George draws attention to *Nostra Aetate*, the declaration of the Second Vatican Council on non-Christian religions, in which much that is good and worthy in other faiths is explicitly commended, as he illustrates with an extensive quotation. Of course, there must be limits, so that gross evil or unspeakable wrongs cannot be committed in the name of religion; however, to restrict religious freedom is so serious that it can only be contemplated through weighty considerations that are themselves grounded in central dimensions of the integral flourishing of human beings.

This is followed by **Marc Gopin**, who draws on decades of diplomatic work and conflict resolution in the Middle East to argue for *compassionate reason* as the most important cultural and religious capacity for a peaceful future in which human beings are competing for increasingly scarce resources. Compassionate reason is not just a state of mind but also a mode of ethical practice, drawing upon both contemporary science and various schools of philosophical ethics. Studies have shown that deep compassion (empathy plus intense identification with the other) is the most significant factor in reducing levels of violence. Its roots have been sought in scientific studies of neurons and within social psychology. He also examines how the main schools of philosophical ethics since the Enlightenment (Kantian deontology, consequentialist utilitarianism, and moral sense theory) enabled human beings to put compassion into universal declarations and laws of human rights. Thus compassion and reason need each other. However, what the Enlightenment and the great philosophers missed was the immense contribution of spiritual commitments and religious habits to the ethically based nonviolent life. Compassion needs to be trained through cultural habits to apply to all human beings, not just one's own group or society—a belief often presented in the Golden Rule. Therefore, today's task is to formulate shared education and habits that will move people toward the internalization of universal laws of compassionate reason. Gopin then sets out eight steps that he has used across many groups and societies, especially in the Middle East, over the last thirty years: be (meditate on peace), feel (explore emotions), understand (learn and study), hear (listen to others), see (observe what is unspoken), imagine (cultivate positive hopes and dreams), do (practice ethical deeds), and speak (find healing words). These eight steps can help people move their mental maps through religious catechisms and habits toward an enlightened practice of nonviolence. Like Hoti, Gopin argues that empathy has to develop the mental habits of compassionate reasons, which will then lead finally to peaceful practices. He concludes by relating a personal story of a visit to a mass grave in Bosnia before a final summary of the need to align the insights of science, morality, and reason with religious wisdom in order to develop the habits of compassionate reason to build a better and more peaceful world.

Concluding this section is **David Sloan Wilson**, the president of the Evolution Institute, who brings his vast experience of evolutionary theory to bear on our topic. While he recognizes that human communities were often compared to a single corporate organism, like a body, in the past, such conceptions were eclipsed by individualist approaches during the twentieth century. This corporate approach has been revived over recent decades, however, so he begins with a brief history of the idea of the superorganism in evolutionary thought. In order to explain group-level adaptations—such as individuals working together for a common good—Darwin suggested that natural selection functioned not just at an individual but also at a group level. However, this merely elevates destructive violence to the group level, so evolutionary scientists have been working with multilevel selection (MLS) theory over recent decades, leading to the concept of *major evolutionary transitions*. Human evolution is best explained in these terms, as our ancestors learned to cooperate in a group for survival and reproduction. Cultural multilevel selection also allowed mental activity, including memory and writing, to be transmitted across generations, providing a strong foundation for the concept of society as an organism. Wilson then applies this concept to understanding selfishness, altruism, and violence within and between groups. In order for evolution to develop, genes have to be expressed by being turned on or off—and this can be represented by a *heat map*. Wilson undertakes a metaphorical transfer in order to apply these theories to human beings and groups as superorganisms. One particular experiment considered the use of all the biblical books within six church congregations, three designated as conservative and three as progressive based on their stance on same-sex marriage. Treating the biblical books like genes, Wilson and his colleague drew up a heat map for the cultural genome of these churches, revealing that the progressive and conservative pastors preached more or less regularly from certain books of the Bible. Regrettably, this study also revealed how violence is built into the DNA of the sacred texts of all religions, meaning that a religious counternarrative to violence is not possible. Instead, Wilson concludes with a brief account of interspirituality as his proposed counternarrative, drawing in multilevel selection to recognize the whole earth as a superorganism which needs to come into being.

Part IV: Theological Reflections

Our final section moves through theological reflections toward practical suggestions for educational practices today. First, **Miroslav Volf**, a Croatian now teaching and researching at Yale, provides twenty-five interlocking theses on the connections between monotheism and nationalism in producing or legitimizing violence. He begins with a study of the resurgence of nationalism in many countries across the globe today, distinguishing between *inclusive nationalism*, which is rooted within universal moral commitments, and *exclusive nationalism*, which argues for the superiority of a particular tribe or race and which is most dangerous. Religion has motivated and legitimized nationalism in the past and can still play a part in different nationalisms today. Monotheism has often been thought to be responsible for nationalist violence because its exclusivist claims can lead to negation and rejection; when allied to political religion, it can become aggressive toward both internal enemies and external competitors. However, monotheism can also be against exclusive nationalism because of its universal application to all human beings without distinction, giving primacy of devotion to God above the claims of family, tribe, ethnicity, or nation. Monotheism also affirms the freedom of religion and its distinction from the cultural domain of politics. A major distortion of monotheism seeks to use God to satisfy human purposes, as illustrated by the stories of Jesus, Abraham, and Job. Instrumentalizing God can take place through prosperity religion or political religion, and in some cases these two forms can merge. Hobbes argued that religion can be employed as a tool of government, while Kant saw it as a marker of communal identity—both of which can tie religion to violence, especially when it is identified with a political project and those striving to realize it. Volf, however, argues that monotheism is not intrinsically violent, but he recognizes that most forms of monotheism have been violent, usually through becoming articulated as political religions. Monotheism is more likely to become violent when it denies the freedom of religion, or refuses to keep religion and politics separate, or becomes itself political. All these possibilities are in tension with the universal core of true monotheism's stress on God's care and love for all people. Accordingly, Volf concludes by noting that while inclusive nationalism can be a possible friend, authentic monotheism is incompatible with exclusive nationalism, which will claim its soul and turn God from "the creator and lover of all people and all creatures into a selfish and violent idol of a particular nation."

Next, theologian **Michael Welker**, from Heidelberg, reflects on the task modern Germany faced in rebuilding itself, after two devastating world wars, through a stress on justice, mercy, and freedom. These are, of course, some of the oldest human concerns, dating back to at least 2400 BCE in Sumer, when the Sumerian king had to set an example and provide mercy, compassion, and care for his people. This contributes to the development of a climate of freedom, solidarity, and harmony in Western cultures. The special protection of orphans, widows, and the poor goes back to the oldest existing law code from Ur in 2100 BCE and was codified by Hammurabi in the eighteenth century BCE. The concern to protect the weak, especially widows and orphans, also finds expression in the early scriptures of Judaism in the Mosaic and Deuteronomistic laws and in the first Christian writings of the New Testament. Although it is a mistake to assume that mercy is a natural tendency of life, since all life survives only at the cost and expense of other life, mercy is particularly essential for human family life, especially for infants and the elderly, leading to the experience of receiving and giving mercy and love at different times. This is also expressed in the biblical motivation of showing mercy because "you were strangers in the land of Egypt" (Exod 22:20 NJPS; see also Deut 23:7). It is codified in the mercy laws affecting widows, orphans, and slaves—laws that connect moral and legal striving for justice with religious orientation. The interconnection of the educational, moral, legal, political, and religious aspects becomes essential for the development of society and culture. It works against the evil spirit of hate and unfreedom that is not just animosity, bitterness, or aggression but also the neglect of others, as is made clear in the Heidelberg Catechism. Therefore, in order to be truly free we have to let go of hate and also we need to become motivated by examples of merciful caring and forgiveness in order to break the cycles of blame, hate, and violence. This requires constant moral communication and especially serious educational enterprises, not just at school but throughout society to root out expressions of hatred and neglect of the other, replacing them with habits of justice, mercy, love, and freedom.

Finally, **William Storrar** picks up Welker's concern and directs our attention to the important task of practical imperatives in theological education, drawing on his experience as the director of the Center of Theological Inquiry at Princeton. This work has led him to integrate a series of practical imperatives—hospitality, honesty, humility, and hope—within a dialogical approach to interreligious theological inquiry. He warns of an inherent tension between the moral urgency of this task and the sheer time and work needed for patient scholarly understanding of the issues and questions across different religions, especially that of violence in the name of God. Storrar then explores these imperatives in more detail, beginning with an account of a three-year project undertaken by sixteen Muslim, Jewish, and Christian scholars on whether their respective scriptures united or divided them. The scholars needed *interpretative hospitality*—the first practical imperative—to grapple with each other's scriptures through friendship across the three Abrahamic traditions. Interestingly, this led not to a diminution to a lowest common denominator but to an accentuation of the distinctiveness of each tradition. The second practical imperative, *honesty*, facilitated the ground clearing necessary before common ground could be established through fellowship. The third and fourth practical imperatives in this enterprise required both *humility* (to acknowledge the limits of one's own understanding) and *hope* for greater understanding through interdisciplinary and interreligious scholarship. Finally, these four imperatives must come together in a fifth, a *dialogue* based on dignity, integrity, and generous respect for the other. This can only happen if we imagine constantly how those others who are listening might hear and interpret what we say and consider how it will make them feel—included or excluded, threatened or welcomed. Only such a dialogue can fulfil the call of Rabbi Sacks' magisterial book and the hospitality of the John Templeton Foundation to lead us further into interdisciplinary and interreligious theological inquiry that seeks to build a counternarrative to violence in the name of God.

Concluding Reflections

The volume concludes with some reflections from **Rabbi Sacks** that develop his original comments made in the final session of the symposium, summing up our conversations. After the rich diversity of the papers, he considers the sheer complexity around violence and terror which arises from so many contrasting factors, including, sadly, religion itself, which can be both a force for peace and also part of the problem at the same time. Reflecting on the interplay of the various disciplines represented around the table and through these papers, Rabbi Sacks draws out three threads: *hope*, which is different from optimism, as seen particularly in the story of the Exodus; the compelling idea of *wisdom* across all the great faiths; and finally the importance of *education*, which links us all together as we seek to go forward into the next chapter of the human story, honoring the Divine Other and allowing God's presence to guide us toward a world at peace.

Revd Canon Professor Richard A. Burridge

It remains only for me to thank, first and foremost, the participants in the seminar, for the depth and vigor of their contributions and for the friendship that emerged so strongly during the time we were together. I am deeply grateful to the John Templeton Foundation for making the seminar possible and to the Principal and staff at King's College London for being such generous and hospitable hosts. Last, but deeply felt, is my indebtedness to the Dean of King's College, Professor Richard Burridge, together with Dr. Meg Warner, for steering the sessions and bringing this volume to fruition. I feel blessed to count them as colleagues and friends, and the book you hold is overwhelmingly the work of their hands.

Rabbi Lord Jonathan Sacks

SETTING THE SCENE

1

THE STORIES WE TELL

Jonathan Sacks

This essay, in an earlier draft, served as an introduction to the seminar that gave rise to the other essays in this volume. In it I tell the story behind my book about religiously motivated violence, *Not in God's Name*.[1] It is a story about the nature of stories, how they help us to understand ourselves in relation to the world and other people, the behaviors to which they give rise, and the potential dangers they pose. Specifically, I want to draw attention to the intellectual and spiritual crisis that occurs when the stories we have told ourselves for many generations no longer make sense, when the world we encounter is not the one we had been led to expect, when, as it were, the latest chapter in the annals of time overturns our narrative expectations. That, I argue, is happening now to the West.

The themes I touch on are large and controversial. For the sake of clarity and brevity, I have painted a picture in the broadest of brushstrokes. Almost every sentence could be challenged as an overgeneralization. Nonetheless I felt the need to sketch this larger picture to contextualize the conversation about how best to think our way through to a future more gracious than the one the twenty-first century has yielded thus far.

I begin with a simple proposition: *we are the story we tell ourselves*.[2] There is an intrinsic, perhaps necessary, link between narrative and identity. In the words of the thinker who did more than most to place this idea at the center of contemporary thought, Alasdair MacIntyre, "man is in his actions and practice, as well as in his fictions, essentially a story-telling animal."[3] We come to know who we are by discovering the story or stories of which we are a part.

Jerome Bruner has persuasively argued that narrative is central to the construction of meaning and that meaning is what makes the human condition human.[4] No computer needs to be persuaded of its purpose in life before it does what it is supposed to do. Genes need no motivational encouragement. No virus needs a coach. We do not have to enter their mindset to understand what they do and how they do it, because they do not have a mindset to enter. But humans do. We act in the present because of things that we did or that happened to us in the past and in order to realize a sought-for future. To explain even minimally what we are doing is already to tell a story. Take three people eating salad in a restaurant, one because he needs to lose weight, the second because she's a principled vegetarian, the third because of religious dietary laws. These are three outwardly similar acts, but they belong to different stories, and they have different meanings for the people involved.

Cultures are in no small measure defined by the range of stories to which they give rise or for which they make space. Some of these have a special role in shaping the self-understanding of those who inhabit them. We call such stories *master narratives*. They are about large, ongoing groups of people: the tribe, the nation, the empire, or the civilization. They hold the group together, horizontally across space, vertically across time, by giving it a shared identity handed on across the generations. Often, in the past, they were provided by religions: recorded in sacred texts, transmitted through education, and recounted ritually at specific times. It was these stories, about founders and followers and their encounters with God, that gave the great religions—the Abrahamic monotheisms in particular—their unrivaled power to bind vast numbers of people in a common purpose, dedicated to collective ideals.

One of the most striking features of modernity as it emerged in the West is that it *sought to do away with master narratives*—at least as an explanation of the human condition. Truth was no longer to be located in texts. Society was no longer to be regulated by religious rules. Other institutions could do the work once done by the church or its counterparts in other faiths. Narratives might still exist—though by now they were seen as "stories" bearing the same relationship to truth as myth did to science. Ironically, though, this entire process gave rise to metanarratives of its own. I want to examine four such narratives by which the West has sought to understand itself from the seventeenth century to today.

The first was what has become known as the *secularization thesis*, that religion would eventually vacate the public square, though it might still have a place in the private life of the human imagination.[5] The second was the *accommodation thesis*, that the forms of religion that would survive would be those that made their peace with secular society and its values.[6] Rather than shaping public culture, religion would be shaped by it. The third was the *end-of-history thesis*, that with the end of the Cold War in the late 1980s, liberal democracy and the market economy would eventually spread throughout the world, replacing national and ideological struggles ("history") with the pursuit of private happiness and individual choice.[7] The fourth was the *Westernization thesis*, that any country or culture seeking to enter the modern world would have to do so the Western way.[8]

These metanarratives worked as accounts of modernity for several centuries. History seemed to confirm the explanation they gave of the processes operating on societies as they entered a post-traditional age. Yet in recent years, each has begun to falter. None can be told with the same confidence that they commanded a half century ago. I want first to explain why this is, and then, in the second half of this paper, to explore some of the implications, especially in relation to identity, the limits of secularization, religion, narrative, and violence. What are the dangers, and what is the intellectual work we have to do if we are to avoid or limit the return of religiously motivated violence?

1. Modernity's Master Narratives

The Secularization Thesis

The first narrative, the *secularization thesis*, had its origins in the seventeenth century, after the great wars of religion that scarred the face of Europe following the Reformation. Secularization began not because people lost faith in God but because they lost faith in the ability of people of God to live peaceably together.[9] It is then that we find people beginning to search for structures of thought and practice that do not rest on potentially contentious doctrinal foundations. It is a story in four acts, each with its own century.

The seventeenth century saw the beginnings of the secularization of *knowledge* in the form of Cartesian philosophy and Newtonian science. Neither Descartes nor Newton disbelieved in God. Descartes makes him integral to his system as soon as he has established that cogito, ergo sum. Newton spent much of his time writing notes on the Bible. Yet both sought to ground knowledge in reason and observation, above the fray of religious disputes.[10]

The eighteenth century saw the beginnings of the secularization of *power*, in the American and French revolutions, in the form of either the First Amendment "separation of church and state" or an avowedly secular nation-state. The foundations for both had been laid in the seventeenth century by thinkers such as Hobbes, Locke, and Spinoza, but America and France were the first to translate them into new political structures.

The nineteenth century saw the secularization of *culture*.[11] Museums, art galleries, and concert halls became alternatives to houses of worship as shrines of the human spirit. Hegel said that reading the morning newspapers had taken the place of daily prayer. Music from Bach to Beethoven changed from an offering to the greater glory of God to an expression of the creative genius of the artist.

The twentieth century saw the secularization of *morality*. Starting in the 1960s in the West, there was a gradual abandonment of many of the elements constitutive of the "Judeo-Christian" ethic, most notably in relation to the sanctity of life and the consecration of marriage. It became progressively harder to understand what morality might mean, other than the avoidance of harm and unfairness. Beyond that the sole remaining value was autonomy. With rare exceptions—the avoidance of harm to others—morality became what we chose it to be.[12]

The dominant assumption was that secularization was linear, irreversible, and universal. Religious belief might remain but only in the private sphere. We no longer needed God to explain the universe, bind citizens into a nation, or organize the way we live our lives. And though this was true of the West, not necessarily of the rest, there was only one road to modernity—and it was the one the West had taken.

There were dissenting voices, but they were few. One was Alexis de Tocqueville, who wrote, near the beginning of *Democracy in America*, that "Eighteenth century philosophers had a very simple explanation for the gradual weakening of beliefs. Religious zeal, they said, was bound to die down as enlightenment and freedom spread. It is tiresome that the facts do not fit this theory at all."[13]

Tocqueville believed that American democracy depended not on the state but on the strong presence of religion in society. Its sphere was marriage, the family, community, and social action—what he called "the art of association" and we now call "social capital." It was the antidote to the new phenomenon that he saw as the danger of democracy. He called it "individualism."

This belief that secularization is linear, inevitable, and irreversible has turned out to be at best a simplification and at worst simply untrue. The twenty-first century is likely to be more religious than the twentieth, if only for demographic reasons.[14] For the past half century or so, as a generality, the more religious you are, the more children you have. The more secular a society, the lower its birthrates. In secular Europe, there is not a single country whose birthrate is even at replacement level. The only way Europe has maintained population levels has been by immigration on an unprecedented scale. Often the immigrants bring with them a strongly religious culture. Often, too, their children are more intensely religious than they are.

The Accommodationist Thesis

That is the first narrative that has not played out as expected: secularization. The second was that the form in which religion would survive would be, for the most part, *accommodationist*. Religion might persist, but it would generally make its peace with the values of the wider society. It would accept a larger place for autonomy and personal choice. The Ten Commandments would become the Ten Constructive Suggestions. Faith was a personal journey that might include periods of involvement with multiple experiences: Buddhism, new age mysticism, "decluttering," and the like. The pilgrim would become a tourist, and religion itself a leisure-time activity. So it seemed in the West in both Judaism and Christianity.

It was not until the 1960s and 1970s that perceptive sociologists began to take note that the pattern was beginning to change. In the United States, Dean Kelley noticed that it was the conservative churches that were growing.[15] In 1965 Charles Liebman was among the first to see that in Judaism, Orthodoxy had stopped dying and become the most energetic element of American Jewish life.[16] Fifty years later, Jews are just waking to the fact that the ultra-Orthodox will be the strongest element in both America and Israel. Likewise, in Islam, extremist theology, once a relatively marginal phenomenon, has become mainstream.

Thus the second story no longer holds. Accommodationist forms of religion are rapidly being outpaced by those opposed and resistant to modernity.

The End-of-History Thesis

The third story began in 1989 with the fall of the Berlin Wall, the end of the Cold War, and the beginning of the collapse of the Soviet Union. The narrative was that the West had won. Communism had failed. People wanted freedom and affluence. The Soviet Union had delivered neither. Politically it was repressive. Economically it was inefficient. For freedom you need liberal democracy. For affluence you need the market economy. The year 1989 marked the victory of both. From here on democratic capitalism would spread slowly but surely across the world. This was the story known as *the end of history.*

Almost immediately it proved false.[17] There was ethnic war in Bosnia and Kosovo; there was 9/11 and the rise of al-Qaeda and its rivals; and there was the failure of the 2011 Arab Spring. In the light of subsequent history, it may be that two other events that happened in 1989 will prove to have been more fateful than the events in Berlin or the Soviet Union. One was the fatwa of February 14, 1989, issued by Ayatollah Khomeini in Iran against Salman Rushdie and his book *The Satanic Verses*, which led to British Muslims burning books in Bradford. It became clear that a religious decree in Iran could affect behavior in Britain, thousands of miles away. It was the first demonstration of the potentially global reach of radical political Islam.[18]

The second event also took place in February 1989, namely, the Soviet withdrawal from Afghanistan. This suggested that a handful of dedicated mujahideen could cause the humiliating retreat of one of the world's two superpowers. Nine months later, the Soviet Union imploded. If that could be achieved, why not do likewise to the other superpower, the United States? It would have to be done in the same place, Afghanistan, from which no superpower has ever emerged without humiliation. How, though, could America be lured into so obvious a trap?

The human brain has an ancient core, the amygdala, activated at moments of extreme threat and capable of flooding out the rational calculations of the prefrontal cortex. Psychologists call this occurrence an *amygdala hijack.*[19] You become blind with rage, and your capacity for thinking through the consequences of actions is disabled. Thus, I believe, 9/11 was conceived. It would provoke an American invasion of Afghanistan that, like Russia's, would end in withdrawal and humiliation. And so the third narrative failed. It was the end of "the end of history."

The Westernization Thesis

Lastly, the *Westernization thesis* has been increasingly called into question as Europe and the United States have seen their influence wane in the twenty-first century. Four ancient civilizations, each of which suffered decline or eclipse in the modern world—China, India, Russia, and Islam (Sunni in Saudi Arabia, Shia in Iran)—have reasserted themselves politically, economically, or both. Each believes that the future belongs to it, not to the West.[20]

2. Time: Linear and Otherwise

What happened? Why did these metanarratives, which had, in some cases, worked for centuries, cease to align with the emergent realities of the twenty-first century? One reason, it seems to me, has to do with the novel concept of time that emerged in the West in the wake of the Enlightenment. For the first time, people began to think of time as linear and unidirectional. The keyword was *progress*.[21] It came to stand for the idea that, for the most part, things were getting better in the human situation and would continue to do so. Knowledge was increasing; so was wealth. Societies were becoming more tolerant. People were becoming more rational, less driven by fear and superstition. Science allowed us to understand the world, and industry and technology to control it. The market promised open-ended economic growth, and the gradual move to democracy meant less tyranny and oppression, perhaps even fewer wars. Kant, in 1795, could speak of a real possibility of "perpetual peace."[22]

History, however, does not work in quite that way, as Giambattista Vico, Bertrand Russell, Will Durant, and other decline-and-fall scholars have pointed out. One of the first was the fourteenth-century Islamic thinker Ibn Khaldun. He argued that every urban civilization becomes vulnerable when it grows decadent from within. People live in towns and get used to luxuries. The rich grow indolent, and the poor resentful. There is a loss of *asabiyah* (social cohesion), a keyword for Khaldun. People no longer think in terms of the common good. They are no longer willing to make sacrifices for one another. Eventually they lose the will to defend themselves. They then become easy prey for the desert dwellers, the people who are used to fighting to stay alive.

Durant eloquently articulated his own version of essentially the same story. After scaling the heights, great civilizations tend to go through the following process:

> The intellectual classes abandon the ancient theology and—after some hesitation—the moral code allied with it; literature and philosophy become anticlerical. The movement of liberation rises to an exuberant worship of reason, and falls to a paralyzing disillusionment with every dogma and every idea. Conduct, deprived of its religious supports, deteriorates into epicurean chaos; and life itself, shorn of consoling faith, becomes a burden alike to conscious poverty and to weary wealth. In the end a society and its religion tend to fall together, like body and soul, in a harmonious death. Meanwhile among the oppressed another myth arises, gives new form to human hope, new courage to human effort, and after centuries of chaos builds another civilization.[23]

In the introduction to his *History of Western Philosophy*, Russell said something similar about the two civilizations he regarded as the peak of human achievement: pre-Christian Athens and Renaissance Italy. In both cases, "the liberation from fetters" made people "energetic and creative, producing a rare florescence of genius." But the "decay of morals" eventually undermined the social sense of shared responsibility and collective action, and people then fell "under the domination of nations less civilized than themselves but not so destitute of social cohesion."[24]

In other words, *the history of civilization is never linear*. If anything, it is cyclical. Virtually every great civilization has seen itself as immortal, but none has proved to be so. Shelley's poem "Ozymandias," about the Egyptian pharaoh Ramses II, is the ironic testament to the hubris of self-belief. What happened before may be beginning to happen now in the postmodern, late-capitalist West, with its moral relativism and hyper-individualism, its political culture of rights without responsibilities, its aggressive secularism and impatience of any morality of self-restraint, and its failure to inculcate the habits of instinctual deferral that Sigmund Freud saw as the basis of civilization. As Robert Bellah memorably put it: "Progress, modernity's master idea, seems less compelling when it appears that it may be progress into the abyss."[25]

3. Escape from Identity

A further and less noticed feature of the Enlightenment was its attempt to *escape from identity*. Europe, in the wake of the wars of the sixteenth and seventeenth centuries, was well aware of the inherent connection between identity and violence. We are social animals. We find our identity in groups. But groups not only unite multiple "I"s into a collective "We." They also divide one group, "Us," from another, "Them." That division into—and competition between—groups is a primary driver of violence, not only among humans but among almost all social animals.

One way of avoiding war and achieving perpetual peace was therefore to seek to abolish identity. The Enlightenment, with its "dream of reason," is often portrayed as a battle against irrationality, but that is a tendentious way of putting it. I have suggested an alternative way of understanding it as a *flight from particularity* in favor of universality: the universals of reason (Descartes), science (Newton), and morality (Kant).[26] One of its highpoints was Schiller's vision, set to music in Beethoven's Ninth Symphony, of a world in which *Alle Menschen werden Brüder* (All people become brothers)—in which we are all simply human. But *there is no such world*, just as there is no universal language. Identities, like cultures and languages, are inescapably multiple and particular, and we cannot be human without them.[27] The Enlightenment dream of an escape from identity was bound to fail.

What happened in the nineteenth century was a collective version of what Freud called "the return of the repressed." The age of universals was succeeded not by the return of Christianity but by the reappearance of older and more pagan gods. Three substitutes for religion emerged as the basis for new identities. One was the nation-state. The second was class. The third was race. The first led to two world wars, the second to Stalin's Russia, the Gulag, and the KGB, and the third to the Holocaust. The cost of these three substitutes for religion was in excess of a hundred million lives.[28] After that, no one who argues that abolishing religion will lead to peace can be taken seriously. The culprit is not religion but identity, and identity is a constitutive feature of the human condition.

Since the 1960s the West has been living through a new attempt to escape identity, in favor not of the universal but of the *individual*. The contemporary West is the most individualistic era of all time. Its central values are: in ethics, autonomy; in politics, individual rights; in culture, postmodernism; and in religion, "spirituality." Its idol is the self, its icon the "selfie," and its operating systems the free market and the post-ideological, managerial, liberal democratic state.[29] This was a danger already foreseen by Tocqueville in his remarks about "individualism," and at the close of the nineteenth century by Durkheim in his study of anomie, the collapse of a shared world of meanings, the result of which would, for example, result in a rise in rates of suicide. A world of anomie, he thought, was for many people unbearable.[30]

This too cannot hold, as we saw in Ibn Khaldun's insight about the loss of *asabiyah* and Bertrand Russell's about the failure of social cohesion. The desecularization of the world in the twenty-first century is in no small measure the result of a search for identity and community of meaning. The twenty-first century is to the twentieth what nineteenth-century Europe was to the Enlightenment of the eighteenth. That is one reason why religion has returned in some sections of society and several parts of the world.

4. Religion and Identity

To understand why religion has returned, it is helpful to understand why it emerged in the first place—and by *religion* I mean not spirituality, which is as old as humankind, but rather formal, structured religions with temples, priests, myths, and rituals. The most compelling account, given by several contemporary scholars, is that it emerged at a particular stage in the evolution of civilization and that it had to do with the logic of altruism and cooperation.[31]

Darwin was puzzled by the phenomenon of altruism. Natural selection seemed to suggest that egoists, who focused on their own survival, were more likely to survive and reproduce than altruists, who put the interests of the group above their own. Yet altruism and those who practice it are valued in virtually every human society. Darwin eventually came up with an answer in *The Descent of Man*:

> There can be no doubt that a tribe including many members who, from possessing in a high degree the spirit of patriotism, fidelity, obedience, courage, and sympathy, were always ready to give aid to each other and to sacrifice themselves for the common good, would be victorious over most other tribes; and this would be natural selection.[32]

Group Formation

To put it in the language of today, we hand on our genes as individuals, but we survive as members of groups. There are three levels of group formation. One, the most fundamental, is kinship: my sense of identity with those with whom I share a genetic heritage. As J. B. S. Haldane famously said when asked whether he would jump into a river to save his brother, "No, but I would do so to save two brothers or eight cousins." Because I share a proportion of my genes with those to whom I am biologically related (a half with siblings, an eighth with cousins), by saving their lives, I help ensure that this genetic heritage will be passed on to the next generation. That is why altruism is most commonly found within families and kinship groups.[33]

The second and wider form of group cooperation is based on what evolutionary psychologists call *reciprocal altruism*. It makes sense to share with others who share with me. However, though this extends beyond kin, it also sets a limit to group size, since it depends on my remembering who has shared with whom in the past. According to Robin Dunbar, that results in a limit of about 150 as the optimal size of a human group.[34]

Hence the problem that arises with the birth of cities—that is, with groups larger than 150 units (families, clans). The problem, essentially, is: how do we establish *trust between strangers*? It is at this stage that large-scale, highly formalized religions begin to appear. A shared moral code, enacted and rehearsed in shared rituals and overseen by cosmic powers, solves the problem of trust between strangers by creating an ontologically based collective identity.

Religion and Society

It is no wonder, then, that over the course of history, nations and even empires have been held together by religion. It forged a common bond and provided a logic for altruistic behavior that went far beyond kin and small face-to-face groups operating on the basis of reciprocal altruism. Under religion's sacred canopy, a universe emerged saturated with moral meaning and the logic of sacrifice of self for the sake of the group, the faith, and ultimately for God himself. Religion both creates and deeply internalizes obligation. Without it the whole project of morality is thrown into question.[35]

Small wonder that James Madison could say that "We have staked the whole of our political institutions upon the capacity of mankind for self-government, upon the capacity of each and all of us to govern ourselves according to the commandments of God,"[36] or that Tocqueville could write, "Religion in America takes no direct in the government of the society, but it must be regarded as the first of their political institutions; for if it does not impart a taste of freedom, it facilitates the use of it."[37] Until relatively recently, even in the West, the idea that you could have a society without a shared moral code would have seemed absurd. As one of Britain's senior judges, Lord Devlin, wrote in 1965, "society means a community of ideas; without shared ideas on politics, morals and ethics no society can exist."[38]

The return of religion to many parts of the world is a hugely complex and multifaceted phenomenon. Michael Walzer has argued that in India, Algeria, and Israel (and surely Turkey) it has taken the form of a religious counterrevolution, driven by public disappointment at the results of secularization.[39] Among radicalized individuals within Westernized societies, it may be the result of what Durkheim saw as the almost unbearable experience of anomie in societies lacking an objective moral order. Certain religious groups within the West, among them Catholics and Orthodox Jews, have opted for the *Benedict option* of partial withdrawal from a society with whose morality they can no longer identify.[40] One of the most interesting contemporary religious expressions is the growth of Christianity in today's China.[41] In short, many forces are at work, and understanding the dynamics of desecularization lies far beyond the parameters of this paper.

This much is clear, nonetheless: religion has proved itself to be unexpectedly well suited to the twenty-first century, not least because the great religions are global, whereas effective political institutions remain national or at best regional. Religious groups, especially radical ones, have been among the most effective users of the new social media. Religion has stepped into the gaps left by secular culture, giving people a sense of identity, consequence, and moral order. Which means, inevitably, that we are thrust back into the world that the West has sought to liberate itself from since the seventeenth century—namely, religiously motivated violence.

Religion and Violence

The connection between religion and violence, I argue in *Not in God's Name*, is oblique rather than direct. Intergroup violence has to do with identity: "Us" defending ourselves against a threat from "Them," the ones not like us. Religion enters the picture only because it is the most potent form of identity yet discovered. The eighteenth-century Enlightenment project of abolishing particular identities in favor of universals failed, as it was bound to do. The nineteenth- and twentieth-century alternatives to religious identity—nation, race, and class—eventually generated more violence than religion itself. The late twentieth-century project of abolishing identity in favor of individual choice is generating its own discontents. So, for some, religion has reentered the frame, which means the return of religious narrative, because—as I noted at the outset—*we are the story we tell about ourselves.* Few institutions in history have told more compelling narratives than the Abrahamic monotheisms, Judaism, Christianity, and Islam.

Those narratives, though, can become deeply problematic. It is one thing to tell yourself who you are when surrounded by fellow believers who are themselves part of the story. It is another thing to tell yourself who others are, when they stand outside the story and its circle of salvation. The enormous danger is that they become, for you, the embodiment of evil, or they must be displaced if you are to enjoy your proper position in relation to the world and to God. From these beliefs flowed the bloodshed of the Crusades and other holy wars from which the West has spent four centuries trying, with limited success, to extricate itself.

5. The Dualism and Displacement Narratives

To summarize as briefly as possible the argument in *Not in God's Name*, I argued that over and above the violence implicit in religious identity as such, there are two features of monotheism that pose specific dangers. One is dualism. The other is displacement.

Dualism

Dualism is one of the occupational hazards of monotheism. It entered sectarian forms of Judaism during the Second Temple period, and some early expressions of Christianity via Iranian Zoroastrianism and Greek Gnosticism. It would seem absurd to be both a monotheist and a dualist, since the two are in clear contradiction to one another. Yet dualism can become an overwhelmingly attractive resolution of the cognitive dissonance that comes from believing in a good God and at the same time witnessing the evils and injustices of the world.

The dualistic solution is to maintain that the evils of the world are the result of a malign power—the devil, Satan, the antichrist, Lucifer, the prince of darkness—independent of and capable of contending with God himself. It is a short step from this metaphysical dualism to an actual identification of specific groups with the force of evil. They become the children of darkness threatening the children of light. They are, in ways mysterious yet undeniable, the source of our present troubles. The argument goes like this: We are good, faithful, pious, yet bad things happen to us. God could not be willing this to happen. Therefore it must be the Devil and his agents—wizards, witches, blacks, Freemasons, or (most often) the Jews.

Dualism is devastating in its ability to overwhelm and incapacitate the moral sense. It casts us—the group to which I belong—as the innocent victims, and they as the guilty perpetrators. When, therefore, I hate, defame, attack, or murder one of the children of darkness, I am innocent—and they are guilty. I am acting to protect my group, while they are threatening to destroy it. This remains true even if the people I murder are innocent civilians or young children. The name I give to this syndrome is *altruistic evil*—that is to say, evil undertaken in a noble cause. This kind of thinking was rife in Germany between 1933 and 1945, where it was promulgated and defended by, among others, distinguished academics, scientists, judges, and doctors. It is equally rife today in Islamist circles. Both propositions are documented in the book.

Displacement and Sibling Rivalry

The other narrative, which has particular relevance to the Abrahamic monotheisms, is *displacement*. By this I mean the belief that to win a cherished place in the affections of God, it is necessary to displace someone else. The classic case of this is sibling rivalry. To win a share of the limited resources of food (in the case of animals) or attention (in the case of humans), the younger must displace the elder, who at the moment occupies the privileged position of first claimant.

This is the basic structure of so-called supersessionist theology in Christianity and Islam. Christianity, in certain early versions, displaces Judaism by constituting a new covenant between God and humanity. The new Israel replaces the old. Islam, in certain versions, does likewise to both Judaism and Christianity. The prophets of both earlier religions are seen as preparing the way for the final prophet and thus for Islam. The result of both theologies is a demotion of the earlier religions and their adherents, at best to second-class citizens and at worst to the unredeemed who deserve no rights. Such was the story of the relation between the faiths for much of history until relatively recent times.

In *Not in God's Name*, I asked some fundamental questions about the displacement narrative. First I asked whether it could be found in Jewish texts, to which my answer was—yes. Indeed it constitutes the basic narrative structure of the four stories of sibling rivalry in Genesis: Cain and Abel, Isaac and Ishmael, Jacob and Esau, and Joseph and his brothers. It now becomes clear why this should be so. Genesis is confronting the roots of human violence, finding them—as does the great contemporary scholar of religious violence René Girard—in sibling rivalry, or what Girard calls *mimetic desire.*

Genesis is, however, doing more than this. It uses a literary technique of great subtlety—what I call the *concealed counternarrative*—to lead the reader beyond sibling rivalry to reconciliation and coexistence. The four-act drama that begins with Cain's fratricide ends with Joseph's monumental act of forgiveness to his brothers who sought to kill him and eventually sold him into slavery. There is, Genesis is teaching us, nothing inevitable about the conflict between brothers. In so doing, it is hinting at a fundamental theological proposition that is the heart of my argument in the book. The idea that God's love might be governed by the logic of scarcity that underlies sibling rivalry among animals and humans is absurd. To be loved by God, I do not have to assume that someone else, of some other religious disposition, is hated or less loved.

I regard this as the theological move necessary in the twenty-first century if we are to avoid a tragedy that might make the Crusades and the European wars of religion look like mere playground episodes in comparison. There is something deadly about dualism on the one hand and narratives of displacement on the other that, in an age fraught with the possibilities of mass destruction, we must confront while there is still time.

Having persuaded itself, for four centuries, that religion was in intensive care, about to die, the West has been caught unawares and unprepared by the return of religion to the global political arena. Even now, after all that has happened in the twenty-first century by way of terror in the West, chaos and barbarism in Syria, Iraq, Afghanistan, Libya, Yemen, Somalia, and other failed or failing states, and religious conflict elsewhere—"Religious hostilities increased in every major region of the world except the Americas" between 2007 and 2012 according to a 2014 Pew report, and 76 percent of the total global population faces some official or informal restriction on their faith[42]—the West is still inadequately prepared to understand quite how dangerous some narratives are, especially the master narratives that form the basis of identity.

That is not because these master narratives are religious, but because we are human. We are social animals; we find our identities in groups; all groups include and exclude; groups encourage altruism toward insiders and suspicion, fear, and potential aggression toward outsiders. *In extremis* narratives can dehumanize the outsider as either a force of evil or a sibling rival for the scarce resource we seek, even when that resource is the love of God.

Conclusion

To return to the point with which I began: *we are the story we tell about ourselves.* There is an inherent connection between narrative and identity. Over the course of history, humanity has developed two fundamentally different ways of thinking: by way of *system* and by way of *story.*[43] Systems are timeless; stories are embedded in time. Systems offer explanations; stories offer meaning. Systems aim at universality; stories are intrinsically particular.

The modern project was predicated on the idea that you could replace stories by systems. The four key systems were science, industry/technology, the market economy, and the liberal democratic state. It follows, however, that none of these can answer the three questions any reflective person will ask at some stage in life: Who am I? Why am I here? How then shall I live? Science can tell us how but not why. Technology gives us power but cannot tell us how to use it. The market economy gives us choices but cannot tell us which choices to make. The liberal democratic state gives us maximal freedom and minimal guidance as to how to live our lives. That is their virtue. They are procedural rather than substantive, thin rather than thick. They cannot give an account of identity, and therefore, eventually, people will search elsewhere. They will take advantage of the systems, but they will still seek a story: *their* story. Narrative always returns. In the twenty-first century, more widely than was expected, the narrative that many have chosen is not a new one but, to the contrary, one of the classic foundational stories of the great faiths.

Therein lies the danger. The relationship between Judaism, Christianity, and Islam has been historically a poisoned one, built on narratives of dualism and sibling rivalry. The three Abrahamic faiths are not simply discrete, incommensurable phenomena. They are inherently related. Each considers itself the true heir of Abraham. Each initially assumed the others would disappear. Their members would either convert or acknowledge the primacy of the new faith. Christians expected that Jews would become Christian because the founder of their faith was a Jew. Muslims expected that Jews and Christians would become Muslims because their faith incorporated Abraham, Moses, Jesus, and elements of their teachings.

But they didn't disappear. Some converted; most did not. Jews remained Jews. Christians remained Christians. The result is that Judaism, Christianity, and Islam are each challenged and threatened by the existence of the others. So long as the West was engaged in a process of secularization, this did not seem to matter much. Why worry about the religious narrative if religion itself was about to disappear? But in an age of desecularization, it matters very much indeed.

Identity has returned—not just in relation to religion but in other ways also, such as the Brexit vote, the American presidential election, and the rise of nationalist parties in Europe. Identity almost always involves narrative; and I have argued in this essay that the stories we tell are among the most important shapers of the worlds we create or destroy. What stories will we tell about who we are and how we are related to the people who are not members of our group, the "Them" to our "Us"? Will they be sibling rivalry stories ("they are trying to take away from us what is rightly ours")? Will they be dualistic stories ("we are suffering because of what they are doing to us")?

Not all of these will be religious stories, but some will be. And it is by looking at those stories and how they have been interpreted—how at times they have lifted people to the heights of altruism and at others plunged them into the depths of evil—that we may best safeguard our future. For at the beating heart of monotheism is an insight that might just save us from ourselves: that if Genesis 1 is to be believed, then even one who is not in my image—whose color, culture, or creed is not mine—is still in God's image. That is the antidote to dualism and sibling rivalry, and we need it now.

PART I

BIBLICAL AND CLASSICAL BACKGROUND

2

(RE-)READING THE NEW TESTAMENT IN THE LIGHT OF SIBLING RIVALRY
Some Hermeneutical Implications for Today

Richard A. Burridge

This paper will consider the first question posed for the symposium about reexamining the "biblical stories about sibling rivalry that appear to be at the heart of the problem of 'them vs. us' enmity" in the hope that this might help "point to a solution." In his important book *Not in God's Name*, Rabbi Sacks (re-)reads the stories of sibling rivalry in Genesis concerning Ishmael and Isaac, Jacob and Esau, Joseph and his brothers, Leah and Rachel, and Cain and Abel, as well as the universal and particular covenants with Noah and with Abraham. Can Rabbi Sacks' repeated conclusions from these Genesis stories that the choice of one does not necessitate the rejection of the other[1] inspire a similar (re-)reading of the New Testament (especially Paul and the gospels), which may impact on the accusation of supersessionism, as posed in the symposium's fourth question? We will also discuss whether a hermeneutic of reading with and for the "voice of the other" in the light of such sibling rivalry might assist our search for answers to the problems of violence in the name of God.

This chapter will employ both a careful historical-critical reading of the New Testament writings in their historical and social context (according to the current consensus reconstruction of biblical scholars) and draw upon some literary readings. I am conscious that this attempt to cover a vast area (most of the New Testament!) must therefore entail some broad generalizations, so in the footnotes I will supply cross-references to some of my other work where this is described in more

39

detail with fuller academic documentation. I would like to offer to these discussions together my experience and training, originally as a classicist specializing in Graeco-Roman literature and history, through my initial studies at Oxford and teaching Latin and Greek, history, literature, and culture as a schoolmaster—and these interests have driven all my work, as well as this paper. During ordination training and the early years of ministry as a parish priest and university chaplain, I completed my doctoral studies on the literary background of the gospels, with regard to their genre, in comparison with Graeco-Roman biography (which is very different from the modern genre).[2] This biographical genre of the gospels inevitably entails an overriding emphasis on the person of Jesus of Nazareth, his deeds and words, life, ministry, and death, which therefore runs throughout my writings,[3] as recognized in my being awarded the 2013 Ratzinger Prize by Pope Francis for establishing the "indissoluble connection between Jesus and the gospels."[4] I have discussed this particular biographical stress on the person of Jesus with Rabbi Sacks on many occasions over the years since we both share an interest in narrative and story, and so now I am delighted to bring it to bear upon the question of how we interpret the New Testament, particularly in the light of the biblical stories of sibling rivalry and the relationship between the emerging early church and first-century Judaism.

The second phase of my work went on to the implications of this biographical genre for the application of the gospels in particular—but also the Bible in general—to moral and ethical issues, including the social and political sphere. This work began with a detailed study of the use of the Bible and the hermeneutics of the interpretation of scripture both to justify and to critique apartheid in South Africa.[5] I have appreciated my conversations about the Bible and ethics with Rabbi Sacks over many years, both during his time as chief rabbi and his more recent tenure as Professor of Law, Ethics, and the Hebrew Bible at King's College London—and he keeps asking me when the second part of my work on ethics is going to appear![6]

It was a privilege to hear Rabbi Sacks' first (re-)reading of these stories of sibling rivalry in 2004 (the 175th anniversary of our founding Royal Charter), as some lectures given for the Associateship of King's College London (AKC, our original award since 1831), which also included lectures from Archbishop Desmond Tutu, to which I and other members of the Theology Department then responded. However, I am delighted to see the much more detailed treatment of the stories now worked out in *Not in God's Name*. By looking at the stories in

Genesis of Isaac and Ishmael, Jacob and Esau, Joseph and his brothers, and finally—and tellingly—Leah and Rachel, Rabbi Sacks analyses the "surface" narrative of the younger sibling supplanting or usurping the elder, leading to the general and popular assumption of the rejection of the elder. However, his careful (re-)reading reveals a counternarrative, that the choice of one does not necessitate the rejection of the other, who is still loved by God who has a purpose for them: "*God rejects rejection* . . . the conclusion to which the whole of Genesis has been leading is *the rejection of rejection*."[7] This is a wonderful example by a devoted and faithful scholar of a close and careful reading—and (re-)reading—of the holy scriptures, especially Genesis and the Torah, which leads to a new interpretation that has significant consequences for popular assumptions about usurping others and religious violence in the name of God. In this chapter, I shall attempt to follow suit with a (re-)reading of the New Testament to determine whether it necessarily leads to similar usurpation or supersessionism—or, at least, to offer a brief sketch of how such a reading might look.

1. Reading the New Testament as a Narrative of Usurpation and Supersessionism

Christianity is sometimes interpreted as an offshoot or descendant of Judaism, as a new religion which then seeks to replace the former and to appropriate all its self-understanding, which leads, of course, to what is rightly called *supersessionism*. At its worst, the "child" turns on the "parent," even committing patricide like Oedipus—killing his father and marrying his mother to appropriate the crown and the rule for himself—which leads to the whole sorry history of anti-Semitism and eventually to the Holocaust.[8]

Chief among sinners in this narrative is Saint Paul (who of course gives us this phrase by describing himself in this way, "first" or "foremost" among sinners, 1 Tim 1:15).[9] January 25 has been viewed from the sixth century—and more widely since the twelfth century—as the Feast of the Conversion of Saint Paul. In this narrative, Paul is interpreted as an "anti-Christian zealot," a "fanatical Pharisee" (and consequently often as a "hypocrite"), and a "persecutor of Christians" who is wonderfully converted by the appearance of the Risen Christ to him on the road to Damascus into the "apostle of Christ to the nations." He thus becomes responsible for founding the new religion of Christianity and also for thrusting Graeco-Roman ideas of divinity onto Jesus of Nazareth, something which Jesus himself, standing within the Jewish prophetic tradition, never intended or foresaw. According to this narrative, Paul is therefore properly to be viewed as the "true founder" of the Christian church, not Jesus. Actually, I would argue that there are both historical and hermeneutical problems with practically every aspect of this interpretation or narrative—but we will come to that shortly.

First, however, I want to consider Rabbi Sacks' important section on Paul in *Not in God's Name*, in which he quite rightly sets Paul in his proper historical context as a Jew: "During his lifetime, there was no such thing as 'Christianity' as we now understand it. The decisive break with Judaism had not yet taken place."[10] Rabbi Sacks' reading of Paul is thus not the simplistic caricature of the surface narrative outlined above; it is careful and nuanced, as we would expect from such a respectful and experienced interpreter of sacred text. However, he rightly draws attention to Paul's treatment of some of the key texts about sibling rivalry, notably the contrast Paul makes between the two sons of Abraham: Ishmael through the "slave woman" Hagar and Isaac through the free wife Sarah (Gal 4:21-31). Rabbi Sacks poignantly describes how it feels to a Jew reading Paul's interpretation: "it feels like being disinherited, violated, robbed of an identity. This is my past, my ancestry, my story, and here is Paul saying it is not mine at all, it is his and all who travel with him."[11] He then goes on to consider the "older and more reflective" Paul writing about this again in his later epistle to the Romans, going on to the other story of sibling rivalry, Jacob and Esau (Rom 9:6-13). This story is then in turn taken up by some of the Church Fathers, starting with Cyprian in the third century and going on though others like Tertullian, Chrysostom, and Augustine, leading eventually to justifications for anti-Semitism and the expulsion of Jews through the Middle Ages from England in 1290 to Spain in 1492.[12]

Our task now is to consider whether this narrative of supersessionism and anti-Semitism is a necessary consequence of these New Testament texts—or, on the other hand, if we can emulate Rabbi Sacks' example of a careful and respectful (re-)reading of the scriptural stories from Genesis, we will discover a similar counternarrative in the New Testament texts that will also lead to the conclusion that the choice of one does not necessitate the rejection of the other.

2. Re-reading the New Testament as a Narrative of Sibling Rivalry

Paul's Prophetic "Calling" and Early Conflict: Galatians

In the narrative just described, using the term *conversion* for what happened on the road to Damascus (see Acts 9:1-30; 22:3-16; 26:2-23; Gal 1:11-17) implies that Saul of Tarsus, a rabbi trained under Gamaliel in the Pharisaic tradition, ceases to be "Jewish" and "converts" to become an "apostle" of Christianity as a different religion. Certainly, this event is central to both popular and scholarly accounts of Paul's life,[13] as well as having inspired generations of artists' depictions. However, these brief accounts do not suggest that Paul himself would have seen it as a conversion away from Judaism itself; it is more likely that he would have interpreted his spiritual experience as a "calling" to a particular commission, in a way similar to many of the prophets before him (compare the accounts of their calling in Isa 6:1-13; Amos 7:14-16; Jer 1:4-10). Meanwhile, the command for Paul to go to the Gentiles would be reminiscent of a similar call to Jonah, even if he did not like it (Jonah 1:1, 4:1-3). Paul's attitude to his Jewish heritage has undergone enormous scholarly debate in recent years.[14] The debate between "call" and "conversion," and whether this is a "commission" or an "act of apostasy," has also provided a focus for discussion about the nature of identity between Christian and Jewish scholars writing about the New Testament; Segal, for example, still prefers to talk of Paul's conversion as the "appropriate term."[15]

The passage quoted by Rabbi Sacks about the two sons of Abraham—Ishmael through the "slave woman" Hagar and Isaac through the free wife Sarah—comes from Galatians 4:21-31, thought by most scholars to be one of Paul's earliest letters. It was probably written in 48–49 CE in the middle of the "Judaizing controversy," in which other teachers from the community of Jewish early believers in Jerusalem were going to some of Paul's groups of Gentile converts in Asia Minor to instruct them to be circumcised and keep all the Law of Moses. In the midst of this internal battle, Paul is very forthright, fighting for his very understanding of the gospel. Therefore, it is not surprising that he paints the Law in a negative light: he wants to combat the influence of the "Judaizers," who think they have to be circumcised and keep "the works of the Law" (Gal 3:2, 10). Paul's response is that "Christ has set us free"—so his readers should not "submit again to a yoke of slavery. . . . If you are led by the Spirit, you are not under the Law" (Gal 5:1-2, 18). However, the traditional interpretation of Paul as having been set free by Christ after

being racked with guilt over his failure to keep the Law (which feeds
some anti-Semitic interpretations of Pharisees, the Law, and Judaism in
general down through history and into today) is now seen by scholars
as a late medieval or early modern interpretation, coming out of the
German Reformation when Martin Luther interprets Paul in the light
of his own sense of guilt and sin. This Lutheran understanding has,
however, been a major influence on Protestant and German views ever
since. The work of E. P. Sanders—especially his concept of *covenantal
nomism* and his distinction between observing the Law for "staying
in" rather than "getting in" the covenant—has been pivotal in a major
reorientation of Paul's attitude to the Law and to his Jewish heritage
in biblical scholarship over the last few decades,[16] while other scholars
have debated and refined the so-called new perspective on Paul.[17]

Later Paul in Reflection: Romans and Philippians

As noted above, and also by Rabbi Sacks himself,[18] Paul returns to these
themes later in the much more reflective and irenic treatment in his
letter to the Romans, preparing the way for his eventual journey under
guard to Rome, where he would be martyred. It therefore dates from
the mid- to late 50s, depending on differing scholarly reconstructions.
The interesting historical background is that, according to the Roman
historian Suetonius in his *Life of Claudius*, the emperor expelled the
Jews from Rome because of disturbances of the peace brought about
over "Chrestus," in either 42 or 49 CE (*Claud.* 25.4). This is usually
thought to suggest controversies between Jewish believers in Jesus as
Christ (= "Chrestus," with the long *e* interchanging with *i*) and non-
believing Jews, which shows how the initial arguments about Jesus
were seen by the Romans as an internal Jewish debate. Paul's letter to a
mixed congregation at Rome suggests that Jewish Christians had been
able to return later (perhaps after Claudius' death in 54), but Gentile
believers had become numerous in the Roman congregation during the
intervening years, thereby becoming more dominant.[19]

As well as returning to the contrast in the sons of Abraham and
considering the text from Malachi about God loving Jacob but hating
Esau (Mal 3:1)—as noted by Rabbi Sacks[20]—Paul makes very clear to
his (predominantly Gentile?) Roman readers both his own continuing
commitment as a Jew himself and God's love for Jews. Thus Paul is
even willing to give up his own salvation for the sake of his people:

> I am speaking the truth in Christ—I am not lying; my conscience confirms
> it by the Holy Spirit—I have great sorrow and unceasing anguish in my

heart. For I could wish that I myself were accursed and cut off from Christ for the sake of my own people, my kindred according to the flesh. They are Israelites, and to them belong the adoption, the glory, the covenants, the giving of the Law, the worship, and the promises; to them belong the patriarchs, and from them, according to the flesh, comes the Messiah, who is over all, God blessed forever. Amen. (Rom 9:1-5)

He makes clear his own desire and prayer: "Brothers and sisters, my heart's desire and prayer to God for them is that they may be saved" (Rom 10:1). Finally, in chapter 11, he poses the same direct question asked by Rabbi Sacks: "I ask, then, has God rejected his people? By no means! I myself am an Israelite, a descendant of Abraham, a member of the tribe of Benjamin. God has not rejected his people whom he foreknew," a clear example of Rabbi Sacks' point that the choice of one does not necessitate the rejection of the other (Rom 11:1-2). So Paul concludes "as regards election they are beloved, for the sake of their ancestors; for the gifts and the calling of God are irrevocable . . . by the mercy shown to you, they too may now receive mercy. For God has imprisoned all in disobedience so that he may be merciful to all" (11:28-32).[21]

Elsewhere, in his letter to the Philippians,[22] also probably written in the mid-50s, Paul continues to be clear about his Jewish identity and heritage—when arguing against his Judaizing opponents—coupled to his total commitment to and confidence in Christ:

If anyone else has reason to be confident in the flesh, I have more: circumcised on the eighth day, a member of the people of Israel, of the tribe of Benjamin, a Hebrew born of Hebrews; as to the Law, a Pharisee; as to zeal, a persecutor of the church; as to righteousness under the Law, blameless. Yet whatever gains I had, these I have come to regard as loss because of Christ. More than that, I regard everything as loss because of the surpassing value of knowing Christ Jesus my Lord. For his sake I have suffered the loss of all things, and I regard them as rubbish, in order that I may gain Christ. (Phil 3:4-8)

It is therefore this total stress on the person of Jesus as Messiah (back to my earlier biographical emphasis) which drives Paul's theology and takes priority over his continuing Jewish heritage and the Law of Moses.[23]

Thus Paul's attitude to his Jewish identity and heritage is much more nuanced than any simplistic ideas of conversion away from Judaism to founding a new religion in Christianity, which then "replaces" Israel in any supersessionist understanding. It is true that while Paul

values his Jewish heritage and draws attention to all his privileges, he
sees his identity and confidence before God as rooted "in Christ" (Phil
3:3-11), through the gospel that God has commissioned him to take to
the Gentiles; however, they have been grafted into God's "olive tree"
alongside Israel, his "kindred according to the flesh," whom God has
"by no means" rejected—so that, at the End, God may be "merciful to
all" (Rom. 9:3; 11.1, 17-24, 32). Thus Paul would be in full agreement
with Rabbi Sacks' point that the choice of one does not necessitate the
rejection of the other. Even Paul's comment at the end of the polemical
argument in Galatians, "peace be upon them, and mercy, and upon the
Israel of God" (Gal 6:16), which has sometimes been interpreted in a
supersessionist way of using "the Israel of God" to refer to the church,
actually distinguishes between those who follow Paul's teaching and
Israel itself; therefore, increasingly scholars interpret this comment as
a blessing on "the Israel of God" as the Jewish people. Thus Barclay
concludes that "Romans 9–11 is a development, not a reversal, of this
aspect of Galatians."[24]

Judaism and Christianity: "Mother-Child" or "Sibling Rivalry"?

Thus we have seen that Paul can at one and the same time be both very
polemical about his Judaizing opponents when he thinks that the whole
basis of the gospel is at stake and also very positive about his Jewish heritage and identity and his love and desire for his own people. Even when
he refers to his "previous way of life" in Judaism (Gal 1:13), this does
not mean that he has left everything Jewish behind; rather it reflects the
different groups and the internal debates that are still common within
Judaism today—and since the days of the patriarchs and matriarchs.
As Rabbi Sacks himself sometimes says, "where there are two rabbis,
there are three opinions"! We have already noted that one problem with
supersessionist or similar "replacement" approaches is that they tend to
see Judaism as a single entity, the parent, or mother who gives birth to
the child who then outgrows, replaces, or—in Oedipean terms—even
kills the father and takes the mother's heritage! But historically this
parent-child matrix is both too simplistic and not quite accurate. We
have already referred to the importance of the groundbreaking work
of E. P. Sanders in revising scholarly approaches to Paul's attitude to
Judaism and especially to the Law. However, this is only part of the
wider revolution of our understanding of Second Temple Judaism in

general and how Jesus, Paul, and the early messianic communities fit into it, again following Sanders' work.[25]

Judaism during the period of the Second Temple—and especially during the years of Roman occupation and rule from 63 BCE until the destruction of the temple in 70 CE—was so multifaceted that many scholars now prefer the plural, "Judaisms." There were lots of different groups such as the Pharisees, Sadducees, Zealots, and Essenes, as well as smaller groups who formed around people like John the Baptist and various prophets of what we now term *restoration eschatology* (i.e., the hope that God was about to "restore the kingdom to Israel" in the "end-times," or *eschaton* in Greek: see the disciples' question to the risen Jesus in Acts 1:6). Such groups differed on practically every aspect of their understanding of Jewish practice and beliefs: compare the Sadducees' acceptance of only the Torah (the first five books of Moses) and their stress on the centrality of the sacrificial system in the temple (linked to the chief priests), plus their little or no understanding of life after death, with, in contrast, the Pharisees' use of all the Hebrew scriptures (including the Prophets and Writings), their attempt to keep ritual purity in daily life, and their belief in a paradise bliss beyond death. On the other hand, they both differed from the Zealots' attempt to bring in the kingdom through violence and "holy war," which was itself a complete contrast to the alternative Essene withdrawal into desert communities like Qumran—from which they issued bitter invectives against the leaders in Jerusalem, whom they described as "children of darkness" while they themselves were the "children of light."

The early communities of Jews who came to believe Jesus' proclamation of the kingdom of God would therefore have looked just like another subgroup within this broad mixture, opposing those who did not accept Jesus as Messiah, and arguing among themselves in good Jewish fashion whether Gentile proselytes were to be included, and on what grounds—baptism or circumcision?—and whether they were expected to keep the Law or not. These debates and arguments are reflected in the stories in Acts about the tensions between the Greek-speaking Jewish believers from the Diaspora and the more traditionalists living in Jerusalem (Acts 6) and the decisions of the council in Jerusalem to impose only the Noachide Commandments about idolatry, sexual immorality, and blood offenses (Acts 15). Acts also depicts the various Roman authorities treating all these disputes as internal Jewish disputes.

Thus in Greece, Gallio, proconsul of Achaia, "said to the Jews, 'If it were a matter of crime or serious villainy, I would be justified in accepting the complaint of you Jews; but since it is a matter of questions about words and names and your own law, see to it yourselves; I do not wish to be a judge of these matters.' And he dismissed them from the tribunal" (Acts 18:12-16). Or the governor Festus on putting Paul before King Agrippa:

> When the accusers stood up, they did not charge him with any of the crimes that I was expecting. Instead they had certain points of disagreement with him about their own religion and about a certain Jesus, who had died, but whom Paul asserted to be alive. Since I was at a loss how to investigate these questions, I asked whether he wished to go to Jerusalem and be tried there on these charges. But when Paul had appealed to be kept in custody for the decision of his Imperial Majesty, I ordered him to be held until I could send him to the emperor. (Acts 25:18-21)

Therefore the relationship between all these different groups, including those Jews who came to accept Jesus as Messiah, is better understood as that of different "siblings" within the greater matrix of Second Temple Judaism than as that of "parent-child"—and the various disputes and arguments between and among them fit into that typical Jewish acceptance of debate and disputes, often conducted, as with the Essenes, in most intemperate language and invective. Furthermore, if the first Jewish groups who believed in Jesus as Messiah can be likened to younger siblings arguing with their elder brothers and sisters like the Pharisees and Sadducees within the wider matrix of Second Temple Judaism, does Rabbi Sacks' idea of sibling rivalry provide a better model for this than the more traditional supersessionist understanding? To answer that important question, we need to examine the gospels in turn, each in their sociohistorical setting.

Mark's Gospel and the Jewish War/Revolt
Leading to the Destruction of the Temple (66–70 CE)

Mark's gospel fits well within this Second Temple milieu, and most scholars think that it was either composed in the 60s during the period of Nero's persecution of some early Christians at Rome (where Mark is traditionally associated with Peter's preaching)[26] or in the run-up to or actually during the Jewish Revolt and the siege of Jerusalem starting in 66 CE, which led to the final destruction of the temple in 70 CE.[27] You did not need divine powers to discern that the Romans' patience was likely to run out sooner or later, and therefore many scholars accept as historical Jesus' prophecy of both the destruction of Jerusalem and the final cataclysm in the so-called Markan apocalypse of chapter 13.[28]

Mark's gospel itself is not seen by New Testament interpreters as particularly "pro-" or "anti-Jewish"; while it does include teachings of Jesus about the observance of the Law, particularly with regard to the controversy over dietary laws (Mark 7:1-23), it seems to reflect a mixed and open community where "Jesus is the absolute authority under God," as William Loader puts it.[29] It is much more concerned with suffering and possible persecution, which reflects its presumed time period in the 60s—and also fits into this mixed and variegated picture of Second Temple Judaism prior to the destruction of the temple. Mark is not usually therefore brought into discussions about supersessionism.

The Jewish revolt against Roman rule led to full-scale war with the legions, culminating in troops surrounding Jerusalem, first under Vespasian, and then (when he went to become emperor in 70) under his son Titus. As Jerusalem was surrounded by the Roman siege works, there was bitter internal fighting going on inside the city between several of the warring factions—which led to many Jews being killed by their fellow Jews, especially as food stocks ran out and starvation was rampant—while the Romans were content to wait for the city to implode. It was then sacked, and the temple destroyed, with all the holy vessels being taken back to an imperial triumph in Rome, as depicted on the column in the Forum.

This brought about the end of the multifaceted nature of Second Temple Judaism, since what held most of the different groups together was a shared respect for the temple. The destruction of Jerusalem, and the temple itself, meant the end of the Sadducees and the priestly families, while the Zealots and their strongholds like Masada were defeated, and the desert communities of Essenes, such as at Qumran, were destroyed. This left only two main groups of survivors, which both had to find a new identity and unity without the temple as the common factor:

- emerging rabbinic Judaism (drawing upon the Pharisaic concern for the Law and all the scriptures, reconstituting around the synagogue, Torah interpretation, and identity markers including circumcision and food laws)
- and messianic Judaism (reconstituting around belief in Jesus, leading to the development of the early church, *ecclesia*, and increasingly Gentile mission).

These two groups may therefore be properly viewed as siblings, descendants from the same parental "matrix" of Second Temple Judaism, and therefore a good parallel to Rabbi Sacks' stories of sibling rivalry in Genesis. Thus we need to examine whether the other three gospels are narratives in which the "younger" sibling (i.e., the emerging church) attempts to displace the "elder" (i.e., the developing synagogue)— leading to the later history of supersessionism and anti-Semitic persecution. Once again, these are huge areas of gospel studies, so here we can only outline the overall argument and provide some footnotes and references to my other work, such as *Imitating Jesus*, for those who wish to follow it up in more detail.

Matthew's and Luke's Gospel
after the Destruction of the Temple (70–90 CE)

Matthew's gospel is a paradox. On the one hand it is (one of) the most Jewish writings in the New Testament. Its opening words, "the Book of the Genesis of Jesus the Christ/Messiah, son of David, son of Abraham" (Matt 1:1), immediately recall the Greek name of the first book of the Hebrew scriptures, and the references to David and Abraham are expanded by a careful genealogy, tracing Jesus' ancestry back through three lots of fourteen generations from Abraham to David, from David to the Exile, and from the Exile to Joseph, with fourteen being the numerical value of the Greek letters of the name of David (1:2-17). Then the account of Jesus' birth and the visit of the wise men, followed by the flight into Egypt, recapitulate the story of Moses, while the adult Jesus delivers his teaching from mountains in five great blocks reminiscent of Moses on Sinai and the five books of the Pentateuch (chs. 5–7, 10, 13, 18, 23–25). As son of David and son of Abraham, Jesus is also the new Moses, the incarnation of all of Israel's history sent to bring God's people back to him. Thus only Matthew makes Jesus tell his disciples to "Go nowhere among the Gentiles, and enter no town of the Samaritans, but go rather to the lost sheep of the house of Israel," a phrase he repeats himself in response to a Canaanite woman who is asking for his help (10:5-6, 15:24). Nevertheless, she persists, arguing that even the "dogs eat the crumbs" that fall from the table—and is finally rewarded for her faith through the healing of her daughter (15:26-28).

However, the central chapter of Matthew's gospel is a collection of the parables of the kingdom, which repeat a constant refrain of judgment and separation, of seeds that bear no fruit or a hundredfold, wheat and weeds, good fish and bad fish (13). As the leaders of the "lost sheep of Israel" reject his message or accuse him of being inspired by demons, complaining that he does not keep "the tradition of the elders" or seeking "a sign" (Matt 12:24-42, 15:1-9, 16:1-4), so a new community that does bear fruit is allowed to eat the food falling from the children's table. Thus we also find, on the other hand, that it is also only Matthew who uses the word *ecclesia* in his gospel as Jesus tells Peter he will build his "church" on this rock and gives instructions for how the church is to behave (16:18, 18:15-17). The rejection of his message, and the failure of the temple and the religious leaders to bear fruit (like the barren fig tree or the tenants of the vineyard withholding their produce, 21:12-13, 18-22, 33-46) results in Matthew collecting together an entire chapter, unique to his gospels, of polemical attacks on the Pharisees, "woe to you, scribes and Pharisees, hypocrites!" (ch. 23). Similarly, only Matthew describes Pilate washing his hands of Jesus while the crowd cry "his blood be upon us and our children" (27:24-25), a verse which gave rise to centuries of appalling persecution and accusations against the Jews as "Christ-killers." The final division takes place after the resurrection when the religious authorities bribe the guards at the tomb and instruct them to tell lies, while the disciples gather on the mountain to receive the commission from the one who was called Emmanuel, "God with us," at the start (1:23), that he will now be with them forever as they "make disciples of all nations" (28:11-15, 19-20).

And so it is that this most Jewish of gospels with Jesus recapitulating Moses and David while teaching about the "law and prophets" ends up with such a bitter denunciation of the Jewish religious authorities. As Graham Stanton puts it, "Matthew's vigorous anti-Jewish polemic is acutely embarrassing to most modern readers of this gospel."[30] Perhaps it is not surprising that Mel Gibson's portrayal of Matthew's account of Jesus' arrest, trial, and death in his 2004 film, *The Passion of the Christ*, should have stirred up so much controversy about it—or Matthew's gospel?—being "anti-Semitic." However, we need to be careful about such terminology. Scot McKnight prefers to use "anti-Semitism for irrational, personal, racial prejudice against Jews because they are Jews; anti-Judaism for the religious polemic exercised especially by early Christians who thought rejecting Jesus as Messiah was abandoning God's covenant with Israel."[31]

A historical analysis of Matthew's first-century context in the aftermath of the destruction of the temple and Jerusalem might help to explain how such a Jewish book ends up fueling anti-Semitism in the future. In an attempt to provide cohesion and a renewed identity, a gathering of rabbis at Yavneh/Jamnia in the mid-80s centered Jewish faith and worship around the Law and the synagogue, giving rise to the rabbinic tradition that has kept Judaism alive all around the world for two millennia. At some point, the so-called *birkat ha-minim* (blessing against the heretics) was included in the synagogue liturgy; if its invocation against the *notsrim* meant "Nazarenes," then from that time Jewish Christians could no longer worship with other Jews without cursing themselves. However the exact dating of the *birkat ha-minim* and the *notsrim* is disputed in current scholarship, so it is better to see the parting of the ways between the synagogue and the church as a gradual process, taking place around the Mediterranean during the end of the first century and beginning of the second.[32] Internal rows within families are often the most bitter, and civil wars the hardest fought. Matthew's portrayal of Jesus as the teacher of Israel reflects the bitterness and pain of this separation: it was not a polite agreement to differ or an amicable settlement. Interestingly, Ulrich Luz also uses the image of sibling conflict for the separation as "the Pharisees and the Jesus movement . . . both tried to define themselves as Israel" after the war.[33] Similarly, McKnight ends with his "contention that Matthew's Gospel, however harsh and unpleasant to modern sensitivities, is not anti-Semitic. It is, on the contrary, a compassionate but vigorous appeal to nonmessianic Judaism to respond to the Messiah."[34] But when it gets read "outside the family," as Christian scripture, it can appear "anti-Semitic" despite all its Semitisms and "anti-Jewish" despite its Jewish context.

Thus a careful (re-)reading of Matthew as a story of sibling rivalry might help to explain the bitterness in his writing and enable us to find Rabbi Sacks' counternarrative that the choice of one does not entail the rejection of the other within the universal love of God.[35]

In contrast to Matthew, Luke's gospel appears to be directed more at a Gentile readership and thus lacks most of Matthew's polemic. Jesus' genealogy is traced back to Adam, and Jesus' ministry is constantly directed at the poor and marginalized, women and non-Jews. Yet Luke is clearly aware of the scriptural background of the Septuagint (LXX) and writes in a Greek style which reflects that background, especially in the early chapters of his gospel with angels appearing to Zechariah and to Mary, and in the songs sung by the principal characters, the Benedictus, Magnificat, and Nunc Dimittis (Luke 1:5-25, 26-38, 46-55, 67-79; 2:28-32). However, once we move into Luke's main account of Jesus' ministry, the Pharisees are depicted in a better light, engaging Jesus in theological debate, often over dinner, and Jesus' criticisms emerge in conversation rather than all at once like Matthew's invective in Matthew 23. However, when we get to Jerusalem, we are told that "the chief priests, the scribes, and the leaders of the people sought to destroy him" (19:45-47). Similarly, in Luke's second volume, the Pharisees are shown supporting Peter and Paul in debates of the council, while the real opposition comes from the Sadducees, chief priests, and other leaders (Acts 4:1-6; 5:17-18, 33-40; 23:6-10; 24:1-9). Meanwhile, as previously noted, the Roman authorities tend to view these disputes as an internal Jewish debate (Acts 18:12-16, 25:18-21). Luke's decision to write his gospel with a sequel means that Luke–Acts provides what Daniel Marguerat calls "continuity *and* rupture."[36] In telling how the story of Jesus emerges out of Israel's history, followed by the growth of the early church, Luke includes both positive and negative material about Judaism—and both are held together. Luke's view of Jesus' universal mission means that his account includes both rejection (especially by the powerful leaders) and acceptance (especially by ordinary people), which leads to the formation of the new community, initially of believing Jews and then increasingly of Gentiles, who form the majority of Luke's probable intended audience.[37] While Luke therefore lacks Matthew's polemic arising from his involvement in the internal Jewish arguments of this period, Luke's narrative could be seen as leading nonetheless to the idea of a later supersessionist reading of the replacement of Israel by the early (Gentile) church, even if that was not his original intention.[38]

John's Gospel (90s): Sectarianism or the Parting of the Ways?

Finally, we come to the most vexed book in the New Testament for this (re-)reading of the narrative of supersessionism and anti-Semitism, which provided several of the key quotations used in persecution of Jews down the centuries, culminating in Nazi justifications for the Holocaust quoting Johannine texts like "you are of your father, the devil" (John 8:44).

First, we must note that, like Matthew, John is indelibly rooted in a Jewish context, with his narrative structured around all the Jewish festivals such as Passover, Tabernacles, and Hanukkah (John 2:13-25; 6:4; 7:2, 14; 10:22; 13:1; 18:28).[39] The main events take place in synagogues and around the temple (7:14; 8:2; 10:23; 18:20), often on a sabbath (5:9-10; 9:14-16). John displays a detailed knowledge of Judaism and the topography and geography of Jerusalem and the holy land. Thus the debates between Jesus and his opponents are conducted according to Jewish customs about witnesses and evidence (see 5:30-47), and great heroes like Moses and Abraham are brought into the arguments. The themes of the Law, the prophets, and the scriptures run constantly just below the surface, and particular quotations and prophecies are used through the passion (see, e.g., 12:15; 19:24, 28, 36).

The paradox is that John provides a biographical narrative of Jesus the Jew (John 4:9), who calls other Jews to be his disciples—yet, as the story progresses, he faces increasingly bitter opposition from a group who are termed simply "the Jews." While this phrase comes only five or six times in the other gospels, John uses it some seventy times. Some of these can be seen as "positive," especially those which refer to believing Jews (4:22, 8:30-31), including a number "of the Jews" consoling Mary and Martha and witnessing the raising of Lazarus, which led to "many of the Jews" believing in Jesus (11:19, 31, 36, 45); later, the chief priests are worried that "many of the Jews were going away and believing in Jesus" because of Lazarus (12:11). Other usages are more "neutral" descriptions, where "of the Jews" is another way of saying "Jewish" as in festivals "of the Jews" or purification and burial customs (2:6, 13; 5:1; 6:4; 7:2; 11:55; 19:40, 42).

However, the majority of the uses of this phrase are hostile, denoting those opposed to Jesus: "the Jews" send people to question John the Baptist and Jesus (John 1:19, 2:20), and they also interrogate those healed by Jesus (5:10-18, 9:18-34). The conflict grows through various debates with Jesus (6:42-52; 7:11-24; 8:22-29, 57), leading to acrimonious accusations that Jesus is a Samaritan and demon possessed, while Jesus says, "You are of your father, the devil" (8:44-48, 52).[40] "The Jews" seek to kill him (5:18, 7:1), stone him (10:31, 11:8), plot against him and Lazarus (11:47-53, 12:10-11), send officers to arrest him (18:12), interrogate him (18:19-23), hand him over to Pilate (18:28-31) and demand his death (18:38–19:15).

There have been various attempts to solve the problem of these hostile references by translating *hoi Iudaioi* as "Judaeans" or "the Jewish leaders." However, the phrase cannot be restricted either geographically or to the authorities, nor can it mean all Jews everywhere, at all times, then and now, given the fact that Jesus, the disciples, and other positive characters are Jews, and given the general Jewishness of the gospel. Therefore, it is clear that John is using this phrase "the Jews" to denote the main opposition to Jesus—which gives rise to the accusations of supersessionism and anti-Semitism. This is probably the biggest ethical challenge about the Fourth Gospel, provoking enormous scholarly debate. The twenty-five collected papers of the Leuven Colloquium in 2000 on *Anti-Judaism and the Fourth Gospel* run to some 550 published pages, while their "select bibliography" contains around four hundred items! As previously, there is much debate about whether this is best described as "anti-Semitism," "anti-Jewishness," or "anti-Judaism."[41] Even if the author himself cannot be accused of being "anti-Jewish" at the same time as writing such a Jewish book, nonetheless "the text itself can generate anti-Jewish prejudice, even if this prejudice was not present in the mind of the author";[42] in addition, there is the entire *Wirkungsgeschichte*, the history of the influence of this text, down to and including the use of it made by the Nazis and how we might interpret it today. Interestingly, the Leuven Colloquium was itself divided, with some contributors who argued that John was anti-Jewish also considering it to be supersessionist, while others who did not accept entirely the charge of being anti-Jewish also rejected supersessionism as well.[43]

Most scholarly attempts to handle this paradox—of such a Jewish book ending up promoting anti-Semitism—entail returning to a careful historical analysis of John's context and setting toward the end of the first century. Once again, it is probably best located within the period after the destruction of the temple and the attempt by the rabbis at Yavneh to provide a renewed focus for Judaism in the synagogue and the Torah, regardless of whether the *birkat ha-minim* was fully formulated then, as discussed above with regard to Matthew. The polemic employed by different sects against each other and especially opposing the religious-political leadership in Jerusalem was extremely bitter in the period of the Jewish War—and this continued after the tragedy of the destruction of Jerusalem and the temple. As Dunn notes, "The character of denunciation and quality of vituperation are remarkably consistent across the range of literature."[44] Therefore John's language and rhetoric, like Matthew's, should be seen as intra-Jewish debate going on within the wider Jewish family during those tumultuous decades after the destruction. However, while Matthew is probably writing during the 80s to an audience which still sees itself as deliberately Jewish, John is likely to be written a decade or so later to a community which has become more sectarian as a result of the tragic divisions and arguments. Thus Adele Reinhartz, as a Jewish scholar, concludes, "This is not to say that the principal goal of the gospel is to promote anti-Judaism. Rather, the gospel's anti-Judaism is a by-product of the evangelist's strong convictions regarding the identity and salvific role of Jesus on the one hand, and his tendency to view not only attributes and actions but also communities in a polarized way."[45]

Finally, we should conclude with the fourth evangelist's main counternarrative of the universal love of God for *everyone*. He summarizes it in his programmatic verse that Jesus "came to what was his own" (*ta idia*, neuter plural) but "his own [people?]" (*hoi idioi*, masculine plural) "did not receive him"; but to "*all* who received him, who believed in his name, he gave power to become children of God" (John 1:11-12). This "all people" is fully inclusive of both Jews and Gentiles alike, as is made clear in John's most famous verse, "For God so loved the world that he gave his only Son, so that everyone who believes in him may not perish but may have eternal life" (John 3:16). As the Leuven editors concluded, "Even if we cannot help but admit that the entire gospel is affected by an anti-Jewish attitude, the text projects an alternative world of all-inclusive love and life which transcends its anti-Judaism. It is the world of the text, and not the world of the author that is a witness to divine revelation."[46] Thus, once again, we are back to Rabbi Sacks' counternarrative that the choice of one does not entail the rejection of the other within the universal love of God.[47]

Conclusions:
Re-Reading Together for the
Counternarrative of God's Universal Love

This paper set out to determine whether a narrative of supersessionism and anti-Semitism is a necessary consequence of reading the New Testament texts. By emulating Rabbi Sacks' example of a careful and respectful (re-)reading of the scriptural stories from Genesis, I have tried to demonstrate a similar counternarrative in the New Testament books, which also leads to the conclusion that the choice of one does not necessitate the rejection of the other. To discover this counternarrative, it is necessary in each case to set the various gospels and letters within their first-century social and historical context.

Firstly, *reading the earlier New Testament writings between the death of Jesus and the Jewish war (40–66 CE)* reveals that they belong within an internal, intra muros, family dispute taking place between all the various siblings and children of multifaceted Second Temple Judaism—or even Judaisms in the plural. Such antagonism and vitriol as may be found in these New Testament writings fits perfectly within that internal Jewish debate and is actually less vituperative than can be found in, for example, the Dead Sea Scrolls and other Jewish literature. In fact, these earlier New Testament books, especially the letters of Paul, still stress God's continuing love and purposes for the Jews, despite the controversies.

Secondly, *reading the New Testament (especially the gospels) during the period after the destruction of Jerusalem and the temple (80s–90s CE)* reveals a (still mostly?) internal, intra muros, family dispute of sibling rivalry between the only two groups surviving the destruction, namely emerging rabbinic Judaism (reconstituting around the synagogue, Torah interpretation, and identity markers including circumcision and food laws) and messianic Judaism/the developing early church (reconstituting around belief in Jesus, leading to the *ecclesia*). This increasingly bitter internal argument can help to explain the paradox whereby Matthew and John's gospels, in particular, can be simultaneously both very Jewish, yet give rise to texts that will later be used for anti-Semitism, without the authors or original audiences intending those consequences. Here we can apply Rabbi Sacks' conclusion about the Genesis sibling rivalry stories that the choice of one does not necessitate the rejection of the other also to this situation; that is to say, the New Testament material about God's choice of an increasingly Gentile church need not necessitate the rejection of Jews and Judaism.

However, thirdly, *reading the New Testament after the Constantinian settlement (312 CE)* takes us into an external, extra muros, dispute of one religion (recently successful and dominant) against a separate (and increasingly despised and discriminated against) minority religious group.[48] This social and historical context makes the New Testament writings look completely different, which leads to the development of supersessionist readings in which the church replaces Judaism, and the rise of anti-Semitism culminates, eventually, in the Nazis and the Holocaust. To understand this process, we might draw a comparison with the fact that Jewish or Irish comedians are the only ones allowed to tell Jewish or Irish jokes—and even Rabbi Sacks himself is fond of many anecdotes and stories about rabbis and their arguments. However, what is acceptable and even normal within a family or group has a nasty tendency to read or sound very different when taken outside that family or group: a white, English or American comedian telling jokes about "the Irish" or "the Jews" or people of color will inevitably be seen as racist and offensive. As Amy-Jill Levine concedes, "The analogy to the ethnic joke is somewhat apt."[49]

Finally, we need to learn *to (re-)read the counternarrative together today in an inclusive community* in order not only to avoid the supersessionist and discriminatory readings but also to discover the counternarrative of God's universal love. Elsewhere I have argued that it was not surprising that white Afrikaners reading and interpreting the scriptures on their own should lead to their theological justification of apartheid, in contrast to the inclusive approach of the Truth and Reconciliation Commission where the victims and perpetrators of all ethnic and social groups had to learn to listen to and understand each other.[50] We might also compare the impact of some senior women being allowed to be present and to be heard in the Church of England's House of (male) Bishops on the eventual decision to consecrate women bishops in recent years. Similarly, the current debates on sexuality within the church are struggling to be able to listen to the experiences of lesbian, gay, and transgender people: as the slogan goes, "don't talk about us without us." If we are to avoid traditional interpretations of supersessionist and anti-Semitic readings of the New Testament, we will need to find ways to (re-)read these writings together today, in order to understand and appreciate what effect such readings have on others and, together, to discover the counternarrative of the universal love of God.

Thus, in conclusion, just as Rabbi Sacks' (re-)reading in his book *Not in God's Name* of the sibling rivalry stories in Genesis of Ishmael and Isaac, Esau and Jacob, Leah and Rachel, and Joseph and his brothers led to the counternarrative of a renewed understanding that "the choice of one does not necessitate the rejection of the other" and to the "rejection of rejection," so a careful (re-)reading of the relevant New Testament passages, especially in their literary and historical context as part of a "sibling rivalry" within first-century Judaism, should also lead to a rejection of later anti-Semitism and supersessionism, to be replaced by a renewed counternarrative in appreciation of the universal love of God, which will not permit violence in his name.

3

OPEN RELIGION AND ITS ENEMIES

Guy G. Stroumsa

Religious violence seems to be winning the day—not only by murdering, maiming, and terrorizing, all around the globe, but also, at the same time, by telling a powerful narrative. We—all the rest of us—are on the defensive and are asked to provide a counternarrative, as if our fight was a rear-guard one. This is the core of our predicament.[1]

One may, of course, disclaim the alarmist whistle: men (and sometimes women) have always been violent, and religion has nothing, or not much, to do with nature and instincts. At worst, one may describe religious beliefs or practices as "fuel" thrown on natural behavior. But the issue of religious violence is one of deep existential urgency—and not only of serious intellectual interest. I may perhaps be able to formulate, at least vaguely, some of the questions. But I also hope to hear some answers, at least tentative.

What is, then, the narrative for which we are seeking a counternarrative? In a nutshell, it is fair, I think, to refer to the universal and perennial battle cry: "Gott mit uns!" It is with it that gods (and sometimes goddesses) have always and everywhere empowered their believers to kill in good conscience, the name of the Supreme Good. One way to disassemble this grenade would be to argue, following Epicurus, that the gods have better to do than getting involved in the pettiness of human affairs. Since Plato, the church fathers, and the rabbis of the Talmud, however, the Epicurean belief has been deemed anathema. If

God, then, insists on being involved with humans, can he manage not to take sides?

As a historian, I can only reflect on a number of striking points relating to early Christianity and, more broadly, to late antique religious history. Since the Christianization of the Roman Empire, with the conversion of Constantine in 312, one can observe a fast, unambiguous rise in religious intolerance and violence. This rise did not end with Theodosius I's proclamation, in 380, of the Edict of Thessalonica (*Cunctos populos*), which made Christian Nicene orthodoxy the state religion of the empire, imposed on all but the Jews. The fifth and sixth centuries, both in the Greek East and in the Latin West, showed the continued limitation of religious freedom and disenfranchisement of the Jews, accompanied with more and more frequent outbursts of religious violence. Could the religion of universal love be responsible for such violence? Such slander (amounting to a crime of *lèse divinité*!) has of course been countered, rather glibly, by a long list of apologetic writers since the church fathers. A contemporary observer may notice some similarity between this apologetic line and that arguing that "true Islam" (or, for that matter, "true Judaism") is a religion of peace and can in no way be held responsible for violent actions of thugs claiming to be true believers.

My title refers, first, to Bergson's famous analysis of *open* versus *closed* religion in his seminal work—alas, almost forgotten today—*The Two Sources of Morals and Religion*.[2] For Bergson, the prophets of Israel represented open religion, while the priestly rituals reflected closed religion. At the same time, the title alludes to Karl Popper's classical *Open Society and Its Enemies*,[3] a work written during the dark years of World War II. In a nutshell, "Open Religion and Its Enemies" reflects my belief that, like cholesterol, religion can be either good or bad, and that the enemies of open religion can be identified. They are, essentially, all beliefs and patterns of behavior according to which religious truth belongs to me, to my group, and is denied from the other. Unsurprisingly, it is in religious intolerance that religious violence finds its roots. Let me reflect first on radical religion in the Christianized Roman Empire. I shall then insist on some psychological and social transformations of identity in late antiquity, highlighting their consequences for our present question.

1. Radical Religion and the Shrinking of Tolerance in Late Antiquity

Searching for the origins of religious intolerance, the Egyptologist Jan Assmann singles out what he calls the *Mosaic distinction* as the major element responsible in the ancient world for the introduction of a Weltanschauung intolerant of alternate conceptions. The Mosaic distinction refers to the Israelite conception of religion as identical with truth. Such a conception entails the view of other religions—in particular, polytheistic systems—as reflecting error. According to Assmann, the Mosaic distinction is the most important source of religious intolerance, as we know it in the Western world.[4]

In a sense, Assmann reaches conclusions rather similar to those who contrast the monotheistic intolerance of ancient Israel with Greek and Roman polytheistic tolerance.[5] According to this view, traditional since the Enlightenment, Christian intolerance is but a by-product of Israelite and Jewish particularism. To some extent, as shown, for instance, by Voltaire's case, such a view can lead to intellectual attitudes rather dangerously close to anti-Semitic conceptions, in which contemporary Jews, as the heirs of the ancient Israelites, are perceived as ultimately responsible for religious (i.e., Christian) violence and intolerance. Whatever conclusion we may reach about the degree to which Judaism informed the early Christian perception of other religious views, there can be no doubt about the importance of the Jewish heritage in early Christianity, and one must therefore start with some remarks on the possible Jewish roots of early Christian intolerance.

Jewish Roots

The God of Israel is a jealous God. He hates the false gods, the idols, and those who render cult to them. More generally, he also hates any false religious attitude and any wrongdoing; ethical behavior, in the Hebrew Bible more clearly than in most other religious systems of the ancient world, is considered to play a central role in religious life. Thus the priest Phinehas follows religious duty when he kills the Israelite man and the Midianite woman with whom he was sleeping (Num 25:7-8). Throughout both the Jewish and the Christian exegetical tradition, Phinehas' behavior would be praised as showing "zeal" for the Lord (the Greek word *zèlos* translates the Hebrew *kin'a*, "jealousy," in the Septuagint), thus imitating a divine quality. Religious zeal, later to become enthusiasm, and then fanaticism, was indeed for a long time a leading religious value in the biblical tradition.

In the Hebrew Bible, such zeal is found in particular in the behavior of the prophets. Even when they strike against official and traditional religion, it is in the name of the Lord that they do it, passionately arguing for a return to God's original ethical and cultic demands from his people. For the prophets, the history of Israel reflects constant betrayal of its calling (*Beruf*), followed, time and again, by repentance. At the public level, the demand for the restoration of the true cult against all usurpations may become a call for combat or for a "holy war" (note that the concept itself does not appear in the Bible). In any case, the Maccabean revolt against both the Seleucid king Antiochus Epiphanes IV and the Jewish elites in Palestine, who supported his cultural and religious policy, clearly reflects the demand of a collective zeal for God and the absolute intolerance of idolatry. During the Second Commonwealth, the call for holy war was echoed mainly in the transformation of prophecy into apocalypticism. At the end of times, the eschatological war would end in the final victory of the forces of good and the defeat of the forces of evil. In the language of the Qumran scrolls, this war would be fought between the sons of light and the sons of darkness.

Early Christianity

The religious trends reflected in apocalyptic literature are, as is well known, very close to the original milieu in which Christianity was born and first developed, as a Jewish sect in the first century. Traces of the eschatological war and of apocalyptic patterns of thought are still visible in both the Synoptic Gospels and in John's Apocalypse. As with all sectarian milieus, which thrive on a combination of violent internal strife and radical rejection of the other, it was a milieu in which there was, manifestly, little room for religious tolerance. In many ways, then, the Jewish heritage of early Christianity was one of rejection and intolerance. Like all outlawed and persecuted sects, and in particular as it thought the end of days was near, earliest Christianity was expressing radical views with great intensity. Such an atmosphere left little room for the development of any notion of religious tolerance.

Yet, unlike the Essenes, the Christians did not remain Jewish sectarians for a long time. Christianity emerged as a type of religion that one may call *secondary*—that is, a religion born out of another religion, in contrast with it and in opposition to it. (Judaism, in this sense, would be called a primary religion.) It is usually assumed that the monotheistic roots of Christianity are responsible for its intolerance of other religious ideas and the later persecution of their proponents. There is no doubt that early Christian patterns of behavior toward outsiders and patterns of thought about outsiders are deeply imbedded in earlier Israelite and Jewish attitudes and ideas. Christianity owed to its biblical background the establishment of identity on religion and the centrality of the concept of a single religious truth as opposed to error (which is polyvalent by nature—Irenaeus can speak about the "hydra" of heresy), and hence the development of both religious thought and ethics as central to religion.

Yet the differences between the two religions under the empire are as significant as the similarities between them. In its rejection of the Law and of the centrality of Jewish ethnicity, mainstream Christianity believed it had suppressed religious exclusivism. The religious structures of Christianity were significantly different from those of Judaism; for the clearly defined collective boundaries was substituted the ambiguity of a dogma meant for all—meant for all, but which of course excluded the many who did not know or accept it.

The fact that Christianity shared with Judaism a deep denial of religious tolerance for false religions, offering a cult to false gods—that is, idols (or demons)—does not explain the fact that Christians, more than Jews, developed strong patterns of religious intolerance in late antiquity. In a study of early Christianity as a radical religion, I employed the Weberian concept of *Entpolitisierung*, which refers to those literati who, pushed aside from political activity or responsibility, could play freely with conceptions artificially detached from their natural social applicability.[6] So, I argued, radical ideas, often presented as hermeneutics of the sacred texts, were developed, without the need to show their concrete applicability. When, all of a sudden, the conditions changed radically, and the literati found themselves "politicized" (*politisiert*), the simplest, easiest, and laziest option was to apply literally the corpus of hermeneutical texts to the new reality. Visions of the end, for instance, stemming from apocalyptic literature, could now be presented as concrete political programs, with their dreams of a cosmic war between sons of light and sons of darkness.

Early Christianity, then, remained for some time a radical religion, harboring intense expectations for the Second Coming of Christ, the Parousia, and redemption of humankind. The first generations of Christians saw themselves as soldiers in the cosmic war between God and his Son and the ruler of this world, Satan, and his acolytes. They were few, engaged in a world war against the powerful forces of evil. In that sense, the earliest Christian communities, despite the profound theological, cultural, and sociological differences between them, and despite the new identity that they were in the process of developing, retained some significant similarities with the worldview of the Jewish sectarians of first-century Palestine, in particular their utopianism and millenarianism.

Like the Qumran covenanters, the earliest Christian communities developed their theological conceptions in radical isolation from, and opposition to, almost anyone else, both Jews and pagans. The Christians considered themselves to be the true Israel, *verus Israel*—that is, their borrowed identity linked them directly to the history of ancient Israel. They interpreted correctly the message of the biblical prophets, whom the contemporary Jews misunderstood, and identified with the ancient history of Israel. Their cultural memory, however, never really became rooted in ancient Israelite society.

In their successful attempt to break the circle of sectarianism and establish themselves as followers of a religion in its own right, the early Christians soon drew their own identity in terms profoundly different from any kind of Jewish identity. The Christians had given up on all the known ingredients of Jewish identity: legal prescriptions of the Torah and the oral law, including kinship rules, language, and territory. They were, indeed, in the words of the second-century Epistle to Diognetus, a *tertium genus* (*triton genos*, a new, "third" kind of people), "from all the peoples," as the Persian sage Afrahat would say in the fourth century. Early Christian cultural memory, then, despite affirmations of being the "true Israel," was deeply different from Jewish cultural memory: it lacked the latter's sense of concrete roots in past Israelite society.

The Christians had voluntarily given up the traditional characteristics of Jewish identity boundaries and had, hence, to build anew identity markers of their own. As they could not use any of the usual identity markers provided by language, territory, or polity, they had to focus on theological ideas. The definition of orthodoxy as the narrow track meandering between the various dangers provided by heresies of all sorts was the backbone of this new identity. Until the fourth century, this would provide the major battlefield of Christianity in the making. More than the blood of the martyrs, the fight for the correct interpretation of the scriptures—the ongoing argument with the Gnostics, dualists, and docetists of all kinds, toward the constantly sharper definition of Christian orthodoxy—would provide the leading story of early Christianity. Clearly, the constant and rigorous watch for unacceptable understandings of Jesus Christ and his message would offer ample space for polemics and rejection of competing views.[7]

Jews and Christians in the Early Empire

The same first centuries also saw the making of rabbinic Judaism and the crystallization of talmudic culture. It is this fact, precisely, that highlights the deep difference between the two orthodoxies: while the rule of faith (*kanōn tēs pisteōs*) is central to Christian identity, the rabbis thrive on polemical discussions about all legal and extralegal matters. The fact that consensus is rarely reached does not usually engender a split: "both are the words of the living God" (*elu ve-elu divrei Elohim hayyim*, i.e., opposing opinions are equally legitimate) is the traditional talmudic way of summarizing legal arguments between two rabbis.

While the church fathers, partakers of an ecumenical faith, are in the business of excluding all dissenters, it is precisely Jewish exclusivism which permits a rather liberal acceptance of dissenting views within the community, together with a deep (and nonpolemical) lack of interest for whatever and whoever lies outside the community. Oddly enough, this paradox does not seem to have been clearly noticed and reflected on. What should be emphasized here is that the systematic fight against heretics takes place together with the dramatic proselytizing movement in Christianity that established it as a world religion, within and without the borders of the Roman Empire. One retains the impression that these two phenomena are not quite disconnected: together with the fast spreading of Christian faith, the need for clear boundaries is intensely felt, and this need cannot be filled with the traditional characteristics of collective identity. Hence the need is felt for more and more stringent arguments against all kinds of deviance from the (single) right belief on any major point of theology. It goes without saying that such arguments repeatedly limit the boundaries of legitimate religious thought, concomitantly enlarging those of rejected heterodox views. It is in that sense that we should first understand the paradox of a Christian universalism reflecting intolerant character more clearly than Jewish exclusivism, which had given up, at least to some extent (and due to the presence and success of Christianity) on the Jewish proselytism of old.

A surprising and rather paradoxical consequence of theological universalism and dynamic proselytism, then, is its strengthening of intolerant trends in early Christianity. But this is not all. As we shall see below, it is also on other, psychological grounds that universal pretenses foster intolerance: when salvation is offered to all and sundry, those daring enough to reject it soon become objects of anger, even hatred, on the part of the Christians who feel that their generous love of humankind is not returned in kind. Such psychological grounds are clearly visible in the development of Christian attitudes toward Jews. The topic of the growth of Christian anti-Judaism, and of its possible transformation into attitudes that one must call anti-Semitic, is obviously much too big to be treated here.[8] What I want to call attention to in the present context is the intolerant side of this attitude. Christian intolerance toward Jews, however, usually remained limited by a modicum of toleration. As mentioned above, the Jews remained tolerated more than other enemies of Christian order, such as heretics and pagans.

Tolerated, perhaps, though not really accepted, and retaining an uncomfortable place on the margins of Christian society: it was impossible for the Christians to completely erase the presence of the Jews, as the memory of Israel loomed large in their own identity. The Jews were a testimony of the divine promise, "living letters of the Law." But they were also the offspring of Christ's murderers, who in their continuous stubbornness refused to recognize the Messiah whom God had sent them, when all around the world people had converted to the new faith. Hence, it proved very difficult not to develop a strong anger, even hatred, against the Jews. This aversion had begun early. John's Gospel had called them "Satan's first born," while Melito, in second-century Sardis, was the first to speak of them as "God killers."

The major transformation of Christian anti-Jewish discourse, however, was effected during the fourth century. Constantine, who only asked for toleration of Christianity, could refer to the Jews as "that deadly sect." Throughout the century, as the progress of Christianity was more and more sensible, the violence of Christian anti-Jewish discourse became clearer. The seeds had been there for a long time, but they could now bloom, as it were, under the new political conditions that were revolutionizing the status of Christianity. The bishops, leaders of the formerly *religio illicita*, were now filling the corridors of power from Constantinople to Milan, and their voice was heard loud and clear. The long-standing accusations against the Jews and their religion, which had over Christianity the advantage of a legal status, had long remained dormant—or in any case devoid of any real power—as long as the Christians had been disenfranchised (or *entpolitiesiert*, to use Max Weber's term). They were now activated and, in the course of the fourth century, we can observe a strange phenomenon: the transfer to the Jews of some qualities (or rather vices) until then identified only with pagans. As soon as the pagan threat to Christianity was perceived as less virulent, the perception of paganism as a cult (or rather a variety of cults) offered to idols or demons was transferred to Judaism. In other

words, we can observe then a "paganization" of the Christian perception of Judaism, as it were, which directly entails a demonization of
the Jews: those who practice a cult of demons in their synagogues, for
the first time identified as pagan temples or theaters, are themselves in
the process of becoming demons, supporters of Satan, indeed, his "first
born." With John Chrysostom's eight sermons *Kata tōn Ioudaiōn*, written in the 380s, this process reaches a new stage, and the passage from
theological anti-Judaism to a much deeper hatred of Jews—what we
call anti-Semitism—seems to be fully accomplished, even with Robert
Wilken's proviso about the rules of late ancient rhetoric, which explain
some of Chrysostom's verbal violence, and the recognition that he was
fighting a still very active Jewish competition for the minds and hearts
of Christian communities.[9]

2. Personal and Social Identity: Transformations and Impact

Individual and Collective Identity

From Paul to Constantine and Augustine, as we have seen, two radical
changes occurred in the perception of identity. The new parameters of
personal identity emphasized the integration of soul and body into the
definition of the human person as a composite. It has been noted above,
however, that in the emerging conception, the person was not quite a
harmonious one. Instead of the divide between soul and body typical
of Platonism, the idea of an original sin brought with it a new break,
this time within the soul itself. This break was due to a sense of guilt,
inescapable because sin was inherited and ever present. This state of
affairs strengthened the need for a salvation that went far beyond the
individual and his or her behavior. Repentance for one's sins, indeed,
expressed this need of salvation only in part. Christian salvation entailed
total removal of sin. Such an attitude was bound to enhance a tension
within the soul unknown among Greek philosophers. In this framework, faith became not only the sine qua non of salvation but also almost
equivalent to it. Faith in Jesus Christ and his redemptive sacrifice, in
itself, saved.

Social identity, on its side, was also submitted in early Christianity
to a radical reinterpretation. For the first time in the ancient world,
identity became defined in religious terms, not in ethnic or cultural-
linguistic ones (as was the case in the Hellenistic and Roman worlds).
This new approach to social identity is perhaps best reflected in the
new corpus of laws being developed from the time of Constantine up

to Theodosius II in the first decades of the fifth century and collected in the Codex Theodosianus.

These laws show the importance of defining the church and the centers of authority within it. This implied a constant effort at defining the boundaries of the Christian community. Since the traditional Jewish criteria, such as ethnicity, language, and halakah, were not available any more, only dogma could provide the definition of the new social identity. Dogma—that is, the proper way to understand Jesus Christ, his nature, and his mission. Hence, for the first time, collective identity was defined in terms directly rooted in interiorization, in belief. True belief—or orthodoxy—was itself defined by its negation and reflected the many faces of error: heterodoxy or heresy from within and Judaism and paganism from without.[10]

The social definition of church boundaries, however, reflected not only opposition to error but also the desire, inherent to Christianity from its very beginnings, to broaden its appeal; in other words, the church boundaries reflect Christianity's very catholicity, its strong and successful urge to convert. Conversion is the other side of the essentially dogmatic definition of the new religion: it implies a choice between truth and error.

The consequences of this state of affairs for our present purpose are as follows:

Both individual and collective identity are redefined in early Christianity in direct relation to the interiorization process. As pointed out above, both also reflect the limitations of this process. The fight between faith and sin within the individual and the fight between truth and error at the collective level seem to follow parallel patterns. Since truth comes from Jesus Christ, error comes from the Antichrist, from Satan. A choice of belief stands at the basis of the formation of both individual and collective identity and establishes an element of intolerance in the very definition of Christian identity. To be sure, intolerance has many faces, not all of them religious, and religious intolerance itself did not start with Christianity. But what seems to happen very clearly in early Christianity, and what will remain an ominous legacy in the Western world, is the following: the two sides of intolerance related to identity formation seem to strengthen each other. A strong sense of the unavoidable presence of sin does not prevent self-righteousness (paradoxically, the contrary seems sometimes to be true), while an interiorized strong feeling of certainty directly leads to religious persecution. These processes, which deserve serious study, are very complex and can be studied only in the *longue durée*. I have been able here only to allude to them.

Therefore, I should like to come back to the revolutionary character of early Christian beliefs with which I began. If the direction followed here is basically correct, it is less these beliefs in themselves than the overall structure and status of interiorization in the new religion that is responsible for the growing religious intolerance that is one of the hallmarks of late antiquity. Like other revolutions, the Christian revolution succeeded to a remarkable extent in suppressing freedom in the name of liberation.

Eristic versus Irenic: Love and Intolerance

I have elsewhere called attention to the influence exerted by what can be called eristic tendencies in New Testament texts.[11] One must now go further and insist also on the following paradox. The absolute and unconditional command of love cannot be considered irenic. Indeed, the hiatus between the attitude dictated by the command of love and social and psychological reality entails a deep and irreducible tension, usually referred to as *cognitive dissonance*. As John Gager has shown, the cognitive dissonance between messianic expectations and the disappointment caused by Jesus' crucifixion is fundamental for understanding the development of first- and second-century Christianity.[12] Anthropologists make use of the term *rituals of reversal* in order to describe the peculiar phenomena observed in some societies in times of particularly intense tensions due to chiliastic expectations.[13] The term might be useful in reference to the command of love for the enemies. The new attitude is perceived as radical and paradoxical by its proponents. It is opposed to any legitimate expectation; in other words, it is utopian. We have seen how this command is linked to the idea of secret hatred in Essene theology. Hence, some links between this command and the esoteric trends in early Christian doctrine (trends ignored by most scholars) cannot be excluded.[14]

Gert Theissen, who speaks of an "introjective aggressiveness turned into self-acceptance," offers a first attempt at a psychoanalytical interpretation of the command of love.[15] Freud himself, however, had already pointed out with great clarity the tragic paradox of this command. In a striking, yet generally unnoticed, passage of *Civilization and its Discontents*, Freud emphasized the direct relationship between the idea of love of mankind and that of intolerance.

> After the apostle Paul made general love of mankind (*die allgemeine Menschenliebe*) the foundation of his Christian community, the greatest intolerance towards those who remained outside this community (*die aüsserte Intoleranz gegen die draussen Verbliebenen*) became the unavoidable consequence. The Romans, who had not established their political collectivity upon love, did not know religious intolerance, although religion was a state matter for them, and the state imbibed with religion.[16]

To be sure, the lack of historical precision of this passage, as well as its rather sweeping generalization, do weaken the statement made by Freud. Indeed, we cannot ignore the limits of Roman religious toleration. Even before their ferocious fight against Christianity, the Romans reacted violently to the second century BCE development of the Bacchic cult in Magna Graecia and to the first century CE rise of the Druidic cult in Gaul.[17] One must also insist upon the deep ambiguity and the limits of any conception of tolerance—be it religious or political—in antiquity. We might perhaps refer here to the idea developed by Paul Veyne concerning belief in the gods in ancient Greece.[18] In order to explain the double attitude of belief and skepticism among Greek intellectuals up to Plutarch, Veyne appeals to what he calls "truth programs" (*programmes de vérité*). The same person can show signs of faith and disbelief at different levels. In this way, it seems to me, one can refer without oversimplification to the complex relationships between tolerance and intolerance in the first Christian centuries. There are no *Idealtypen* in historical reality. It is, in each case, the specific equilibrium between tolerance and rejection of the other that distinguishes between the different attitudes.

These remarks however should not overshadow the original intuition of Freud (who seems here to extrapolate on 1 Cor 13). He does not say what would be only partly true—that Christian monotheism, confronted with Roman polytheism, shows clear signs of intolerance. The roots of Christian intolerance, according to Freud, should be found not in the idea of a single God but in the totalitarian character of a universal command of love. In other words, it is the very universalism of Christianity that is shown here to be threatening. By right, the Christian community must include all mankind. A refusal to join the community of believers reflects a perverse and shocking vice. While ethnic or religious particularism tends to turn rather quickly into exclusivism that ignores or despises outsiders, ecumenical inclusivism entails the delegitimization of the other's existence and hence generates tensions and violent intolerance. For Arnaldo Momigliano, the roots of religious intolerance in the Western world are to be found to a large extent in Christian universalism.[19] Momigliano comes close to the conclusions of Paul Hacker in his analysis of what he called Indian *inclusivism*, an attitude to be strongly distinguished, Hacker argues, from true religious tolerance.[20]

One should also note that the duty of perfection central to Jesus' teaching ("Be perfect as your Father in heaven is perfect," according to Matt 5:48) entails the highest ethical and spiritual standards, and hence harsh disappointment upon the inevitable failure in meeting these standards. In other words, it is the *combination* of the idea of love—and the duty of love—and the universalist nature of Christianity that Freud finds to be so threatening, almost totalitarian in its unattainable expectations.

Last but not least, Freud's intuition about the deep-seated ambiguity of the Christian idea of total love refutes a central thesis of René Girard, according to which only Christianity, through the love sacrifice of Jesus, avoids the violence intrinsic to any other form of expression of the sacred.[21]

3. Activism and Conviction

"The letter kills, but the spirit gives life." Paul's lapidary dictum (2 Cor 3:6) soon became a cornerstone of Christian thought and sensitivity. Prima facie, it would seem to preempt the danger of "fundamentalism" (in the broader sense of a literal reading of the scriptures) within Christianity. Paul's words, indeed, have always been understood as referring to the Old Testament, while the New Testament, reflecting the teaching and actions of Jesus, means for Christian consciousness, above all, an *exemplum*, to follow in the *imitatio Christi*.[22] But the imitation of Christ entails an activist attitude. When the reading of the gospels became politicized, as was the case in the fourth century, the ambiguities, the tensions, and the contradictions in the figure of Jesus would soon be reflected in Christian life. Side by side with the ascetical and mystical *imitatio Christi*, one would find the *zèlos* of religious activists in late antiquity, these monks whom Gibbon, although he avoided the term, considered to be fanatics.[23]

The tragedy of ancient Christianity is not directly dependent on the cognitive dissonance created by the delay *sine die* of the Second Coming. Rather, this tragedy reflects the Christians' lack of sensitivity to the dissonance caused by the reading of utopian texts in a new political context and their new power to activate them. I wish to insist here on the importance of *actualization*, a concept opposite to *neutralization*, in order to understand various phenomena in the history of religions.

Christian utopia lies at the very heart of New Testament kerygma.[24] The French ancient historian Fustel de Coulanges could say how, together with Christianity, "the spirit of propaganda replaced the law of exclusion." The problem here stems from the very fact that Christianity is a religion of conviction, based on the spirit rather than on the letter, in contradistinction with the religions of the ancient world and even to some extent with Judaism. Conviction, indeed, entails the duty to convince, but also, too often, the urge to conquer. The strength of the Christian message is an inherently ambiguous force, which is also at the root of an ineluctable, though spiritual, will to power.

Paradoxically, then, the universal drive in religion (traditionally, unreflectively considered in a positive light) has often led to religious intolerance and violence, more so than has religious exclusivism, which has traditionally retained room for other religious identities beyond the community boundaries.

Conclusion

The preceding pages are far from having offered a full-fledged analysis of the rise of religious violence in late antiquity. As a historical case study, early Christianity might offer us some perspective on our present predicament. In conclusion, I can only call attention to a number of points relevant to our present discussion.

(1) Since 1957, social scientists have spoken—following Leon Festinger and his associates—of *cognitive dissonance*, referring to deep shocks in the belief systems of people after events dispelled those beliefs (for instance, the coming of the Messiah). I propose to introduce the corollary concept of *cognitive consonance*. What happens to the belief systems of people when events suddenly, or surprisingly, confirm their beliefs? The first Christian communities, like the Qumran covenanters, could retain radical, violent eschatological beliefs in check as long as they were *entpolitisiert*. Although they read radical texts (such as the *War Scroll* or John's Apocalypse) through a literal hermeneutic, this reading did not endanger anyone, as they were totally powerless. The real problem started with the Christianization of the Roman Empire, when they retained the same simplistic hermeneutics, while political and military power was now on their side. Hence, the direct responsibility for holy violence should not be attributed to religious texts (even when they are indeed violent) but rather to unsophisticated hermeneutics.

(2) Religion belongs at once to the private and to the public sphere. In other words, there are both individual and collective aspects to religious identity. While the spectrum of the impact of religion on both the private and the public domain varies greatly between internalized religion and universalized religion—according to the nature of the religion involved and to each historical and cultural context—no religious life can ignore either private or public life. A lack of balance between the private and the public expression of religion is bound to create tensions leading to violence. Similarly, the dialectical interplay between religious (and ethnic) and cultural identities may lead to religious violence when the chasm between the two is too great, creating dissociation between religious and cultural identity. Open and closed modes of religiosity are found in all religious traditions. To some extent, those can be seen as reflecting centrifugal and centripetal forces. The present struggle is set, essentially, not between "religions," but between modes of religiosity, within each religious tradition.

(3) In modern societies (and the same is true in the postmodern "global village"), open religion entails embracing religious pluralism in the public sphere. Hence traditional religious identities must undergo deep hermeneutical transformations in order to become full and active participants in their societies (rather than passive onlookers, tolerated by and tolerating the other faute de mieux). The core of these transformations is represented by the passage *from religious to cultural memory*. While the first is centered on the experience of the group, the second integrates the religious memories of other groups within a given society. The transformation of religious memory into cultural memory will be the counternarrative to that breeding religious violence.[25] In this transformation, the main enemy of open religion is its closest neighbor: closed religion. Whether open religion will be successful in its fight against closed religion is not a prediction which historians can make. But we must try.

PART II

REFLECTIONS FROM THE FRONT LINE

4

RADICAL ENCOUNTERS
Climate Change and Religious Conflict in Africa

ELIZA GRISWOLD

Ours is an age of unprecedented radical change, and people search for something that doesn't change, that is eternal. And of all such things, God is the ultimate. And there is a specific factor in the Middle East, Africa and Asia, and that is the perceived failure of Western regimes. That is leading to a whole series of religious counterrevolutions. That's what's happening in Iraq and Syria. It's what happened in Iran. To some extent it is happening in India with Hindu nationalism.

—Rabbi Lord Jonathan Sacks[1]

Not so long ago, most people thought that theologians were largely irrelevant to our contemporary culture. Most of us in the West believed that the world, led by the United States and Europe, had grown beyond a need for God. Belief was naive, a stage in development, the thinking went. "Third Worlders" would soon abandon their churches and mosques and temples in favor of the more sophisticated understanding of human existence that accompanied technological advancement. This was the "God is Dead" camp—a group that believed that devotion was irrelevant and that believers were, to put it in its starkest terms, dangerously stupid.

Of course, from the start, some of us understood that this kind of thinking was entirely wrong. In terms of demographics alone, the majority of humans on the planet believed strongly in God. And, due to the very secular factor of birthrates, the numbers of believers were

77

growing such that the center of Global Christianity was no longer Europe or the United States but Nigeria. We didn't take such believers seriously enough, as we knew little about who they were and less about the practices that patterned their devotion.

At its root, this chauvinism was born of a misunderstanding about development. Many Western thinkers viewed what we call now call the Global South through a prism of single-track development. Everyone was moving from third to first world. This, in itself, was naive. Africa and South Asia weren't chugging along happily behind the United States and the United Kingdom on the same inexorable march toward development. In terms of technology, vast regions were outpacing the West— leapfrogging us—moving from no electricity to solar panels, jumping from no phone lines to smart phones, and skipping dial-up completely.

To assume that we in the West were somehow further along technologically and ideologically—that belief in God was a symptom of poverty and poor education—was thickheaded. It was a mistake. Unfortunately, it has taken paroxysms of violence from North Africa to the Middle East to South Asia waged in the name of God to sharpen our understanding that, for the vast majority of the world's inhabitants, belief isn't dead. Instead, it is the single determining factor that patterns peoples' lives— more than race, ethnicity, and nationality combined.

Throughout the Global South, in countries where national boundaries exist only as arbitrary lines drawn on the maps of colonial administrators, religion (I will argue here) has become the primary form of identity. When these identities are constructed along brittle ideological lines which posit that one religion must have primacy over another—as determined by divine revelation—then these identities often become violent.

In *Not in God's Name*, Rabbi Sacks offers us an intellectual invitation to think beyond the front pages of our newspapers and the squawk of a few loud talking heads on our televisions in order to engage Westerners in rereading these ideological fault lines through not only the scriptures but also Freudian logic. If each Abrahamic sibling is born with a self-schema founded on the need to outdo the previous one, then the conflict between them is inherent in divine revelation. What is one to do?

As usual, Rabbi Sacks is inviting us into a new frame of thinking that allows us to shake off the limitations of our own ideas and apply a new story to the logical and ideological challenges before us. In this essay, I will offer three other close observations I have gathered on the ground after fifteen years of work in places where the hardening of religious identity has led to violence. In political elections, droughts, floods, and even fights over cacao (the principle ingredient in chocolate), I've asked believers of all stripes why it is people believe what they do and what factors—other than scripture—determine the competition or coexistence through which they view their perceived rivals. The observations I offer make no claim to exclusive truth. Instead, in the spirit of Rabbi Sacks, they are invitations to think beyond the self-limiting frameworks through which we view ardent believers within other faith traditions and within our own. *First,* religious identity has surpassed ethnic, racial, and national identity in the Global South. *Second,* part of the solution to unteaching religious violence is to restore the historical context of coexistence in Africa and beyond. *Third,* the most overlooked factor in violence in God's name today is climate change, which not only helps to drive the largest human migration since World War II but also brings people of different religions into competition and conflict over both land and limited resources.

1. Religious Identity in the Global South: Beyond Ethnicity and Nation

In Africa and in Southeast Asia, nearly half of the world's two billion Christians meet a similar number of the world's Muslims. (I have focused on these two faiths due to the fact that in most of the places where my work as a journalist has taken me—as in Iraq for instance—ancient Jewish communities have already largely fled.)

Take Nigeria, for instance, Africa's most populous country. With a population of 182 million people, Nigeria is home to one in seven Africans. For most, the state is largely absent from daily life and often rapacious. In response people put religion in the center of their lives and use both prayer and the practical relationships of their faith communities to meet their basic needs. "You have car insurance, but I have nothing but prayer to rely on," a Catholic priest told me some years ago. In communities with poor roads and access to water and electricity, belonging to the local church or mosque often helps people safeguard access to the means of survival. In places where resources are scarce and growing scarcer—as a result of swelling populations and climate change—conflicts over resources often take on a religious dimension.

Religion often seems to provide the answer to government crises as well. As Rabbi Sacks points out in his observations above, religion in the Global South is often viewed as the answer to the failure of Western systems. Dependence on religious identity is a direct result of the failure of colonial power to make positive change in the daily lives of Africans and Southeast Asians and of the widespread corruption that has come in the wake of decolonization. In North Africa, which has been predominantly Muslim for centuries, Islamic law is often viewed as an antidote to failed Western legal systems that can be corrupt and inefficient. From a distance, the desire to adopt sharia can seem frightening. The little that the West understands of sharia is grounded in images of amputations or stonings. We often forget that the notion of punishing a woman for adultery by stoning predates the Qur'an. Instead, the edict is laid out in Deuteronomy 22:21 and reflects ancient legal codes, including Hammurabi's, rather than solely religious ones. These punishments certainly exist within the sharia criminal code called the *hudud*, but they do not make up the majority of Islamic edicts, which also provide property rights for women and welfare for widows and orphans. Often, reporters—my tribe—play a role in deepening misunderstandings. After the devastation wrought by the 2004 tsunami in Indonesia's Banda Aceh, for instance, local government leaders turned to Islamic law to mete out property rights for female survivors. Although there was much ink spilled about the new sharia police—and they certainly were eagerly pursuing young couples canoodling on beaches—there was relatively little written in the Western press about the challenges of safeguarding rights of women and children after the disaster.

In many cases, at the core of this drive toward the adoption of Islamic law lies a desire to return to an idealized past—a peaceful time that never really existed when uniform belief in an Islamic God reigned supreme. For millennia, particularly in the Middle East, societies have been pluralistic rather than homogenous. Zoroastrians, Jews, Christians, and Muslims have lived alongside one another. Yet this rich and multifaceted religious and cultural history is under existential threat as subsets of believers across faith traditions distort their own histories in a drive for supremacy in the future.

Since 2011 the Arab Spring has intensified this pattern—pushing religious minorities out of their ancient communities and leading to deeper tribalism. The fall of military dictators, many of whom protected religious minorities, hasn't led to the "democratization" the West hoped for. Once again, the Western notion that democracy means godlessness has been confounded. Instead, in these fraught places—Egypt, Libya, Syria, and Iraq, to name a few—contested political space has given rise to competition between various religious groups over power and resources.

2. Religious Violence in Africa: An Historical Perspective

The encounter between Christians and Muslims in Africa dates to 615 CE, and it began largely peacefully. In 615, as one of the first cases of political asylum in history, the Prophet Muhammad sent more than a dozen of his followers from his hometown of Mecca to Africa in search of safe haven. They landed in Abyssinia, today's Ethiopia, at the court of a Christian king. To guarantee their passage, these early Muslims told the king the story of Mary giving birth to Jesus beneath a date tree, which occurs in the Qur'an. More than any tie of blood or nation, the refugees relied on a shared understanding of one, true God to keep them safe. For most of the past fourteen centuries, Christians and Muslims have lived side by side in Africa relatively peacefully.

Recently, however, some of the long-standing patterns of religious coexistence and intermarriage seem to be shifting. Over the past several decades, religious revivals unfolding within both Christianity and Islam have led to an explosive growth of numbers of believers in Africa and a greater awareness of religious identity. In many places where the two faiths meet on the ground, Christians and Muslims have come in increased competition over dwindling resources. Fights over access to water, grassland, electricity, and other basic tools of survival have taken on the color of holy war.

The fighting between Christians and Muslims has taken place largely within a fraught band that lies between the equator and the line of latitude some seven hundred miles to the north. This band, about which I have written in *The Tenth Parallel*,[2] marks the space where Africa's dry north meets the more fertile south. Historically, North Africa has been predominantly Muslim, while the south has belonged to those who follow traditional religions and those who have come to embrace Christianity.

In terms of numbers, this band marks the center of Global Christianity. Again and again, we hear about the skyrocketing numbers of believers in the Global South. The face of Christianity isn't changing; it has already changed. According to numbers, the average Christian today is no longer a rich, white American man. She is a poor, black woman in sub-Saharan Africa.

Yet, beyond digits on a page, what do such numbers really mean?

The Case of Nigeria

No single nation represents this shift in the face of Global Christianity more powerfully than Nigeria, where nearly half of its 182 million citizens are Christians.

Of Nigeria's Christians, Pastor James Wuye is one of the finest leaders. Graced with a warm chuckle and a preacher's gift for spinning stories, Pastor James—as he is known—is a vocal and charismatic evangelical leader. He lives and works in a northern Nigerian town called Kaduna, which means "crocodile." Like Nigeria itself, the town of Kaduna is nearly evenly split between Christians and Muslims.

The River Kaduna divides the two faiths. The Christians live in neighborhoods called Haifa and Jerusalem. The Muslims live in Afghanistan and Baghdad. For both groups, these neighborhood names reflect a deeper understanding of their respective faiths. As Pastor James and others explain it, on a local level, being a Christian or a Muslim guarantees people the right to vote in local elections and the ability to safeguard their basic rights. On a global level—as the neighborhood names reflect—religion allows those isolated and living in poverty to ally themselves with those on a world stage.

Pastor James has a painful and visceral understanding of what it means to be a Christian. He has only one arm. The other was cut off in an attack by militant Muslim thugs more than a decade ago. Back then, Pastor James' current business partner, Imam Nurayn Ashafa, a handsome and eloquent religious teacher, was the leader of this bunch of thugs. Pastor James was his counterpart: he led the young Christian fighters.

Now these two religious leaders, former blood enemies, work together to bring peace to their hometown of Kaduna, as well as to other violence-stricken communities in Nigeria and worldwide. The story of their reconciliation centers on each man's relationship with God. One Friday, at prayer, the imam heard a sermon about the Prophet Muhammad being pelted with stones when he went to preach to a village called Taif. According to tradition, the archangel Gabriel appeared to the wounded Prophet Muhammad and asked if he wanted to take revenge on the villagers. But Muhammad said no, he would forgive them instead.

A newfound desire for reconciliation drove the imam to seek out his nemesis, the pastor, and to find a way to make peace. After some time, the pastor, still wary given the loss of his arm, had his own experience of God's will, which energized him to work with the imam to rebuild the community both men had helped to destroy. The two founded an organization, the Interfaith Mediation Centre (IMC), which solves crises between these two rival groups in Nigeria.

The IMC is located in Kaduna's tallest building, a broken-down high-rise, built for a kind of prosperity that never arrived. Due to a lack of electricity, the elevator rarely works. When I first visited several years ago and climbed the stairs to their office, I knew I had arrived when I saw a plastic sign that read Peace Hall.

Waging peace entails teaching ex-fighters how to reread their own holy books and those of their enemies to understand them more fully than the usual catchphrases about killing unbelievers, or selling cloaks to buy swords, on which militant groups usually focus. "Our secret is spiritual intimidation from the holy books," Pastor James wrote to me in a recent email. That doesn't mean that either the pastor or the imam has strayed from strict interpretation of his respective faith tradition. Both are still self-avowed fundamentalists—each believes the other will go to Hell if he doesn't convert from his faith.

Pastor James speaks first to his fellow Christians in Nigeria. From Catholics to Pentecostals to Anglicans, the Christian community is varied and vibrant; it encompasses so many manifestations of worship. Sunday morning is a veritable smorgasbord of old and new traditions. The breadth of beliefs within Nigerian Christianity is wide enough to make room for a new religion called Chrislam, which, as its name indicates, is an amalgam of the two religions that frequently run into conflict in Nigeria's booming religious marketplace.

Over the past decade, confrontations between Christians and Muslims have led to bloodshed. This violence has been at its worst not only in Kaduna, but also across a wider swath where the two religions meet. This is Nigeria's Middle Belt: the horizontal ribbon of land that runs across the middle of the country between the latitudes of the seventh and tenth parallels, which means roughly between five hundred and seven hundred miles north of the equator. Pastor James' town of Kaduna is at the top of this area.

This band roughly coincides with the edge of Africa's dry north and the beginning of sub-Saharan jungle. Most of Africa's roughly four hundred million Muslims live to the north of this band, and the majority of the continent's more than three hundred million Christians live to its south. It is the fault line where Christianity and Islam meet.

The patterns emerging along it, especially in Nigeria, raise unnerving questions. Is the kind of violence we see in Nigeria a harbinger of the future between the two great faiths? Is this what happens in places where swelling populations of different faiths come head to head over resources such as land, water, and even oil, or political power?

In Nigeria, as in many other countries where Christians and Muslims collide, largely between the equator and the tenth parallel, religious difference has contributed to long-standing fights over who has the right to land, education, and the most basic services. In some neighborhoods of the Middle Belt capital of Jos, religious identity— whether you're a Christian or a Muslim—has even come to determine whether your community has the right to electricity or running water.

These are the kinds of rights a state usually provides. But Nigeria is one of the world's most corrupt democracies. And although Nigeria is America's fifth-largest supplier of oil, that massive influx of petrodollars doesn't reach most Nigerians. Because the state neglects to supply clean water, medical care, or free education, people try to find other ways to provide for themselves and their children. Now, more than ever, they turn to their respective religions to guarantee those most basic rights. Religious groups serve as voting blocs or pressure groups: collective organizations that help members survive in practical ways. Thus a shared belief in God becomes the means to survive in the workaday world and also enables people to look to the hereafter for eternal salvation. This pattern holds true for both Christians and Muslims in Nigeria.

Paradoxically, democracy has intensified the troubles between them. Democracy is less about freedom than survival. It is as if being a Democrat or a Republican meant the difference between being able to drink the tap water or not. Imagine how divisive politics could become.

Since the end of military rule in 1999, religion has become a rallying cry in a fierce competition for political power. Frequently, secular events trigger these skirmishes. And global conflagrations frequently have local impact in Nigeria, too. For instance, following the 2001 U.S. bombing of Afghanistan, violence broke out when local Muslims believed that America and the world's Christians had gone to war against their brethren. Riots between Christians and Muslims have broken out over such issues as the 2002 Miss World competition. Isioma Daniel, a Christian reporting for Nigerian paper *This Day*, inadvertently outraged Nigerian Muslims by saying that the Prophet Muhammad would have picked a wife from among the contestants. Following the 2006 Danish cartoons that depicted the Prophet Muhammad with a bomb on his head, among other controversial images, riots unfolded in many places with Muslim populations. In those riots, more people were killed in

Nigeria (more than one hundred) than anywhere else in the world. The instances go on and on and on.

"When the West sneezes, Africa catches the cold," Pastor James told me. He meant that global issues lead to local troubles in Nigeria. When a Florida pastor claims that he is going to burn copies of the Qur'an, the people who suffer are fellow Christians in the Global South. This bumper crop of believers, many of whom are ethnic minorities, frequently become scapegoats for the Christian-seeming West. When we, far away, say that we are at war with Islam, then local Christians become the enemies of their Muslim neighbors, too. That is how global contagion works, and it is also why, thanks to the ever-more-powerful airwaves, we have to be careful about how we talk.

Yet in Nigeria, and elsewhere, such seeming religious grievances almost always have worldly—or secular—causes underlying them, since in Nigeria, as in many countries in the Global South, the federal government does almost nothing for its people. There are thirty-six states in Nigeria, which functions largely on a federal system. Among other things, this system is supposed to make sure that the oil wealth of the south reaches all Nigerians. But it doesn't. (According to Human Rights Watch, more than $4 billion have been embezzled from the government *each year* since the end of military rule.)

But faith in Nigeria, for both Christians and Muslims, means much more than the ballot box or the distribution of resources. On my visits to the country, I have been repeatedly silenced by the eloquence with which people speak of their experiences with God. Yes, people pray to keep their cars safe in the absence of auto insurance, but suffering also brings people in daily contact with the divine.

Take Pastor James, for instance. One morning in Kaduna when I climbed the concrete stairs to visit Peace Hall, I found the pastor standing in the middle of a group of Christian and Muslim women who were tinkering with some very newfangled hardware, which turned out to be stoves. The din was near deafening as the women turned the knobs and peered at what looked like space-age camp stoves. One of the things Christians and Muslims wrestle over in Nigeria is firewood. Despite the vast deposits of oil, wood remains the cheapest source of fuel for many Nigerians. But in the north especially, there is scant wood left, and so children have to walk for miles to fetch enough scraps of wood for their mothers to cook each day.

This is one of the unexpected ways in which religion becomes woven into resource conflict. As the two groups vie for survival, they can see one another as the enemy in a race for wood. So, on this day, Pastor James was piloting a program that would bring Christians and Muslims together—to share the stoves and therefore ensure each other's survival. This is one of the strongest—and simplest—examples of interfaith work I have ever seen. The project succeeded because it introduced a third element—stoves.

The project also targeted women, who are both less likely to commit violent acts in Nigeria and more committed to safeguarding resources for their children. They are involved in efforts that target more than one issue at a time, like the stoves, which helped stop violence and also addressed the growing pressure of deforestation due to dwindling numbers of trees.

In many cases, both Christian and Muslim women are also the main breadwinners in families. Cooking isn't simply a means to feed their families. Selling food on the street is also a ready business. But the fuel was expensive, and these women spent roughly a dollar a day acquiring enough fuel to cook. The shiny stoves in Peace Hall cost about $200, a steep price that would pay for itself in less than a year—but still, it was a lot.

Over the past few years, I have thought often of these women squatting on the floor of Peace Hall, while Pastor James, sweating slightly, stood among them—wondering how to distribute these stoves and if the women would ever be able to pay for them. Recently, I checked in with the pastor via email to find out how this pilot project was going. Very well, he wrote back. They had managed to cut the price of the stoves in half, so now they only cost about $97. And the group had begun to stretch out beyond the town of Kaduna, which was still at peace, and into the larger area of the Middle Belt—some of the areas of greatest conflict where suspicion and animosity were at their worst. And another thing, he wrote, the women had found a name for their collective, which had nothing to do with either religion but made it clear that their efforts began with the environment. Together, these Christians and Muslims now called themselves "Green Women."

Beyond Nigeria: The Case of the Central African Republic

The problems stretch beyond Nigeria. Nearby, in the failing nation of the Central African Republic (CAR), religious identity, resources, and climate change have collided to hasten the near collapse of an ailing nation. The CAR provides us a recent and troubling instance of a larger pattern of religious violence across much of the continent. And yet, in the CAR, as elsewhere, the root causes of conflict have little to do with religion.

First, the CAR's arbitrary postcolonial borders situate the struggling nation in the middle of a rough neighborhood between Congo, Darfur, South Sudan, Cameroon, and Chad. Since national borders have never meant much in the first place, these neighbors threaten to join in the violence in the name of protecting fellow Muslims and Christians, as massacres perpetrated in the name of religion continue. Regional chaos has contributed to the political mess in the CAR, and it could easily make things much worse.

Second, since the country gained independence from France in 1960, a catalogue of corrupt military leaders—including the self-proclaimed "Emperor" Bokassa, who wore a crown of golden laurel leaves fashioned after Caesar's—stuffed their pockets with diamonds and other natural resources while leaving their people to starve.

Third, there is the power vacuum left by the end of the Cold War on Africa's proxy battlefields. Take Michel Djotodia, the erstwhile president and first Muslim leader who was recently exiled to Benin. Before donning a turban and leading the mostly Muslim rebel group Seleka on a rampage against his political enemies—who happened, like 75 percent of the country, to be Christians—he lived in the former Soviet Union for a decade. He married there and fathered two children before returning to pursue his push to lead the country. His transformation from a Soviet civil servant into a Muslim rebel leader who espouses vague ideas about political Islam mirrors a larger shift in the CAR and throughout the surrounding region, which lies within a uniquely sensitive zone where Christianity and Islam meet and often collide across much of inland Africa.

CAR lies within one of the most environmentally sensitive belts on the planet. The problem begins with geography. As its name suggests, landlocked Central African Republic, which is almost as big as Texas, lies just about smack in the center of the African continent, within the Middle Belt. In CAR, home to less than five million people, the mostly Muslim north comprises only 15 percent of the population. Fifty percent is Christian, and the remaining 35 percent follow indigenous beliefs.

As elsewhere across the Middle Belt, in CAR the history of this religious encounter was forged by the weather. The belt lies within the intertropical convergence zone where hot, dry air dropping from the northern hemisphere hits warm, wet air rising from the southern hemisphere. The Middle Belt marks the end of the continent's dry, desert north and the beginning of the steamy, jungle south. Where the dry land ceases, so, too, does Islam. The Muslim traders and missionaries who spread the faith over the northernmost third of the continent by the fourteenth century were forced to stop moving south when they reached the edge of dry land. Where the jungle began, so did the tsetse fly belt. Along this belt, sleeping sickness, which the tsetses carried, killed off the traders' camels. So this, in effect, is where Islam stopped its southern spread.

Many African Christians stress that their faith arrived in Ethiopia as early as 37 CE when, according to the Bible, an Ethiopian eunuch was baptized on the road between Jerusalem and Gaza (Acts 8:26-39). But Christianity really flourished in what is today CAR and across the Middle Belt during the nineteenth and early twentieth centuries. Protestant and Catholic missionaries worked alongside French colonial administrators and sowed the seeds for a contemporary confrontation with Islam along this geographic fault line.

3. Secular Drivers of Religious Violence in the Global South: Climate Change and Mass Migration

With sixty million people on the move, we now have more people fleeing the weather worldwide than fleeing war. These shifting weather patterns play a role in a deepening religious divide across much of inland Africa. They are visible in the CAR, as in other countries along this fault line— the already arid north, which is plagued by the moisture-sucking trade wind called the Harmattan that carries a powdery red dust from the Sahara, and which is growing hotter and drier.

Over the past seventy-five years, the amount of rainfall within this belt north of the equator has dropped by between 6 and 7 percent. In effect, Africa's desert north is creeping south. This pattern, paired with deforestation, means that many of the Muslims who live in the north must push south into land already settled by Christians.

In the CAR, as in many other nominal nations along this band, the Muslims of the north, who are ethnic Fula or Peulh, tend to be traders and herders, while the Christians of the south account for most of the nation's farmers. (Although timber and diamonds make up most of the nation's exports, more than half of the GDP is agriculture.)

This deepens the very real specter of starvation. Farmers cannot harvest crops if they are forced to flee their land. And a season of war makes it impossible to plant for the next year. Climate change plays a role here, too. Shifting weather patterns contribute to the worsening disaster. Extreme and unpredictable rainfall renders growing seasons unreliable. Flash flooding wipes out crops and villages, as rising temperatures push the storms borne by the intertropical convergence zone farther south.

These extreme storms in the CAR and elsewhere in the Middle Belt have a direct impact on the United States. The collision of hot air and wet air creates Hadley cells, cycles of wind that move westward and carry with them cataclysmic storms. If they are strong enough, these storms spin off of the west coast of Africa at Cape Verde and head over the Atlantic Ocean. They pass through the doldrums or horse latitudes—so named by becalmed sailors forced to throw horses overboard—and if the storms are strong enough to survive, they strike the Eastern Seaboard of the United States as hurricanes.

As these severe weather patterns intensify, they wreak havoc on cotton, coffee, and tobacco crops, among others, in a region where the population is growing at a rate of over 2 percent a year. This mushrooming birthrate helps drive the fact that both Christianity and Islam are growing in Africa faster than anywhere else on the planet. Birthrates, alongside the fact that the fastest-growing forms of each faith are the most fervent ones, means that the two groups of believers will bump up against one another in a deepening struggle to survive.

Now, religion—more than nation, race, and ethnicity—has come to define who is an ally and who is an enemy. Village by village, religion is becoming a means to safeguard access to the most basic rights: food, a job, even education. This has long been the case in neighboring countries, including Sudan and Nigeria, where violence in the name of religion, ethnicity, and race has left tens of thousands dead over the past several decades.

However, labeling the violence simply "religious" obscures our role and responsibility in creating the conditions for conflict, which lies in part in the wreckage of the colonial project and in postcolonial support for despicable puppet leaders. The factor unfolding right now is the pressure brought by the extreme weather born of a rapidly warming planet. We blame the creeds when the conflict is driven by the failure to address the man-made environmental crisis unfolding around us.

In addition, the death of nomadism also plays an important role here in the rise of militancy. In Somalia, and in Chad, Niger, Nigeria, and across North Africa, young men can no longer support their families tending herds of cattle. Both climate change and the Arab Spring— particularly in Libya, where Qaddafi's overthrow sent thousands of

Tuareg mercenaries home to Chad and Niger—have exacerbated this confrontation and contributed to the rise of groups like Boko Haram, al-Qaeda in the Islamic Maghreb, and ISIS, which are based on the myths of eternal return to an idealized version of the past. By pushing notions of nineteenth-century jihad, in which Islamic reformers in West Africa successfully overthrew Western colonial powers, recruiters target vulnerable young men with no other viable futures. This is not about the scriptures; this is about survival.

And yet we must acknowledge the role that religious identity—reinforced by globalization—is playing in fomenting violence. In this, those of us of different stripes within our faith communities have a responsibility to act as some of these key divisions are born of deep fractures that begin much closer to home than the Central African Republic might be.

Conclusion

In closing, this is the problem of the Divide Within. As a lay observer, I have come to see that we often overlook the fact that the most important religious struggles of our time are those *within*, not *between*, our respective faith traditions. These are the fights over who has the right to speak for God and why. Often, these take the form of sectarian struggles which turn violent, for instance in the deepening divisions between Sunni and Shia in the Middle East. Yet, in other instances, even when these struggles within do not turn violent, they are no less formative. Take, for instance, divisions within the Anglican tradition over homosexuality and how these arguments play into the culture wars of the West. This is just one of the many issues that represent theological positions that are often so entrenched that people within the same faith find it difficult to find common ground.

If we are to grow serious about the future of coexistence, then we will have to learn to speak to one another within our faith traditions even when we disagree over the fundamental tenets of our worldview and practice. These are often uncomfortable conversations as they involve issues of political and cultural difference between neighbors, and yet they are essential. Interfaith dialogue is important—but *intra*faith dialogue is essential as well. Often such conversations are successful when they take, as a point of departure, a social issue such as health or human trafficking which allows for a broad base of support across ideological lines. Increasingly, given its pressing realities, climate change is one of these issues.

I will end with a memory of a man from my travels named Dr. Amin al Amin, an Islamic teacher and medical doctor who traveled to conservative religious schools across Africa to talk about the role that humans play in climate change. These schools, called *almajiri* schools, exist across much of North Africa. In them are young boys who have traveled for thousands of miles for a free education in exchange for helping their teacher farm. As a result of warming temperatures and desertification, however, many of these schools no longer function as farms. Islamic teachers are forced to abandon their farms and move instead to the edges of slums, where their students are sent out to beg instead of farm. These boys are easy recruits into militant cells. To combat the dual problems of militant ideology and ignorance about climate change, Dr. Amin gives lectures at schools where he is not always welcome—but uses these opportunities to tell young students to care for the scant trees around them. The desert is spreading due to cutting down trees, not to sins like sex and drinking, he tells them. Once, a group of hostile teachers threw stones at him and cut his face. "I felt like the Prophet Muhammad at Taif," he told me. At Taif, the Prophet was stoned for sharing his message to those who did not want to hear him. Dr. Amin is confronting the division within, which takes courage. Such divisions lie within each of our communities and, until they are addressed, we have little hope of reconciling with others. Let us hope that nimble minds can serve to open hearts.

5

EMPATHY AS POLICY
IN THE AGE OF HATRED

Amineh A. Hoti

Contrary to predictions of a peaceful world order in the post–Cold War era, our planet is facing division and conflict on a scale not seen in generations. With leaders like President Trump in America and President Modi in India and other rising right-wing party leaders, policymakers must give serious thought to how their decisions can affect the lives of millions of ordinary human beings.[1] The refugee crisis unfolding before our eyes is said to be one of the worst humanitarian disasters since World War II, as warfare in many parts of the world rages unabated. In the exodus, refugee families are finding themselves bewildered, desperate, and traumatized—an estimated ten thousand refugee children have been lost or killed according to BBC News.[2] Meanwhile, countries around the globe find themselves in retreat from the rest of the world as a massive influx of immigrants and refugees—the so-called Other— spurs many to question their responsibilities to themselves and others. In the context of increasingly forced large-scale migrations and globalization, the interrelated challenges of preserving cultural and interfaith dialogue assume a new prominence and urgency.[3]

Some social scientists say that "this is the Age of Empathy," with the Age of Reason behind us.[4] Yet, I would disagree because the unprecedented level of global migration in recent years has tested the empathy of many policymakers, the media, and host communities. Studies show that since the beginning of the twenty-first century, there has been an alleged ninefold increase in the number of deaths from terrorism,

93

and communities such as the Rohingya in Burma and the Kashmiris in South Asia have been victims of genocide due to false labeling of terrorism.[5] Instead, it seems that we have entered what I would call "the Age of Hatred." In this age there is a desperate need for empathy because scholars say that these are conditions not dissimilar to Germany in the 1930s prior to the Holocaust.[6] They also talk about an internal enemy—"the Jews"—and an external enemy—"the Muslims."[7]

Anti-Semitism still rears its ugly head in the world, both in the East and in the West.[8] Its counterpart, Islamophobia, sensationalized in the media, has victimized Muslims in the West and has arguably led to the rise of the right-wing from America to Europe.[9] With hate crimes on the rise, humanity needs to remind itself of its value of acceptance. But far from acceptance, there is a vicious, nightmarish anti-migrant mood in Europe. The Hungarians have forcibly locked arriving migrants in asylum prisons and given them a drug called Rivotril (Clonazepam), in which, "you become a zombie."[10] Inmates of the asylum prisons, which are said to be worse than ordinary prisons, become addicted and have tried to commit suicide. Migrants who become ill and need to see a doctor are led through the town on a leash and in handcuffs.[11] Czech social media posts and newspaper reports that state that "all refugees and 'darkies' should be executed, drowned or sent to gas chambers" are regular features.[12] On September 3, 2015, human rights advocates and Jewish groups expressed outrage after Czech authorities wrote numbers on the skin of two hundred Syrian migrants who were pulled off trains—they protested that this summoned memories of the Nazis and the Holocaust.[13]

The media has helped xenophobia spread by not giving full and accurate information on refugees, Muslims, and the Muslim world—albeit with a few outstanding exceptions—and governments have dragged their feet in decision making in terms of the refugee crisis and have failed to show swift, compassionate acceptance, falling short of human rights and biblical standards of loving one's neighbors. Many rabbis from their synagogues and priests from their churches have, however, reached out to refugees and continue to do so.

Not all hope is lost in building peace in our tumultuous world, however. Some of the leading minds of our time have reminded us of both the challenges and the beauty of bridging differences and seeking common ground. The 2009 *UNESCO World Report: Investing in Cultural Diversity and Intercultural Dialogue* maintains that

> Divergent memories have been the source of many conflicts throughout
> history. Although intercultural dialogue cannot hope to settle on its own
> all the conflicts in the political, economic, and social spheres, a key element
> in its success is the building of a shared memory—based through the
> acknowledgement of faults and open debate on competing memories. The
> framing of a common historical narrative can be crucial in conflict preven-
> tion and post conflict strategies in assuaging "a past that is still present."[14]

I argue that the swift implementation of policy toward immigrants, refugees, and minority groups, crafted with compassion and empathy at its heart, is essential to fostering harmonious coexistence with the Other in today's turbulent and fractured world, particularly in the context of the so-called refugee crisis. Such policy must be well thought out and inextricably interlinked with the most cutting-edge, culturally sensitive tools of teaching acceptance, as refugees come with their own cultural and religious backgrounds that must not be dismissed or demonized but be understood and respected.

In our increasingly fragmented world, this paper is a plea for more compassion and empathy, particularly for the consideration of poli-cymakers, academic and religious leaders, and the media. We must embrace all human communities with compassion and empathy. This is the pressing need of our time.

1. Empathy and Recent Initiatives

As some social scientists have termed the present time "The Age of Empathy,"[15] the sophisticated concept of empathy needs to be better understood so that it may be employed in policy when making deci-sions regarding interactions with the Other—in this case, immigrants, refugees, and minority groups. Empathy, which comes from the Greek *empathia* (feeling with people), is the ability to understand and share the feelings of another person.

Empathy is distinct from sympathy—whereas sympathy is me-ori-ented, empathy is you-oriented and is the result of understanding.[16] The skill of empathy is thus vital in making sense of human behavior and relating to others effectively—it helps us walk in someone else's shoes. The opposite of empathy is a vacuum where insecurity looms large; hence, as psychologist Daniel Goleman explains, "Self-absorption in all its forms kills empathy, let alone compassion. When we focus on ourselves, our world contracts as our problems and preoccupations loom large. However, when we focus on others, our world expands. Our own problems drift to the periphery of the mind and so seem smaller, and we increase our capacity for connection—or compassionate action."[17]

As the refugees coming to Europe are human beings and not just numbers, we must give them a voice and place value on their stories so that we may meet their challenges with empathy. The media does not always successfully allow this to happen. Yet social scientists can strengthen and empower the media to do their job better by educating on the value of empathy. Reflexive anthropology is one way in which the social scientist can go beyond foundational notions of objectivity and analytical distance—it allows for researchers to step into the context of the subject so as to arouse one's own consciousness and to explore and reflect the feelings, emotions, multiple voices, and challenges of the people being observed, rather than simply report statistics.

In media discussions today, I see very little reflexive analysis, and even many so-called experts do not reflect a sense of empathy for the people involved and their challenges. Of course, there are notable exceptions. I have had the privilege of working with top interfaith scholars, including the former Chief Rabbi of the United Kingdom, Lord Jonathan Sacks, who has presented, through his profound work, alternative ideas that encourage empathy through respecting the dignity of difference. This emphasis on the dignity of difference has become a core seed concept in the peacebuilding courses I have taught at universities across the world.

Recently, there have indeed been numerous initiatives to foster dialogue and empathy between students and professors from different cultures on campuses around the globe—these include educational and exchange programs that incorporate participatory cultural, artistic, and sports activities. Over the last two years, I have been involved in the President's Interfaith and Community Service Campus Challenge at the White House, which brings together professors and students from different countries on college campuses in the United States, mainly in Washington, D.C.[18] Rabbi Sacks was himself on a similar dialogue panel with my father, Professor Akbar S. Ahmed, in Washington, D.C. This Muslim-Jewish friendship has led to many fruitful outcomes. Prince Charles from the United Kingdom has also played a major role in bridge building. Other multicultural practices and events such as "global city" networking and cultural festivals help transcend these barriers through experiences of "urban communion and entertainment."[19]

While these initiatives have had a positive impact, anti-Semitism and Islamophobia remain rampant, and further efforts are necessary to combat prejudice. The *UNESCO World Report* notes that education plays a major role in determining the fate of cultural diversity, as education is not just about knowledge transmission but also about value transmission. As such, it advocates that policies must seek to "promote education *through*" and "*for* diversity."[20] This means meeting the diverse needs of learners through a diverse set of methods and contents in order to "enable us to acquire the intercultural competencies that will permit us to live together with—and not despite—our cultural differences."[21] The report continues to argue that "the four pillars of [quality] education identified by the International Commission on Education for the Twenty-First Century—'learning to be,' 'learning to know,' 'learning to do' and 'learning to live together' "—can be successfully implemented only if cultural diversity is situated at their core.[22] This can be achieved only through an approach to education that is culturally competent and that responds to cultural change, promotes human rights, and implements teaching methods that reach marginalized groups.

2. Peace Education at
the Centre for Dialogue and Action

It is in this context that I will explore some of the interdisciplinary courses that the Centre for Dialogue and Action (CD&A) pioneered and taught in Pakistan and in the United Kingdom. The courses—and interactions through them—emphasize multiple identities of individuals by raising awareness of the layers of our history and identities; this in turn encourages a deeper understanding and respect for the Other. In order to demonstrate to students the possibility of coexistence in the present, these courses highlight periods of pluralism and multiculturalism from the past, including La Convivencia (the Coexistence), a period often called the Golden Age in which Muslims, Jews, and Christians lived together in relative harmony in Al-Andalus,[23] and La Benevolencia (the Benevolence), when a Sarajevo synagogue and its rabbis gave shelter to persecuted Muslims in war-torn Bosnia in the mid-1990s. I will propose that ideas from these courses must be implemented in policymaking in countries worldwide in order to understand and accept refugees and the Other.

The CD&A, which I initiated with my team at the University of Cambridge and later opened at Forman Christian College University (FCCU) in Lahore, has enrolled hundreds of students at FCCU in coursework on understanding and respecting the Other. Having led the designing of the course, I gave the subject a local name, calling it in Urdu, "Ilm, Adab aur Insaaniyat" (Knowledge and Respect for Humanity).[24] This course encourages respect for the Other—the religious other, the ethnic other, and the gendered other. It is aimed at teaching and cultivating male and female undergraduate students to serve as peacebuilders, while introducing concepts of diversity. We made a special effort to address UNESCO's "*three challenges* relating to cultural diversity that will confront the international community in the years ahead: combating cultural illiteracy, reconciling universalism and diversity, and supporting new forms of pluralism resulting from the assertion of multiple identities by individuals and groups."[25]

In 2014 this course had participants from Punjab, Quetta, and Waziristan, as well as from the northern areas of Pakistan, such as Gilgit and Hunza. The students were enthusiastic. But a few came into class with negative perceptions of not only themselves, but also the Other. This is reflective of the wider attitudes in the region and in the context of a divided world. One boy from the tribal belt said he did not feel included by the central government as a citizen and felt left on the periphery of society. His behavior in class often showed signs of unease. Another student at the beginning of the course confidently told me that his uncle from the village said to him that all non-Muslims were *wajib ul qatal* (*wajib* equates to a necessary or compulsory religious task; *qatal* means to kill).

This statement by one third-year student reflects how a few young people and students can hold dangerous thoughts in their heads even in university. On the other end of the spectrum, reports came in from America of how young, innocent Muslims had been shot by white supremacists. This reflects how global is the problem of hate and how necessary are ideas of *ilm* (knowledge), *adab* (respect), and *insaaniyat* (humanity) in educational institutions, in the media, and for policymakers. By the end of the course at FCCU, the students from Pakistan's remote economically disadvantaged tribal areas had studied the complex concept of empathy and understood the value of stepping into someone else's shoes to see from their perspectives. Students had debated the dialogue—rather than the clash—of civilizations.[26] They had studied the foundations of peacebuilding in the Abrahamic faiths. Young, twenty-two- and twenty-three-year-old boys had also learned to walk in the shoes of the gendered other. Keep in mind that many of the terrorist attacks in Europe have unfortunately been by young people of about this age group.

The course was strategically designed—it was interdisciplinary and drew on such subjects as religion, anthropology, sociology, history, law, and human rights. Along with designing the new course, my team and I worked tirelessly on innovative textbooks and booklets that emphasized the three building blocks of dialogue: learning to understand what others believe and value; avoiding violent action and language (this includes avoiding labeling religious others as violent in contrast to the self); and preventing disagreement from leading to conflict.

At the end of the course, when students gave their feedback, the same student mentioned above—who thought all non-Muslims were *wajib ul qatal*—said, "Ma'am, I am a changed man! This course has changed me." As a consequence of the course structure and content, as well as our discussions, he said he now wanted to change his world by seeking knowledge and using his pen (the *qalam*), not by using violence. There were many students who admitted to a change of perspective. A female student called Annie even said that she felt "empowered" and that the course got her to think, "we've got to do something about it"; she went on to open a women's empowerment society at FCCU.

As a director of three peacebuilding centers, I have doubled my efforts in recent years to write about and teach the subjects of empathy and respect for humanity—these courses are offered to retrain teachers as well as students. The challenges, however, are grave—there is a lot of funding for bombs and drones but a lack of funding for such peace-building projects, and people, especially donors, are skeptical of their impact as qualitative data is harder to measure.[27]

My teams and I, however, have developed innovative peace courses on deeper understanding and respect for humanity. In the United Kingdom, through our courses at the Centre for the Study of Muslim-Jewish Relations (CMJR), rabbis and imams began to form bonds of friendships and, through this, worked in their communities to build bridges. Our CD&A team put together textbooks on valuing diversity and teaching acceptance and reached out to religious communities in Pakistan. I discovered the first Jewish community in Pakistan and had the privilege of encouraging the youth—some of whom lacked self-assurance—to assume the confidence of peacebuilders.[28]

3. Policies Fostering Acceptance of Others and of Cultural Diversity: Finding Solutions

The *UNESCO World Report* points out that there is "a need to promote awareness among policy- and decision-makers about the benefits of intercultural and interfaith dialogue, while bearing in mind its potential instrumentalization."[29] There are a number of key strategies that are essential to formulate and introduce in order to increase understanding of the Other and integrate peacebuilding methods in formulating policy toward immigrants, refugees, and minority groups. Considering the caution of Muslim scholars on how to treat Muslim refugee communities, I too would emphasize, "The dignity of the Muslim population must be restored. The increasingly open attacks against the Muslim population, their religion, and their culture push them further and further away from non-Muslims and feed anger which too often encourages violence."[30] In order to prevent this, policymakers and scholars must turn their focus to key areas:

(1) *Religious Leaders*: Administrations must work much more closely with imams and local community leaders. Imams and community leaders in the West must be given lessons in the local culture, language, and history, and they must interact with religious scholars and leaders of other communities, especially rabbis and priests, so that they understand the culture they are working in and can help others in the community understand their context better too. This is already happening on a small scale.

(2) *Youth*: Faced with growing Islamophobia and anti-Semitism and a lack of respect for the religious identity of young people, the youth in minority communities can feel alienated. More focus on the young generation is needed because this is the generation that is facing a cultural crisis. It is essential to involve the young together in interfaith sports, conferences, and debates and to help them to seek gainful employment so they feel a sense of responsibility and belonging in their community—in their religious, local, and global communities.

(3) *The Media*: In order to balance the negative image of Islam and Muslims, the media must focus on the positives of the faith and global community and work to bridge the divide between the West and Muslims. Such coverage will allow Muslim citizens to feel more included and less marginalized in mainstream society. As the *UNESCO World Report* notes, "The limited range of representations" tends to promote "the creation of stereotypes through what is often called the process of 'othering,'" whereby the media tend to fix, reduce or simplify.[31] Strategic "information literacy" is needed to eliminate stereotypes to allow audiences to become more critical when consuming media and also help to combat unilateral perspectives.[32]

The media must work more closely with Muslim scholars and bring them into the fold to represent themselves and their own ideas, rather than inviting so-called experts who barely understand Muslims or Islam to speak for them. These "experts" have given misleading information, which has led to serious misrepresentation of the faith and the community. The power of empathetic scholarship and interfaith education is essential content for the media today. The media must ask itself how it can be a genuine bridge between world communities. How can the media foster confidence in all people regardless of faith and empower the marginal and minorities? For peacebuilding and understanding, the media must serve as an informer of knowledge, positivity, and—above all—peacebuilding.

(4) *Coexistence Courses*: Mosques and synagogues have to engage in coexistence courses for the young and for women, and they must open doors to local communities, not just to members of their own faith. The courses of the CD&A and textbooks focus on themes such as the following:

- Developing better understanding of European/Western ideals/ values and Abrahamic/Islamic ideals/values of coexistence. The film *Journey into Europe* is a good peacebuilding tool to screen in the presence of policymakers, religious leaders, and scholars.[33]
- Exploring the difference between religion and culture. For example, honor killings are cultural, not religious; *jihad* is not as simple as defined by many orientalist scholars. Anthropology may help us understand this complexity of diverse Muslim cultures and religious nuances. We (scholars and others) have to stop labeling and dehumanizing the Other.
- Emphasizing role models of peacebuilders within the Muslim world and in Europe. Young people need to have more role models and not to be told that their society or religious community is violent. Extremists or terrorists are not "Muslims"; they are simply criminals.[34]
- Exploring the subject of empathy.[35] The CD&A team developed an entire curriculum on empathy and acceptance of the Other. This is key to peace and social cohesion.[36]

(5) *Combating Hatred*: Anti-Semitism and Islamophobia together "pose a great risk to the democratic foundations of European constitution and social peace as well as the coexistence of different cultures." The *European Islamophobia Report* emphasizes, "Both civil society actors and states should acknowledge the seriousness of this issue and develop concrete policies to counter [this racism]" by sensitizing policymakers and teachers.[37]

"You are civilized if you protect weaker groups within your society, otherwise you're not," concludes the intellectual Dr. Haris Silajdžić, former prime minister of Bosnia and Herzegovina, whose people faced genocide two decades ago.[38] Learning from past periods when different cultures lived and thrived together (as in Al-Andalus), Europeans must reject all forms of religious intolerance and accept Muslims and the Muslim contributions to European civilization that happened through the Renaissance—and there are many stunning contributions including algebra, medicine, and philosophy. Acceptance will lead to healing of an ailing and fragmented world community. And Muslims, inspired by Al-Andalus, must rediscover a love for knowledge and acceptance of the Other found in a pluralist understanding of Muslimhood. Anti-Semitism and Islamophobia will be overcome by celebrating universal humanism and treating other human beings with dignity, respect, and justice.[39]

Conclusion

With reports of serious and growing Islamophobia and anti-Semitism in the West,[40] there is—as the *UNESCO World Report* points out—a need for new and dynamic ways of introducing tools of cultural diversity in education, media, and policy. To counter the dangerous trends at work throughout the world, there is a need for increased influence of empathetic educationalists and compassionate leaders in the media and a focus on empathy-centric curricula and policies—these will be the keys to successful coexistence and conflict resolution in the twenty-first century. Unless we connect global messages given out in the media with intellectual thoughtfulness inextricably interlinked with ideas of empathy and respect for others, we will be heading straight, in this "Age of Hatred", toward a global disaster characterized by racially motivated dislike of the Other and possibly by war. All of us, therefore, must heed and disseminate the valuable concept of healing our fractured world, or what we may say in Hebrew, *Tikkun Olam*.

6

DEVOTED ACTORS IN AN AGE OF RAGE
Social Science on the ISIS Front Line and Elsewhere

SCOTT ATRAN

Anxiety is the dizziness of freedom.

—Søren Kierkegaard

Introduction: A Fragmenting World Order

The Western creations of the nation-state and relatively open markets that today dominate the global political and economic order (and to which non-Western powers like China and Russia now also subscribe) have largely supplanted age-old forms of governance, social formations, and economic activity. The accompanying rising populations and urbanization, extensive and rapid communications and transportation, and science and technology have transformed people in the farthest reaches of the planet into competitive players seeking progress and personal satisfaction through material expansion and success. But the increasingly unavoidable tension in the quest for material comfort and security, via participation in market-driven competition that constantly agitates for innovation and change, often comes at steep personal and social cost. This is especially so for communities and regions with little time to adapt and where aspirations show scant promise of fulfillment. As the spiritual values of long-standing cultures and religions have been eclipsed under newer institutions that lack stability or are corrupted, redemptive violence is prone to erupt from the resulting anxiety and alienation along prevailing political fault lines.[1]

103

Transnational Terror circa 1900

This was apparent in the actions of social revolutionaries and anarchists in the first wave of modern transnational terror that began shortly before the assassination of Russia's czar Alexander II (1881). This terrorist wave extended through the assassinations of the prime ministers of France (1894) and Spain (1897), the empress of Austria (1898), and the king of Italy (1900), and the killing of U.S. president William McKinley (1901). It involved bombings of "bourgeois" civilians in cafes and theaters across Europe and North America, before abating with the onset of World War I. Affected nations reacted by adding or reinforcing state security organizations: like Russia's Okhrana (1881), precursor of the NKVD and KGB; Britain's New Scotland Yard (1890); France's Brigade des Renseignements généraux (1907); and the U.S. Bureau of Investigation (1908), precursor of the FBI. Initially, however, states lashed out in stunned bafflement, often missing their illusive targets but hitting those unrelated to terrorist acts, and also using the cover of the fight against terror to mask the settling of scores against more traditional enemies.

Thus, in his first annual message to Congress after McKinley's death, Theodore Roosevelt declared that "When compared with the suppression of anarchy, every other question sinks into insignificance."[2] He then offered a corollary to the Monroe Doctrine: anarchy's "general loosening of the ties of civilized society, may in America as elsewhere, ultimately require intervention by some civilized nation, and may lead the United States, however reluctantly . . . to the exercise of an international police power."[3] Most tellingly, the war against anarchy and terror helped to justify the brutal repression of a native insurgency against America's "civilizing mission" and rule in Muslim areas of the Philippines.

The countercultural pressures toward salvational violence against the international order are arguably similar for many who now join or support al-Qaeda and ISIS. And quite similar, too, has been the character of the international reaction to these vanguards of the recent post–Cold War wave of transnational political violence.

There are, in fact, striking political, social, and economic parallels—and arguably continuities—between the pre–World War I unraveling of the European order and present challenges to the global order established after World War II. Before the Napoleonic Wars, the nation-state system was quasi-anarchic, with each nation playing close to a zero-sum game with all competitors and neighbors. The massive bloodletting and upside-down implications of the French Revolution and Napoleonic

Wars (1789–1815) compelled Europe's governing elites to develop a quasi-institutional consensus for how Europe, and the expanding colonial world it dominated, should be managed to avoid chaos. In the century from the Congress of Vienna (1815) to the outbreak of World War I (1914), this informal international consensus persevered to maintain the integrity of existing empires and nation-states; and this, despite important multinational popular uprisings (e.g., the revolutions of 1830 and 1848), the mass-casualty multilateral Crimean War (1843–1846), and bilateral wars (e.g., Austro-Prussian War, 1866; Franco-Prussian War, 1870–1871), which intermittently reconfigured the balance of power within and between polities. Britain, especially, recurrently intervened abroad to maintain the Ottoman Empire's integrity and the overall European balance of great powers. But the increasingly obvious gap separating elite values and actions from popular needs and wants, and the willingness of one, then the other, of Europe's powers to break the consensus (e.g., as with Russia around its borders and in the Balkans and then, in 1911, with Italy seizing parts of Ottoman North Africa to make Libya), speedily unwound the world order.

Globalization

This order had attained spiraling levels of globalization in transportation (worldwide construction of roads and railroads, steamshipping of waterways, and later automobiles), communication (e.g., telegraph and later telephone, film, and radio), unfettered capital flow (not recovered to 1912 levels until the 1990s), movements of people (Russia and Turkey alone required passports), and scientific prowess and reach (with new sources of technology and energy freeing human material effort and creation from muscle power). Yet, when nations again focused narrowly on self-interests (as with other great powers like Germany, which felt unduly left out of colonial quest for empire), and the failed crusades for international brotherhood devolved into anarchism to become a transnational scourge, the world order rapidly degenerated into world war, with disregard for red lines only accelerating in the lead-up to World War II. In *Escape from Freedom*, Eric Fromm[4] argued that the anxiety that results from what religious philosopher Kierkegaard called "the dizziness of freedom"[5] and the resultant social disruption impelled many people to seek the elimination of uncertainty in authoritarian systems, as with fascism, Nazism, and Stalinism in the period between the two world wars.

Indeed, the quest for elimination of uncertainty, coupled with a yearning for significance, are the personal (nonpolitical) sentiments most readily elicited in our research with both volunteers for violent jihad and militant supporters of populist ethnonationalist movements. For today, the speed, scale, and scope of change in a globalization movement is again unsettling Western societies. Yet, the spiraling impact of globalization now extends to the rest of the world whose populations have much less prior experience than the West in adapting to the political, social, and economic effects of market-driven "creative destruction." In the West, traditionally left-leaning working-class communities who have been disadvantaged by economic globalization, and traditionally right-leaning believers in cultural ideals that they feel are threatened by multicultural globalism, have joined populist movements that reaffirm the primacy of the nation-state, reject international alliances, abhor political correctness and the push for cultural diversity, and distrust traditional governing elites. In other parts of the world, there has been a multiplication of failed states, insurgency and war, and massive population displacements. This, in turn, has fostered the implantation of transnational terrorist movements in these regions, enabling such movements to reach out from their bases and into increasingly marginalized immigrant communities in Europe and elsewhere in order to destabilize those host societies, increase hostility against immigrants and other marginalized groups, and encourage people from those groups to enlist into the cause.

The situation is not irredeemable, but it is approaching a dangerous threshold, with mainstream middle classes (the mainstay of democracies everywhere) experiencing a collective loss of community and increasing alienation from governmental elites and joining the underemployed working class in blaming marginalized immigrant groups for societal ills. Radical Islamists are earnestly, and with increasing success, driving mainstream sympathies away from Muslims with brutal acts intended to heighten sentiments of blame among the mainstream and victimhood among immigrant Muslims who come to realize that trying to live in peace brings only pain. All of this is happening against a backdrop of general demographic decline (replacement rate of only 1.6 children per couple) that increasingly hampers European countries' possibilities of sustaining a large middle class—much less armies—without massive immigration, to which the European mainstream is increasingly opposed.

Increasing Nationalism

The values of liberal and open democracy increasingly appear to be losing ground around the world to those of radical Islam and narrow, xenophobic ethnonationalisms in a tacit alliance that is clobbering societies in ways similar to the hatchet job done on republican values by the fascists and communists in the 1920s and 1930s. According to the World Values Survey (Waves 5 and 6, 2005–2014), only 40 percent of Europeans under thirty years old believe that living in a democratic country is "absolutely important" to them.[6] In Hungary, a revanchist, expansive nationalism is advocated by the ruling national conservatives (Fidesz) and far-right Jobbik Party (claiming rights to "protect" large communities of ethnic Hungarians in nearby countries). Prime Minister Orbán, who was expelled from Liberal International, a global coalition of centrist liberal democrats, is now Europe's leading apostle of what he calls "the illiberal state," citing Russia and China as examples.[7] (Jarosław Kaczyński, head of the populist Law and Justice Party, Poland's largest parliamentary block, promised to follow suit and create "Budapest in Warsaw.") Hungary's leadership does not shy from its authoritarian past, having established "National Day of Cohesion" in 2010 to mark the "unfair and unjust dismemberment of the Hungarian nation" following the fall of Miklós Hothy's fascist and pro-Nazi regime (1920–1944). Fidesz avowedly seeks to end "the two-party system with ongoing division as to values" and create a "permanent government" devoted to genuinely "Hungarian" values—a praiseworthy "rethinking of values" according to Vladimir Putin,[8] but inconsistent with EU membership. In a May 2017 poll of residents in Hungary, Czech Republic, Slovakia, and Poland, substantial minorities in each country also think that the EU is pushing them to abandon traditional values, and Russia has taken the side of traditional values.[9]

Fearful of undermining the mission to escape from the chauvinism and xenophobia that fed two world wars, many pro-EU leaders and press simply denounce as "bigoted" or "racist" concerns with national identity or cultural conflict linked with mass immigration from societies whose large majorities oppose the liberty and tolerance of irreligious ideas and gender equality,[10] and who view Westerners as "greedy" and "immoral."[11] Instead of seeking alternatives to leaving defense of heartfelt patriotism and value preference—including traditional religious values—to political fringe groups that increasingly encroach on the mainstream, there is an ostrichlike blindness to these panhuman preferences for one's own that arguably contributes to a crisis of faith in the EU, its prevailing liberal values, and its institutions.

"Is it not that God and society are one and the same?" French sociologist Emile Durkheim famously conjectured.[12] By instilling tribal trust and common cause, imagined kinship and faith beyond reason, religions enable strangers to cooperate in a manner than gives them an advantage in competition with other groups. In so doing, religions sanctify and incite fear (which is the father of cruelty) but also hope (which is the friend of happiness). This has been especially true since the advent of the "Axial Age" more than two millennia ago, when large-scale civilizations arose under the watchful gaze of powerful divinities who mercilessly punished moral transgressors to ensure that even strangers in multiethnic empires would work and fight as one.[13] Call it "God" or whatever secular ideology one prefers, including any of the great modern salvational –*isms*, such as colonialism, socialism, anarchism, communism, fascism, and liberalism. This commitment to a transcendent ideal is "the privilege of absurdity; to which no living creature is subject, but man only," of which Thomas Hobbes wrote in *Leviathan*.[14] Indeed, humans make their greatest exertions and sacrifices, for ill or good, for the sake of ideas that give a sense of significance. In an inherently chaotic universe, where humans alone among organic species recognize that death is unavoidable, there is an overwhelming psychological impetus to overcome this tragedy of cognition: to realize *why I am* and *who we are*.

Virtues and Violence

In *The Descent of Man*, Darwin cast this devotion as the virtue of "morality . . . the spirit of patriotism, fidelity, obedience, courage, and sympathy" with which winning groups are better endowed in history's spiraling competition for survival and dominance.[15] Across cultures, the strongest forms of primary group identity are bounded by sacred values that are immune to material tradeoffs—carrots or sticks—like unwillingness to sell off one's children or sell out one's religion or country. Devotion to such values leads some groups to prevail because of a nonrational commitment from at least some of its members to actions that drive success independent of—or all out of proportion to—expected rational outlays and outcomes, risks and rewards, costs and consequences.

Often such values are attributed to Providence or Nature and embedded in notions whose meaning one can never quite pin down, and which cannot be ever definitively verified or falsified by logic or empirical evidence,[16] such as "God is great, bodiless but omnipotent" or "free markets are always wise."[17] Thus, while the label *sacred values* intuitively denotes religious belief, as when land or law becomes holy, it also includes the *secularized sacred*, as when ground or rights become hallowed (think Gettysburg or the Bill of Rights). For example the foundational doctrines and beliefs of the great ideological *–isms*; the quasi-religious notion of the nation itself, ritualized in song and ceremony and sacrifice; and those "self-evident" aspects of "human nature" that humankind is supposedly endowed with, such as "inalienable rights of life, liberty and the pursuit of happiness," which are anything but inherently self-evident and natural in the life of our species (cannibalism, infanticide, slavery, oppression of minorities, and male domination of women were more standard fare). It wasn't inevitable or even reasonable that conceptions of individual freedom and equality concocted by eighteenth-century European intellectuals should emerge, much less prevail. They did only through revolution, intensive social engineering, economic competition, and belief in "just war."

In our preferred world of liberal democracy and human rights, violence—especially extreme forms of mass bloodshed—is generally considered a pathological or evil expression of human nature gone awry, or collateral damage as the unintended consequence of righteous intentions. But across most human history and cultures, violence against other groups is universally claimed by the perpetrators to be a sublime matter of moral virtue.[18] For without a claim to virtue, it is difficult, if not inconceivable, to kill large numbers of people innocent of direct harm to others. Besides, brutal terror scares the hell out of enemies and fence sitters—let us not forget the rationale for nuclear carnage at Hiroshima.[19]

1. The Trembling and Fear of Transnational Terrorism

The 9/11 attacks cost al-Qaeda $400,000 to $500,000,[20] whereas the United States Government (USG) has likely spent $4–5 trillion or more in the "War on Terror" in the years since.[21] Despite this investment, the global threat arguably has not abated. In just two years, the so-called Islamic State (ISIS, ISIL, or ISISL) created the largest foreign volunteer force since World War II, drawing fighters from the majority of the world's nations, and inspiring attacks that have killed or wounded thousands across the globe.[22] Overwhelming military force by a large coalition of nations will likely destroy the so-called Islamic State's territorial base in the Middle East, but inasmuch as ISIS is more a symptom than a cause of political fragmentation and social turmoil in the Sunni Arab world and beyond, that is unlikely to end the jihadi threat.

Nevertheless, the war-fighting capabilities of ISIS and al-Qaeda combined do not even approach, say, the manpower and firepower of the Belgian army alone. Perhaps never before in history have so few, armed with such relatively small material means, frightened so many across the planet. The shutdown of Brussels in the wake of the Paris attacks, or of Boston in the aftermath of the marathon bombings in 2013, speaks to a comparable fear and contributes to an underlying lack of faith in our own societies and values, something that terror attacks are designed to promote. During World War II, not even the full might of the German Luftwaffe at the height of the Blitz could compel the British government and the people of London to cower so. Today, mere mention of an attack on New York in an ISIS video has U.S. officials scurrying to calm the public. A rumor that someone heard a cry in Arabic of "Allahu Akbar" (God is great) in a shooting or a stabbing—ignoring the many thousands of more lethal or damaging events—is often enough for the major news services to post breathless "breaking news" alerts. Media exposure, the oxygen of terror in our age, not only amplifies the perception of danger but, in generating such hysteria, makes the bloated threat to society real.

This is especially true today because the media is mostly designed to titillate the public rather than inform. Thus, it has become child's play for ISIS to turn our own propaganda machine, the world's mightiest, into theirs—boosting a novel, highly potent jujitsu style of asymmetric warfare that we *could* counter with responsible restraint and straight-forward information.

The outcome is preposterous and dangerous. The U.S. Department of Justice, with overwhelming support from Congress and the media, now considers the common kitchen pressure cooker to be a "weapon of mass destruction" if used for terrorism. This ludicrously levels a cooking pot with a thermonuclear bomb that has many billions of times greater destructive power. It trivializes true weapons of mass destruction, making their acceptance more palatable and their use more conceivable. In this present hyperreality, messaging is war by other means. ISIS' manipulation of our media has created a sense of foreboding of mass destruction where it is not really possible, at the same time obscuring greater, real threats: even with ISIS driven from its territorial centers in Raqqa and Mosul, the specter of ISIS has loomed much greater in the popular press or in political discourse than the far greater menace of nuclear holocaust.

2. Devoted versus Rational Actors
on the ISIS Front Line and Elsewhere

Perhaps a deeper problem, though, concerns the conceptual framework that our society and political culture use to understand human nature in its dealings with transnational terrorism. On one side, we have a culture that has built an awesome military capability to defeat or neutralize any other state's military threat, but whose key decision makers (as well as many others) have a fairly narrow view of human motivation and action. That analytic framework for interpreting human behavior is based mainly on utilitarian (cost-benefit) presumptions about *rational actors*. Rational actor theories generally assume that individuals select among available preferences (depending on potential costs and benefits in determining those preferences with the information at hand) to act in ways consistent with chosen preferences and the likelihood of outcomes expected from such action. If people fail to meet such *rational* expectations, then they are considered *irrational*, unless their behavior also can be explained as bounded by cognitive processing limitations,[23] lack of cultural awareness,[24] intrinsic indivisibility of resources,[25] or other biases and ecological constraints.[26]

Political reactions to transnational terrorism thus alternate between either trying to find the material, self-interested motivation driving terrorists' behavior or else viewing them as crazy. We expend enormous resources to find technological solutions to problems of transnational terrorism (e.g., through detection of improvised explosive devices and possible chemical, biological, and nuclear weapons, or the use of supercomputers to find a needle in a haystack); however, there is relatively scant attention to terrorists' actual motivation or psychology, few resources committed to studying people in the field, and comparatively little intimate and sustained engagement with the personal networks that terrorist groups feed off of and wherein may reside the most useful information for preventing violence. In short, the focus is on rational deterrence, a strategy more applicable to state-on-state power rivalries than to conflict in which opponents are non-state actors fighting for a sacred cause. Decision making is hierarchic and bureaucratic, and funding for counterterrorism is politicized and required to produce short-term, quantifiable results.

On the other side, transnational terrorist groups are often only loosely hierarchical, horizontally intricate and based in personal networks, and nimble. This side focuses less on mass messaging an ideology or narratives to a general audience and more on personal engagement with the aspirations and grievances circulating in particular kinship and friendship networks. The bonds created within a militant group are of imagined kinship—brotherhoods, motherlands, and the like. The overall conceptual framework views good people as righteous and spiritually motivated, and enemies as moral nihilists lacking in spiritual strength. The focus of action is on the long term rather than the here and now: "You have the watches but we have the time."[27]

The Role of Sacred Values

With transnational terrorism, as with other violent expressions of seemingly intractable conflict—with Israelis and Palestinians,[28] Saudis and Iranians,[29] and blood feuds in southern Europe or the southern United States[30]—ample historical and cross-cultural evidence shows that perceived insults to faith, dignity, or honor, or, generally, one side's failure to show respect to another side's cherished values can lead to intergroup violence that may persist for decades, even centuries. Disputes over otherwise mundane phenomena (people, places, objects, events) then become existential struggles immune to the utilitarian logic of risks and rewards, costs and consequences.[31]

In this regard, a utilitarian and instrumental approach to transnational terrorism may be insufficient to explain, predict, or parry willingness to fight and die for a cause if such willingness is shaped by duty-bound devotion to sacred values and identity groups that people are fused with, as, for example, with some suicide bombers.[32] Sacred values are preferences, beliefs, and practices that communities deem protected from monetary or other material trade-offs, as when land or law becomes holy or hallowed. Within this framework people most willingly engage in costly sacrifices and extreme actions when motivated to protect nonnegotiable sacred values[33]—whether religious (e.g., holy law) or secular (e.g., democracy)—and such values are associated with a group with which they feel viscerally connected and that imbues members with a collective sense of invulnerability.[34] Ever since World War II, on average, revolutionaries and insurgents willing to sacrifice for their cause and group have prevailed with up to ten times less firepower and manpower than the state armies and police forces (which rely mainly on material incentives and disincentives such as pay, promotion, and punishment).[35]

Our research team of academics, policymakers, former military, and artists has been exploring why people refuse political compromise, go to war, attempt revolution, or resort to terrorism, focusing on what Darwin called virtues "highly esteemed and even sacred" that give "immense advantage" to any group inspired by devoted individuals willing to sacrifice for them.[36] The theoretical frame emerges from our prior online, lab, and field studies of conflict situations, most recently among combatants on the ISIS front line in Iraq.[37] The studies suggest that seemingly unconditional cooperation and intractable conflict are best understood within a *devoted actor* rather than *rational actor* framework that integrates research on sacred values[38]—whether religious or secular—and identity fusion, which gives a visceral sense of group oneness and invincibility.[39] Consider the following:

In September 2014 U.S. president Barack Obama endorsed the declaration of his national intelligence director: "We underestimated ISIL and overestimated the fighting capability of the Iraqi army . . . It boils down to predicting the will to fight, which is an imponderable."[40] This shortfall may arise, in part, from undervaluing certain aspects of what may be considered the nonutilitarian dimension of human conflict, which combatants themselves deem "sacred" or "spiritual," whether secular or religious. Over the last two years, members of our research group at ARTIS International and the Centre for the Resolution of Intractable Conflict (CRIC) at the University of Oxford have been working in Western Europe, North Africa, and the Middle East to understand people's willingness to make costly sacrifices for their groups and their values, including the will to fight and die.

Interviews with Pro- and Anti-ISIS Fighters

To examine this dimension of intergroup conflict, we developed measures based on ethnographic fieldwork and interviews with two groups on the USG list of terrorist organizations in northern Iraq in February–March 2015: captured ISIS fighters and combatants of the Kurdistan Workers' Party (PKK) fighting against ISIS. Next, we tested and refined these measures with large-sample online studies in Spain to understand people's willingness to make costly sacrifices for their groups and their values.

The preoccupation with understanding those who seek to join ISIS has led us largely to overlook a related phenomenon. Just as foreigners from around the globe have flocked to ISIS' so-called Caliphate, so too have others, and for different reasons, rallied to *fight* ISIS. Accordingly, we followed with a quantitative field study in February–March 2016 on the same front line with Peshmerga (Kurdish Regional Government forces), Iraqi Army Kurds, and Arab Sunni militias. Further online studies in Spain with Western Europeans then examined cognitive mechanisms underlying frontline results in the Middle East.

From our studies, three interrelated factors appear to be critical to willingness to kill and sacrifice: (1) commitment to nonnegotiable sacred values with which the group's actors are wholly fused, (2) readiness to forsake commitment to kin for those values, and (3) perceived spiritual strength of one's own group versus foes. The following paragraphs briefly describe the experimental measures and results for each factor.

To measure sacredness, we probed willingness to trade off values in exchange for material benefits, whether for individual or collective gain. Much more is known about economic decision making than value-driven behavior. But here are some features of sacred values that we, and others, have empirically identified:

1. *Disregard for material incentives or disincentives*: attempts to buy people off from their cause ("carrots") or punish them for embracing it through sanctions ("sticks") do not work and even tend to backfire.[41]

2. *Blindness to exit strategies*: people cannot even conceive of the possibility of abandoning their sacred values or relaxing their commitment to the cause; this fosters unconditional cooperation and intractable conflict in ways that social contracts born of shared convenience and utility do not. Offering material incentives, however reasonable or rewarding, or sanctions and punishments to abandon or compromise sacred values increases anger, violence, and opposition to peace.

3. *Resistance to social pressure*: it matters not how many people oppose your sacred values, or how close to you they are in other matters; sacred values are not social or cultural norms but defining and circumscribing features of culture itself.[42]

4. *Insensitivity to discounting*: according to most economic and political theory, and usual in most everyday affairs, distant events and objects have less significance for people than things in the here and now; but matters associated with sacred values, regardless of how far removed in time or space, are more important and motivating than mundane concerns, however immediate.[43]

5. *Privileged link to emotions*: for example, people feel anger and rage when sacred values are threatened, or joy and happiness when successfully defending sacred values, including by way of revenge.[44]

6. *Distinct neural signatures*: for example, our brain scans of supporters of al-Qaeda affiliate Lashkar-e-Taiba on willingness to fight and die for sacred values show diminished activity in areas associated with utilitarian reasoning, indicating inhibition of deliberative reasoning in favor of rapid, duty-bound decision making.[45]

Absolute refusal to contemplate such trade-offs was taken as an indicator of a sacred value.

Identity Fusion

In relation to identity fusion, participants were asked to indicate their relationship to a number of groups. They were shown a series of increasingly overlapping circles, one of which represents them, the other a given group.[46] Respondents who picked the figure displaying completely overlapping circles were considered fused with the group, leading to a dichotomous measure. For example, those who chose the last pairing in figure 6.1, "E," expressed actions markedly different from those who chose other pairings, indicating that their personal identity is bound to a unique collective identity, with each individual ready to sacrifice for every other.

Our previous online and field studies in North Africa and Western Europe had shown that commitment to sacred values and identity fusion independently affect willingness to make costly sacrifices, but that their interaction maximizes such willingness under real or perceived threat (fig. 6.2). For example, among 260 Moroccans who lived in either of two city neighborhoods with a history of support for militant jihad (Jemaa Mezuak in Tetuan and Sidi Moumen in Casablanca), individual testing in the field indicated that about 30 percent were *devoted actors* (i.e., driven by duty-bound, deontological considerations rather than rational anticipation of costs and consequences, risks or rewards). In the Moroccan case, these were people who viewed strict imposition of Islamic law, or sharia, as a sacred value, and who identified closely with a kin-like group with which they were *fused*. They were also the most willing to kill and die for Islamic law. A parallel study of 644 people in Spain identified only 12 percent as devoted actors willing to sacrifice for democracy, and few willing to kill, die, or forsake family, even when reminded of threats by ISIS and al-Qaeda. Those most likely to make costly sacrifices saw democracy as a sacred value and identified closely with a kin-like group of friends.[47]

3. For Cause and Comrade:
Will to Fight on the ISIS Front Line and Elsewhere

In February–March 2016 we interviewed combatants near the village of Kudilah, the first engagement in the offensive to retake Mosul, the largest ISIS-controlled city.[48] At Kudilah, some ninety ISIS fighters with no heavy weaponry managed to prevent a sustained advance by

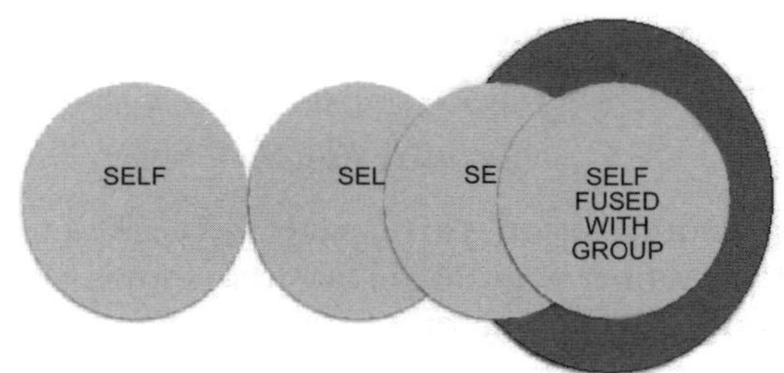

Pictorial Measure of Identity Fusion used with Islamic State Fighters

FIG. 6.1. MEASURES OF IDENTITY FUSION.

Top: *generalized dynamic slider version for tablet or smartphone.*
Bottom: *static pictorial version used with Islamic State fighters on plastic card.*
People who choose the fused option (placing the "self" circle entirely within the "group"
circle) think and behave differently than people who choose any other option.[49]

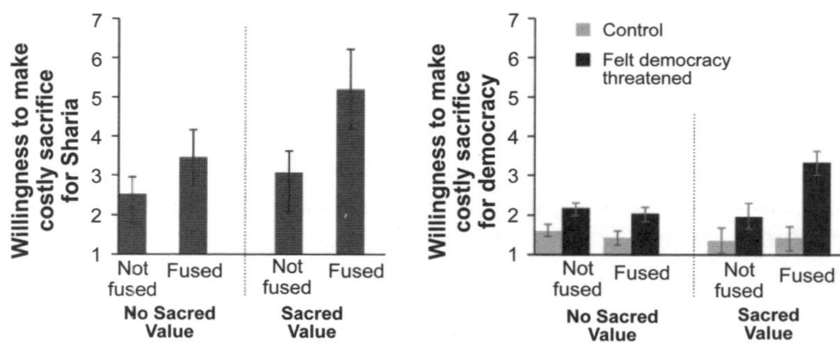

FIG. 6.2. THE DEVOTED ACTOR:
INTERACTION OF SACRED VALUES AND IDENTITY FUSION.

Left: *in ISIS-supporting Moroccan neighborhoods, people who viewed strict imposition*
of Islamic law, or sharia, as a sacred value and who identified closely with a kin-like
(fused) group most expressed willingness to kill and die for Islamic law.
Right: *a sample of Spaniards reported a weaker willingness to kill and die for*
democracy as a sacred value when identifying closely with a kin-like group of friends
and only under an explicit threat priming.[50]

several hundred coalition forces of Arab Sunni militias, Iraqi Army, and Kurdish Peshmerga, aided by U.S. and German advisors and repeated air strikes. This, despite the fact that more than fifty ISIS fighters were killed in the battle, including a score of *inghamasi* ("those who plunge deep," suicide attackers trained for piercing enemy positions and for covering retreat), yelling that they would die so that "The Caliphate is enduring and expanding!" Many who fought in the battle, including some who had been fighting in various wars since the 1960s, told us this was the fiercest combat of their lives.

We wondered whether there were common traits that explain the fierce devotion of ISIS fighters as well as fighters opposing ISIS. As we noted, researchers usually treat extreme sacrifice for others in utilitarian terms, weighing pros and cons in ways that best satisfy their own interests even if others benefit as well. But it is difficult to see how that applies to *inghamasi* or to Kurdish fighters who have already lost limbs and left their families behind in ISIS territory to defend "Kurdeity" (their term). Calling one side "losers/nihilists/insane/barbarians/cowards," as our press and politicians frequently do, while on the other hand labeling the other side "heroes/altruists/courageous/civilized/brave," may be relevant for mobilizing sentiment, but has little apparent scientific worth for distinguishing sides.

We examined the will to fight among the three anti-ISIS groups who fought at Kudilah. Both the Peshmerga and Iraqi regulars were Kurds, and all groups identified as Sunni Muslims. We intended to interview twenty combatants from each group, but difficulties in getting to the front, the wounding or death of planned interviewees, and changes in military scheduling prevented achieving total parity between the groups before the second battle of Kudilah began in late March 2016. Values considered sacred for Peshmerga and Iraqi Army Kurds were mainly "Kurdeity" (a cultural concept denoting a sense of Kurdish language, heritage, and land; 63% and 41%, respectively) and Independent Kurdistan (a political goal, 26% and 47%, respectively). For Sunni Arab fighters, maintaining the integrity of the Iraqi nation (a political goal, 55%) and Arabness (a cultural concept, 20%) were considered sacred. The different groups with which Peshmerga, Iraqi Army Kurds, and Arab Sunni militia participants might be fused were: family (95%, 94%, 100%, respectively), kin-like group of friends (95%, 82%, 94%), Muslim Ummah (26%, 19%, 39%), Iraqi people (0%, 12%, 61%), and own group (79%, 100%, 56%).

All anti-ISIS combatants were fused with at least one group whose members were perceived as sharing at least one sacred value. All were constantly under threat and were putting their lives on the line, as evident from the fact that more than half of frontline participants had been wounded in battle (table 1). Those wounded expressed greater willingness to make costly sacrifices, indicating convergence between stated and actual willingness for costly sacrifices on the front.

Group	n	Wounded	Sacrifices M (SD)
Peshmerga	19	12 (63%)	2.56 (1.07)
Iraqi Army Kurds	17	8 (47%)	1.82 (0.95)
Sunni Arab militia fighters	20	9 (45%)	1.70 (1.13)

TABLE 1. WILLINGNESS TO FIGHT AMONG ANTI-ISIS FIGHTERS.

Peshmerga are more likely to express willingness to make costly sacrifices than Iraqi Army Kurds or Sunni Arab militia fighters.[51]

Sacred Values Compared
with Kinship and Other Fusion Groups

We tested our measures of sacred values and fusion online ($N = 816$). Participants responded to measures of fusion with country (Spain) and democracy as a sacred value. Under an explicit threat condition highlighting the 2004 Madrid train bombings, an interaction of identity fusion and sacred values characteristic of devoted actors appeared: devoted actors in the threat condition displayed the strongest willingness for costly sacrifice.[52]

Previous studies of combat soldiers stress devotion to comrades over cause,[53] as do online studies of Western Europeans.[54] However, this may be otherwise when combatants consider the cause sacred. In in-depth interviews with (captured) ISIS and PKK (Kurdish Marxist) combatants in Iraq in 2015, some told of how they had to give up their families to fight for their cause (Islamic Caliphate, Kurdish homeland).[55] In fact, ISIS has divulged that some children have even publicly executed their parents for opposing the Caliphate and its leader.[56]

From a material and evolutionary perspective, one should prioritize kin or kin-like groups over abstract ideals. Yet one finding of our qualitative frontline interviews is that combatants make painful decisions when prioritizing value over group. We empirically tested how people reason over such trade-offs, and to what extent they predicted willingness to fight, in a sequence of studies. We asked participants to choose between sacred values and fused groups. All combatants were devoted actors who regarded relevant values as sacred and who were fused with at least one larger group: comrades, Muslim Ummah, kin-like group of friends (often comrades in arms), Iraqi people, or their own groups (Peshmerga, Iraqi Army Kurds, Sunni Arab militia fighters). Most were also fused with their families (> 90% for all three groups). We pitted their two most important groups against their two most important sacred values whenever possible. Most combatants chose at least one value over a group (86%), with more than half of them choosing at least one value over their families (59%). Combatants scored more highly in the costly sacrifice scale if they chose the value over the group in general (fig. 6.3).

On a more general plane, these findings of apparent preference for value over kin by devoted actors provides empirical support for the thesis that humans may form their strongest (and potentially most expansive) political and religious ties by subordinating devotion to kin to a more abstract ideal. Indeed, a founding parable of the monotheistic

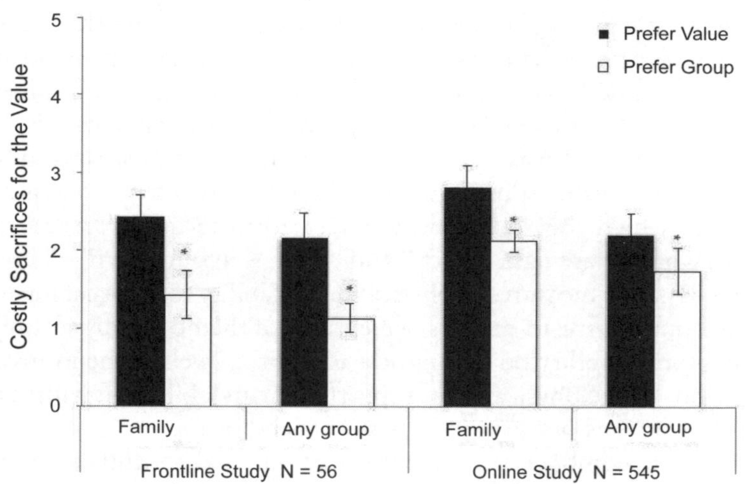

FIG. 6.3. WILLINGNESS TO SACRIFICE
AMONG COMBATANTS AND NONCOMBATANTS.

An illustration of willingness to make costly sacrifices for participants who forsake their fused groups for sacred values in frontline and online studies. An asterisk (*) indicates significant differences between preferences for value versus group (p<.001).[57]

religions (Judaism, Christianity, and Islam) involves Abraham's willingness to sacrifice beloved progeny to signal devotion to a sacred value (absolute commitment to God).[58] The very term *Islam* (submission), refers to sublimation of tribal and all other prior group affinities to God's message. Historically, willingness to sacrifice family and tribe was arguably critical to construction of larger groups founded on political principles.[59]

Physical and Spiritual Formidability

Within a rational actor framework, perceived intergroup difference in material formidability would strongly relate to willingness to engage in costly sacrifices. In contrast, within a devoted actor framework, perceived spiritual formidability would be most relevant when sacred values are in play. Although the term *spiritual formidability* may have religious connotations to some, it more properly refers to nonmaterial strength. In the frontline and online studies, we find that relative spiritual formidability of groups, compared to relative physical formidability, is more related to willingness to sacrifice.

Using techniques to judge physical formidability that assessed the perceived strength of various combatant groups in Iraq,[60] we found that both avowedly pious ISIS fighters and avowedly secular PKK fighters (the only force that held fast against the ISIS onslaught in summer 2014) disregarded consideration of in-group and out-group physical formidability. They argued during our initial experiments in early 2015 that most important was spiritual formidability (*ruhi bi ghiyrat* in both Arabic and Kurdish, "spirituality with bravery" to defend what is most cherished, which they recurrently described in terms of "strength of belief in what we are fighting for" and "what is in our heart"). Thus we adapted dynamic measures of physical formidability to spiritual formidability to compare the in-group's perceptions of their own physical versus spiritual formidability on willingness to fight, as well as the in-group's perceptions of the physical versus spiritual formidability on willingness to fight of various out-groups, whether friend or foe.

Frontline combatants' perception of spiritual formidability positively correlated with willingness to make costly sacrifices. These costly sacrifices to defend the value were: dying, letting their family suffer, killing civilians, undertaking a suicide attack, and torturing women and children. Combatants also judged the United States high in physical formidability but low spiritually, while judging ISIS low physically but high spiritually (fig. 6.4). A fighter typically remarked, "They are weak now because they have used up their resources but their fighters don't retreat even if the battle is lost."[61]

Follow-up online studies in Spain (N = 1,434) further explored possible effects of spiritual and physical formidability on willingness for costly sacrifices and armed intervention. Participants responded with their willingness to engage in actions to defend the sacred value using a five-item Likert gradated scale: *lose my job or source of income / go to jail / use violence / let my children suffer physical punishment / die.* (Quest for

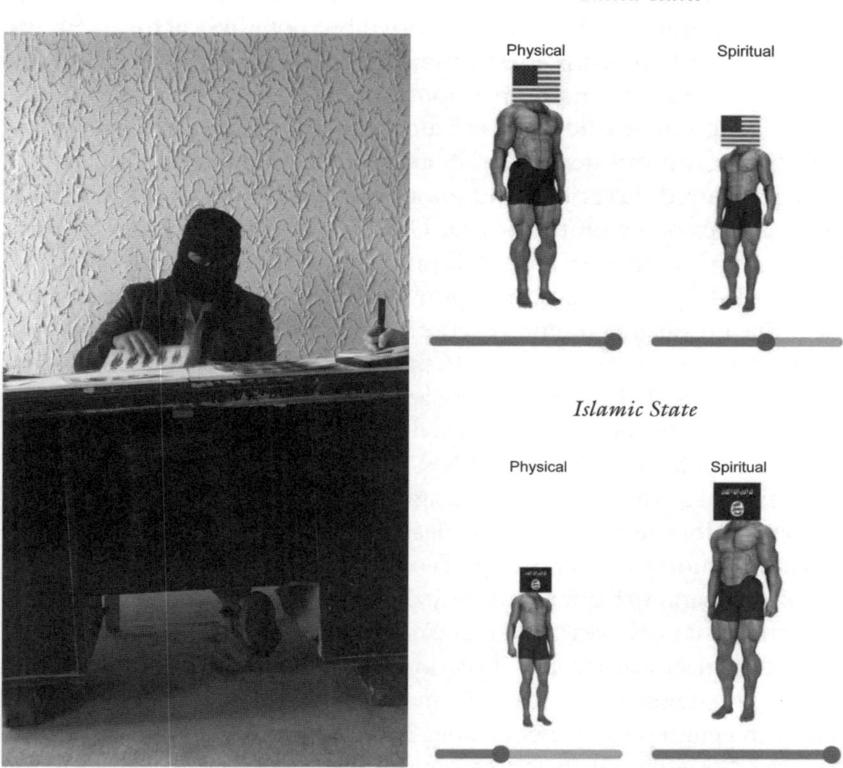

FIG. 6.4. COMPARING COMBATANT FORCES IN IRAQ: PHYSICAL VERSUS SPIRITUAL FORMIDABILITY.

In testing in Iraq, a captured ISIS fighter, left, chose how to mask himself to ensure anonymity to conform with human subjects' safety protection. ISIS fighters (here using a static paper measure with discrete choice) and Kurdish fighters (using either a static measure or a dynamic measure on the iPad allowing continuous choice) depict U.S. military physical force as strong and its spiritual force as middling (top). The same men portray ISIS physical force as weak and spiritual force as strong (bottom).[62]

variance in responses motivated use of different sets of costly sacrifices for frontline combatants and European noncombatants.) Participants who perceived ISIS as spiritually strong were least willing to sacrifice for democracy and support the country in an armed intervention.[63] When participants were asked to estimate the spiritual formidability of Spain versus ISIS, they invoked negative emotions (fear, panic, defenselessness, anger) when perceiving ISIS as spiritually stronger than the in-group. Together, the Spanish findings suggest that perception of an adversary's great spiritual strength relative to one's own may hamper and deter willingness to sacrifice in opposing the adversary. In sum, we consistently find that the relative spiritual but not physical formidability of groups predicts willingness to engage in costly sacrifices. This was true for combatants and online noncombatants.

Although these studies do not directly focus on transnational terrorism, they were motivated by earlier and parallel ethnographic fieldwork, semi-structured interviews and pilot experiments with ISIS and PKK (both groups being on the official USG list of terrorist organizations). This research with ISIS and PKK proved highly relevant to how those fighting ISIS perceive and act upon ISIS' will to fight relative to their own. The unsolicited responses (controlling and monitoring for possibilities of deception) of captured ISIS fighters and of PKK fighters holding the line against ISIS regarding what they considered to be sacred and spiritual were spontaneously echoed by other frontline combatants.

The numbers of ISIS and PKK fighters interviewed were too few for statistical analyses; however, insights gained with them were directly responsible for the elaboration of measures that we validated in a number of studies among a wider group of combatants and a much larger group of noncombatants from an entirely different cultural context. The fact that these hypotheses-driven measures reliably elicited statistically significant responses in the direction intimated by the ISIS and PKK interviews suggests that the information from ISIS and PKK fighters was both genuine and generalizable. More broadly, our findings suggest that insights gained from studies on the ISIS front line are theoretically and methodologically robust among large samples of noncombatants in an entirely different cultural context.

Understanding the will to fight in the face of lethal danger may remain imponderable—and attendant security challenges seemingly intractable—as long as we view such actions through a narrow lens of instrumental rationality.[64] This optic tends to disregard the immediate and remote consequences of actions motivated by highly esteemed, even sacred, spiritual and moral virtues that, as Darwin noted, "will certainly give an immense advantage" to one group over another when possessed by devoted actors who would "by their example excite . . . in a high degree the spirit"[65] in others to sacrifice self for cause and comrades—whether for ill or good.[66]

4. The Importance of Social Networks: Counter Engagement versus Counternarratives

There is a pervasive belief in governments and NGOs that—short of physical elimination—offering jobs or education or spouses to volunteers for value-driven militant groups would be the best way to reduce violence and counter the jihadi pull. But long-term analyses by the World Bank indicate no reliable relationship between job production and violence reduction. If people are ready to sacrifice their lives or their family—the totality of their self-interests—then it is not likely that offers of greater material advantages will stop them. Although such incentives may provide viable alternative life pathways at initial stages of radicalization, research shows that fully radicalized individuals who are fused with their group and its values are not particularly susceptible to such material incentives or disincentives (punishments, sanctions), which often backfire by increasing support for violence.

Research also shows that most who originally joined al-Qaeda were married,[67] and prior marriage does not seem to be a deterrent to those now volunteering for ISIS. Among the senior ranks of such groups, there are many who have had access to considerable education—especially in scientific fields such as engineering[68] and medicine[69] that require great discipline and a willingness to delay gratification. Indeed, ever since the anarchist movement began in the late nineteenth century, this sort of specialized preparation has held for much of the leadership of insurgent and revolutionary groups.

Commitment to absolute values that cannot be refuted by logical argumentation or empirical counterevidence—as with core religious precepts and axiomatic secular ideologies—may be paramount in sustaining extreme behaviors for the betterment or harm of others.[70] But such values can only generate successful actions by being embedded in social networks, inspiring and mobilizing groups of people bound by those values as "imagined kinship" (think brotherhood or motherland) and ready to sacrifice for one another unto their last measure of devotion.

A very senior member of President Obama's administration told our research team that when the operations to eliminate bin Laden were successfully concluded,

> I told Congress that this won't be the end of the problem, that we have to find a message to pull people away from this movement, and we need research and funding to do this because we don't know what will work and what won't. But Congress said: "How do you quantify this. Can you produce quantifiable results for the budget?" And of course we couldn't, because this is a long-term thing whose means and results we really can't predict in advance. So we've had a very dispersed and inadequate effort by the U.S. Government to understand causes and come up with some effective messaging. . . . To deal with this we can't just let a thousand flowers bloom. We need a coordinated, global effort to meet the security challenge in the realm of ideas.

The fitful and often feckless USG counterterrorism focus in the realm of ideas is on *counternarratives*, intended as alternative to the ideologies held to motivate terrorists. This strategy treats ideas as disembodied from the human conditions in which they are embedded and given life, thereby animating social groups. In their stead, research and policy might better focus on personalized *counter engagement*, addressing and harnessing the fellowship, passion, and purpose of particular people within their specific social contexts, as ISIS often does. This focus stands in sharp contrast to the current reliance on negative mass messaging and on sting operations to dissuade young people in doubt through entrapment and punishment (the most common practice used in U.S. law enforcement)[71] rather than through positive persuasion and channeling into productive life paths.

5. The Role of Social Groups

Reports from the Soufan Group, the International Center for the Study of Radicalisation (King's College London), and the Combating Terrorism Center (West Point) indicate that approximately three-quarters of those who join ISIS at home or abroad do so in groups. These groups often involve preexisting social networks and typically cluster in particular towns and neighborhoods.[72] This clustering suggests that much recruitment does not owe primarily to direct personal appeals by organization agents or individual exposure to social media (which would entail a more dispersed recruitment pattern). Rather, recruiting often critically involves enlisting clusters of family, friends, and fellow travelers from specific locales (e.g., neighborhoods, universities, prisons), indicating a public health rather than strictly criminal approach to violent extremism as most appropriate.

Consider, for example, the evolution of the Paris-Brussels attack networks (2015–2016) in terms of their increasing operational effectiveness via increasing reliance on local facilitation networks involving preexisting social ties (fig. 6.5).[73] In 2014 at least twenty-one ISIS

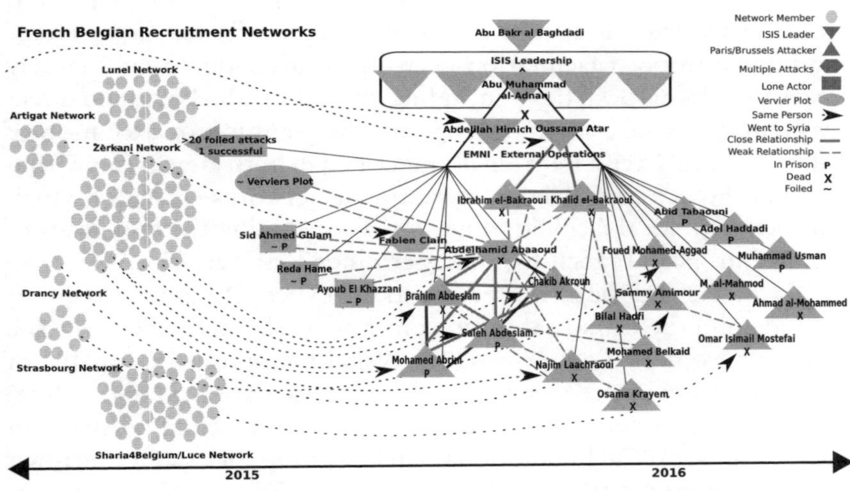

FIG. 6.5. EVOLUTION OF PARIS-BRUSSELS ATTACK NETWORKS (2015–2016).

Initially, authorities did not figure out the link between these attacks until they identified a common middleman, Abdelhamid Abaaoud. Abaaoud was again implicated as a middleman in a series of foiled Emni-directed group and lone actor attacks in France in early to mid-2015. By this time, Abaaoud became known as "the most wanted terrorist in Europe." As a result, his ability to be an effective logistical middleman was diminished (ISIS faked his death to help his operations), and he needed to outsource his role to others. Five of Abaaoud's childhood friends from Molenbeek, fellow Zerkani network recruits, began exploiting family, friends, and underworld connections in Belgium and France to set the stage for the attacks. Salah Abdeslam's low or nonexistent profile in European terrorism databases allowed him to take over the crucial middleman role. He arranged housing and transportation, picked up attack network members returning from Syria, and so forth. Many members of the attack network contributed facilitation sources, but the Molenbeek friends with the closest social ties were the primary coordinators of these resources. In the months following the attacks, over two hundred individuals were arrested in over twenty countries on charges of facilitation. In 2016 at least twenty more attack plans in France were either inspired or directed by ISIS, seventeen being foiled. In most cases, attackers were recruited, coordinated, and instructed online with limited offline facilitation in preexisting social networks, which may account for their limited effectiveness.[74]

operatives were sent back from Syria into Europe to carry out attacks on soft targets. All were Francophone; most were French and Belgian while others were citizens of former French colonies. They reentered individually or in pairs. All attacks, except one, were foiled. All were directed by ISIS' external operations branch, Emni (a.k.a. Amn al-Kharji). The attackers' lack of local facilitation networks partially contributed to their failings. In contrast, the "success" of the November 2015 Paris and March 2016 Brussels attacks can be partially attributed to an extensive inter-European facilitation network of overlapping, and largely preexisting, local social ties—including many individuals with no direct involvement in, or even knowledge of, the planning or execution of violent actions. Twelve individuals implicated in both attacks came from disparate French and Belgian recruitment networks—each of which had their own local facilitation networks—including the two heads of Emni's European branch that "masterminded" the attacks.

To understand the intricate networking of people and ideas requires an epidemiology of radical notions in host social networks.[75] At the very least we need field research in actual communities, capable of capturing the evidence to reveal which strategies are working, failing, or backfiring. A necessary focus of that research effort must be on youth, who form the bulk of today's terrorist recruits and tomorrow's most vulnerable populations. Volunteers for al-Qaeda, ISIS, and many extreme nationalist groups are often youth in transitional stages in their lives—immigrants, students, and people between jobs and before finding their mates.[76] Having left their homes, they seek new families of friends and fellow travelers to find purpose and significance. Ability to understand the realities facing young people will determine whether the scourge of transnational terrorism continues, abates, or surges. Presently, though, young people, especially young men (although increasingly young women), are viewed mostly as "youth bulge" and a problem to be pummeled rather than as a "youth boom" and the world's most creative force, which holds the promise of a solution to violent extremism. We need prevention research, fostering positive youth development through concrete possibilities for realizing young people's hopes and dreams—research that goes beyond seeing youth only as perpetrators, beneficiaries, or victims of others' initiatives, but instead as people potentially having political agency (as ISIS allows) with decision-making roles in shaping their own futures.

Conclusion

The "Clash of Civilizations" is an idea born in the intellectual circles of Harvard and *Foreign Policy*,[77] and then purposely nurtured both by al-Qaeda and ISIS and many who oppose them, including xenophobic ethnonationalist movements that play off them. It is a woefully misbegotten idea for our times. For transnational jihadi terrorism and right-wing violent extremism represent not the resurgence of traditional cultures but their collapse, as young people unmoored from millennial traditions flail about in search of a social identity that gives personal significance and glory. This is the dark side of globalization. Individuals radicalize to find a firm identity in a flattened world. In this new reality, vertical lines of communication between the generations are replaced by horizontal peer-to-peer attachments that can span the globe, albeit in vanishing narrow bandwidths of information.

The counternarrative strategies developed in think tanks and used by governments are largely ineffective. They try to dissuade youth with mass negative messaging. "So DAESH wants to build a future; well, is beheading a future you want, or someone controlling details of your diet and dress?" As I noted in an address to the UN Security Council: "Can anyone not know that already? Does it really matter to those drawn to the cause despite, or even because of, such things?"[78]

In contrast, ISIS may spend hundreds of hours enlisting single individuals and their friends, empathizing instead of lecturing, turning personal frustrations and grievances into moral outrage. ISIS understands that young people empathize with each other; they generally do not lecture. From Syria, a young woman messages another:[79]

> I know how hard it is to leave behind the mother and father you love, and not tell them until you are here, that you will always love them but that you were put on this earth to do more than be with or honor your parents. I know this will probably be the hardest thing you may ever have to do, but let me help you explain it to yourself and to them.

As one imam who was a former recruiter for ISIS explained to me:

> The young who came to us were not to be lectured at like witless children; they are for the most part understanding and compassionate, but misguided. We have to give them a better message, but a positive one to compete. One in our religious frame. Otherwise, they will be lost to Daesh.

If we ignore these passions, we risk fanning them, to our likely detriment and that of others across the world.

For our singularly self-predatory species, success has depended on willingness to shed blood, including the sacrifice of one's own, not merely for family and tribe, wealth or status, but for some greater group cause that promises personal significance and glory in the eyes of one's peers. George Orwell, in his review of *Mein Kampf,* in 1940, described the essence of the problem of radicalization:He [Hitler] has grasped the falsity of the hedonistic attitude to life. Nearly all western thought . . . certainly all 'progressive' thought, has assumed tacitly that human beings desire nothing beyond ease, security and avoidance of pain." In such a view of life there is no room for greatness and glory, which as Darwin noted motivates heroes and martyrs to motivate others to survive and even triumph against great material odds. "Hitler knows . . . that human beings *don't* only want comfort, safety, short working-hours, hygiene, birth-control and, in general, common sense; they also, at least intermittently, want struggle and self-sacrifice."[80]

At the 2017 World Economic Forum in Davos, Switzerland, where I presented some of our research findings[81]—while listening to China's president, the managing director of the International Monetary Fund, the U.S. secretary of state, and others—I had the impression that most people in attendance thought that the vicious spiral of jihadism and xenophobic ethnonationalist populism were just atavistic blips in the ineluctable progress of globalization that were destined to soon go away. That to me was the most worrisome feature of Davos, whose denizens basically run the world (or try to). Few at Davos seemed willing to change their behavior. They seemed to view the left-behinds of the dark side of globalization as simply losers that might be given a handout when robotization denies them any chance for a decent living. To end these worries, there was earnest talk among the spectacularly wealthy of a universal guaranteed income for the economically disadvantaged. Yet poor people rarely instigate violent overthrows of established order.[82] A guaranteed income for people without purpose or significance in life, however, would more likely make all these lumpen laborers revolutionaries rather than quiet sheep. Not, as Marxists would have it, because they rebel against the exploitation of their labor, but because the prevailing powers just want them to quietly consume or fall off the face of the earth.

Civilizations rise and fall on vitality of cultural ideals, not material assets alone: after the Visigoths sacked Rome over 1,500 years ago, Augustine sought in *The City of God* to describe the abiding city or commonwealth which would outlast the fall of earthly cities; only

"The Republic of God," he surmised, would endure under whatever material guise. With the defeat of fascism and communism, have our lives defaulted to the material quest for comfort and safety on ever-shifting sand? Is this endless, despiritualized gambling for gain enough to ensure the security, much less triumph, of the open societies that we seem to take for granted and believe our world should be based on? Reenchantment and perhaps communitarian rerooting of our own once transcendent values in an engaged and educated citizenry for the cooperative pursuit of individual happiness—the values of open society (e.g., representative government that protects the rights of the individual through the rule of law, independent judiciary, a free and vigilant press, fair and competitive elections, and which affords equal protection of civil liberties and political freedoms), values which Jefferson deemed "sacred" (before Franklin called them "self evident")[83]—measured in terms of our willingness to make costly sacrifices to defeat threats from violent extremists of all sides, may be the key existential issue for our futures.

PART III

MORAL, PHILOSOPHICAL, AND SCIENTIFIC REFLECTIONS

7

RELIGIOUS FREEDOM AND HUMAN FLOURISHING

ROBERT P. GEORGE

Why honor religious freedom?[1]

What is the point of respecting and protecting the right of people to act on their religious convictions and fulfill what they judge to be their religious duties (absent truly compelling reasons for governments to prohibit or compel acts whose performance or omission is required by some citizens as a matter of religious duty)?

1. Religious Freedom:
Social Contract or Human Right?

The way some people see it, the reason for respecting religious freedom is purely instrumental and self-interested. If you and I disagree in matters of religion, I should tolerate your beliefs and religious practices so that you will tolerate mine. Religious freedom, in this view, is not so much a moral or *human right* as it is the product of a social contract. It is a kind of mutual nonaggression pact. Everyone fears what will happen to members of their own group. And so each group agrees to tolerate the other groups so that it, too, will be tolerated. The moral force of the obligation to respect religious liberty is precisely as stringent as the force of an obligation to keep a contract.

It is easy to see the attraction of this view or to explain why some people hold it. A world in which members of each community live in fear that members of another will seize power and oppress them is hardly an ideal state of affairs. But that, of course, is what happens where there is little or no protection for religious freedom.

133

But there is a problem with this view. It ignores the fact that at its core, religious freedom means something far deeper and more profound than people grudgingly tolerating each other in a kind of modus vivendi. Simply stated, religious freedom means nothing less than the right to be who we truly are as human beings. The fact is that as human beings we are drawn to ponder life's deepest questions and seek meaningful, truthful answers: Where do we come from? What is our destiny? Is there a transcendent source of meaning and value? Is there a "higher law" that pulls us above personal interest in order to "do unto others as we would have them do unto us"? No matter how these existential questions are answered, one thing is indisputable: human beings cannot stop asking them, and they would be diminished precisely as human beings if they were to try to do so. This suggests that the religious quest is a constitutive part of our humanity—an irreducible aspect of our flourishing as the kind of creatures we are—namely, rational, intelligent, and free actors.

This, in turn, suggests that we must cherish and honor, preserve and protect the right of persons to ask and answer these questions as best they can, and, within the broadest limits, to lead their lives with authenticity and integrity in line with their best judgments of conscience. And so, both as individuals and together with others in communities of faith, religious freedom means the right to ponder life's origins, meaning, and purpose; to explore the deepest questions about human nature, dignity, and destiny; to decide what is to be believed and not to be believed; and, within the limits of justice for all, to comply with what one conscientiously judges to be one's religious obligations—openly, peacefully, and without fear.

The great English theologian and man of letters John Henry Newman once observed that "conscience has rights *because* it has duties."[2] We honor the rights of conscience in matters of faith because people must be free to lead lives of authenticity and integrity by fulfilling what they believe to be their solemn obligations. But authenticity and integrity are directly threatened whenever there is coercion or compulsion in matters of faith or belief. Indeed, coercion does not produce genuine conviction but merely pretense and inauthenticity. A coerced faith is no faith at all. So, as the Qur'an says, "there can be no compulsion in religion" (Q Baraqa 2:256). Compulsion may cause a person to manifest the outward signs of belief or unbelief, but it cannot produce the interior acts of intellect and will that constitute genuine faith. Therefore it is essential that freedom of religion include the right to hold any belief or none at all, to *change one's beliefs and religious affiliation*, to bear witness to these beliefs *in public*, as well as in private, and *corporately* as well as individually, and to act on one's religiously inspired convictions about justice and the common good, as Martin Luther King Jr.—about whom I will have more to say in a moment— did in carrying out the duties of citizenship. And it is vital that religious liberty's full protections be extended to those whose answers to life's deepest questions reject belief in the transcendent.

Because the right to freedom of religion is so central to human well-being and fulfillment, and thus to the dignity of human persons, we would expect that in places where it is dishonored, societies would be less contented and secure. And such is the case across the world. Countries that protect religious liberty tend to be more secure and stable than those that do not, and nations that trample on this freedom provide fertile ground for war and poverty, terror and radical movements. In other words, not only do religious freedom abuses violate the core of our humanity, they do grave harm to the order and well-being of societies.

They do so *politically*—as religious freedom abuses are highly correlated with the absence of democracy and the presence of other human rights abuses.

They do so *economically*—as religious persecution destabilizes communities and marginalizes the persecuted, causing their talents and abilities to go unrealized, robbing a nation of added productivity, and reducing that nation's ability to fight poverty and create abundance for its citizens.

They do so *morally*—since wherever religious freedom is dishonored, the benefit of religion in molding character is diminished, and with it, the self-discipline necessary to handle the rights and responsibilities of citizenship.

And finally, they do so *socially*—since wherever religious freedom is abused, peace and security become ever more elusive.

So individually and corporately we all have an interest in promoting and protecting religious freedom and securing religious freedom as an honored human right. But for this to be achieved, people need to understand that, despite theological and religious differences, they are bound together in the distinctively human quest for meaning and value. This is part of what it means for us to recognize each other as members of the same family—*the human family*—and as, in that way, equals and bearers of fundamental rights (including the right to engage in the religious quest and fulfill one's religious duties) that others are morally bound to respect.

2. Religious Freedom and Mutual Understanding

If I am right about all this, then mutual understanding among people of different faiths is imperative—mutual nonaggression pacts (the "liberalism of fear") are not enough. And that aspect of the work needing to be done on behalf of religious freedom and other human rights cannot primarily be the responsibility of governments. This is not to say that governments have no significant role to play in securing these rights. Obviously, that is the very reverse of the truth. It is merely to say that the promotion of mutual understanding among people of different traditions of faith is not something governments on their own are equipped to do. The primary duty falls, rather, on the leaders of the various communities of faith to engage with each other and to encourage the faithful of their respective communities to engage with each other, precisely in the pursuit of mutual understanding.

Now when I say mutual understanding, I do not mean theological agreement. I mean just what I say: understanding. Understanding what people believe and why they believe it. And, sometimes even more importantly, clearing away *mis*understandings—misunderstandings that are often rooted in ignorance or even bigotry; misunderstandings that are often *at the root* of suspicion, hostility, and contempt.

Theological agreement is not necessary for mutual understanding or, in most cases, even for mutual respect. As I will explain more fully later in this essay, theological agreement is certainly not necessary in order for people of different traditions of faith to appreciate each other as fellow truth seekers, fellow questers, people who share a desire to know the truth and bring their lives fully into line with the truths they discern—even if that means meeting difficult challenges and making great sacrifices.

Of course, if some religious believers think that the truth is that God wants them to kill people who do not practice the right religion, there is not a lot that can be said to them. They simply have to be stopped. And, alas, there are indeed people in the world who think that God wants them to murder infidels.

Not nearly so bad, but still not helpful, are people who believe that God does not want them to engage with, much less respect, people of other faiths (or that God wants them to engage with "infidels" only with a view to converting them, not merely to enhance mutual understanding, respect, empathy, and so forth). Fortunately, the majority of the world's people do not fall (or do not necessarily and inevitably fall) into either of these camps but are (or could be made) open to understanding and appreciating people of other faiths and even those traditions of faith themselves. About this I will say a good deal more later in this essay, but first let me offer a more detailed account and defense of the idea of religious freedom as a human right.

3. Human Goods, Just and Unjust Laws

The starting points of all ethical reflection are those fundamental and irreducible aspects of the well-being and fulfillment of human persons that some philosophers refer to as *basic human goods*.[3] These goods—as more than merely instrumental ends or purposes—are the subjects of the very first principles of practical reason that control all rational thinking with a view to acting, whether the acts performed are, in the end, properly judged to be morally good or bad.[4] The first principles of practical reason direct our choosing toward what is rationally desirable because humanly fulfilling (and therefore intelligibly available to choice) and away from their privations.[5] It is, in the end, the integral directiveness of these principles that provides the criterion (or, when specified, the set of criteria, viz. the moral norms) by which it is possible rationally to distinguish right from wrong—what is morally good from what is morally bad—including what is just and unjust.[6] Morally good choices are choices that are in line with the various fundamental aspects of human well-being and fulfillment integrally conceived; morally bad choices are choices that are not.

To say the very abstract things I have just said is simply to spell out philosophically the point made by Martin Luther King Jr. in his *Letter from Birmingham Jail* about just and unjust laws—laws that honor people's rights and those that violate them. You will, perhaps, recall that the great civil rights champion anticipated a challenge to the moral goodness of the acts of civil disobedience that landed him behind bars in Birmingham. He anticipated his critics asking: How can you, Dr. King, engage in willful law breaking, when you yourself had stressed the importance of obedience to law in demanding that officials of the southern states conform to the Supreme Court's desegregation ruling in the case of *Brown v. Board of Education*? Let us listen to King's response to the challenge:

> The answer lies in the fact that there are two types of laws: just and unjust.
> I would be the first to advocate obeying just laws. One has not only a legal
> but a moral responsibility to obey just laws. Conversely, one has a moral
> responsibility to disobey unjust laws. I would agree with St. Augustine
> that "an unjust law is no law at all."
>
> Now, what is the difference between the two? How does one determine
> whether a law is just or unjust?
>
> A just law is a man-made code that squares with the moral law or the law
> of God. An unjust law is a code that is out of harmony with the moral law.
> To put it in the terms of St. Thomas Aquinas: An unjust law is a human
> law that is not rooted in eternal law and natural law.
>
> Any law that uplifts human personality is just. Any law that degrades
> human personality is unjust. All segregation statutes are unjust because
> segregation distorts the soul and damages the personality. It gives the
> segregator a false sense of superiority and the segregated a false sense of
> inferiority.[7]

So: just laws elevate and ennoble the human personality, or what King
in other contexts referred to as the human spirit; unjust laws debase and
degrade it. Now his point about the morality or immorality of laws is a
good reminder that what is true of what is sometimes called "personal
morality" is also true of "political morality." The choices and actions
of political institutions at every level, like the choices and actions of
individuals, can be right or wrong, morally good or morally bad. They
can be in line with human well-being and fulfillment in all its manifold
dimensions, or they can fail, in any of a range of ways, to respect the
integral flourishing of human persons. In many cases of the failure of
laws, policies, and institutions to fulfill the requirements of morality,
we speak intelligibly and rightly of a violation of human rights. This
is particularly true where the failure is properly characterized as an
injustice—failing to honor people's equal worth and dignity, failing to
give them, or even actively denying them, what they are due.

But, contrary to the teaching of the late John Rawls and the extraor-
dinarily influential stream of contemporary liberal thought of which
he was the leading exponent,[8] I wish to suggest that good is prior to
right and, indeed, to rights. Here is what I mean: To be sure, human
rights, including the right to religious liberty, are among the moral
principles that demand respect from all of us, including governments
and international institutions (which are morally bound not only to
respect human rights but also to protect them). To respect people, to
respect their dignity, is to—among other things—honor their rights,
including, to be sure, the right that we are gathered today to lift up

to our fellow citizens and defend, that of religious freedom. Like all moral principles, however, human rights (including the right to religious liberty) are shaped and given content by the human goods they protect. Rights, like other moral principles, are intelligible as rational, action-guiding principles because they are entailments and—at some level—specifications of the integral directiveness or prescriptivity of principles of practical reason that directs our choosing toward what is humanly fulfilling and enriching (or, as Dr. King would say, uplifting) and away from what is contrary to our well-being as the kind of creatures we are—namely, human persons.

And so, for example, it matters to the identification and defense of the right to life—a right violated not only when the death of another is sought as one's end or as a means to one's end, but also in cases in which someone's death is foreseen and accepted *unfairly* as a side effect of one's action in pursuit of an end—that human life is no mere instrumental good, but is an intrinsic aspect of the good of human persons—an integral dimension of our overall flourishing.[9] And it matters to the identification and defense of the right to religious liberty that religion is yet another irreducible aspect of human well-being and fulfillment—a basic human good.[10]

4. But What Is Religion?

In its fullest and most robust sense, religion is the human person's being in right relation to the divine—the more than merely human source or sources, if there be such, of meaning and value. Of course, even the greatest among us in the things of the spirit fall short of perfection in various ways; but in the ideal of perfect religion, the person would understand as comprehensively and deeply as possible the body of truths about spiritual things, and would fully order his or her life, and share in the life of a community of faith that is ordered, in line with those truths. In the perfect realization of the good of religion, one would achieve the relationship that the divine—say God himself, assuming for a moment the truth of monotheism—wishes us to have with him.

Of course, different traditions of faith have different views of what constitutes religion in its fullest and most robust sense. There are different doctrines, different scriptures, different structures of authority, different ideas of what is true about spiritual things and what it means to be in proper relationship to the more than merely human sources of meaning and value that different traditions understand as divinity.[11]

For my part, I believe that reason has a very large role to play for each of us in deciding where spiritual truth most robustly is to be found. And by reason here, I mean not only our capacity for practical reasoning and moral judgment, but also our capacities for understanding and evaluating claims of all sorts: logical, historical, scientific, and so forth. But one need not agree with me about this in order to affirm with me that there is a distinct basic human good of religion—a good that is uniquely architectonic in shaping one's pursuit of and participation in all the basic human goods—and that one begins to realize and participate in this good from the moment one begins the quest to understand the more-than-merely-human sources of meaning and value and to live authentically by ordering one's life in line with one's best judgments of the truth in religious matters.

If I am right, then the existential raising of religious questions, the honest identification of answers, and the fulfilling of what one sincerely believes to be one's duties in the light of those answers are all parts of the human good of religion—a good whose pursuit is an indispensable feature of the comprehensive flourishing of a human being. It follows, then, that man is intrinsically and by nature a religious being, or at least a religious quester, and the flourishing of man's spiritual life is integral to his all-round well-being and fulfillment.

5. Denying Religious Freedom for Religious Reasons

But if that is true, then respect for a person's well-being, or more simply respect for the person, demands respect for his or her flourishing as a seeker of religious truth and as a man or woman who lives in line with his or her best judgments of what is true in spiritual matters. And that, in turn, requires respect for his or her liberty in the religious quest—the quest to understand religious truth and order one's life in line with it. Because faith of any type, including religious faith, cannot be authentic—it cannot be *faith*—unless it is free. Respect for the person—that is to say, respect for his or her dignity as a free and rational creature—requires respect for his or her religious liberty. That is why it makes sense, from the point of view of reason, and not merely from the point of view of the revealed teaching of a particular faith—though many faiths proclaim the right to religious freedom on theological and not merely philosophical grounds—to understand religious freedom as a fundamental human right.

Interestingly and tragically, in times past, and even in some places today, regard for persons' spiritual well-being has been the premise and motivating factor for *denying* religious liberty or conceiving of it in a cramped and restricted way. Before the Catholic Church embraced the robust conception of religious freedom that honors the civil right to give public witness and expression to sincere religious views (even when erroneous) in the document *Dignitatis Humanae* of the Second Vatican Council, some Catholics rejected the idea of a right to religious freedom on the theory that "only the truth has rights." The idea was that the state, under favoring conditions, should not only publicly identify itself with Catholicism as the true faith but should also forbid religious advocacy or proselytizing that could lead people into religious error and apostasy.

The mistake here was not in the premise: religion is a great human good, and the truer the religion the better for the fulfillment of the believer. That is true. The mistake, rather, was in the supposition made by some that the good of religion was not being advanced or participated in outside the context of the one true faith, and that it could be reliably protected and advanced by placing civil restrictions enforceable by agencies of the state on the advocacy of religious ideas. In rejecting this supposition, the Fathers of the Second Vatican Council did not embrace the idea that error has rights; they noticed, rather, that *people* have rights, and they have rights even when they are in error.[12] And among those rights, integral to authentic religion as a fundamental and irreducible aspect of the human good, is the right to express and even advocate in line with one's sense of one's conscientious obligations what one believes to be true about spiritual matters, even if one's beliefs are, in one way or another, less than fully sound, and, indeed, even if they are false.[13]

6. The Second Vatican Council and Religious Freedom

When I have assigned the document *Dignitatis Humanae* in courses addressing questions of religious liberty, I have always stressed to my students the importance of reading another document of the Second Vatican Council, *Nostra Aetate*, together with it. I do not think it is possible for someone—whether Catholic or not—to achieve a rich understanding of the Declaration on Religious Liberty, and the developed teaching of the Catholic Church on religious freedom, without considering what the council fathers proclaim in the Declaration on Non-Christian Religions. In *Nostra Aetate*, the fathers pay tribute to all that is true and holy, implying and then explicitly saying that there is much that is good and worthy in non-Christian faiths, including Hinduism and Buddhism, and especially Judaism and Islam. In so doing, they give recognition to the ways in which religion (even when it does not include the defining content of what the fathers, as Catholics, believe to be religion in its fullest and most robust sense—namely, the Incarnation of Jesus Christ) enriches, ennobles, and fulfills the human person in the spiritual dimension of his or her being. This is to be honored and respected, in the view of the council fathers, because the dignity of the human being requires it. Naturally, the nonrecognition of Christ as the Son of God must count for the fathers as a falling short in the non-Christian faiths, even the Jewish faith in which Christianity is itself rooted and which stands according to Catholic teaching in an unbroken and unbreakable covenant with God—just as the proclamation of Christ as the Son of God must count as an error in Christianity from a Jewish or Muslim point of view. But, the fathers teach, this does not mean that Judaism and Islam are simply false and without merit (just as neither Judaism nor Islam teaches that Christianity is simply false and without merit); on the contrary, these traditions enrich the lives of their faithful in their spiritual dimensions, thus contributing vitally to their fulfillment.

Now, the Catholic Church does not have a monopoly on the natural-law reasoning by which I am today explicating and defending the human right to religious liberty.[14] But the church does have a deep commitment to such reasoning and a long experience with it. And in *Dignitatis Humanae*, the Fathers of the Second Vatican Council present a natural-law argument for religious freedom—indeed they begin by presenting a natural-law argument before supplementing it with arguments appealing to the authority of God's revelation in sacred scripture. So let me ask you to linger with me a bit longer over the key Catholic texts so that I can illustrate by the teachings of an actual faith how religious leaders and believers, and not just statesmen concerned to craft national or international policy in circumstances of religious pluralism, can incorporate into their understanding of the basic human right to religious liberty principles and arguments available to all men and women of sincerity and goodwill by virtue of what Rawls once referred to as "our common human reason."[15]

Let me quote at some length from *Nostra Aetate* to give you an appreciation of the rational basis of the Catholic Church's affirmation of the good of religion as manifested in different faiths. I do this in order to show how one faith, in this case Catholicism, can root its defense of a robust conception of freedom of religion not in a mere modus vivendi, or mutual nonaggression pact, with other faiths, or in what the late Judith Shklar labeled a "liberalism of fear,"[16] or, much less, in religious relativism or indifferentism, but rather in a rational affirmation of the value of religion as embodied and made available to people in and through many traditions of faith. So here is what *Nostra Aetate* says:

> Throughout history even to the present day, there is found among different peoples a certain awareness of a hidden power, which lies behind the course of nature and the events of human life. At times there is present even a recognition of a supreme being or still more of a Father. This awareness and recognition results in a way of life that is imbued with a deep religious sense. The religions which are found in more advanced civilizations endeavor by way of well-defined concepts and exact language to answer these questions. Thus in Hinduism men explore the divine mystery and express it both in the limitless riches of myth and the accurately defined insights of philosophy. They seek release from the trials of the present life by ascetical practices, profound meditation and recourse to God in confidence and love. Buddhism in its various forms testifies to the essential inadequacy of this changing world. It proposes a way of life by which men can with confidence and trust, attain a state of perfect liberation and reach supreme illumination either through their own efforts or by the aid of divine help. So, too, other religions which are found throughout the world attempt in their own ways to calm the hearts of men by outlining a program of life covering doctrine, moral precepts and sacred rites.
>
> *The Catholic Church rejects nothing of what is true and holy in these religions.* She has a high regard for the manner of life and conduct, the precepts and doctrines which, although differing in many ways from her own teaching, nevertheless often reflect truths which enlighten all men. Yet she proclaims and is in duty bound to proclaim without fail, Christ who is the way, the truth and the life (Jn. 1:6). In him, in whom God reconciled all things to himself (2 Cor. 5:18-19), men find the fullness of their religious life.
>
> The Church therefore, urges her sons to enter with prudence and charity into discussion and collaboration with members of other religious. Let Christians, while witnessing to their own faith and way of life, acknowledge, preserve and encourage the spiritual and moral truths found among non-Christians.
>
> The Church has also a high regard for the Muslims. They worship God, who is one, living and subsistent, merciful and almighty, the Creator of heaven and earth, who has also spoken to men. They strive to submit themselves without reserve to the decrees of God, just as Abraham submitted himself to God's plan, to whose faith Muslims link their own. Although not acknowledging Jesus as God, they revere him as a prophet; his virgin Mother they also honor, and even at times devoutly invoke. Further, they

await the Day of Judgment and the reward of God following the resurrection of the dead. For this reason they highly esteem an upright life and worship God, especially by way of prayer, almsgiving, and fasting.

Over the centuries many quarrels and dissensions have arisen between Christians and Muslims. The sacred Council now pleads with all to forget the past, and urges that a sincere effort be made to achieve mutual understanding; for the benefit of all men, let them together preserve and promote peace, liberty, social justice and moral values.

Sounding the depths of the mystery which is the Church, this sacred Council remembers the spiritual ties which link the people of the New Covenant to the stock of Abraham.

The Church of Christ acknowledges that in God's plan of salvation the beginning of her faith and election is to be found in the patriarchs and in Moses and the prophets. She professes that all Christ's faithful, who as men of faith are sons of Abraham (cf. Gal. 3:7), are included in the same patriarch's call and that the salvation of the Church is mystically prefigured in the exodus of God's chosen people from the land of bondage. On this account the Church cannot forget that she received the revelation of the Old Testament by way of that people with whom God in his inexpressible mercy established the ancient covenant. Nor can she forget that she draws nourishment from that good olive tree onto which the wild olive branches of the Gentiles have been grafted (cf. Rom. 11:17-24). The Church believes that Christ who is our peace has through his cross reconciled Jews and Gentiles and made them one in himself (cf. Eph. 2:14-16).[17]

Of course, from the point of view of any believer, the further away one gets from the truth of faith in all its dimensions—what the council fathers refer to in the passages I just quoted as "the fullness of religious life"—the less fulfillment is available. But that does not mean that even a primitive and superstition-laden faith, much less the faiths of those advanced civilizations to which the fathers refer, is utterly devoid of value, or that there is no right to religious liberty for people who practice such a faith. Nor does it mean that atheists have no right to religious freedom. The fundaments of respect for the good of religion require that civil authority respect (and, in appropriate ways, even nurture) conditions or circumstances in which people can engage in the sincere religious quest and live lives of authenticity reflecting their best judgments as to the truth of spiritual matters. To compel atheists to perform acts that are premised on theistic beliefs that they cannot, in good conscience, share, is to deny them the fundamental bit of the good of religion that is theirs, namely, living with honesty and integrity in line with their best judgments about ultimate reality. Coercing them to perform religious acts does them no good, since faith really must be free, and dishonors their dignity as free and rational people. The violation of liberty is worse than futile.

Of course, there are limits to the freedom that must be respected for the sake of the good of religion and the dignity of the human person as a being whose integral fulfillment includes the spiritual quest and the ordering of one's life in line with one's best judgment as to what spiritual truth requires. As I noted near the beginning of this essay, gross evil—even grave injustice—can be committed by sincere people for the sake of religion. Unspeakable wrongs can be done by people seeking sincerely to get right with God or the gods or their conception of ultimate reality, whatever it is. The presumption in favor of respecting liberty must, for the sake of the human good and the dignity of human persons as free and rational creatures—creatures who, according to Judaism and Christianity, are made in the very image and likeness of God—be powerful and broad. But it is not unlimited. Even the great end of getting right with God cannot justify a morally bad means, no matter the sincerity of the believer. I do not doubt the sincerity of the Aztecs in practicing human sacrifice, or the sincerity of those in the history of various traditions of faith who used coercion and even torture in the cause of what they believed was religiously required. But these things are deeply wrong, and they need not (and should not) be tolerated in the name of religious freedom. To suppose otherwise is to back oneself into the awkward position of supposing that violations of religious freedom (and other injustices of equal gravity) must be respected for the sake of religious freedom.

Still, to overcome the powerful and broad presumption in favor of religious liberty, and thus to be justified in requiring the believer to do something contrary to their faith or forbidding the believer to do something their faith requires, political authority must meet a heavy burden. The legal test in the United States under the Religious Freedom Restoration Act is one way of capturing the presumption and burden: to justify a law that bears negatively on religious freedom (or even a neutral law of general applicability), it must be supported by a compelling state interest and represent the least restrictive or intrusive means of protecting or serving that interest. Scholars and citizens can debate, as a matter of American constitutional law or as a matter of policy, whether it is, or should be, up to courts or legislators to decide when exemptions to general, neutral laws should be granted for the sake of religious freedom, or to determine when the presumption in favor of religious freedom has been overcome. But the substantive matter of what religious freedom demands from those who exercise the levers of state power should be something on which reasonable people of goodwill across the religious and political spectrums should agree on—precisely because it is a matter capable of being settled by our common human reason.

Conclusion

And so it seems to me that we have reasons—good reasons, indeed, conclusive reasons—to honor religious freedom as a true human right, one grounded in central dimensions of the integral flourishing of human persons, and not to regard it merely as the fruit of a modus vivendi or mutual nonaggression pact. The human right to religious freedom imposes stringent obligations on governments and other institutions and on individuals to respect the liberty of others to believe and act on their best judgments in religious matters, including those pertaining to their moral obligations. At the same time, we have reasons no less sound and compelling to understand that religious freedom is not an absolute: the presumption in favor of religious freedom, though broad, can be overcome by sufficiently weighty considerations—requirements of justice—that are themselves grounded in central dimensions of the integral flourishing of human beings.

8

COMPASSIONATE REASON

The Most Important Cultural and Religious Capacity
for a Peaceful Future

MARC GOPIN

I will argue in this essay that the cultivation of compassionate reason is the key to a less violent planetary future, a future in which secular and religious communities can collaborate constructively for a new path of education and shared ethical practices for individuals, families, communities, and nations. Compassionate reason will be enhanced and strengthened within the human being the more that religion, philosophy, and neuroscience consciously collaborate on understanding and increasing this most vital human capacity.

I am defining *compassionate reason* as compassionate thoughts, experiences, and regular practices that lead the mind inexorably toward higher reasoning and universal principles for equal ethical treatment of all sentient beings. The compassion that extends to all leads the mind naturally to use reason to employ moral principles that can apply compassion to all beings equally in order to adequately and reasonably fulfill the drive to compassion. Compassionate reason constitutes, therefore: first, the cultivation of a state of mind and, second, a mode of ethical practice. I will argue that the experience and practice of compassion can with proper guidance lead the mind to build principles for compassion to be applied to all sentient life. The mind, influenced by the moral sense and experience of compassion, is challenged by its very emotional universality to then use reason to apply those feelings toward building universal principles for a diverse, divided, and conflicted world. This is essentially what Kant referred to as a *good will* but devised through

147

a path that combines the mind's emotional capacity for compassionate action and its capacity for reason-based will and behavior.

I will also argue that both science and significant schools of philosophical ethics make the case that the will and universal principles of reason for ethics are inextricably connected to prosocial emotions, especially compassion. Emotions and principles of reason are indissolubly related, challenging and changing each other. I am claiming that the combination of compassionate feelings and behaviors, and reason's development of universal principles of application therefrom, is the only sure way to achieve a less violent world shared by all, regardless of race or creed.

Human beings are constantly competing for increasingly scarce resources and are embroiled in a great variety of conflicts that have reached tragic proportions in a world of seven billion people. Negative emotions such as fear, greed, and jealousy can push the mind to only violent solutions to scarce resource challenges. Prosocial emotions such as compassion and hope, however, induce the mind to search for new approaches to survival and flourishing, as well as toward trust, solidarity, and shared enterprises with fellow human beings.

1. Scientific and Philosophical Foundations of Compassionate Reason

Roots in Neuroscience and Psychosocial Studies

A psychological analysis of ethics, and particularly the ethics of nonviolence, was gathered into an exhaustive study in recent years, with the aim of isolating the most essential elements of moral behavior leading to less violence.[1] This analysis, performed across many cultures and societies, discovered that a prevalence of compassion, related to ethical feelings and actions, was the most significant factor leading to reduced levels of violence. Empathy is vital as well, but predators and sociopaths also have empathy in the sense of using an empathic understanding of victims in order to destroy victims, often with great acumen (more on this below). Compassion, however, is defined as empathy plus an intense kind of solidarity or identification with the other being, which results in thoughts and acts of kindness, benevolence, and love.

The biochemical and neurological foundations of this experience are not so simple to isolate. Some have posited a particular kind of neuron referred to as a *mirror neuron*, but this is not conclusive. Mirror neurons explain much of the human and animal tendency to copy one another and be deeply affected by one another, but this does not yield the results always of compassionate feelings and moral actions. Others have searched for particular neurotransmitters that seem to be especially associated with compassion, such as oxytocin, but this is a topic beyond our scope.

Compassion and Reason as Psychological Partners

More important for our argument is that compassion by itself has not been shown to be enough to develop the moral human being capable of being peaceful with everyone, for the simple reason that compassion for some and not others is often a *catalyst* for violence rather than an inhibiter. Sometimes the more compassion I feel only for my own group, the more violence I want for enemy groups. Furthermore, for compassion to embed itself in all human life, reason is essential, for it transforms principles into laws that apply to all. Also, for nonviolence to embed itself, self-control and higher reason are essential. These are abilities strongly associated with various parts of the neocortex, especially as it regulates and controls the amygdala, the latter being most associated with "fight or flight," fear, hatred, and violence. In sum, it is a subtle combination of compassion and reason that seems to be critical for the generation of the peaceful human being who conceives and adheres to universally applied ethical principles. This is the person who calculates his or her ethical actions with prudence, caution, and a careful attention to all the possible consequences.

From Neuroscience to Philosophy

This synchronicity of compassion and reasoning has its exact parallel in the history of philosophy and the history of religious ethics in particular. Let me explain. The Enlightenment was a pivotal moment in the history of human evolution. Western civilization was turned upside down by unprecedented worldview-changing scientific discoveries and by classical empirical investigation that led to a rethink of everything about the human being and humanity. It had its effects as well on our evaluation of and recommendations for human behavior—in other words, our ethics. All thinkers of the Enlightenment came out of civilizations steeped in religious traditions, where those traditions stood in tension with fundamentalist or antiscientific dogmas.

There are fascinating parallels in the evolution of philosophical ethics, religious ethics, and today's neuroscience and psychology; these parallels hold the seeds for a new alignment on the ethics of violence reduction. Three relevant schools of ethics include:

1. the less well-known moral sense theory,
2. consequentialism/utilitarianism, and
3. deontology, or Kantian ethics.

All were profoundly important to the political institutions that would rise out of the Enlightenment. All are important to why and how people of diverse religiosity and color can sit around the table today as equals.

Moral sense theory, with its perception of prosocial emotions—especially sympathy—as the foundation of ethics, had enormous influence and positive effect. Many theorists explaining the five-hundred-year decline of domestic violence and public torture in Western Europe suggest that the movement toward empathy for all, even the most "miserable" human beings, culminated in the runaway success of those who we may call "empathy" novelists—Dickens, Hugo, Clemens, and Proust. This massive move toward empathy for strangers led to legislation and democratic movements to lessen the violence of society as a whole, and especially the horror of slavery and punishment.

Consequentialism, pioneered especially by utilitarians like Jeremy Bentham, James Mill, and his son John Stuart Mill, had the effect of taking this feeling of empathy to the next level—namely, calculation of the maximization of happiness for all. This extended to all who experience happiness and suffering, even prisoners, for example, in terms of what kind of rehabilitation would reduce the most suffering and create the most happiness of all in society. Put the way the Dalai Lama might express it, utilitarianism's goal is the minimization of suffering for the greatest number of human beings. The Dalai Lama extends this calculus to all sentient beings. In fact, the prevention of animal suffering through rights legislation is seen already in Ireland in 1635 and in the Massachusetts Bay Colony in 1641, well before abolition of human slavery.[2] Classical utilitarianism involved a somewhat ill-defined but well-intentioned calculus to anticipate future consequences of our actions, which strengthened the critical role of the neocortex in ethical thinking but also stayed rooted in the human passion to bring happiness to oneself and others.

Finally, Immanuel Kant and the deontologists took ethics to the next level and insisted that the truly unassailable good is the good will. The good will in turn formulates with reason universal imperatives that treat all human beings as ends in themselves, not means.

From these three approaches—moral sense theory, consequentialism, and deontology—to the revolutionary international documents of civil and human rights was a clear progression that has changed the way in which we all relate to each other today across the globe. Tens of thousands of domestic and international laws of human rights exist today around the world that never existed before in human history, and they affect billions of people.

This movement from compassion to universal law has utterly changed what we consider better and worse governments in every part of the globe. It drives many of our political struggles, as people demand more and more extensions of rights. For example, it is now becoming increasing clear that most developed nations have populations that consider health care a basic human right to be provided by the state through common taxation, but that was not the case just a few years ago. Human rights are an amazingly resilient frame for the human mind that just keep expanding.

The philosophical schools of ethics that formalized a movement toward less violence dovetail nicely with what we have outlined above about the science of ethical behavior. Taken together, these philosophical schools embrace the two essential qualities of ethical behavior leading to less violence—the feelings of compassion combined with the use of calculation and practical reason to try to spread that compassion evenly and fairly to everyone. Finally, deontology comes in with its exercise of the neocortex for self-control, for higher reasoning, and especially for universal rules that are the bedrock of human progress.

Why Compassion and Reason Need Each Other

Here is the most important point for the psychology and philosophy of successful nonviolent ethics: *compassion and reason cannot exist without each other; compassion and reason need each other.* Think of compassion without reason, while I suggest something shocking. If you really face it, compassion without reason was the foundation of Nazism. It was an absolute and complete love of and compassion *for Aryans* that led to the need to destroy everything else standing in their way. All nationalism, nativism, and triumphalism, secular or religious, is guilty of the sacrifice of reason and universal rules before an excessive compassion for one's own family, tribe, or nation. Compassion needs reason, just as surely as the amygdala needs the neocortex, for self-control, for the logical extension of the best senses and emotions to all people, all sentient beings, even the earth itself, as a way of guaranteeing the survival and flourishing of all. Only reason—either through the deontological development of universal principles or through consequentialist moral calculus and pragmatism—can promise a channeling of the precious sense of compassion into universal law and an intellectually compelling force that makes society into a better place where violence and hate steadily decline. From this perspective Enlightenment philosophy provided humanity with an irreplaceable service, moving us from tribal and religious rituals and practices to the hope of universal principles that can govern governments and international systems. This was Kant's dream in *Perpetual Peace*, and such dreams have produced impressive results.

2. What the Enlightenment and the Great Philosophers Missed: Enter Religion

What the great philosophers and scientists have missed, however, is the immense power of spiritual commitments, wisdom literature, and religious habits to complete the road to ethically based nonviolent life. Every moral sense theorist knew that habit and education were critical to compassion exercising its power over human life. Furthermore, it is a basic fact of psychology that self-control is one of the deepest challenges for human beings, no matter how educated we become. The amygdala can be easily driven to violence without the habituated positive effects of a well-trained independent neocortex. Twentieth-century history has tragically taught us that powerful, magnetic leaders can make us subordinate to their deadly will unless our minds and bodies are trained in the habits of independent ethical thought. The Enlightenment propounded a historic universal application of ethical values, but did it prepare us as a global community for the challenges to democracy from totalitarianism, nihilistic abandon, and demagoguery?

Where today is the Enlightenment's effect on childhood and adult education? Where is education for enlightenment? Education for compassion? Education for the evolution of universal reason ethically committed to all? The Enlightenment fell down when it came to education for universal commitments of citizenship. The remnants of enlightened education that we have today in public education, focused on math and science in the service of capitalism or the state, has nothing whatever to do with the mind working in the service of a nonviolent, compassionate society, a rule-based society.

It is very well understood that the advance of the brain in terms of math skills or chess or physics has absolutely no effect on ethics, especially in atmospheres of stress, fear, or authoritarian pressures. For that you need education in and habituation to:

1. Ethical ideas and mental constructs, and
2. Ethical practices, habits so convincing that you want to do these things and believe in them as if your life depended upon it, as if it were fundamental to what your community is or to whom you are as an individual.

The Task of Spiritual Beings and Religious Society

For compassionate reason to be inculcated in the individual and in society itself, there needs to be an investment of precious resources of time, energy, and broad commitment. It must be a fundamental task of the society, a matter of national security in the broadest sense of that term.

Here is the most important point: this is something that can become a joint venture between religious and secular members of society. The task of spiritual people and religious societies is to mine the depths of their traditions, look into themselves, and emphasize educational systems, inspirational systems, and legal systems that centralize the importance of two things: compassion and universal commitments to all people, to all sentient life. Kant knew this as a Christian pietist, and so did Rabbi Samuel David Luzzatto, the only Jewish moral sense theorist of the Enlightenment period. Oddly enough, Luzzatto and Kant—the moral sense philosopher and the deontologist—had in common a search for one sure component of human nature that could be relied on to build a courageous ethics, something that would withstand all of life's sorrows and all the violent social assaults on the ethical personality. For Luzzatto, compassion was not just a moral sense but a real pleasure, an empowering act. The experience and practice of compassion was the one pleasure, a real gift, that even the worst sufferings could not take away from the person. He or she could be as poor and miserable as could be, assaulted by tyranny, but no one and nothing could take away the joy of helping another human being.

In this regard Luzzatto anticipated Viktor Frankl's ingenious discovery a hundred years later of meaning and purpose that even a concentration camp could not take away. Today there is very good evidence that discovering a meaningful life in such a way leads to the deepest and most permanent kind of human happiness.[3]

The deontologists such as Kant, by contrast, found their answer in a good human will, a will that would naturally develop categorical principles that apply to all human beings no matter what the circumstances. Science has confirmed that both moral sense theorists and the deontologists were right: a highly developed compassion and a strong self-controlled good will that commits to universal ethics were both necessary to create the nonviolent person.

One thing was missing, however—deeply ingrained cultural habits of the mind, body, and heart that would make the prosocial emotions victorious over the antisocial ones, the neocortex victorious over the amygdala. This is where religion has seen its finest successes in history, when and only when compassion is trained, daily and even constantly, to apply to all human beings, even all sentient life, without any hesitation.

The Golden Rule and Compassionate Reason

The Golden Rule, doing unto others what you would want done to you—or its negative formulation, to not do to others what is hateful to you—is a classic expression of compassionate reason. The Golden Rule appeals to the compassionate identification with another, and then it extends that identification with the other to all neighbors; this is a clear appeal to our reasoning capacity. The Golden Rule also happens to express itself in numerous major religions across the planet.[4]

Although compassionate reason is present this way in most religions, unfortunately it by no means dominates at the present time. Most importantly the *scope* of its application to all people is often severely circumscribed, often limited to "neighbors," which can mean the faithful in good standing, as I or my cleric interpret "good standing." This can easily mean it is fine to hate everyone else who is not from that club. I see this constantly in religious debates on the internet, internal to each religion, and this is not limited to my Jewish experience. Due to thirty-three years of work in the Middle East, I have often found myself in the middle of fierce Muslim debates, where one group is destroying the other while adhering to principles of their interpretations. To this day, I can find myself in fierce debates with those who claim universal values but hate every single Shia, Alawite, feminist, homosexual, and so forth. I stand on the side, exasperated, generally reverting to my peace partners who are usually Sufi or progressive Muslims of one kind or another.

Ben Azzai, thousands of years ago, understood that "love" mandated by religion—the core action of the Golden Rule—was not necessarily subject to universal application because we so often hate one another, or another group. Therefore, he made the universal principle regarding other human beings based on the religious fact that we are all created in the image of God.[5] It is indeed difficult to discover and implant in the religious consciousness an unconditional "ought" for compassion that extends to all without exception.

We have only begun to think about how we can formulate religions of the future that will rise to the challenge of compassionate reason universally applied. The Golden Rule's spiritual authenticity and meaning can overcome dangerous descents into amygdala-driven tribalism, hate, and murder, if and only if it is pedagogically inculcated to apply to all.

This is our task today in terms of the future of religion and society. Society needs a more redemptive expression of religion that inculcates and habituates us to compassionate reason. Many of us have spent a lifetime working on the hermeneutics of integrating traditional religious sources with universal expressions of compassion and reason. We must however make it a more collective and intentional effort *between* religions. We must also make it a more intentional campaign *between* secular and religious citizens, to save the earth together, to save humanity and help it evolve to its highest potential. Not only are we divided, as we always have been, by religious extremists of all stripes, we are also divided by secular versus religious constructs of the world that have made it very difficult to combine energies and talents to create the good society for all. It will take a self-conscious secular and religious covenant to realize this combination of energies and talents.

In *Perpetual Peace* Kant knew that society was facing an uphill battle as it struggled with tribal psychology and tribal struggles that would continue to tear the globe apart. He was not impressed finally with enlightened absolute rule, nor would he be impressed by nation-states or even liberal states calling themselves superpowers. He focused rather on a vision of the future, constructs of the future. His vision, buttressed by his spiritual faith, built the basis of critical legal foundations of nonviolent globalization today that has now taken the form of thousands of international laws and treaties. He was joined in this grand vision by dozens of courageous thinkers such as Grotius and Locke. These were religious men who also understood the severe dangers of fundamentalism and sectarian abuse of religion.

It is our task today to go further, to formulate *shared education and habits* that will move the masses away from demagogues and toward internalization of universal laws, toward shared compassion and reason, across cultures, across religions, across the globe itself. Liberalism, championing freedom as the only ethical value of supreme importance, has relied too much on modern legal structures to ensure freedom, but those are not continually reinforced by other ethical values. This is where religion has the educational structures and the global crosscutting ties that will move us forward ethically. Adam Smith, the most important harbinger of the modern capitalism that has seized control of all the earth's cultures, made it very clear that the freedom of capitalism depended on the inculcation of compassion. We took his capitalism, jettisoned the compassion, and got greed alone.

3. The Necessary Steps toward Less Violence

In my recent book *Healing the Heart of Conflict: Eight Crucial Steps to Making Peace with Yourself and with Others*,[6] I outline eight steps toward educating the human being in less violence, a form of training that I have utilized in many settings and conditions, including for many years in difficult conditions in Damascus, Syria. The steps evolved out of both secular and religious wisdom and are based on my field experience of thirty years. The work in Syria continues to this day with refugee activists who valiantly build crosscutting ties between Christian, Sunni, Shia, Alawite, secular, and conservative men and women, all in the worst of conditions. The methods work, despite the overwhelmingly terrible effect on Syria of so many outside destructive forces that buttress the most criminal elements in that tragic land.

Here are the steps for healing conflict that constitute the training:

Step 1: Be
Step 2: Feel
Step 3: Understand
Step 4: Hear
Step 5: See
Step 6: Imagine
Step 7: Do
Step 8: Speak

These steps entail building the following clear but emotionally challenging mental habits:

1. Build a Peaceful Identity and Character
2. Make Your Emotions Essential to Healing
3. Make Knowledge an Ally of Healing
4. Listen to Everything
5. Observe Everything Not Spoken
6. Build Visions of Your Future Without Conflict

7. Practice Ethical Deeds and Gestures that Transform
8. Find the Words that Heal

I am proposing that these steps become the hermeneutical foundation of best practices in all our religions. Articulating the textual and ritual religious analogues to these habits can generate compassionate reason in our coreligionists. I am also proposing that such practices can be a good bridge between religious and secular orientations as this will be essential for the future of global coexistence.

Let us look at them individually:

1. Self-examination is an ancient core practice of both wisdom and world religions that is essential for less violence and essential for the power of the neocortex over the amygdala, but also essential for religious growth. Much interesting science is being established on the power of meditational practice or prayer. When done intentionally meditation has been shown to lead to an increase in calm self-control and an increase in compassion.[7]
2. The exploration of feelings is critical to discovering compassion within, as well as facing and challenging darker emotions; many religious traditions have essential habits for facing the inner self.
3. Learning and study are essential to religious experience and to secular wisdom; they clearly increase the capacity of the neocortex for self-control, especially when learning and knowledge are focused on how to make peace and heal conflicts.
4, 5. Listening and observation, as well as the humility and quiet that they require, is a mainstay of spiritual and monastic traditions.
6. The power of positive imagination, of hope, of appreciative inquiry, and of positive dreams is almost essential to every great religious tradition.
7, 8. The sacred centrality of deeds and words as transformative is self-evident in religious traditions of good deeds, commandments, and imitation of God or prophetic figures.

These steps can also constitute forms of religious education of the mind, but they hinge on their universal commitment to (a) compassion and (b) principles of ethics that apply to all human beings. With compassionate reason as the central focus, world religions can employ their finely honed skills and habits to inculcate peaceful religion for the future. But we must invest heavily in expanding the reach of these universal religious teachings to every quadrant of religious communities worldwide. There can be no exceptions or loopholes where religious elites say this is what they are teaching but in fact distribute something different to the masses or to specific countries where they dominate. On the contrary, it is precisely where one form of religion dominates that the universal commitments of compassionate reason must be most disseminated by new habits and practices.

Religious hermeneutics must be courageous and flexible, clever and conservative, but insistent on basic commitments to compassion and reason that are nonnegotiable. This is a path to a less violent, more peaceful future that will complete the cultural and moral evolution of recent centuries. We now need an evolution of spirituality solidly grounded in religious traditions, from where we can move much more easily to a global society equally shared.

From Mental Maps to Religious Catechisms and Habits: Coherence, Habitual Thoughts, and Enlightened Practices

One way of framing the challenges we have had in coordinating a religious response to violence and hate with a secular response is at the very basic level of how we determine reality. Epistemology, the philosophical study of knowledge or knowing, has always been divided by the approaches of *coherence* and *correspondence*. Coherence argues that we come to know through a process of all that we know cohering into some intelligible reality. Correspondence, however, focuses on a reality "out there," a reality that is independently true and knowable, while we as knowers do the best we can with our senses and our abstract reasoning to come to know that reality. The effects of the Enlightenment from its inception have been to move us away from coherence systems of truth that were not able by definition to be challenged by science and inquiry. Religions by contrast have prospered by creating attractive systems of coherent truth for their believers, and their frequent insistence on coherence versus correspondence has made them an enemy of free thinkers and scientists throughout history. This war between epistemologies remains for many adherents of science and free thinking—as well as for millions of fundamentalist leaders and followers—a war that brooks no compromise, where only one side can win.

The truth, however, is that the science of psychology has taken a hard look at the reality of what humans actually do with knowledge. This has very far-reaching consequences for the future of human ethics and politics, in terms of our subject. George Lakoff, for example, has argued strenuously through his career that relatively impenetrable neural nets govern our worldview and our reasoning, and that neural nets strongly resemble coherence as truth.[8] He argues that this in turn has serious consequences for ethics and politics. Lakoff is a passionate progressive who clearly follows the epistemic structures of the Enlightenment and believes in the priority of social justice and compassion in human ethics, governance, and political struggle.[9]

Lakoff's argument for what is to be done today about the fragile nature of democracy and elections and the manipulations of millions toward selfishness or cruelty by demagogues is that we must confront and accept a coherence theory of truth as the governing way in which the minds of millions work. Embracing the power of this coherence through neural nets means that if you are trying to persuade millions of people to be reasonable, self-controlled, and compassionate, you cannot use logical argumentation. The only real way to break neural nets that are hardened is through engaged inquiry into the lives of others, and through care for those with grievances or hostile approaches to others. Those qualities break into the universe of the other and provide some basis for creating new worldviews, new moral opinions, and fresh reevaluations of what is right in politics.

If Lakoff and others open their own minds to it, their best allies in this journey just might be enlightened religious representatives in every major religion, who are quite accustomed to centuries or even millennia of religious principles and practices designed for compassion, for care, and for an embrace of others. It is true that there are places of tension between free thinking secularism and religion that must remain a contest. But there is perhaps more here that unites than divides in terms of moving masses of people away from violence and closed neural nets of suspicion and hate.

Perspective Taking: The Perfect Combination of Mental Training for Compassion and Religious Experience

Finally, I would like to add that some of the most amazing achievements in our peace work in the field come from the deceptively simple exercise of perspective taking. When people play each other's roles, practice at adopting each other's perspectives, the mind moves inexorably toward compassionate reason. First comes the emotional understanding of the other, and then comes the mind's natural interest in fair rules that govern relations between so many different people—in other words, enlightened reason. We have seen this technique work even in the most difficult places in the world. I have done this work with thousands of students from war zones over the past twenty years. It works in powerful ways that science is only beginning to explain. We need religious and secular education to move in the direction of these revolutionary practices and habits with a particular emphasis on the cultivation of compassion.

From Empathy to Compassion: The Next Stage of Emotions Leading to Peace Practice

Something has emerged in recent years that is refining our practice of compassion and reason globally. Many of us who have worked in conflict resolution for decades now have come to notice how debilitating this work can be. We have experienced how continual empathy for those who suffer in war can shatter you, can deplete you, can make you cynical, angry, or lost in despair. And yet there are others among us in this work who practice a life of altruism and compassion but who seem continually energized and ever ready for more experience.

It was hard for me to understand the destructive experience of empathy as a scholar and practitioner until I started to study—or reevaluate—my field and practice of conflict resolution through the eyes of medical intervention. In previous works, I have raised the analogy of medicine and conflict resolution as an effective way to discern complicated questions of ethics and intervention.[10] Now I want to raise the matter of how and why some caregivers and emergency doctors flourish under the worst of circumstances while others fall apart.

In the course of immersing myself in my sister's care when she fought for months the H1N1 virus several years ago,[11] I watched a very large number of doctors and caregivers over months. I was also dealing with my own grief and trauma in an immediate way every day, and it took me a long time to recover. What I learned is that there are those who focus on the tasks of healing, who use all their mind and heart in those tasks. It is not just that the pain of empathy with the victim did not affect them. It was the opposite: they evinced strength, power, exhilaration. I was astonished, but it started to make perfect sense.

This led to changing many of my own habits in international interventions. Every time I felt despair, overwhelmed by the pain of the victims, I redirected it to what is to be done at every moment, especially at the moments of my deepest pain. Later I started to realize that religious traditions and wisdom traditions had made a fine distinction between empathy and compassion, between the *feelings* of the pain of the other and the *actions* of care.

I had written my dissertation on Luzzatto, the much-overlooked nineteenth-century theologian mentioned above, as he centralized compassion as the core of Judaism.[12] I will publish soon a book based on that dissertation, entitled *A Compassionate Judaism*. Luzzatto had argued, like Viktor Frankl would argue a hundred years later after surviving the death camps in the Holocaust,[13] that discovering meaning through altruism or compassion was a pleasure that no one could ever take away from you, no matter how battered you were by life, no matter what you lost. I wrote on these matters; I argued their value; but I never felt it in my fieldwork with victims for thirty years. I found work with victims to be devastating to me personally, to my body, to my state of mind. I persisted in the work anyway for very Kantian and Jewish halakic reasons of duty, as I had been so influenced by my teacher Rabbi Joseph Soloveitchik. My risky work came out of a place of duty, not joy. On the contrary, it was hell.

Let me divert for a moment. Something has happened of late in neuroscientific and medical research,[14] perhaps inspired by increasing interest in compassion and altruism in both animal and human life. There came to be a keen interest in the *destructive* aspects of empathy, that powerless feeling of the pain of others, versus compassion, that active joy of embracing and helping others.

The work on this distinction is just beginning, but it will change the way that we do work on healing conflicts, and I am arguing that it will produce yet another powerful link between religious ethics and cutting-edge science, all in the service of compassionate reason. Let me quote at length from this research on the brain's response to feeling or practicing empathy versus the response to feeling or practicing compassion.[15]

> The development of social emotions such as compassion is crucial for successful social interactions as well as for the maintenance of mental and physical health, especially when confronted with distressing life events. Yet, the neural mechanisms supporting the training of these emotions are poorly understood. To study affective plasticity in healthy adults, we measured functional neural and subjective responses to witnessing the distress of others in a newly developed task (Socio-affective Video Task). Participants' initial empathic responses to the task were accompanied by negative affect and activations in the anterior insula and anterior medial cingulate cortex—a core neural network underlying empathy for pain. Whereas participants reacted with negative affect before training, compassion training increased

positive affective experiences, even in response to witnessing others in distress. On the neural level, we observed that, compared with a memory control group, compassion training elicited activity in a neural network including the medial orbitofrontal cortex, putamen, pallidum, and ventral tegmental area—brain regions previously associated with positive affect and affiliation. Taken together, these findings suggest that the deliberate cultivation of compassion offers a new coping strategy that fosters positive affect even when confronted with the distress of others.

This line of research is in its preliminary phases, and this only focuses on the neuroscientific evidence. Other researchers have suggested to me in conversations that this is just the neuroscience, but the metabolic indicators of debilitating stress (heart rate, blood pressure, sweat, etc.) that suggest advantages of compassion over empathy are equally compelling.

This is all preliminary, but—in a word—we may be on the edge of learning how to train people in compassion in a scientifically supported way that leads to exhilaration and joy; this is a promising way to make this work sustainable. Most importantly, it will be exciting to demonstrate the parallels to religious ethics. For example, one of the highest experiences of Judaism, with rewards in this world and "the next world" (whatever that may mean) is *Gemilut Hasadim*, the bestowal of abundant kindness (Pirkei Avot 1:2).[16]

I propose further that if empathy is debilitating, then it prepares the mind more for despair and apathy, not for reason and universal laws applied to all. It can even breed rage and hatred. I certainly fought this in myself working with thousands of war victims near the battlefront. But the exhilarating experience of compassionate action, as opposed to passive and debilitating empathy, will be more likely to prepare the mind and heart for rational reasoning, which leads to the creation of shared rules of behavior for a peaceful society. The positive experience of compassion and healing across enemy lines, across the lines of diversity, will encourage the mind in the direction of a reason-based approach to coexistence, despite obvious religious differences between many peoples.

It has always been a mystery how in some eras very conservative adherents to multiple religions in proximity will kill each other, but in other eras multiple religions exist side by side and flourish. Misdirected empathy leading to anger and despair, misdirected excessive empathy for one's own people and hatred of others, may be to blame. By contrast, good habits of compassionate action, habits that prevented outbreaks of violence, may have provided crucial bridges in other places and circumstances.

It seems to me that a marriage of science and religious ethics emphasizing both the healthful pleasures and the duties of compassionate action will lead secular and religious minds together to form the basis of a pluralistic and good society.

4. A Personal Story

I want to end with a story from June 2017 in Bosnia. I run classes in different parts of the world as a form of field education for conflict resolution but also as a way to intervene and support peaceful change makers. I had struggled during the years of horror in Bosnia, 1991 to 1995, to stand up to genocide from a distance. I fought in Washington to organize attention to the genocidal war crimes taking place. In all the years since then, my professional attention was focused on peacebuilding in the Middle East, and so this was the first time I went on the ground to Bosnia with students. We look on these trips to meet those who have really sacrificed, struggled, and done heroic things.

We found our way by bus to a tiny village in the Serb Republic called Kevljani to meet a forty-four-year old man by the name of Kemal Pervanic, a survivor of the infamous Omarska concentration camp. Kemal sat us down to the most harrowing half-hour film I had ever seen. We saw everything that had happened to him and his community; we saw him confront after the war his Serbian professor who had interrogated him during the war and sent untold numbers to a terrible fate. I heard of the roundups, the emaciated bodies in the camp, so familiar to me from a lifetime studying the Holocaust of my own people.

When we finished, Kemal stood before us with the most peaceful and plaintive blue eyes, a survivor of everything we had just seen, a survivor of torture. We sat with him in one of the many village houses that had been destroyed and rebuilt, his family home. I was broken by the stories; nevertheless we were there to support him. I asked him, "What can we do to help you?" and he responded, "You already have by coming." And it broke me further.

Nothing prepared me, however, for what was about to come. We left with Kemal to go to the larger town of Prijedor. Everything as far as the eye could see was beautiful, quiet, peaceful, as bucolic a scene as one could imagine. Just down the road, he stops us and asks us to get out of the car near the mosque that was recently rebuilt. He shows us where he is building a peace center, where the sports field was where he was forced to gather with everyone to go to the concentration camp, where his Serb kindergarten teacher, sporting a gun, ordered them to line up. Then, turning around, he looks into my eyes and says, "And this is where the mass grave was. Bodies from the Muslim village, and also from the concentration camp." I started shaking, stunned.

I was not prepared for a mass grave. I saw the ruins of the old mosque, I looked at the graveyard, and then I saw the depression in the ground, covered over by beautiful grass, but a clear, rectangular depression in the ground heading off into the distance. I did not know what to do; I am a professor, I had a class with me, and I was breaking down completely inside. The rage in me, the sheer rage. For, you see, it is in exactly this kind of bucolic, rustic village that three hundred Jews had been rounded up on one day in the tiny hamlet from which my Gopin clan came, all shot on one day, by some Ukrainian fascists with perhaps a couple of Nazis present, all between Rosh Hashanah and Yom Kippur 1943, during the Ten Days of Repentance. It was a beautiful tiny hamlet, my family's hamlet, just like this one.

I looked at the scene with the mosque in front of me; I crossed the road; I asked Kemal to accompany me to the mass grave; I stood on it with him. Ever since I was little I had an intense uncontrollable and sometimes crippling empathy for those in pain. I could not stop thinking—what would the six hundred people there, in their last moments, their blood still in the ground beneath my feet, what would they want from me? What would I have wanted at the last moments of my life in a ditch, abused and killed as if my life meant nothing? The answer that came to me in that moment was that I would want to be remembered, I would want my soul to be prayed for, I would want to not be forgotten.

And so I put on my Jewish kippah which I use for prayers, I held Kemal close, and I said the Jewish prayer for the memory of the dead, a quite universal prayer for the holy souls of the dead to achieve eternal rest under the wings of the Divine Presence.

I did not want my class to see what I was doing, I did not want anyone to see, except Kemal. I needed to bear witness, but I also needed to not make it into a public spectacle in the middle of my professional role as professor. I needed it to be an act of intimacy with the dead and the survivor. That is what my heart demanded, but also what my reason told me the situation allowed for.

For so many decades, my work has brought me face to face with victims, and the pain of what they went through debilitated me. But now, I have achieved far greater calm, healing, and rapid recovery. The course of my life has allowed me to merge the best of religious values, from my own Judaism all the way to the Dalai Lama's Buddhism, together with learning from medical healers.

Conclusion

There is a greater wisdom that we have achieved, more every day, as we align the insights of science into compassion, empathy, morality, and reason, together with the wisdom we have garnered from religions. I now understand—thanks to science and to the role model of doctors— why my pure empathy with victims was destructive, causing so many problems in my life. But I also have come to understand that the answer is compassion and solidarity with the clear intention at every moment to care, to be kind, to be constructive, to educate, and to do some- thing with deep meaning. I learned that good interventions are not just righteous deeds in the religious sense, but they are clearly rooted in mental and physical health, and that as such these actions build the good society based upon a combination of compassion and reason.

From training our minds and hearts to focus on compassionate action and practical aid, we can build the rational principles necessary for the good society and the good civilization, and we can do it with the mental and physical health necessary to be strong and sustainable.

My empathy does me no good when it just creates rage against perpetrators. I watch Kemal—I watch what he tries to do every day with his pain, to heal, to change perpetrators, to enlighten all—and I feel that the best in science and the best of our spiritual habits can work together on building a far better world than we have inherited. Compassion, whether its source be motivated by simple human reac- tions, philosophical training, or religious training, is the core ingredient that must unite with reason to create a world shared by religious and secular citizens of the earth.

9

THE SUPERORGANISM CONCEPT AND HUMAN GROUPS
Implications for Confronting Religious Violence

DAVID SLOAN WILSON

Comparing a human community to a single organism has an ancient history. It is how religious believers often describe their own communities and how scholars of religion such as Emile Durkheim also described them. It is reflected etymologically in words such as *corporation*, in phrases such as *the body politic*, and in the legal designation of corporations as individuals.

Despite its ancient pedigree, however, this superorganismic conception of human society was eclipsed by individualistic schools of thought during the middle of the twentieth century, including methodological individualism in the social sciences and rational choice theory (a form of methodological individualism) in economics, which makes individual self-interest a grand principle for explaining all aspects of human behavior and society. As the British Prime Minister Margaret Thatcher famously put it, "There is no such thing as society, only individuals and families."[1] Theories of religion were also influenced by methodological individualism during this period, with Rodney Stark and William Bainbridge as prominent examples.[2]

A renaissance of evolutionary thinking in relation to human affairs during the last three decades has revived the concept of human groups as superorganisms and placed it on a stronger theoretical foundation than ever before. In this essay I will first review what it means to take the superorganism concept seriously for human groups. Then I will

167

review implications for confronting human violence at all scales and
in all kinds of groups, including but not restricted to religious groups.

1. A Brief History of the Superorganism Concept
in Evolutionary Thought

The Judaeo-Christian worldview that preceded Darwin's theory of
evolution assumed that God created a harmonious universe at all scales,
from the tiniest insects to the stars in heaven. At first, Darwin thought
that his theory of natural selection could explain all examples of design
in the living world that had been attributed to a Creator. On further
reflection, however, he came to a disturbing realization. If natural selection favors individuals that survive and reproduce better than other
individuals, it would seem to select against traits that are regarded as
morally virtuous, such as altruism, honesty, and bravery, which almost
by definition benefit others at the expense of the morally virtuous individual. Unless he added something to his theory, he could explain only
the evolution of *individual-level* adaptations such as the sharp teeth of
the tiger or the thick fur of the polar bear, not *group-level* adaptations
such as individuals working together to produce a common good.[3]

That "something" was not far to seek. Darwin realized that social
behaviors are almost always expressed in groups that are small compared
to the whole evolving population, such as a colony of bees, a flock
of birds, a troop of primates, or a human tribe. While it is true that
benefiting others at the expense of oneself would be selectively disadvantageous within a single group, it is equally true that a group of
cooperators would robustly outcompete a group whose members cannot
pull together. Natural selection can be imagined to operate at two levels:
among individuals within groups, favoring self-serving behaviors in all
their forms, and among groups in a multigroup population, favoring
cooperative behaviors in all their forms.

Darwin's elaborated theory of two-level selection is easy to understand and has the potential to explain the evolution of group-level
adaptations, but it also has some major limitations. First, not only is
group-level selection required to explain the evolution of group-level
adaptations, but it must be strong enough to outweigh opposing selection within groups. Otherwise, selfishness prevails. Second, even when
cooperation within groups does evolve by between-group selection, it
can often be used in destructive competition with other groups. Group-
level selection does not *eliminate* conflict so much as *elevate* it to the
scale of between-group interactions, where it can potentially take place

with even more destructive force than before (Darwin was curiously silent on this implication in his own writing). The only solution to this problem would be to add another level of selection (among groups of interacting groups), turning two-level selection theory into multilevel selection (MLS) theory (something that Darwin was also silent about). Given these limitations, Darwin's theory can explain the evolution of higher-level adaptations only when special conditions were met, which might be quite restrictive. Over the last century and a half, such theories have challenged the previous Judeo-Christian worldview that harmony and order exists at all scales.

As important as these issues were, they did not occupy center stage during the decades following the publication of *Origin of Species*, compared to other pressing issues such as the mechanisms of heritable variation.[4] Those who did think about social adaptations were not always as discerning as Darwin; some assumed that adaptations evolve at all tiers of a multilevel hierarchy without requiring special conditions. This could be called "The Age of Naive Group Selection," which came to an end in the middle of the twentieth century.[5] The single most influential book of this period was *Adaptation and Natural Selection* by George C. Williams.[6] Williams accepted the logic of MLS theory but argued as an empirical fact that lower-level selection almost invariably outweighs higher-level selection. As he put it, "group-level adaptations do not, in fact, exist."[7] Thus, during this period, evolutionary theory was marching in step with methodological individualism in the human social sciences.

The widespread rejection of group selection, by others in addition to Williams,[8] challenged evolutionary biologists to explain how behaviors that *seemed* to be altruistic, and which had been attributed to group-level selection, could have evolved. A number of theoretical frameworks were developed to meet this challenge, including inclusive fitness theory,[9] evolutionary game theory,[10] and selfish gene theory.[11] Inclusive fitness theory explains altruism as individuals helping their own genes in the bodies of others. Evolutionary game theory explains altruism as individuals benefiting others to obtain return benefits for themselves. Selfish gene theory explains altruism as a form of gene-level selfishness. In all cases, altruism was permuted into a form of lower-level selfishness that was only *apparently* altruistic. All three theoretical frameworks were regarded to be consistent with each other and collectively to provide a robust alternative to group selection. It became almost mandatory for authors to assure their readers that their theoretical model or empirical study did not invoke group selection.

Almost as soon as the ink was dry on the rejection of group selection, new developments began to prove otherwise. It must be remembered that the age of computer simulation models and desktop computing was only dawning during this period. The theoretical models that made group-level selection appear unlikely were riddled with simplifying assumptions that were necessary to make the mathematics tractable. A new generation of computer simulation models that could make more realistic assumptions suggested an important role for group selection after all.[12]

In addition, a subtle but widespread confusion began to be recognized that Sober and Wilson called the *averaging fallacy*.[13] To appreciate the averaging fallacy, imagine a situation (no matter how far-fetched) where between-group selection actually does outweigh within-group selection. The fact that altruism evolves in the total population means that the average altruist is more fit than the average selfish individual, all things considered. If you only take note of this fact, without comparing fitness differences within and between groups, it is easy to label fitness differences at the scale of the total population individual-level or gene-level selection, even though the selective disadvantage of these traits within groups and the need for between-group selection is plain for anyone to see. In retrospect, it has become clear that all theories of social evolution that were developed as alternatives to group selection commit this fallacy. They all include the basic ingredients of an MLS model: a total evolving population that is subdivided into groups, cooperative behaviors that are selectively disadvantageous within groups, and the most cooperative groups differentially contributing to evolution in the total population as a counterweight to within-group selection. This fact went unnoticed because the fitness of the lower-level entities (individuals or genes) was averaged across the higher-level entities (groups), and the average effect was called individual- (or gene-) level selection.

Today, the averaging fallacy is largely recognized and avoided in the peer-reviewed literature on social evolution. This passage from Birch and Okasha describes the consensus view:

> In earlier debates, biologists tended to regard kin and multilevel selection
> as rival empirical hypotheses, but many contemporary biologists regard
> them as ultimately equivalent, on the grounds that gene frequency change
> can be directly computed using either approach. Although dissenters from
> this equivalence claim can be found, the majority of social evolutionists
> appear to endorse it.[14]

This passage represents a sea change in the acceptance of MLS theory, compared to earlier decades when authors felt compelled to say that they were not invoking group selection.

I have reviewed the history of thinking about MLS in a fair amount of detail because, while the issue is largely settled among authors of the peer-reviewed literature within evolutionary biology, there is still wide-spread confusion in the human social sciences and popular literature, where group selection is still often portrayed as heretical.[15]

2. Major Evolutionary Transitions

Having set the stage, I can quickly show how MLS theory places the concept of social group as like an organism on a stronger foundation than ever before in its long history. The concept of a major evolutionary transition notes that the balance between levels of selection is not static but can itself evolve. When mechanisms evolve that suppress the potential for disruptive competition within groups, then between-group selection becomes the dominant evolutionary force. The group becomes such a cooperative unit that it qualifies as a higher-level organism in its own right, as an analogue to the cooperation of specialized genes or cooperation between specialized cells that comprise a well-functioning organism.

This concept was first proposed by the cell biologist Lynn Margulis in the 1970s to explain the evolution of nucleated cells (called eukaryotic) not by small mutational steps from bacterial cells (called prokaryotic), but from symbiotic associations of bacterial cells.[16] It was radical at the time and would have been beyond the imagination of Darwin, but it has now become the accepted view. Then the concept was generalized by the theoretical biologists John Maynard Smith (a former critic of group selection) and Eörs Szathmáry in the 1990s to explain other events such as the first cells, multicellular organisms, eusocial insect colonies, and possibly even the origin of life itself as groups of cooperating molecular reactions.[17] These too have become widely accepted as cases of major transitions, thanks to the evolution of mechanisms that suppress (without entirely eliminating) the potential for disruptive competition within groups, so that between-group selection becomes the dominant evolutionary force. In other words, every entity that is currently labeled with the word "organism" is in fact a social group that has evolved by between-entity selection to be so cooperative that the interactions among the parts only make sense in terms of the welfare of the whole. In addition, eusocial insect colonies such as ants, bees, wasps, and termites richly deserve their designation as superorganisms as products of between-colony selection.[18] If that is not a strong scientific foundation for the concept of a social group as like an organism and an organism as like a social group, what would be?

Human Genetic Evolution as a Major Transition

Maynard Smith and Szathmáry were somewhat timid in speculating about human evolution as a major evolutionary transition,[19] confining themselves to the genetic basis of language. The work of Christopher Boehm and others presents a much more solid case.[20] In many nonhuman social species, including our closest ape relatives, between-group selection operates to a degree, but there is also intense and disruptive within-group selection. Even the cooperation that evolves often takes the form of small alliances that compete against other alliances within the same group.[21] What set our ancestors apart was the evolution of mechanisms that suppress the potential for bullying and other forms of disruptive competition within groups, so that cooperating as a group became the main strategy for survival and reproduction. Boehm calls this *reverse dominance*, and it describes the kind of guarded egalitarianism found in most extant hunter-gatherer societies and many other small-scale traditional societies. It is the social organization that asserts itself in small-group settings in modern life, whenever there is a relatively equal balance of power among the group members. We will have much more to say about it in subsequent sections of this chapter. For now, it should be obvious that Boehm's concept of reverse dominance is nothing more or less than human genetic evolution as a major evolutionary transition.

Cultural Multilevel Selection

Cooperation in hunter-gatherer groups (both today and in the distant past) includes physical activities such as hunting, gathering, childcare, defense against predators, and offense and defense against other human groups. Cooperation also includes mental activities, such as memory, decision making, maintaining an inventory of symbols with shared meanings (including but not restricted to language), and the transmission of large amounts of learned information across generations. When we combine both physical and mental forms of cooperation, the concept of human genetic evolution as a major evolutionary transition has the potential to explain nearly everything that is distinctive about our species.[22]

Our ability to transmit large amounts of learned information across generations became nothing short of an inheritance system in its own right that coevolved with the genetic inheritance system.[23] This enabled our ancestors to adapt to their environments much faster than by genetic evolution alone, allowing them to colonize all habitable regions of the planet and dozens of ecological niches. It also led to a positive feedback loop between the production of resources and the scale of human society, leading to the megasocieties of today. This thesis has been developed in considerable detail by Peter Turchin in his book *Ultrasociety: How 10,000 Years of War Made Humans the Greatest Cooperators on Earth.*

According to Turchin and others, our genetic adaptations for suppressing disruptive self-serving behaviors, which evolved in the context of small groups, tend to break down in larger groups. This has resulted in phases where societies became despotic, ironically more like chimp societies than small-scale human societies. However, cultural evolution is a multilevel process no less than genetic evolution. In other words, sizable human groups varied in how well they functioned as cooperative units, and the best replaced or were copied by the worst (imitating the best practices of a group qualifies as a form of cultural group selection). Cultural group selection resulted in the evolution of cultural mechanisms that interface with previously evolved genetic mechanisms to regulate societies at ever larger scales. As Turchin puts it: "Such a multilevel nature of economic and social life has profound consequences for the evolution of human societies—just how profound we are only now beginning to understand, thanks to cultural evolution. The central theoretical breakthrough in this new field is the theory of Cultural Multilevel Selection."[24]

As with genetic multilevel selection, special conditions are required for cultural between-group selection to prevail against within-group selection. There is also a back-and-forth quality to cultural multilevel selection, as Turchin analyzes for the rise and fall of empires in his earlier book *War and Peace and War.*[25] Empires tend to form in geographical regions with chronic between-group conflict, which acts as a crucible for the cultural evolution of cooperative societies. Once one forms (often with the help of new military technological innovations), it spreads to become an empire. Then cultural evolution takes place within the empire, favoring self-serving behaviors and factionalism in all their forms and ultimately leading to a collapse. This dynamic is eerily similar to cancer, which is a process of disruptive lower-level selection that takes place during the lifetime of multicellular organisms.[26]

To summarize, the concept of a society as like an organism stands on a stronger foundation than ever before in its long history. It should be seen not as entirely metaphoric but as a result of similar evolutionary forces operating on a multitiered hierarchy of units, which provides a theoretical framework for explaining both increases and reverses in the scale of human societies over the last ten thousand years. Against this background, we can begin to examine the implications of MLS theory for confronting human violence at all scales and in all kinds of groups, including but not restricted to religious groups.

3. Thinking like an Evolutionary Ecologist about Violence and Nonviolence

Forget about humans for a moment, and try to imagine that you are an evolutionary ecologist studying nonhuman species. Some species display more violence than others. Within species, some individuals display more violence than others. Any given individual is likely to behave more violently in some contexts than others. How can you explain the presence and absence of violence at all these scales? *By thinking about violence and nonviolence as social strategies that succeed under some conditions and not others.* That is how evolutionary ecologists structure their inquiry for all evolved traits, behavioral or otherwise. Adaptationist explanations are only informed guesses because not everything that evolves is adaptive, but to the extent that the behaviors of nonhuman species have been molded by natural selection, then adaptationist explanations often prove to be correct.

Hundreds of empirical studies and theoretical models confirm that natural selection can favor either violent or nonviolent social strategies, depending on the social environment. The contest takes place at a miniature scale in two-person game theory models, where violent "hawks" prey on nonviolent "doves," but doves can succeed to the extent that they interact with each other and avoid the depredations of the hawks, who are then forced to interact with each other by default. More sophisticated strategies such as "tit-for-tat" are capable of both violence and nonviolence, which they employ conditionally, and so on.[27]

Edward O. Wilson and I concluded our 2007 article titled "Rethinking the Theoretical Foundation of Sociobiology" with the following statement that pays homage to the famous description of Rabbi Hillel summarizing Jewish law while standing on one foot: "Selfishness beats altruism within groups. Altruistic groups beat selfish groups. Everything else is commentary."[28] Implicit in this statement is that altruism is primarily a within-group social interaction that evolves by some form of between-group competition, which includes but is not restricted to violent conflict. Just as drought-resistant plants outcompete drought-susceptible plants in the desert without the plants directly interacting at all, groups that work harmoniously can outcompete groups riven by internal conflict without any direct interactions. Another way to make this point is to imagine all the ecological relationships among species in a natural ecosystem. They include negative interactions such as competition, predation, and parasitism, but also positive interactions such as mutualism or no direct interactions at all. The full range of ecological interactions exists for social species (such as eusocial insect colonies) in addition to solitary species. For example, some species of ants engage in violent between-colony conflict, while others do not. The reasons are due to ecological factors that cause violent between-group conflict to be an evolutionarily successful strategy in some species but not others.

Everything that I have stated in this chapter is commonplace for an evolutionary ecologist who studies nonhuman species, but it becomes novel when applied to human groups as superorganisms, as we shall see.

4. Thinking like an Evolutionist about Proximate Mechanisms

The pioneering ethologist Niko Tinbergen wisely observed that four questions need to be asked about all products of evolution, concerning their function, history, mechanism, and development.[29] Function concerns why a trait exists, compared to the many other traits that could have existed, often (but not always) based on its contribution to survival and reproduction. History concerns the evolution of the trait over multiple generations, which is a highly contingent process, starting with the chance mutation that gave rise to the trait. Mechanism concerns the physical basis of the trait, since all traits (including behaviors) have a physical basis. Development concerns how the trait comes into being during the lifetime of the organism. Tinbergen's fourfold distinction maps onto a twofold distinction made independently by Ernst Mayr between ultimate (function and history) and proximate (mechanism and development) causation.[30] These distinctions are part of the conceptual toolkit of evolutionary theory.

Focusing on mechanism, imagine that you're an evolutionary ecologist studying combat among males for females. Two males size each other up. If they are unevenly matched, the weaker yields to the stronger without much of a fight. If they are evenly matched, a protracted fight might occur. Whatever happens at the behavioral level is accompanied by physical events within the two males, such as changes in hormone levels. Increasingly, we are discovering that gene expression can be rapidly turned on and off by environmental events. The genes are like the keys of an organ being played by the environment, with the score scripted by natural selection. When a behaviorally flexible individual exhibits different behaviors (such as attack vs. flee), it is expressing different genes within its genome. At a different timescale, we know that specialized cells such as a liver cell and a heart cell share the same genes. What makes them so different from each other is differences in their gene *expression* during the process of development.

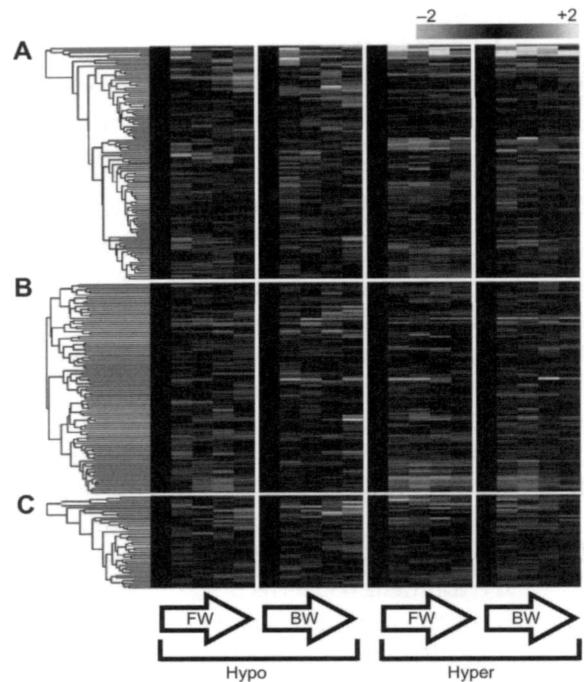

FIG. 9.1. A STUDY OF GENE EXPRESSION IN TWO POPULATIONS OF A FISH SPECIES THAT INHABIT FRESH WATER (FW) AND BRACKISH WATER (BW), RESPECTIVELY.

Individuals can physiologically adapt to changes in salinity through changes in gene expression. Each vertical bar represents a gene, and the degree to which it is colorized represents the degree to which it has been up-regulated or down-regulated by its environment. This visual representation is called a heat map.[31]

Technological advances enable biologists to measure changes in gene expression and visualize them in the form of "heat maps." The heat map in figure 9.1 is from a study of a small-fish species that lives in estuaries.[32] Local populations are adapted to different levels of salinity, but individuals from each population can also physiologically adapt to an extent through changes in gene expression. The lighter gray bars show genes that are up-regulated, and the darker gray bars show genes that are down-regulated. The details need not concern us, other than to make the points that organisms are impressively flexible in their response to their environment (called *phenotypic plasticity*), that their patterns of flexibility are molded by natural selection, and that flexibility at the phenotypic level is orchestrated by physiological mechanisms, including changes in gene expression.

5. Performing the Metaphorical Transfer

With this background information in mind, I am now in a position to describe what it means to take the superorganism concept seriously for human groups. It means performing a *metaphorical transfer* so that everything I wrote about nonhuman species in the last two sections is applied to the internal organization of human groups and their inter-actions with each other. This includes asking all four of Tinbergen's questions concerning function, history, mechanism, and development. This has been the aim of my research funded by the John Templeton Foundation, beginning with my first "forgiveness" grant in 1998, which led to my book *Darwin's Cathedral: Evolution, Religion, and the Nature of Society*, and continuing through my most recent grant (with Harvey Whitehouse) that examined religion and spirituality in the context of everyday life.[33]

For the rest of this essay, I will apply the metaphorical transfer to the theme of this symposium, which is based on the premise that "the violence committed in God's name is always an act of desecration." Since desecration is a key word for the premise, let us be clear about its definition: "The act of depriving something of its sacred character, or the disrespectful, contemptuous, or destructive treatment of that which is held to be sacred or holy by a group or individual."[34]

This premise is deeply problematic from an evolutionary and ecolog-ical perspective. If human groups are functionally organized units that interact with each other in multigroup "ecosystems," then we should expect the full range of ecological interactions, including predation, competition, parasitism, mutualism, and coexisting without any direct interactions, depending on the circumstances. We should expect to observe violent social strategies whenever they win out over nonviolent social strategies in a Darwinian contest. When violence between groups evolves, it becomes as sacred for perpetrators of the violence as does nonviolence when it evolves.

To be *sacred* means "dedicated or set apart for the service or worship of a deity," with the secondary meaning "entitled to reverence and respect."[35] Thus, the word is central to religious meaning systems but is also widely used in nonreligious contexts. All human groups have meaning systems that place obligations on the behaviors of their members. Whatever is normative requires reverence and respect, hence calling for words such as "sacred" or equivalent words. In multigroup human ecosystems, some groups are organized by religion more than others. The fact that violence is part of the behavioral repertoire of most human groups, regardless of whether they are classified as "religious," goes without saying from an ecological and evolutionary perspective. This background presents major challenges to the premise that "violence committed in God's name is *always* an act of desecration."

6. Sacred Text as Cultural Genome

Just as technological advances in biology have led to heat maps of gene expression, advances in the study of cultural evolution enable us to think about the mechanisms of transmission and expression of learned behaviors more clearly than ever before. The sacred texts of the major world religions bear an intriguing resemblance to genomes. They are transmitted across generations with high fidelity and even have a segmented structure, similar to genes on chromosomes. At any particular time and place, the sacred text is related to current environmental circumstances by citing and interpreting selected passages—similar to the differential expression of genes in phenotypically plastic organisms.

Thinking of sacred texts as cultural genomes helps to answer a fundamental question about religious diversity. Within a given tradition, how can religious communities be so different when they draw on the same sacred text? The answer is by the differential invocation and interpretation of the sacred text, just as liver and heart cells become different despite relying on the same genome.

As part of my most recent John Templeton Foundation grant, Yasha Hartberg and I borrowed techniques from genetics to create heat maps for cultural genomes.[36] Figure 9.2 is a comparison of six American Protestant religious congregations. Three are conservative (designated C), and three are progressive (designated P). They were classified according to their stance on same-sex marriage but differed in many other respects associated with American conservatism and progressivism.

C3 and P3 are United Methodist churches located within ten miles of each other in a small city in upstate New York. Hence, their main difference was their conservative versus progressive outlooks. The other congregations were located in separate states, and their denominations were Baptist (C1 and P2), United Church of Christ (P1), and nondenominational (C2).

For each congregation, we collected a large number of biblical citations from sermons and church bulletins, enabling us to create the heat maps of biblical expression shown in the figure. Each vertical bar is a book of the Bible. The brighter the color, the more that book was cited. There is clearly a family resemblance between the three conservative congregations and the three progressive congregations, which as groups are more different from each other. The conservative United Methodist Church in upstate New York (C3) is more similar to conservative

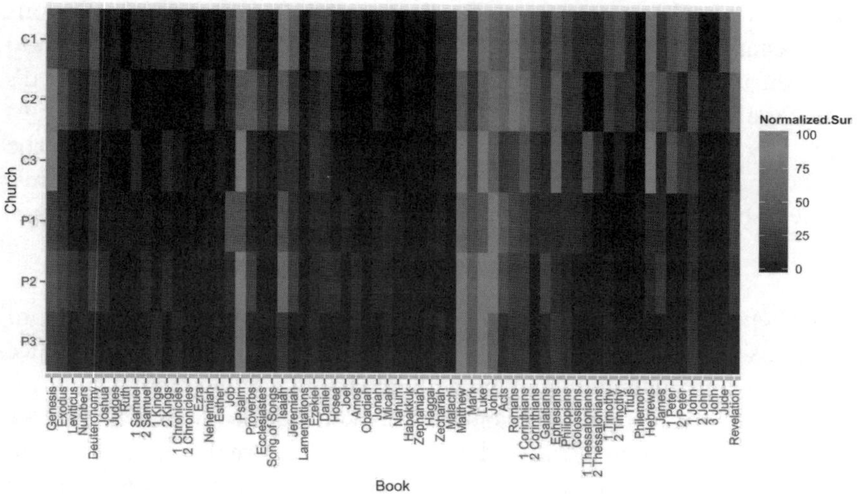

FIG. 9.2. A HEAT MAP FOR A CULTURAL GENOME.

Each vertical bar is a book of the Christian Bible, and each horizontal bar is a church congregation. Three are designated conservative (C), and three are designated progressive (P), based on their stance on same-sex marriage. The lightness of the bar indicates the degree to which each book was cited during sermons.[37]

churches of other denominations in other states than to the progressive United Methodist Church ten miles away (P3).

It is possible to create similar heat maps for chapters within each book and verses within each chapter.[38] The bottom line is that there is very little overlap in the passages of the Bible cited between the conservative and progressive congregations. One of the few passages cited by both is John 3:16: "For God so loved the world that he gave his one and only Son, that whoever believes in him shall not perish but have eternal life" (NIV). However, even this passage was subjected to contrasting interpretations by progressive and conservative pastors in their sermons. A progressive pastor used it to argue for unconditional love. A conservative pastor stressed that when this passage is combined with other passages, it plainly shows that God does not love everyone equally or even at all. Thus, when differential citations are combined with differential interpretations, progressive and conservative churches become as different as heart and liver cells, or estuarine fish placed in fresh or salt water.

Thinking of sacred texts as cultural genomes provides a powerful new tool for studying religious diversity. Since the citation and interpretation of sacred texts are well preserved in the historical record, it becomes possible to measure the "expressed phenotype" of religious congregations at any time or place in history. However, the same method calls into question the premise that "the violence committed in God's name is always an act of desecration." Like it or not, violence is built into the "DNA" of the sacred texts of all the major religions, along with the functional equivalents of sacred texts in nonreligious meaning systems, ready to be expressed whenever warranted by environmental conditions.

Conclusion

The theme of this symposium clearly has a normative goal: to confront religious violence. However, the idea of confronting religious violence with a counternarrative can be problematic for two reasons. First, if we have a commitment to scientific and scholarly knowledge, then we cannot let a counternarrative depart from factual reality. Second, even the best counternarrative will fail in an environment that favors violence as a social strategy.

The premise of this symposium might provide a counternarrative, but one that is challenged by evolutionary and scientific knowledge. While I have approached the subject from a modern ecological and evolutionary perspective, scholars from other disciplines have argued that violence is part of the cultural DNA of all of the major world religions, for example, Bruce Chilton in his book *Abraham's Curse: The Roots of Violence in Judaism, Christianity, and Islam*.[39] Recently, Peter Turchin has provided a compelling account of the role of warfare in the cultural evolution of both religious and nonreligious meaning systems during the last ten thousand years of human history.[40]

Books such as *Sacred and Secular: Religion and Politics Worldwide* by Pippa Norris and Ronald Inglehart show that the violent side of religion is expressed in conditions of existential insecurity.[41] That is what makes the difference between geographical regions, such as the Middle East compared to Western Europe, or between modern Western Europe and the same region several centuries ago. The Middle East does not lack narratives arguing for peace, in both religious and nonreligious idioms. These narratives already exist, but they lose out in competition with narratives arguing for war. If religious extremism is spreading worldwide, it is because existential insecurity is spreading worldwide. Thinking like an evolutionary ecologist shows that a good narrative is only necessary and not sufficient to evolve nonviolent social strategies in a Darwinian world.

I will end this chapter with a counternarrative called *interspirituality* that I find especially persuasive and personally appealing.[42] The narrative begins by noting that all religious and spiritual traditions converge on a common awareness of rich interconnectedness. Of course, numerous scientific traditions converge on the same awareness, such as physics, complex systems theory, and ecosystem ecology. Once a person becomes truly aware of rich interconnectedness, then certain ethical conclusions follow—namely, it becomes difficult to use one part of the system to attack another part of the same system.

Common awareness of rich interconnectedness and its ethical implications provides a common language that can be spoken across religious, spiritual, and scientific traditions. This is called *second-tier consciousness*, in contrast to *first-tier consciousness*, which is rooted in a particular tradition. Second-tier consciousness does not replace first-tier consciousness. Instead, people can feel free to draw on the strengths of a particular tradition and also sample other traditions, a bit like appreciating multiple cuisines.

I find interspirituality personally appealing because it is fully consistent with scientific knowledge. Also, it naturally leads to an ethic that recognizes the whole earth as the entity that is not yet—but that needs to become—the superorganism. This is the ultimate message of MLS theory, which states unequivocally that adaptation at any given level requires a process of selection at that level and tends to be undermined by selection at lower levels. This means that "Peace on Earth" requires consciously striving for it and coordinating all lower-level units with that objective in mind. Anything less will almost certainly lead to discord. MLS theory therefore adds scientific authority to the many other whole-earth ethics that emerge from the appreciation of rich interconnect-edness, which provides a counternarrative to violence in all its forms.

PART IV

THEOLOGICAL REFLECTIONS

10

MONOTHEISM, NATIONALISM, VIOLENCE
Twenty-Five Theses

Miroslav Volf

In this essay, written in the form of twenty-five interlocking theses, I approach the problem of religiously motivated or legitimized violence by exploring the relation between monotheism and nationalism.[1] The first is allegedly the most violent of all forms of religion, and the second one of the most violent forms of political arrangements, especially when it is cut loose from universal moral commitment and tied to some form of tribal identity (exclusive nationalism). I argue that monotheism is a universalist creed and that it is compatible only with inclusive nationalism, a nationalism that is a form of special relations framed by a universal moral code. When monotheism is aligned with exclusive nationalism—when it becomes a *political religion* aligned with exclusivist nationalism—monotheism betrays its universality, a feature which lies at its very core, and morphs into violence, generating and legitimizing henotheism: our god of our nation in contrast and competition to other nations with their gods. Alternatively, if monotheism keeps its universality while being associated as political religion with exclusive nationalism, it will tend to underwrite dreams of nationalist imperialism: our god and our nation as masters of the world.

1. Resurgence of Nationalism

1. Nationalisms are surging today across the globe. Only a decade ago, nationalism seemed a marginal phenomenon, mainly a reaction to the loss of local power in an increasingly globalized

185

world. But globalization processes, driven as they are by the markets, have left in their onward march a trail of suffering and melancholy, exemplified most potently by extraordinary discrepancies of wealth and power, progressive ecological devastation, and loss of a sense of personal, cultural, religious, or national identities and purposes.[2] Today, nationalist sentiments have conquered the world, and in many countries nationalists have taken the levers of political power—in China, India, Russia, Turkey, and the United States, for instance. Nationalism has gradually emerged as the main alternative to the current, morally unacceptable, global arrangements.

2. When firmly rooted in universal moral commitments, nationalism *can* be a way of living out particular loyalties within the larger human—and therefore global—community. Such *inclusive nationalism* (sometimes called *civic nationalism* or *patriotism*) is a form of special relations framed by universal moral commitments, of which the central one is the equal dignity of all human beings. As one loves one's own family in the framework of a universal love of neighbor, so one loves one's own nation in the community of all nations. But when nationalism is divorced from universal moral commitments and becomes *exclusive* (sometimes described, though too narrowly, as *ethnic nationalism*)—a nationalism which is based on the superiority of tribe, race, or history, and which operates on the principle of international exceptionalism—it is one of the most dangerous forces in the world.[3] National and geopolitical upheavals in Europe and the Far East in the middle of the previous century provide frighteningly vivid examples of nationalism's aggressive hatred for what threatens the perceived purity, greatness, and destiny of the nation and its possible world-destructive effects.

3. The main inspiration for most nationalisms today is not religious. The current American and Chinese nationalisms, for instance, are not religious in any significant sense. In some cases nationalism in fact posits itself as a pseudoreligion (i.e., the object of ultimate longing and the foundation of ultimate trust) while being explicitly antireligious. Depending on the circumstances, however, nationalism can take on a religious expression or, more often, make religions serviceable to its cause. Phrases like, "God and the Croats," "heavenly Serbia," "German Christians," "the city set on a hill"—all widespread

slogans in the countries in which I resided over the past sixty years—name forms of religiously (in these cases: Christianly) inflected or legitimized exclusive nationalism. Today Indian, Russian, and Turkish nationalisms are of such kind. Religions have motivated and legitimized nationalism in the past, and they continue to do so in the present.

2. Monotheism and Negation

4. More than any other religious expression, monotheism has borne the brunt of critique for allegedly fomenting and legitimizing violence, with the blame being placed squarely on monotheism's exclusivism. Jan Assmann has persuasively argued that monotheism introduced the question of truth into the world of religions.[4] Less convincingly, he has argued that the denial of the truth of other religions, which is implied in the affirmation of the one true God, fosters violence.

5. There are inclusive forms of monotheism ("all gods are One"), but today's major monotheisms are all of exclusive type ("no god but the One"). This is true of Islam: "no god but God" are the very first words of the most basic Islamic profession of faith. It is also true of Judaism: "you shall have no other god besides me" is the key prohibition of the very first of the Ten Commandments (Exod 20:3).[5] Christianity is no different: "no God but One," wrote the first Christian theologian, the apostle Paul, repeating in his own way the Jewish commitment to God's unicity (1 Cor 8:4). Monotheism's exclusivism is the necessary obverse of its universalism. The singular and the universal are identical: the one God is the God of everything that is not God.[6]

6. To recognize the gesture of negation and rejection at the heart of monotheism is to note its iconoclastic edge. When exclusive monotheism enters the field of forces in which religious claims are tied to economic, political, cultural, and reputational interests, it inspires struggle against pagans and atheists as well as monotheists of an alternative stripe (namely those monotheists whose idolatry consists in the erroneous conception of the one true God[7]). "Negation" at the level of epistemic claims and "struggle" at the level of social power that monotheism implies can be practiced in different ways. For negation to take the form of dogmatic assertions of unquestionable truths is very different from its taking the form of witness or of reasoned

argument. Similarly, for the struggle for social power to involve coercion and persecution is very different from it being regulated by commitment to the equal dignity and freedom of every human being.

7. When monotheism becomes a political religion (see thesis 14), iconoclasm will not just be exclusive at the level of religious convictions and practices. As history clearly shows, such monotheism will seek to avail itself of the power of the state to eliminate competitors and achieve universal acceptance. Monotheism might then become defensively aggressive, seeking to neutralize or eliminate internal enemies and, if sufficiently strong, striking preemptively against external enemies it sees as posing an imminent threat. Or, worse, monotheism might then become actively imperialistic, motivating and legitimizing the armed struggle for world domination ("no god but God" as the planetary political reality).

3. Monotheism against Exclusive Nationalism

8. Like other types of religion and/or philosophies whose emergence is part of the centuries-long axial transformations,[8] monotheisms address people primarily as human beings and only secondarily as members of a particular family, tribe, ethnicity, or nation.[9] This is true of Islamic and Christian monotheisms;[10] in a qualified way, this is also true of Jewish monotheism.[11]

9. Though a monotheism introduces a division between those who worship the one God and those who do not, its *moral precepts apply to all human beings without distinction* because they are commands of a single God of the whole world. For instance, according to the Christian faith, all human beings ought to obey the Golden Rule; according to Judaism, Noachide laws, such as the command to worship the one true God and prohibitions from murder and theft, are universal. The prophet of what Muslims believe is the last universal religion, Muhammad, enjoins on all human beings "that which is right and forbid(s) that which is wrong" (Q Al-A'raf 7:157). To the extent that monotheism addresses human beings *as* human beings, it undercuts in principle the apportioning of human beings into moral insiders and outsiders.

10. Having at its foundation a categorical distinction between the creator and the creature (or, more abstractly, between

transcendent and mundane realms) and insisting on the *primacy of devotion to God* by any and all creatures, monotheism relativizes belonging to family, tribe, ethnicity, or nation. The willingness of Abraham, the progenitor of all three great monotheistic traditions, to sacrifice Isaac at God's command (Gen 22:1-19) illustrates most vividly (and frighteningly!) the primacy of the commitment to God over all earthly ties and hopes.

11. All monotheisms affirm *freedom of religion*, if for no other reason than because their very existence is predicated on de facto exercise of such freedom by their founders. Abraham left behind his own land, kin, and religion (see Gen 12:1; Josh 24:2);[12] Jesus practiced a form of Judaism deemed blasphemous/idolatrous by his contemporaries (see Mark 14:60-64); Prophet Muhammad, like Abraham, rejected the idolatry of his time and was persecuted by his contemporaries.[13] Consequently, all three monotheisms explicitly affirm the freedom to *embrace* the true religion. Throughout their long histories, all three monotheisms have predominantly rejected the freedom to *leave* the true religion—or what its guardians deem to be the true religion. But the stance of affirming the freedom to embrace the true religion while rejecting the freedom to leave a religion one no longer considers to be true is not consistent. The most compelling versions of all three monotheisms reject the prohibition from leaving the true religion, affirming instead the freedom to exercise, publicly practice, and bear witness to the religion people deem true, *as well as* to leave that religion if they cease to consider it to be true.

12. Monotheisms assume the distinction (*distinction*, not complete separation) between the cultural domains of politics and religion.[14] Such a distinction is implied (a) in the primacy of the allegiance to the creator over love for creatures, (b) in monotheisms' addressing the person primarily as a human being rather than as a member of family, tribe, ethnicity, or nation, (c) in the insistence that the moral code applies universally, and, finally, (d) in the (implicit) affirmation of the freedom of religion. When monotheistic religion enters a social space for the first time—or when a rival version of monotheism enters a social space in which another form of monotheism functions to mark ethnocultural boundaries, integrate political entities, and legitimize governments—it inevitably creates a fissure in that

social space. For the person who embraces it, the allegiance to the one God redefines all other allegiances, including political ones. The result is a new and foreign social body within the existing one.[15]

4. Distortions of Monotheism

13. A major and prevalent distortion of monotheism consists in treating God as if God were a tool to be used for human purposes; in a word, the instrumentalization of God. The Source of all creaturely existence who, by definition, has no private interests is turned into a servant of human private interests, whether individual or collective. The great tests of the towering monotheistic figures centered on that issue. Will the famished Jesus attempt to use God to turn stones into bread for himself? (No, humans do not live by bread alone.) Is Abraham obedient to God primarily so as to secure for himself the promised blessing? (No, he will take Isaac on the three-day journey to Mount Moriah.) Is Job in fact serving God because God made him the greatest man in the East (as Satan maintained) rather than doing so "for nothing"? (No, Job will stay faithful to God—argumentatively faithful!—through loss of everything.) If humans are interested in God only as long as God serves their purposes, they worship their purposes rather than God—and monotheism is hollowed out from within.

14. The first of the two main ways of instrumentalizing God is practicing monotheism as a *prosperity religion*.[16] The main purpose of religion is then to deliver material blessings, to help secure production and acquisition of wealth. Using an image from the teaching of Jesus, Mammon here takes on the appearance of the one true God. The second main way of instrumentalizing God is practicing monotheism as *political religion*. The main function of religion is then to express the moral unity of the nation and furnish its political order with a sacred aura.[17] Using an image from the book of Job, Leviathan here takes on the appearance of the one true God. The two ways of instrumentalizing God can reinforce one another, especially when the main goal of the state becomes to increase prosperity through market means, or, in the terminology of Philip Bobbitt, when, as today, nation-states become market-states.[18] The two great

distortions of monotheism—monotheism as prosperity religion and as political religion—then merge.

5. Political Monotheism

15. Two great political philosophers of the Western tradition held two distinct but complementary positions on the political function of religion. Thomas Hobbes argued that religions are employed as *tools of government.* To aid rulers, religious elites—or, today, in an age of democratized religion, charismatic religious personalities—craft religious convictions to legitimize oppressive rule and justify unjust wars.[19] Immanuel Kant observed that religions function as *markers of communal identity.* In addition to diversities of languages, diversities of religions are the primary ways in which "nature" separates people into groups. As markers of identity, religions "bring with them the propensity to mutual hatred and pretexts for war," he argued.[20] Both of these political functions of religion, which often merge into one, tie religion to the deployment of violence.[21]

16. Partly building on Hobbes' and Kant's combined accounts of the political function of religion, David Martin, a sociologist, identified the circumstances under which religions tend to turn violent. These occur, he argued, when "religion becomes virtually coextensive with society and thus with the dynamics of power, violence, control, cohesion, and marking out of boundaries."[22]

17. The single most significant factor determining whether a religion will be implicated in violence is this: the level of its *identification with a political project and its entanglement with the agents striving to realize that project.*

6. Political Monotheism and Violence

18. Monotheism is not violent qua monotheism,[23] that is, on account of its affirmation of the singular commitment to the one God, the obverse of which is the negation of all other gods. Monotheism is no more violent on account of its exclusivity than is the affirmation of the distinction between truth and falsehood or justice and injustice. To the contrary, the distinction between true and false religion and the concern for justice that goes with monotheism are presuppositions of responsible peace and not,

as such, causes of violence.[24] It is true, however, that historically, most forms of monotheistic religions have been violent—above all because they have been practiced, and therefore also articulated, as political religions.[25]

19. A monotheism which *denies the freedom of religion*—freedom to embrace, freedom to publicly practice, freedom to bear witness to, and freedom to leave a religion—is likely to be violent. Notwithstanding the present strong sentiments against globalization, we live and will continue to live in an interconnected and interdependent world in which people with different ultimate allegiances and clashing lifestyles live under a common roof. To deny freedom of religion in such a world is to discriminate and persecute.

20. A monotheism which *refuses to affirm that religion and politics are two related, but distinct, cultural systems* is likely to be violent. In assuming the unity of religion and politics, instead of seeing itself as a force shaping cultural sensibilities and thereby influencing politics, it will more likely end up being coopted by politics and used to legitimize and motivate the state's deployment of violence.

21. A monotheism which *functions as political religion*—a nationalistic monotheism—will likely be violent; its implicit or explicit claim is that the one God belongs more to one family, tribe, ethnicity, or nation than to others. It is then likely to enlist God to oppose all those who oppose a given family, tribe, ethnicity, or nation.

22. Denying the freedom of religion, blurring the distinction between religion and the state, conceiving a particular monotheism as a political religion—all these stances are in taut tension with the core convictions of monotheism, namely that one God is the God of all people, that the transcendent God has primacy over all mundane goods, and that God has created each person in God's image and calls each person to find fulfillment in God, in the universal reign of God, or in both, which would be the world become "God's home among mortals," as the final book of the Christian Bible describes God's goal for history (Rev 21:3).

Conclusion:
Monotheism, Nationalism, and Violence

23. Inclusive nationalism is a possible (though historically contingent) way of honoring the particularities of human life at a given time and place, of taking seriously the essential temporality, sociality, linguisticality, historicity, and finitude of human beings. Affirmation of the goodness of such particularities, and therefore positive relation to boundaries and boundary maintenance, is a condition of the possibility of concrete identities of finite beings.[26] Authentic monotheism—a belief in the one God who creates human diversity rather than opposing it—can have inclusive nationalism as a friend.

24. Authentic monotheism is incompatible with exclusive nationalism. The construction and deployment of monotheism as a political religion in service of exclusive nationalism presupposes a tacit transformation of monotheism into henotheism (allegiance to a single God without denying the reality of other gods), transforming an essentially universalist creed into an exclusivist particularism with either dormant or active imperialistic aspirations.

25. The price monotheism always has to pay for its alliance with exclusive nationalism is the loss of its soul. When monotheism embraces exclusive nationalism, monotheism's God morphs from the creator and lover of all people and all creatures into a selfish and violent idol of a particular nation.

11

COUNTERING RELIGIOUS, MORAL, AND POLITICAL HATE-PREACHING
A Culture of Mercy and Freedom against the Barbarism of Hate

MICHAEL WELKER

After the horrors of the Nazi dictatorship, countless murders of innocent people, and two devastating world wars, Germany tried to regain trust and recognition among the peoples of the world by establishing itself as "Rechtsstaat" and "Sozialstaat," a state of law and a welfare state. This was a good move, deeply rooted in the value systems of ancient oriental cultures and, later, in both the Jewish and the Christian biblical law and moral traditions. It is the intrinsic connection of *justice, mercy, and freedom* that has to be emphasized here. This connection of justice, mercy, and freedom exhibits deep religious and moral logics and transformative powers. It has been formative for the Western ethos and has become one of the most important impulses in the positive shaping of societies, freedom-loving civil societies, and their ethos in the West.

1. Discerning and Strengthening the Spirit of Justice, Mercy, Love, and Freedom

As early as around 2400 BCE, the Sumerian emperor Urukagina claims to have "established freedom" and to have "protected the orphans and the widows" in Lagash,[1] one of the oldest cities of the Ancient Near East, northwest of the junction of the Euphrates and Tigris Rivers. The protection of the weak in general, and of widows and orphans in particular, and the establishment of freedom go hand in hand. The king thus

195

not only sets a great example of mercy, compassion, and care, nor does he only promise to provide relief for people in situations of poverty and need. He also offers relief for the strong and the healthy with respect to their fear for their beloved ones should they themselves die or become in other ways helpless in the future. In addition, he comforts their souls at least to some degree and recursively wins their loyalty and trust. All this contributes to generating a climate of freedom, solidarity, and harmony. Thus the establishment of freedom through the protection of the orphans and widows does not simply mean feeding the poor and the hungry so that they and their environments remain somehow satisfied and silent. Rather, the establishment of freedom happens when a good spirit—a spirit of trust and hope, a spirit of philanthropy and care—is evoked and promoted. Memories and imaginations, attitudes and practices are shaped by the example of the emperor.

A network of memories, imaginations, attitudes, and practices constitutes a spirit and is recursively sustained and animated by this spirit. Impressed by Aristotelian and related thought and metaphysics, Western cultures associated spirit with self-referential reflexivity and rationality. Other traditions of thought regarded the spirit just as a numinous, vague, and fleeting power. The interconnection of reliable care for the helpless and the weak and the generation of societal freedom challenges us to focus on another type of spirit, a spirit which was and has been an enormous shaping power in Mesopotamian and Western religion, culture, ethos, and history.

This spirit cannot adequately be grasped by bipolar relations, be they simple notions of reflexivity or interpersonal communication. It is very well expressed by the biblical notion of the "outpouring of the Spirit," namely the beneficial constitution of a polyphonic constellation, of a network of interdependent, mutually strengthening relations.[2] This impressive spiritual power was already grasped and expressed in important ancient Mesopotamian law codes.

In the laws of Ur-Nammu, king of Ur, the oldest existing law code from around 2100 BCE, the special protection of orphans, widows, and the poor is already proclaimed in the prologue.[3] The Codex Hammurabi, the emblem of Mesopotamian civilization, established in the eighteenth century BCE, is the most important legal compendium of the Ancient Near East, even of antiquity in general. The prologue says that Prince Hammurabi, "who feared God," is elected "to bring about the rule of righteousness in the land . . . so that the strong should not harm the weak." And the epilogue repeats that this law code is put on the memorial stone so "that the strong might not injure the weak, in order to protect the widows and orphans."[4]

Protecting the Weak and the Mercy Laws

The topic of the protection of the weak and of the widows and orphans in particular becomes a most important and normatively shaping topic in the biblical traditions, the holy scriptures of both Judaism and Christianity. God "executes justice for the fatherless and the widow" (Deut 10:18)[5] and expects similar attitudes, also to be adopted toward strangers, from his people; this is a constant refrain throughout both the Hebrew scriptures and the New Testament (see, e.g., Deut 14:29; 16:11, 14; 24:19-20; 26:12-13; Ps 68:6; 146:9; Isa 1:17; 9:16; Jer 7:6; 49:11; Zech 7:10; Sir 4:10; 1 Tim 5:3; Jas 1:27; etc.). This topic is not only essential for the biblical law traditions, but also for the central commandment to love one another. I propose to speak of the "mercy code of the biblical law" and to acknowledge the tremendous political, moral, and religious power of the connection between justice and mercy. I also propose to define mercy as "the free, creative self-withdrawal in favor of [another person] or in favor of others."[6]

Many people assume that mercy is a natural tendency of life. This, however, is highly questionable, at least without further strong qualifications. For all natural life lives at the cost and expense of other life. Even if we are vegetarians, we have to destroy an enormous amount of natural life to sustain ourselves. As Alfred North Whitehead, mathematician, scientist, and philosopher, states, "life is robbery."[7] Mercy, however, is not just self-limitation in the midst of this natural predatory tendency of life to sustain itself at the expense of others. Mercy is a *creative, supporting, and freeing activity in favor of the frail, the weak, the poor, the person in need.*

The activity of mercy is essential for family life. No baby, no child could be raised without massive free and creative self-withdrawal in their favor. The solidarity between the generations is also expressed in mercy for the sick, the frail, the old, and the dying. In family life and in contexts of friendship, mercy is often blessed by love and then often turns into a *joyful,* free, and creative self-withdrawal in favor of others. The experience of receiving and giving mercy and love and the acknowledgment that we are all in need of mercy, at least in specific phases of our life, leads to a differentiated and subtle self-experience. Human beings are thus enabled to see themselves as weak and strong, as frail and healthy, as vulnerable and protected at the same time.[8]

The biblical traditions very often cultivate such a self-experience by using most impressive dualisms, rooted in paradigmatic historical experiences. One of the most famous dualism is the double identity of the Israelites, that is, to have been slaves in Egypt and to have become free persons who live in the blessed land. What is known as the *motive clause* of the Old Testament traditions argues for the practice of mercy with the poor and the stranger because "you" know how it feels to be a stranger and because "you" are grateful to God who has freed "you" from slavery in Egypt with mighty hand and outstretched arm.[9] Basic human experiences rooted in family life are thus moved into the broad social realm and gain moral, political, and even legal and religious importance and weight.

Mercy and the Law

The mercy laws in favor of widows and orphans, the poor and the weak (not only in one's own family and among close friends, but in one's whole social environment) gain an enormous normative shaping power. The normativity of the Law reaches beyond the capacity of conflict solution into the capacity of social transformation. This becomes particularly clear in what is known as the *slave laws*, which require the freeing of slaves, at least of Hebrew slaves, after six years of slavery: "When you buy a Hebrew slave, he shall serve six years, and in the seventh he shall go out free, for nothing" (Exod 21:2). This is a revolution in antiquity, a period in history in which all societies were self-evidently slaveholder societies.

The mercy code of the Law makes it clear that slaves are no longer just "speaking tools," but that they are potentially free human beings. The mercy code thus organizes processes of social transformation in the direction of enhanced freedom and toward a more harmonious society. The legal routinizing of almsgiving and tithing in favor of the poor and needy, especially widows and orphans, points in the same direction (Deut 14:28-29; 26:12-13). The laws of mercy become instruments for creative and freeing social transformation. Not only the king but society as a whole should participate in the cultivation of justice and mercy, thus enjoying and spreading a spirit of freedom.

The mercy laws do not only learn from family ethos, they recursively strengthen this ethos and the radiating power of family life and love. They also strengthen the legal culture and the religious symbolisms and practices. With respect to the juridical law, the laws of mercy both strengthen and challenge its competence. On the one hand, no case can fall outside the purview of the Law; no person, however weak, poor, and miserable can fall beyond the reach of the Law. On the other hand, the systematic orientation of the Law toward mercy and compassion demands the continual refinement of the legal culture and its progression toward humanization. In addition, the mercy code of the Law enables human societies to deal with a strange paradox that plagues all moral and legal evolution. Many human societies have the desire to improve the juridical law and to develop the quality of their moral matrices. However, how can this transformation be done without destroying the binding forces of law and morals, their capacity to provide normative "security of expectations"?[10] The mercy code of the Law allows for transformation of the Law and human morals without relativization. It allows for the balancing of normative stability and creative innovation.

Mercy Laws and Justice

Mercy laws finally connect the moral and legal attempts to strive for justice and to care for the weak with a creative religious orientation. In the religious perspective on the just and merciful God, the biblical traditions encourage the development of a subtle individual and communal identity. They also open broad historical horizons. Not only in the celebration in cultic contexts, the grateful memory of God's freeing and saving acts of mercy in the midst of God's people becomes nourished and sustained. Precious shared memories and expectations of liberation are established and extended over vast historical time spans.

Here again we can speak of the fact that a spirit is at work, a spirit which gives history direction and meaning. Educational, moral, legal, political, and religious mentalities, habits, and practices are connected and intertwined. In serving the common good in justice-, mercy-, love-, truth- and salvation-seeking communities, they mutually strengthen each other. This interconnection strengthens concrete moral, legal, educational, political, and religious orientations. It guides the human mind through phases of trial and error and even normative failure. As the history of God with his people reveals and teaches: the just and righteous God will deal with human beings in time spans that reach far beyond the imagination of human courts or of concrete individual and communal moral memory.

Again, we see a recursive strengthening of the religious, legal, and moral imagination and communication. The parental mercy, the care for justice, and love provide an understanding of the powers of the divine, of powers which can deal with the very sobering insight that natural life has to live at the expense of other life, that experiences of violence and death are sad factors of all natural existence.[11] Above all, enormous counterforces to this latter fact are discovered and set free that shape a mutually supportive and humane culture. Sensitivities for grave social distortions (the areas of sin, trespasses, temptations, and evil) and for moral refinement (the areas of love, forgiveness, and ennoblement in many forms) are cultivated, can become taught, and can shape many areas of individual and communal lives.

Not only the practice of justice, mercy, and love, but also its teaching—the moral, legal, and religious education—becomes essential for all of society and its culture. The cultivation of memories and expectations becomes part of the value system. Truth-, justice-, and salvation-seeking communities are established in many forms. Schooled work and wisdom and general education spread the insights gained into the normative and freeing powers of the law for the general public and on through future generations. Not only political, religious, and legal leaders, but in principle every person in a society should participate in cultivating the freeing normative moods and forms of behavior and action.

2. Working against the Evil Spirit of Hate and Unfreedom

In order to grasp the good spirit of love in all its glory and the evil spirit of hate in all its horror, it is advisable to consider not only the dramatic forms of love and hate but also their inconspicuous appearances. Although the bipolar romantic love, igniting joy and excitement between "an I and a Thou," is often seen as the exemplary form of love, at least in contemporary Western cultures, it covers only a small spectrum of the spirit and the reality of love. Similarly, sacrificial and kenotic love—a most important and moving topic in religious and morally edifying experiences and narratives—is only a boundary phenomenon in the vast realm of love. In family affairs, in parental relations, in good constellations among relatives and friends, what is known as covenantal love, a faithful love that goes "through thick and thin," is the dominant phenomenon.[12] Beyond that, cool and inconspicuous love in many forms of philanthropy and humanitarianism should be acknowledged and respected as a tremendous blessing for humankind. This is the general "love of the neighbor," a love of which Paul says: "Owe no one anything, except to love one another; for the one who loves another has fulfilled the law. . . . Love does no wrong to a neighbor; therefore love is the fulfilling of the law" (Rom 13:8, 10 NRSV).

The Spirit of Hate

In a similar way, we should look at the evil spirit of hate. By "hate" we should not only think of aggressive anger and acts of violence, persecution, curses, and attacks. The field of meaning of "hate," particularly in the biblical languages, is significantly broader than these extreme examples. It includes the broader sense of "not being able to love" and "not wanting to love." And here again, we should not just think about romantic, covenantal, and kenotic forms of love. Hate therefore does not just mean animosity, loathing, bitterness, and aggression, but also neglect, underestimation, or lack of willingness to endure the other person, persons, or groups. Hate stands for finding someone or others unpleasant, having little interest in or care for someone, not wanting anything to do with someone, not being able to suffer someone, and not liking others.[13] The famous Heidelberg Catechism[14] displays a strong sensitivity to the broad field of the meaning of "hate." It expresses the human "misery" in the words of the answer to Question 5: that I am unable to keep the twin commands to love God and my neighbor. In a stifling way, the Catechism states, "I have a natural tendency to hate God and my neighbor." This sounds strange and totally unconvincing if we do not see the broad spectrum of hot and cool forms of hate. For the Heidelberg Catechism, hate includes, for example, "being silent bystanders" in the discussion of blasphemy (Q. 99). When discussing love for our neighbor, the catechism urges its readers to promote their neighbor's honor (Q. 112) and calls on us "to do good even to our enemies" (Q. 107).

It will be important to develop "short sharp views" on the roots of the barbarisms of hate in many parts of the world in order not only to develop a counternarrative confronting religious, political, and moral violence, but also to show that a counternarrative and a healthy counternormativity and counterpraxis have been present in our history and have been operative in many beneficial and blessing ways over millennia: the culture of mercy, love, and humane justice—its documents and its many experiences and achievements in individual lives and in social and institutionalized forms. But this does not spare us from asking the pressing question: How can we deal with the most extreme forms of hate that have caused so much suffering in our contemporary environments?

And how can we deal with instrumentalized religious pretensions that support the exercise of moral, political, and physical violence?

Letting Go of Hate

In his most impressive book *Not in God's Name: Confronting Religious Violence*,[15] Rabbi Jonathan Sacks offers a chapter on "Letting Go of Hate."[16] He brilliantly shows that hate is an expression of enslavement, even of self-enslavement. "To be free, you have to let go of hate."[17] He points out that the famous motive clause—"Love the stranger for you yourselves were strangers in Egypt" (Deut 10:19)—and the "very counter-intuitive command"—"Do not hate an Egyptian, because you were a stranger in his land" (Deut 23:7)—are messages and commands that are intended to promote freedom in the minds of the Israelites, in their memories, their imaginations, and their executed social actions.

Rabbi Sacks underlines this powerful message in reports about encounters with Holocaust survivors.[18] But he also signals how hard it can be to overcome inclinations to hate and to seek blame and revenge and even violent retaliation. An important religious contribution in these processes is the "affirmation of God's vengeance," the affirmation that "the belief that God will avenge wrongs spares human beings from having to do so."[19] He also sees the potentials of monotheism to encourage people to move out of a "blame culture into a penitential culture,"[20] to resist and counter in nonviolent ways, and, if possible, to flee and escape "conditions of oppression, corruption, economic stagnation and educational underachievement,"[21] which bind suffering peoples in the barbaric cycles of hate and self-hate. The darkest expression of this state of mind is the suicidal murdering of innocent people.

In my view, the great wisdom of Rabbi Sacks' book is the message that only examples of merciful caring and forgiving, invitations and encouragements to move out of enslaving and self-enslaving cycles of blaming, hate, and violence and to search for and practice individual and communal freedom will protect us from religiously motivated moral, political, and physical violence.[22] This does not only require a passion for freedom and peace. It will be quite easy to win most people for abstract moral, political, and religious declarations: "I am and we all are for freedom and peace—individually and among all humankind." If we want to exorcise the evil spirit of hate and unfreedom, it will be most important to control, to restrict, and to try to avoid all strategies of blaming and shaming. Our moral communication in all areas of life needs our attention and care.[23]

Moral Communication and Education

All moral communication (and it starts with the education of infants) communicates respect; that is, it gives or withdraws respect, promises respect or threatens to withdraw it. ("If you do this or that, mom will be happy! If you don't do this, grandpa will be sad.") Respect in moral communication comes in many forms, reaching from a sharp short view to enthusiastic admiration. All interpersonal relations, small or large, are—latently or overtly—morally coded and loaded. Since moral communication is unavoidable in interpersonal relations, and since it steers human action and behavior, it usually is associated with the predicate "good." Sadly, reality presents a different picture. It depends very much on the governing values, on the guiding spirit, whether the moral communication directs human beings toward the good or the evil. All too often we see the development of robber morals, which spread and reinforce the evil spirit of hate.

To counter the spirit of hate, to exorcise it without entering the vicious cycles of shaming and blaming, we need gigantic educational enterprises. They have to start in family life and have to continue in early childhood and in school education. Civil societal, political, and religious communication, and above all mass media communication, have to develop the responsibility to identify, to name, and to purge mentalities and utterances of hate in the different spheres of individual and communal life. It will be crucial to develop processes of gaining political loyalty and media resonance without seeking support through the rhetoric of shaming, blaming, and hating. Even the areas of law and religion, not to mention the defense systems, will have to control inclinations to use or at least to tolerate strategies of hate in order to specify and justify their tasks. It will be important to acknowledge that as a rule all reactive activities which try to deal with the evil spirit of hate have a very limited capacity. Rather, it is the proactive spirit of love that creates a climate of freedom and peace in which the energies of hate can vanish and dry out.

Conclusion

The project of "confronting religious violence with a counternarrative" cannot just mean telling impressive stories of nonviolent reactions to violent behavior in the religious orbit and beyond. Neither will it suffice to invest such stories in more or less empathetic moral appeals to specific individuals, groups, or general publics. And even joyful talk about the moral and political overcoming of religious violence and stories of forgiving and healing cannot be strong enough for a helpful confrontation of religious violence, because the success stories of the past may just generate melancholy and skepticism in present times.

This contribution tries to identify powerful spirits of love and hate that have permeated human history and have shaped not only impressive narratives and normative codifications, but also moral, political, educational, and religious practices. It reflects on the inner logics of the connection of justice and mercy with the creation of a climate of social harmony, freedom, and peace. It sees examples of such logics and normative binding powers and witnesses to them in Mesopotamia as early as 2400 BCE, and it follows further instances through the biblical law traditions up to attempts in modern and late modern societies to regain and preserve a humane ethos.

Although rooted in the family ethos of love and care, the spirit of justice, mercy, love, and freedom generates educational, moral, legal, political, and religious mentalities, habits, and practices which are connected and intertwined and which strengthen each other. The contribution argues that it will be most important not to focus exclusively on dramatic appearances and forms of love and hate, but to center as well on their inconspicuous, "cool" appearances. In order to identify and then to counter the evil spirits of hate, one should not only think of aggressive anger and acts of violence, persecution, and attack. As shocking as the darkest barbaric cycles of hate and self-hate in the suicidal murdering of innocent people are—a convincing counter development should give them nothing but a short sharp view. Moral, political, and religious communication and education should concentrate on the many cool forms of hate grasped in the expressions "neglect, underestimation or lack of willingness to endure the other person, persons or groups . . . finding someone or others unpleasant, having little interest in or care for someone, not wanting anything to do with someone, not liking others."[24] And it should teach appreciation, support, and even admiration for the many cool forms of love that have permeated moral, legal, educational, political, and religious thoughts, habits, and practices under the guidance of the spirit of justice, mercy, love, and freedom.

12

BETWEEN URGENCY AND UNDERSTANDING
Practical Imperatives in Theological Education

WILLIAM STORRAR

In this chapter, I wish to consider the "practical imperatives in theological education . . . that stem from a commitment to using theology to combat religiously motivated violence."[1] I shall do so by drawing on the educational insights gained by the Center of Theological Inquiry (CTI) in Princeton, New Jersey, a research institute that is committed to theology as an interreligious and interdisciplinary field of inquiry on global concerns, including religious violence. While I shall quote extensively from scholars engaged in our program to illustrate these insights, let me begin with a personal story.

When I accepted an invitation to become director of the CTI, I had to apply for a work visa as a UK citizen in the United States. I duly made an appointment with a visa lawyer and found myself sitting in the reception lobby of his law firm. When the time came for our meeting, the receptionist called through to the lawyer and announced, "Dr. Storrar from the Center for Theological Injury." The receptionist spoke truer than she knew. We need centers of theological inquiry in the world because we live in a world of theological injury: injury done to God's creation; injury done to humanity in God's image; and above all, injuries perpetrated in God's name. In this volume, we are considering one contemporary form of theological injury, "the phenomenon of religious extremism and violence committed in God's name."[2] What can institutions like CTI do to prevent this particular injury?

205

1. The Work of CTI

As an independent research institute with no permanent faculty or specialization in any one field, CTI fosters wide-ranging work that is carried out and carried forward by visiting scholars from across disciplines, religions, and nations, whom we gather together in resident seminars at the Center in Princeton. As a result, our research conversation is continually being renewed and replicated by the higher education institutions around the world from which our seminar members come and to which they return. For this reason, our work may be of wider relevance in considering the fundamental question for theological education in this volume: how can our educational institutions help to create a *counternarrative* on religiously motivated violence in dialogue with the sciences and humanities? In our experience, we can best do so by creating a *counterculture* for interreligious scholarship.

Five Practical Imperatives

CTI has convened three recent theological research projects that have considered the problem of religion and violence from the different perspectives of scriptural interpretation in the Abrahamic traditions, Islamic law and international human rights law, and the scientific study of cooperation and prosociality in human nature and moral behavior.[3] That research experience has led us to identify five practical imperatives in theological education to combat religiously motivated violence. We have seen the importance of hospitality, honesty, humility, and hope in theological inquiry across religious and disciplinary boundaries. Even more importantly, we have learned of the need to integrate these four practical imperatives in a dialogical approach to interreligious theological inquiry (which I will refer to, below, as "the dignity of dialogue," the fifth practical imperative). It is an approach which we are seeking to put into practice in running a CTI project on religion and violence in 2018–2019.

Moral Urgency and Theological Understanding

Before considering each of these five practical imperatives in theological education to combat religiously motivated violence, we should note that educational institutions face a distinctive dilemma in their work on such problems. The dilemma has been well named by CTI's senior fellow in theology, Robin Lovin. It is the tension between a sense of moral urgency to resolve the questions we study and the need for slow, patient scholarly work to understand them. Having already co-led an inquiry at the Center on Christian theology and international law with the philosopher Jeremy Waldron, Lovin was invited to serve as the rapporteur at a meeting of scholars in Islamic law and international human rights law which the Center convened in Princeton. We did so on behalf of an initiative of the International Bar Association and the Salzburg Global Seminar to find common ground between these two fields of law. Reflecting on that experience, Lovin wrote in the subsequent published volume,

> The search for common ground has an urgency in the law. Advocates for the oppressed and dispossessed know that until they can find a shared vocabulary for justice with which to make their appeal, they are unlikely to gain ground in the courts or among the public, and the abuses they are trying to combat will continue . . . When the authors met [at CTI] to discuss the essays which have been collected in this volume, however, they began to see that the search for common ground had become perhaps a little too urgent. The importance of justice and peace was obvious enough but it was not clear that anyone understands international human rights law or Islamic law well enough to do more than build superficial connections between them . . . As an observer at the authors' workshop at the Center of Theological Inquiry, I took a particular interest in *the tension between moral urgency and theoretical understanding*, because it had arisen in [the Center's] discussions of Christian theology and international law. Like those concerned about the relations between Islamic law and international law, theologians and lawyers were initially drawn to the topic by an urgent question [of] religious responses to torture . . . Some of the participants in these discussions, however, recognized a need for further exploration of the relationship between Christian moral traditions and the principles of international law. An interreligious approach to the legal issues surrounding imprisonment and interrogation was clearly urgent, but it raised the question whether the Christian scholars understood their own tradition well enough to think through its application to these questions and the further implications for religious understandings of human rights.[4]

Lovin has named a key educational insight and operational axiom for our work of fostering interreligious scholarship at CTI: we are always caught in the tension between moral urgency and theoretical understanding in addressing the global concerns that are the focus of our educational mission. Aryeh Cohen, one of the Jewish scholars in our CTI research project on interpreting scriptural texts in the three Abrahamic traditions, has described his own resolution of this tension in a moving personal reflection:

> As I write, the Middle East is once again in flames. War is the massive deployment of uncontrolled violence for short-term goals. It is essentially its own defeat. Scriptural reasoning in an atmosphere of trust, as a counterpoint, is a minute and controlled deployment of intellectual and spiritual tools for a long-term goal of friendship. Its existence is a first step toward the establishment of that world which might mirror the kingdom of God.[5]

Mindful of the moral urgency of responding to the latest abhorrent act of "altruistic evil in God's name," theological scholarship must remain steadfastly committed to the longer-term work of conducting basic research and cultivating interreligious scholarship, without losing its sensitivity to the human suffering caused by religious extremism.[6] The following five practical imperatives in theological education to combat religious violence must therefore be seen as ways of handling this inherent tension between urgency and understanding in a vocationally appropriate manner—theological inquiry as a counterpoint to theological injury.

2. Theological Education as Hospitality: A Model for Inter-Abrahamic Peace

How, then, can scholars in the Abrahamic traditions confront religious violence with a counternarrative? This was the task that a group of sixteen Muslim, Jewish, and Christian scholars set itself in a three-year CTI project to answer one question: "Do our three scriptures unite or divide us?" Under the coleadership of the Jewish scholar Peter Ochs and the Christian theologian William Stacy Johnson, this CTI research group addressed this question by celebrating each of the three Abrahamic traditions and examining their capacity for mutually enriching dialogue through the study of medieval commentaries on the Hebrew Bible, Qur'an, and New Testament, respectively. In part, this was the group's way of retrieving the legacy of the profound religious dialogues pioneered in Muslim Spain and late medieval France and Italy, restoring them to their honored if regrettably unusual place in the counternarrative to religiously motived violence in the Abrahamic traditions.

At the outset, the group acknowledged that finding such hospitable spaces for productive dialogue was not so simple in the contemporary world because of the tensions among the three communities:

> We are living in a time of crisis. In many parts of the world, Jews, Christians, and Muslims dwell in profound tension with one another. As we know, these tensions sometimes break out into violence. Such hostilities are never purely religious in origin. . . . Nevertheless, the power of religion may

add volatile fuel to already smouldering embers. As British rabbi Jonathan Sacks has wisely noted, religion "is a fire—and like fire, it warms but it also burns. . . . Religious leaders must take responsibility for being 'guardians of the flame.'"[7]

My concern here is with the educational context that fostered the group's fruitful dialogue across the three Abrahamic traditions rather with than their study of the medieval commentaries on the three scriptures. In this inquiry, CTI learned the practical imperative of hospitality in ensuring that religion warms the cause of peace rather than causing fourth-degree burns to the body politic. The understanding of hospitality in theological education developed by the group is a rich and nuanced one.

Interpretative Hospitality

First, it means *interpretative hospitality*, adopting a term used by the scriptural reasoning movement among Jewish, Muslim, and Christian scholars to describe their methods:

> Participants from all three religious traditions read, struggle over, challenge, and interpret texts from their own and the others' traditions with a sense of openness and mutuality. There may arise argument, to be sure—debate, discussion, questioning—but this takes place in a spirit of mutual respect and of wonder—and, throughout, of love for God's word as embodied in our respective scriptures.[8]

Such interpretative hospitality is not a comfortable and comforting practice. As Muslim scholar Mehdi Aminrazavi described his experience of such scriptural reasoning across traditions at CTI, it can be "a spiritual odyssey in the intellectual wilderness," at least for a while:

> It was not another ecumenical and interreligious dialogue for the sake of peace, love, and universal brotherhood. It was a cathartic process, exploring the complex interaction between unity and multiplicity of the Abrahamic traditions, seeing oneself through others and how perceived commonalities might well be the sources of divergence.[9]

And yet the practice of interpretative hospitality can also offer models for addressing the common problems of theological scholarship across Abrahamic traditions and lead to a deeper understanding of one's own tradition. Maria Massi Dakake, for example, has written about the challenge of interpreting the Qur'an in light of modern concerns. She described the relevant insights she gained from her Jewish colleague

Elizabeth Alexander's work on a talmudic narrative about Abraham and the sacrifice of Isaac: "Joining our group discussions of her work, I was impressed by her ability to make the traditional sources respond to the modern critics, addressing the very same texts that challenge modern readers."[10] Dakake also found that the Abraham in the Torah, Talmud, and New Testament helped her rediscover important aspects of the Qur'anic Abraham. Significantly, she describes such group work as participation in a "fellowship," which leads us to a further understanding of hospitality that we gained from this interreligious inquiry.

Friendship across Traditions

The practical imperative of hospitality in theological education is secondly an invitation to friendship across the Abrahamic traditions and not just to dialogue. As the coleaders of this CTI project, Jewish scholar Peter Ochs and Christian theologian Stacy Johnson, have put it:

> The importance of friendship cannot be overemphasized. Participants discovered ways in which the scriptural traditions called them to fellowship as a dimension of study itself. They were instructed, for example, by the rabbinic tradition of *chevruta*, or "fellowships of study," in which the scripture and commentary texts were discussed back-and-forth by study partners.[11]

The friendship of these study partners was lightened by the joy they found in the texts they read together, and in each other's company, but never at the expense of their shared sense of moral responsibility for the crisis of conflict among their three traditions. As the director of CTI who hosted the final year of their inquiry, I had the privilege of witnessing this dual dimension of their hospitality:

> Joy bubbled up in study and also around it. The participants' study was often punctuated with laughter, and in the evenings after study, they were wont to play; there was guitar playing and song and word games and more laughter. Throughout, however, they were also driven by the sense of crisis that brought them together; and they were instructed by each scripture's traditions about how to respond to the crisis.[12]

Accentuation of Distinctiveness in Dialogue

Third, we learned from this inquiry that hospitality in theological education means the accentuation and not the diminution of the distinctive content of each Abrahamic tradition:

> The participants agreed that scriptural reasoning is dialogue *from out of* the three scriptural traditions, rather than any amalgam. The group's model of peace is dialogue among different voices and traditions, not a loss of individual voice. Its model of scholarship is not to replace the many with one, but to provide a context of sustained fellowship within which the many may be transformed from mere multiplicity to many-in-relationship.[13]

This CTI project hoped that its work would offer "another model for inter-Abrahamic peace," beyond mere agreement or shared declarations of belief. It is a hospitable model of "shared space on which Jews, Muslims, and Christians inspired by the word of God may share, discuss, and debate their inspirations in the spirit of fellowship and love that each sacred text demands."[14] It leads us to see shared space as a practical imperative in theological education for peacemaking among the Abrahamic traditions. Ochs and Johnson conclude their overview of the CTI project on that note:

> In sum, the most significant findings of the authors' three years of fellowship are that the three scriptures, indeed, offer resources for peace as well as occasions for potential conflict and that to examine the sources of peace is at the same time to join the practices of peace these sources inspire. Within the realm of scriptural scholarship, this is the practice of face-to-face study and fellowship.[15]

The practical imperative that should have priority in theological education is the need to set up and sustain hospitable spaces for face-to-face study and fellowship among scholars in the Abrahamic traditions. CTI is only one such space in the academy, around the world, and over the centuries. Such spaces demonstrate the importance of the four other practical imperatives we have discerned at CTI.

3. Theology Education as Honesty:
Clearing Ground in One's Own Backyard

A few months before the Arab Spring, the International Bar Association and the Salzburg Global Seminar convened a weeklong seminar in Salzburg to explore the potential for common ground between Islamic law and international law on human rights. The papers presented at that timely seminar for lawyers, judges, and human rights activists from the Muslim majority world had been prepared in the earlier authors' workshop for legal scholars in Islamic law and international law to which I have referred, hosted by the CTI in partnership with the International Bar Association and the Salzburg Global Seminar. Once again, the

practical importance of providing hospitable space for face-to-face study
and fellowship was affirmed by the participants. As the legal scholar
Anver Emon commented in his introduction to the volume of essays
published as the fruit of the workshop and Salzburg seminar:

> The Center of Theological Inquiry . . . sponsored a workshop in May 2010
> where the authors . . . found a unique space that allowed them to explore
> important topics and draw upon resources that spanned reason and faith,
> theology and philosophy, law and morality.[16]

As with the scriptural reasoning inquiry, the work of this group at
CTI was transformed through fellowship; in this case, the shared transcendence of a classical music performance before the shared pleasure
of a halal meal, after an intensive day of sometimes tense, face-to-face
discussions. But CTI provided more than a hospitable space for this
pioneering scholarly exchange between the two legal systems on the
contested question of Islam and human rights. As we noted earlier,
Robin Lovin, CTI's senior fellow in theology, acted as a rapporteur to
the group. At a critical juncture on the third day of their conversations,
he suggested that the impasse they had reached could be overcome by
reframing their dialogue as an exercise in ground clearing rather than
in seeking common ground. Neither Islamic law nor international law
offered uncontested perspectives on human rights within their own field
of legal inquiry, far less in an exchange with one another. Before any
fruitful exchange could happen, each legal system had to be honest about
the disagreements in its own backyard. In the published proceedings
of the workshop and global seminar, Lovin noted:

> By clearing ground, they create a space that Islamic law and international
> law can both occupy, though neither of them holds the territory on their
> own terms. The common ground is not a space where all questions have
> been settled. The common ground is where both systems of law continue
> to pose questions to one another, but each understands the other better
> and understands itself differently because of the ground clearing that has
> taken place.[17]

Given the globalization of commerce and culture, Lovin concluded,
"The kind of ground clearing undertaken here may show the best way
under those circumstances to create common ground on which an
ongoing discussion can be sustained."[18] The importance of this preliminary ground-clearing exercise in each tradition of thought, conducted
openly and frankly in the company of the others in the dialogue, is
the second practical imperative that CTI has learned as an educational

institution in countering the hegemonic narrative of religious violence. Such ground clearing is an exercise in intellectual honesty by all the parties in the dialogue and scholarly exchange. In an environment of mutual trust, scholars in different disciplines and religions can acknowledge and explain the internal debates and disagreements in their own tradition as the essential prolegomena to better mutual understanding across disciplinary and religious traditions. In theological education, as in life, honesty pays. How much more important, then, for scholars to acknowledge the internal debates within their own religious traditions over the moral and hermeneutical challenge of violence in each of their scriptures and histories. That ground must be cleared as a practical imperative before common ground can be found and shared.

4. Theology Education as Humility . . . and Hope: The Interdisciplinary Virtues

Humility and hope are the third and fourth practical imperatives in theological education to counter religious violence, based on our experience. In three interdisciplinary inquiries funded by the John Templeton Foundation, CTI considered what theology and theologians had to learn from dialogue with scientists and legal scholars on questions of human nature, moral identity, and religious freedom. In the subsequent coauthored volume by theologians, scientists, and legal scholars in these inquiries, the habits of mind that make for fruitful inquiry across disciplinary boundaries were stressed: "We might call these habits of mind 'interdisciplinary virtues.' Like the virtues that Aristotle first catalogued for us, these habits are both essential to success in the activity to which they relate and cultivated by participation in it."[19]

This CTI research project identified two interdisciplinary virtues which are important in any theological inquiry that acknowledges the tension between moral urgency and theoretical understanding: humility and hope.

Humility

The habit of humility disposes theologians to acknowledge the limits of their own understanding and the value of collaboration with other disciplines to expand their knowledge and identify some of their errors. In particular, the practical imperative of humility in interdisciplinary or interreligious inquiry requires us to respect the assumptions of our colleagues in another discipline or religious tradition as our starting point, rather than our own:

In practice, humility in interdisciplinary inquiry means that we engage the prevailing assumptions of other disciplines as the starting point for discussion. A theology that proclaims the abundance of God's grace may nevertheless take the economists' assumption of scarcity as a starting point for discussion, and a theology that speaks of God's purposes in creation may, in search of understanding, engage a scientific materialism that traces all outcomes to prior physical causes.[20]

In CTI's inquiry on evolution and human nature, for example, the theologians of human nature in the group were challenged by their colleagues in evolutionary anthropology, biology, and psychology to take seriously the growing body of evidence for the centrality of cooperation and prosociality in human evolution, challenging the dominant assumption about the evolutionary survival of the fittest. The scientists in the inquiry had to set out on an even more demanding intellectual journey to enter the unknown territory of theology and take its assumptions about human nature into account, often for the first time. This experience is well described by Celia Deane-Drummond, one of the senior fellows in this inquiry, who describes what she witnessed at CTI with "the emergence of a new kind of dynamic among those who would not, habitually speaking at least, have come into contact with one another. For example, in our group, at the start of the year, some of the scientists present did not really know what theology meant and had never encountered theologians."[21] How much more important is this practical imperative of humility in interreligious dialogue, starting with the assumptions of another religious tradition with which one may not be familiar or may even be encountering for the first time.

Hope

With the related interdisciplinary virtue of hope, the Center found a way of combining a sense of moral urgency with its work of theoretical understanding across disciplinary boundaries:

> Part of the way that we engage people from other disciplines is by emphasizing the moral significance of the questions we can discuss with them. People will be willing to risk the loss of methodological rigor and even have their basic assumptions challenged if they think it will make a difference to important issues of justice and human dignity. Regardless of their own faith or skepticism, people measure such choices by what they hope for. . . . As a practical matter . . . the engagement of theology with other disciplines favors those who hope.[22]

Transposing these virtues from interdisciplinary to interreligious scholarship, they become practical imperatives in the work of theological education on our problem: recognizing the moral significance of combating religious violence and the need to learn from one another's assumptions in creating a counternarrative. Hospitable spaces for honest exchange in any field cultivate these habits of humility and hope.

5. The Dignity of Dialogue: Cultivating a Counterculture

As CTI convenes its resident seminars on religion and violence during the 2018–2019 academic year, I am conscious that we are seeking to create an educational counterculture, one which scholars in the Abrahamic traditions, other religions, and the wider academy will find hospitable and safe for face-to-face study and fellowship. That is our hope, and we hold it with an acute sense of institutional humility at our limitations for the task and need to learn from those who have given much more thought to the problem. However, we shall be welcoming the scholars selected for this inquiry into a research institution with forty years of experience in convening conversations across boundaries. In closing, therefore, I wish to reflect on what we have learned about the fifth practical imperative in our work of theological education that stems from our commitment to using theology to combat religiously motivated violence: the dignity of dialogue, echoing another resonant phrase of Jonathan Sacks.[23]

Integrity in Dialogue

Deane-Drummond, reflecting on the experience of coleading an interdisciplinary inquiry at CTI, stresses the importance of maintaining one's disciplinary integrity while practicing what she calls the art of dialogue:

> This method required a patience and intellectual generosity that presupposes those entering it will have a sense of ignorance of the field of the other in the dialogue, but at the same time, a willingness and openness to learn. Raynhout puts it well when he claims that "sometimes we find ourselves talking about what we assume is the same thing only to discover that we are talking past one another because we actually mean different things." Hence, this opens up a new kind of methodological approach that is the true *art* of what I prefer to call transdisciplinarity; by which I mean paying close attention to the other discipline(s) in a way that has substantial and mutual impact, but at the same time retaining a clear sense of disciplinary integrity. What that integrity might mean is, of course, contested, but each of us operates within what could be termed a "comfort zone," and the

challenge is how far to move away from that while respecting limits. That is why I prefer to call this process an art; there is an aesthetic judgement here that is much harder to delineate compared with setting specific rules for conduct, and will depend on the particular group in question.[24]

Deane-Drummond's account of disciplinary integrity in the art of transdisciplinarity captures the key characteristics of the dialogue across disciplines and denominations at CTI. Inviting scholars who display patience and intellectual generosity to participate in conversation with colleagues in other fields or faiths is a sine qua non in our work. They acknowledge that they have much to learn about the other discipline or religion and are willing to make the effort to do so. It is a sign of effort rather than a failure of communication when the dialogue partners acknowledge that a shared term does not mean the same thing for everyone in the conversation. This is a healthy sign that participants are wrestling with the tension between allowing one's own thinking and very self to be challenged and maintaining the integrity of one's own deepest convictions. The judgment on how far to let the tension pull in one or other direction is an aesthetic one, according to Deane-Drummond. She notes:

> The term *art* is relevant in another sense, in that what emerges in mutual understanding is something that is rather closer to the truth as a result of the encounter, premised on the classical connection between goodness, beauty, and truth. Those taking part in this process are therefore not just changed in the way they think, but also, to some extent at least, changed inwardly as well.[25]

Generous Respect

All these characteristics of the art of dialogue have been borne out in the interreligious dialogues that CTI has convened to challenge the narrative of religiously motivated violence. One of the most profound moments of intellectual generosity and aesthetic judgment that I have witnessed in such conversations was during our authors' workshop on Islamic law and international human rights law. Among the invited participants was a lecturer in human rights at an official government university in a Muslim-majority country in the Near East, who was not able to acquire a visa for the United States to attend the workshop in person. We arranged for him to present his paper by telephone conference call. Just before the call was due to start, another workshop participant very intentionally called her colleagues around our table to attention. She reminded them of how intrepid and even dangerous it was for the lecturer to make his contribution to our dialogue on human rights in these circumstances, with a high likelihood that his every word was being monitored in his home country. They should therefore be sensitive to his situation and respectful of his views in responding to the paper. Who was showing this exceptional level of empathy for an absent and unknown dialogue partner? None other than a legal scholar who was herself a forced political exile from the same country and regime, with every reason to resent the views of one of its academic spokespersons. She was practicing the dignity of dialogue: not abandoning her own secular convictions about human rights but reaching out to understand the assumptions of someone who was seeking to reconcile those same rights with a particular reading of his religious tradition.

Conclusion

The philosopher Iris Marion Young exhorts us to bear in mind that, when speaking in public, we should always do so as if third parties are listening, asking ourselves how they will hear, interpret, and feel what we say: as inclusionary or exclusionary of them. In the context of interreligious dialogue in theological education, what we might call a fourth public audience for theology (to use David Tracy's analysis),[26] we should always ask ourselves how the exposition of our own beliefs, texts, values, and practices will be heard by fellow scholars in other religions: as violent and threatening or honest and irenic. In convening resident seminars on religion and violence at CTI, we are consciously seeking to implement these five practical imperatives of hospitality and honesty, humility and hope, and the dignity of dialogue in our advanced program of theological education. We have been enormously helped in our endeavor to balance moral urgency and scholarly understanding by the honest ground-clearing exercise of Jonathan Sacks on behalf of all the Abrahamic faiths in his seminal study of religion and violence, *Not in God's Name*; and, as ever, by the hospitality of the John Templeton Foundation to interdisciplinary and interreligious theological inquiry.

CONCLUDING REFLECTIONS

Jonathan Sacks

Listening to the multiplicity and variety of voices in this volume, one can sometimes feel overwhelmed by the sheer complexity of the forces operating in the phenomena of religiously motivated violence and terror. Is religion itself dividing the world into believers and infidels? Are sacred texts to blame, with their call to holy war? Or does violence always have other causes, psychological, political, economic, or even—as Eliza Griswold suggests in her essay—climate change and the movement of populations it brings about?

The truth is that, often, all or most of these factors are involved. After all, for much of the time, people of different faiths have learned to live peaceably together. It is only when circumstances change, the prevailing order is challenged, and people feel threatened and destabilized that they turn to the available *maps of meaning* to make sense of what is happening, often imposing dangerous simplicity on history's complexity. Those maps can be secular, as they were in the nineteenth and early twentieth centuries—nationalism, racism, or Marxism—or they can be religious, as they often are today.

It is not religion as such that leads to violence. That is embedded as a permanent possibility within human nature itself. But when it is involved and used as a vindication of violence, then we cannot ignore or deny that fact, saying instead that religion is a force for peace. Sometimes it is, but sometimes it is not, and we must be honest enough to admit that when it is not, it is part of the problem. That is what several of these essays have been about.

But only part: hence the other essays, several of the most powerful of which came from people in the field as observers, analysts, or as individuals involved in conflict resolution. It was this variety of perspectives that made our encounter so rich and enlarging. Often, when all the speakers represent a single discipline, you can feel that a problem is intractable because you are conscious of the factors not being addressed. That was not the case in our gathering. The very fact that we were able to communicate across so many disciplines was itself a signal of hope.

1. Hope

Indeed, *hope* was the first outcome I sensed in our deliberations. Hope is not optimism. Optimism is the belief that things will get better. Hope is the belief that if we work hard enough together, we can make things better. It needs no courage, only a certain naiveté, to be an optimist, but it often needs a great deal of courage to maintain hope. No one with a sense of history can, in this turbulent age, be an optimist; but no one with deep religious faith can be without hope. Hope itself can be a transformative force in long-standing conflicts where the participants are coming close to despair.

One of the gifts of Abrahamic monotheism to the world has been the story of the exodus, which, for many oppressed peoples, has become the West's metanarrative of hope. The faith it engenders has often led to real, historic change: the abolition of slavery, the civil rights movement, and so on. Hope is a signal of transcendence because it testifies to a conviction that history is not what Joseph Heller called it—"a trash bag of random coincidences torn open in a wind."[1] There is a larger providence at work. In Theodor Parker's words, made famous by Martin Luther King Jr., "The arc of the moral universe is long, but it bends toward justice."[2] Apocalyptic violence is often the fruit of despair, and its antidote is hope grounded in real political and existential possibility.

Violent religiosity can and often does give way to moderation and realism once true believers become fully aware of the failures of extremism and its desecrations. So it happened in Europe in the seventeenth century. So it happened in Al-Andalus in Islam. So it happened in rabbinic Judaism after the failures of several revolts against Rome in the first and second century.

2. Wisdom

The second feeling I sensed in the course of our deliberations was the presence of the ancient yet still compelling idea of *wisdom*. All the great faiths—indeed almost all civilizations—have wisdom literatures, represented in the Hebrew Bible, for example, by books such as Proverbs, Job, and Ecclesiastes. Wisdom traditions tend to be the most universal aspects of a culture. They are the points at which different systems of thought converge. Wisdom is integrative—and we tend to be short of it today because of the extreme specialization that exists in most Western universities. Knowledge in the twenty-first century is often divided and parceled out into nonintercommunicating silos, leaving us bereft of those who, in Matthew Arnold's phrase, "see life steadily and see it whole."[3] I felt that, in the coming together of so diverse a range of perspectives, we had each come closer to wisdom.

3. Education

Lastly, what linked us was our commitment to *education*. If we can think our way through conflict, guided by history, instructed by anthropology, informed by the experience of those who have seen conflict at first hand, and if we can teach what we have learned to future generations of leaders, religious, academic, or political, then we are not condemned endlessly to repeat the failings of the past. If there is one thing the Mosaic books insist on, it is the task of teaching our children: "Impress them [these teachings] upon your children. Recite them when you sit in your home and when you walk on the way, when you lie down and when you rise up" (Deut 6:7, NJPS with author modification). The nations of the world spend trillions of dollars on weapons and wars yet comparatively little on education for peace, coexistence, and conciliation. If Jewish history tells us anything, it is that a nation that sees education as a sacred duty and its highest priority can never be defeated. It will survive every tragedy, triumph over every setback, and stay creative and young. In the end the power of ideas is greater than the idea of power.

So, in a tense and troubled age, when religion is so often recruited as a justification for brutality and barbarism, whether by way of memory of a golden past that never was or in pursuit of a utopian future that never will be, a combination of hope, wisdom, and education is an altogether better alternative.

That will, however, depend on the ability of religious leaders and educators to confront the sources of violence in their own traditions and to show courage in rereading hard texts that lead to hatred of the religious other. To my mind, one of the most powerful examples of this is Moses' command, at the end of his life, "Do not despise [or 'abhor'] an Egyptian, for you were a stranger [or 'alien'] in his land" (Deut 23:8 [NJPS; 23:7 NRSV and other versions]). The Egyptians had oppressed and enslaved the Israelites. Yet Moses understood that if the Israelites continued to hate their former persecutors, they would still be slaves, in spirit if not in body. *To be free, you have to let go of hate.* That is the great truth exemplified in modern times by Martin Luther King Jr., Nelson Mandela, and the Holocaust survivors I have had the privilege to know.

We are the story we tell ourselves, and the next chapter in the human story must be more generous than those that came before it if it is not to be the last. Talking together, deliberating together, and sharing our hopes and fears, as a group of us did, courtesy of the John Templeton Foundation and King's College London on January 29–30, 2017, is the way forward. May we learn to honor the human other as the truest way of honoring the Divine Other, allowing his presence to guide us toward a world at peace.

NOTES

FOREWORD

1 Jonathan Sacks, "Faith in the Future: The Promise and Perils of Religion in the 21st Century," *Rabbisacks.org*, November 30, 2016, available at http://rabbisacks.org/faith-future-promise-perils-religion/.

2 Jonathan Sacks, *The Dignity of Difference: How to Avoid the Clash of Civilizations* (London: Continuum, 2002), 20–21.

3 Chapter 12, below.

4 Sir John Templeton, *Possibilities for Over One-Hundred Fold More Spiritual Information* (Philadelphia: Templeton Foundation Press, 2001), 28.

1 THE STORIES WE TELL

1 Jonathan Sacks, *Not in God's Name: Confronting Religious Violence* (London: Hodder & Stoughton, 2015).

2 See Alasdair MacIntyre, *After Virtue: A Study in Moral Theory* (London: Duckworth, 1981); Dan P. McAdams, *The Stories We Live By: Personal Myths and the Making of the Self* (New York: Guilford, 1997); and Jonathan Gottschall, *The Storytelling Animal: How Stories Make Us Human* (Boston: Mariner, 2013). For a theological perspective, see Stanley Hauerwas and L. Gregory Jones, eds., *Why Narrative? Readings in Narrative Theology* (Grand Rapids: Eerdmans, 1989).

3 MacIntyre, *After Virtue*, 201.

4 Jerome Bruner, *Actual Minds, Possible Worlds* (Cambridge, Mass.: Harvard University Press, 1986).

5 Among the key texts are Max Weber, *The Protestant Ethic and the Spirit of Capitalism* (New York: Charles Scribner's Sons, 1958); Peter L. Berger, *The Sacred Canopy: Elements of a Sociological Theory of Religion* (Garden City, N.Y.: Doubleday, 1967); Harvey Cox, *Secular City: Secularization and Urbanization in Theological Perspective* (New York: Macmillan, 1966); and Brian Wilson, *Religion in Secular Society* (London: Watts, 1966).

6 See Berger, *Sacred Canopy*.

7 Francis Fukuyama, *The End of History and the Last Man* (London: Free Press, 2006).

8 See, e.g., Perin Gurel, *The Limits of Westernization: A Cultural History of America in Turkey* (New York: Columbia University Press, 2017).

9 See Stephen Toulmin, *Cosmopolis: The Hidden Agenda of Modernity* (Chicago: University of Chicago Press, 1990).

10 See, e.g., Anthony Gottlieb's recent study, *The Dream of Enlightenment: The Rise of Modern Philosophy* (London: Allen Lane, 2016).

11 See Owen Chadwick, *The Secularization of the European Mind in the 19th Century* (Cambridge: Cambridge University Press, 1975); and Don Cupitt, *The Sea of Faith* (London: SCM Press, 1994).

12 Key texts here are Alasdair MacIntyre, *A Short History of Ethics* (London: Routledge & Kegan Paul, 1967); and idem, *After Virtue*.

13 Alexis de Tocqueville, *Democracy in America*, abridged and with an introduction by Thomas Bender (New York: Modern Library, 1981), 185.

14 Eric Kaufmann, *Shall the Religious Inherit the Earth? Demography and Politics in the Twenty-First Century* (London: Profile Books, 2010). See also Peter L. Berger, *The Desecularization of the World: Resurgent Religion and World Politics* (Washington, D.C.: Ethics and Public Policy Center, 2008); and John Micklethwait and Adrian Wooldridge, *God Is Back: How the Global Revival of Faith Is Changing the World* (New York: Penguin, 2010).

15 Dean M. Kelley, *Why Conservative Churches Are Growing: A Study in Sociology of Religion* (New York: Harper & Row, 1972).

16 Charles Liebman, "Orthodoxy in Modern Jewish Life," in *Dimensions of Orthodox Judaism*, ed. Reuven Bulka (New York: Ktav, 1983), 33–105.

17 The classic text here is Samuel Huntington, *The Clash of Civilizations and the Remaking of World Order* (New York: Simon & Schuster, 2011). See also Michael Ignatieff, *Blood and Belonging: Journeys into the New Nationalism* (London: Vintage, 1994).

18 Kenan Malik, *From Fatwa to Jihad: The Rushdie Affair and Its Consequences* (London: Atlantic Books, 2010).

19 Daniel Goleman, *Emotional Intelligence: Why It Can Matter More than IQ* (London: Bloomsbury, 1996).

20 See Huntington, *Clash of Civilizations*; Niall Ferguson, *Civilization: The West and the Rest* (London: Allen Lane, 2011); and Henry Kissinger, *World Order* (London: Allen Lane, 2014).

21 For a fascinating study of the transformation of meaning of the word "progress" and associated terms, see Raymond Williams, *Keywords* (London: Flamingo, 1981), esp. 243–45.

22 Immanuel Kant, *Toward Perpetual Peace*, in *Immanuel Kant: Practical Philosophy*, trans. and ed. Mary J. Gregor (Cambridge: Cambridge University Press, 1996), 311–52

23 Will Durant, *The Story of Civilization*, vol. 1 (New York: Simon & Schuster, 1935), 71.

24 Bertrand Russell, *History of Western Philosophy* (London: Allen & Unwin, 1962), 18–19.

25 Robert Bellah et al., *Habits of the Heart: Individualism and Commitment in American Life* (London: Hutchinson, 1988), 277.

26 See, e.g., Jonathan Sacks, *The Politics of Hope* (London: Vintage, 2000), 98–108.

27 See Jonathan Sacks, *The Dignity of Difference: How to Avoid the Clash of Civilizations* (London: Continuum, 2002), esp. chap. 3.

28 See Jonathan Glover, *Humanity: A Moral History of the Twentieth Century* (London: Jonathan Cape, 1999).

29 See, e.g., Will Storr, *Selfie: How We Became So Self-Obsessed and What It's Doing to Us* (London: Picador, 2017).

30 Emile Durkheim, *Suicide* (London: Routledge, 1951).

31 See Ara Norenzayan, *Big Gods: How Religion Transformed Cooperation and Conflict* (Princeton, N.J.: Princeton University Press, 2015); Dominic Johnson, *God Is Watching You: How the Fear of God Makes Us Human* (Oxford: Oxford University Press, 2016); David Sloan Wilson, *Darwin's Cathedral: Evolution, Religion, and the Nature of Society* (Chicago: University of Chicago Press, 2002); and Scott Atran, *In Gods We Trust: The Evolutionary Landscape of Religion* (Oxford: Oxford University Press, 2002).

32 Charles Darwin, *The Descent of Man* (Princeton, N.J.: Princeton University Press, 1981 [1871]), 166.

33 See Robert Wright, *The Moral Animal: Evolutionary Psychology and Everyday Life* (New York: Vintage, 1995); and Matt Ridley, *The Origins of Virtue* (London: Viking, 1996).

34 See Robin Dunbar, *Grooming, Gossip, and the Evolution of Language* (London: Faber & Faber, 1996).

35 This was the point made by Elizabeth Anscombe in her landmark article "Modern Moral Philosophy," *Philosophy* 33, no. 124 (1958): 1–19. The most compelling alternative to divine command as the basis of morality in the West has been the case, argued by Anscombe, Philippa Foot, and Alasdair MacIntyre, for a renewed Aristotelian ethic of virtue. That, however, is problematic for precisely the point argued above: the sense of community atrophies in an individualistic age, and virtue is predicated on community.

36 Quoted in Leon G. Stevens, *One Nation under God: A Factual History of America's Religious Heritage* (New York: Morgan James Faith, 2013), 39.

37 Tocqueville, *Democracy in America*, 184.

38 Patrick Devlin, *The Enforcement of Morals* (Oxford: Oxford University Press, 1965), 10.

39 Michael Walzer, *The Paradox of Liberation: Secular Revolutions and Religious Counterrevolutions* (New Haven, Conn.: Yale University Press, 2016).

40 Rod Dreher, *The Benedict Option: A Strategy for Christians in a Post-Christian Nation* (New York: Penguin Random House, 2017). See also my lecture on the subject, "Cultural Climate Change: The Role of Religion in a Secularised West" (lecture, Chautauqua Institution, Lake Chautauqua, N.Y., July 21, 2017), www.youtube.com/watch?v=2GC_xLuKl5Q&t=169s.

41 Described in Micklethwait and Wooldridge, *God Is Back*.

42 Reuters, "Religious Conflict in Global Rise—Report," *Telegraph* (London), January 14, 2014, www.telegraph.co.uk/news/worldnews/middleeast/10572342/Religious-conflict-in-global-rise-report.html.

43 I explore this distinction in my book *The Great Partnership* (London: Hodder & Stoughton, 2012).

2 (RE-)READING THE NEW TESTAMENT IN THE LIGHT OF SIBLING RIVALRY

1 Jonathan Sacks, *Not in God's Name: Confronting Religious Violence* (London: Hodder & Stoughton, 2015), 124, 142, 168–69.

2 Later published as Richard A. Burridge, *What Are the Gospels? A Comparison with Graeco-Roman Biography*, SNTSMS 72 (Cambridge: Cambridge University Press, 1992; 2nd rev. ed., Grand Rapids: Eerdmans, 2004; 3rd/25th anniv. ed., Waco, Tex.: Baylor University Press, 2018).

3 See Richard A. Burridge, *Four Gospels, One Jesus? A Symbolic Reading*, three editions (London: SPCK; Grand Rapids: Eerdmans, 1994, 2005, 2013/2014).

4 "del legame inscindibile dei Vangeli a Gesù di Nazaret." Citation from Cardinal Ruini, *L'Osservatore Romano* (Vatican City), October 27, 2013, p. 5. See Richard A. Burridge, "Graeco-Roman Biography and the Gospels' Literary Genre," in *I Vangeli: Storia e Cristologia. La ricerca di Joseph Ratzinger-Benedetto XVI/The Gospels: History and Christology. The Search of Joseph Ratzinger-Benedict XVI*, ed. Bernardo Estrada, Ermenegildo Manicardi, Armand Puig I Tarrech, and Fondazione Vaticana Joseph Ratzinger-Benedetto XVI (Vatican City: Libreria Editrice Vaticana, 2013), 151–98; and Richard A. Burridge, "Biographies of Jesus: Joseph Ratzinger and the Gospels," in *Cooperatores Veritatis: Tributes to Pope Emeritus Benedict XVI on His 90th Birthday*, ed. Pierluca Azzaro and Federico Lombardi (Vatican City: Libreria Editrice Vaticana, 2017), 47–88.

5 Later published as Richard A. Burridge, *Imitating Jesus: An Inclusive Approach to New Testament Ethics* (Grand Rapids: Eerdmans, 2007).

6 Provisionally entitled *Money, Sex, Power, Violence, and the Meaning of Life: Following Jesus Today* (forthcoming, due 2019).

7 Sacks, *Not in God's Name*, 168–69 (emphasis original).

8 For a good account of how this developed through the first centuries of the church's history, especially after the Christianization of the Roman Empire from Constantine onward, see the following chapter by Guy G. Stroumsa.

9 1 Timothy is one of the most disputed letters in the Pauline corpus, often thought to be written or finally edited by a disciple after his death; if that includes this description, it is all the more remarkable for that. Scripture translations are the author's own.

10 Sacks, *Not in God's Name*, 92–98, quotation from p. 94.

11 Sacks, *Not in God's Name*, 96.

12 Sacks, *Not in God's Name*, 97–98; see also the following chapter by Stroumsa.

13 See Gerd Lüdemann, *Paul, Apostle to the Gentiles: Studies in Chronology* (London: SCM Press, 1984); Martin Hengel, *The Pre-Christian Paul* (London: SCM Press, 1991); Martin Hengel and Anna Maria Schwemer, *Paul between Damascus and Antioch: The Unknown Years* (London: SCM Press, 1997); Rainer Riesner, *Paul's Early Period: Chronology, Mission Strategy, Theology* (Grand Rapids: Eerdmans, 1998); Ben Witherington III, *The Paul Quest: The Renewed Search for the Jew of Tarsus* (Downers Grove, Ill.: Inter-Varsity, 1998); Jerome Murphy-O'Connor, *Paul: A Critical Life* (Oxford: Clarendon, 1996); idem, *Paul: His Story* (Oxford: Oxford University Press, 2004); John Ashton, *The Religion of Paul the Apostle* (New Haven, Conn.: Yale University Press, 2000); and David G. Horrell, *An Introduction to the Study of Paul*, 2nd ed. (London: T&T Clark, 2006), esp. 27–43.

14 Note Krister Stendahl's essay "Call Rather Than Conversion" in his collection *Paul among Jews and Gentiles* (London: SCM Press, 1977), 7–23. See also W. D. Davies, *Paul and Rabbinic Judaism: Some Rabbinic Elements in Pauline Theology*, 3rd ed. (London: SPCK, 1970); F. F. Bruce, *Paul: Apostle of the Free Spirit* (Exeter: Paternoster, 1977); E. P. Sanders, *Paul and Palestinian Judaism* (London: SCM Press, 1977); Francis Watson, *Paul, Judaism and the Gentiles: A Sociological Approach*, SNTSMS 56 (Cambridge: Cambridge University Press, 1986); Jürgen Becker, *Paul: Apostle to the Gentiles* (Louisville, Ky.: Westminster John Knox, 1993); Terence L. Donaldson, *Paul and the Gentiles: Remapping the Apostle's Convictional World* (Minneapolis: Augsburg Fortress, 1997); Troels Engberg-Pedersen, ed., *Paul beyond the Judaism/Hellenism Divide* (Louisville, Ky.: Westminster John Knox, 2001); and S. J. Chester, *Conversion at Corinth* (London: T&T Clark, 2003). For a historical analysis of how Paul's conversion has been interpreted from the time of the early church, see Bruce Corley, "Interpreting Paul's Conversion—Then and Now," in *The Road from Damascus: The Impact of Paul's Conversion on His Life, Thought, and Ministry*, ed. Richard N. Longenecker (Grand Rapids: Eerdmans, 1997), 1–17. For more discussion, see Burridge, *Imitating Jesus*, 84–85.

15 Alan F. Segal, *Paul the Convert: The Apostolate and Apostasy of Saul the Pharisee* (New Haven, Conn.: Yale University Press, 1990); see pp. 6, 72, for example. See also Pinchas Lapide and Peter Stuhlmacher, *Paul: Rabbi and Apostle* (Minneapolis: Augsburg, 1984); L. W. Hurtado, "Convert, Apostate, or Apostle to the Nations: The 'Conversion' of Paul in Recent Scholarship," *Studies in Religion/Sciences Religieuses* 22 (1993): 273–84; and Daniel Boyarin, *A Radical Jew: Paul and the Politics of Identity* (Berkeley: University of California Press, 1994).

16 See Sanders, *Paul and Palestinian Judaism*; idem, *Paul, the Law, and the Jewish People* (Philadelphia: Fortress, 1983); idem, *Paul* (Oxford: Oxford University Press, 1991); and Hans Hübner, *Law in Paul's Thought: A Contribution to the Development of Pauline Theology* (Edinburgh: T&T Clark, 1984), esp. 36–42. For more discussion, see Burridge, *Imitating Jesus*, 110–12.

17 See, e.g., Douglas Campbell, *The Quest for Paul's Gospel* (London: T&T Clark, 2005); James D. G. Dunn, *The New Perspective on Paul* (Grand Rapids: Eerdmans, 2007); Chris Tilling, *Beyond Old and New Perspectives on Paul: Reflections on the Work of Douglas Campbell* (Eugene, Oreg.: Cascade, 2014); Stephen Westerholm, *Perspectives Old and New on Paul* (Grand Rapids: Eerdmans, 2004); N. T. Wright, *Paul: Fresh Perspectives* (London: SPCK, 2005); and Kent L. Yinger, *The New Perspective on Paul: An Introduction* (Eugene, Oreg.: Cascade, 2010).

18 Sacks, *Not in God's Name*, 96–97.

19 For this historical reconstruction, see Francis Watson, *Paul, Judaism, and the Gentiles: Beyond the New Perspective*, 2nd ed. (Grand Rapids: Eerdmans, 2007), 163–91; for an alternative and further discussion, see John Barclay, *Paul and the Gift* (Grand Rapids: Eerdmans, 2015), 455–59.

20 Sacks, *Not in God's Name*, 97.

21 For Romans generally, see C. E. B. Cranfield, *The Epistle to the Romans*, 2 vols., ICC (Edinburgh: T&T Clark, 1975–1979); James D. G. Dunn, *Romans*, WBC 38 and 38A (Milton Keynes: Word, 1991); and Joseph A. Fitzmyer, *Romans: A New Translation with Introduction and Commentary*, AB 33 (New York: Doubleday, 1993).

22 For Philippians, see Peter T. O'Brien, *Commentary on Philippians*, NIGTC (Grand Rapids: Eerdmans, 1991); Markus Bockmuehl, *The Epistle to the Philippians*, 4th ed. (London: Black, 1997); and Gerald F. Hawthorne, *Philippians*, WBC 43 (Nashville: Nelson, 2004).

23 On Paul's attitude to the Jewish law, see Burridge, *Imitating Jesus*, 107–15.

24 Barclay, *Paul and the Gift*, 421; see 418–21 for fuller discussion.

25 See Sanders, *Paul and Palestinian Judaism*; idem, *Paul, the Law, and the Jewish People*; idem, *Jesus and Judaism* (London: SCM Press, 1985); *Jewish Law from Jesus to the Mishnah* (London: SCM Press, 1990); and idem, *Judaism: Practice and Belief 63 BCE–66 CE* (London: SCM Press, 1992). For Sanders' more accessible introductions, see *Paul*; and *The Historical Figure of Jesus* (London: Penguin, 1993).

26 See, e.g., Robert A. Guelich, *Mark 1–8.26*, WBC 34A (Dallas: Word, 1989), xxix–xxxii; Ernest Best, *Mark: The Gospel as Story* (Edinburgh: T&T Clark, 1983), 21–36; and Ben Witherington III, *The Gospel of Mark: A Socio-Rhetorical Commentary* (Grand Rapids: Eerdmans, 2001), 20–31.

27 See Howard C. Kee, *Community of the New Age: Studies in Mark's Gospel* (London: SCM Press, 1977), esp. 100–105, 176–77; Ched Myers, *Binding the Strong Man: A Political Reading of Mark's Story of Jesus* (Maryknoll, N.Y.: Orbis, 1988), 39–87; H. N. Roskam, *The Purpose of the Gospel of Mark in Its Historical and Social Context*, NovTSup 114 (Leiden: Brill, 2004), 74–114; Petr Pokorný, "Das Markusevangelium: Literarische und theologische Einleitung mit Forschungsbericht," *ANRW* 2nd ser., 25, no. 3 (1985), esp. 2019–22; and Morna D. Hooker, *The Gospel according to St Mark* (London: Black, 1991), 5–8.

28 For a robust argument that this material is authentically Markan and reflects the historical Jesus, see Adela Yarbro Collins, *The Beginning of the Gospel: Probings of Mark in Context* (Minneapolis: Augsburg Fortress, 1992), 73–91; see also Willem S. Vorster, "Literary Reflections on Mark 13:5-37: A Narrated Speech of Jesus," *Neotestamentica* 21 (1987): 91–112, reprinted in *The Interpretation of Mark*, ed. William Telford, 2nd ed. (London: SPCK, 1995), 269–88.

29 William Loader, *Jesus' Attitude towards the Law: A Study of the Gospels* (Grand Rapids: Eerdmans, 2002), 134; for further detailed discussion about Mark's setting and attitude to the Jewish law, see Burridge, *Imitating Jesus*, 166–72.

30 See chap. 6, "The Gospel of Matthew and Judaism," in G. N. Stanton, *A Gospel for a New People: Studies in Matthew* (Edinburgh: T&T Clark, 1992), 146–68, quotation from 146; see also Warren Carter, *Matthew and the Margins: A Sociopolitical and Religious Reading* (Maryknoll, N.Y.: Orbis, 2000), 459–61. For a Jewish reading of how Matthew feels, see Samuel Sandmel, *Anti-Semitism in the New Testament?* (Philadelphia: Fortress, 1978), 49–70.

31 Scot McKnight, "A Loyal Critic: Matthew's Polemic with Judaism in Theological Perspective," in *Anti-Semitism and Early Christianity: Issues of Polemic and Faith*, ed. Craig A. Evans and Donald A. Hagner (Minneapolis: Augsburg Fortress, 1993), 55–79, quotation from p. 56. Similar distinctions are used in William R. Farmer, ed., *Anti-Judaism and the Gospels* (Harrisburg: Trinity International, 1999), see, e.g., 45 and 49; on Matthew, see its opening articles, Amy-Jill Levine, "Anti-Judaism and the Gospel of Matthew," 9–36, with responses from Philip L. Shuler, 37–46, and Warren Carter, 47–62.

32 See chap. 5, "Synagogue and Church," in Stanton, *A Gospel for a New People*, esp. 118–24 and 142–45 on the *birkat ha-minim* and how this hypothesis developed and more recently has been challenged again; see also Steven T. Katz, "Issues in the Separation of Judaism and Christianity after

70 C.E.: A Reconsideration," *JBL* 103, no. 1 (1984): 43–76; Pieter W. van der Horst, "The *Birkat ha-minim* in Recent Research," *ExpTim* 105, no. 12 (1994): 363–68; and Anthony J. Saldarini, *Matthew's Christian-Jewish Community* (Chicago: University of Chicago Press, 1994), 3, 18–19, 220–21. See also Craig S. Keener's detailed treatment of both the *birkat* and local disagreements in his introduction to his *The Gospel of John: A Commentary*, 2 vols. (Peabody, Mass.: Hendrickson, 2003), 171–214.

33   Ulrich Luz, "Anti-Judaism in the Gospel of Matthew as a Historical and Theological Problem: An Outline," in *Studies in Matthew* (Grand Rapids: Eerdmans, 2005), 243–61, quotation from p. 255.

34   McKnight, "A Loyal Critic," 7.

35   For further detail about Matthew's gospel, see Burridge, *Imitating Jesus*, 193–96.

36   Daniel Marguerat, *The First Christian Historian: Writing the "Acts of the Apostles*,*"* SNTSMS 121 (Cambridge: Cambridge University Press, 2002), 151–54 (emphasis original).

37   For further discussion, see Daryl D. Schmidt, "Anti-Judaism and the Gospel of Luke," in Farmer, *Anti-Judaism and the Gospels*, 63–96, and the responses from David L. Balch, 97–110, and Allan J. McNichol, 111–19. See also David L. Tiede, " 'Fighting against God': Luke's Interpretation of Jewish Rejection of the Messiah Jesus," in *Anti-Semitism and Early Christianity: Issues of Polemic and Faith*, ed. Craig A. Evans and Donald A. Hagner (Minneapolis: Ausburg Fortress, 1993), 102–12; Eric Franklin, *Luke: Interpreter of Paul, Critic of Matthew*, JSNTSS 92 (Sheffield: Sheffield Academic, 1994), 210–43; David Ravens, *Luke and the Restoration of Israel*, JSNTSup 119 (Sheffield: Sheffield Academic, 1995), passim; François Bovon, *Studies in Early Christianity*, WUNT 161 (Tübingen: Mohr Siebeck, 2003), 28–32; and M. Rese, "The Jews in Luke–Acts: Some Second Thoughts," in *The Unity of Luke–Acts*, ed. J. Verheyden, BETL 142 (Leuven: Peeters, 1999), 185–201. Also see Michael Wolter, "Israel's Future and the Delay of the Parousia, according to Luke," Robert C. Tannehill, "The Story of Israel within the Lukan Narrative," and I. Howard Marshall, " 'Israel' and the Story of Salvation: One Theme in Two Parts," all in *Jesus and the Heritage of Israel: Luke's Narrative Claim upon Israel's Legacy*, ed. David P. Moessner (Harrisburg: Trinity International, 1999), 307–24, 325–39, 340–58.

38   For further detail, see Burridge, *Imitating Jesus*, 251–53.

39   See G. A. Yee, *Jewish Feasts and the Gospel of John* (Wilmington, Del.: Glazier, 1989); and Stephen Motyer, "The Fourth Gospel and the Salvation of Israel: An Appeal for a New Start," in *Anti-Judaism and the Fourth Gospel: Papers of the Leuven Colloquium, 2000*, ed. Reimund Bieringer, Didier Pollefyt, and Frederique Vandecasteele-Vanneuville (Assen: Royal Van Gorcum, 2001), esp. 97–103.

40 See Urban C. von Wahlde, "'You Are of Your Father the Devil' in Its Context: Stereotyped Apocalyptic Polemic in John 8:38-47," in Bieringer, Pollefyt, and Vandecasteele-Vanneuville, *Anti-Judaism and the Fourth Gospel*, 418–44.

41 See "Select Bibliography," 549–70; and esp. Judith M. Lieu, "Anti-Judaism in the Fourth Gospel: Explanation and Hermeneutics," in Bieringer, Pollefyt, and Vandecasteele-Vanneuville, *Anti-Judaism and the Fourth Gospel*, 128–31; also see James D. G. Dunn, "The Question of Anti-Semitism in the New Testament Writings of the Period," in *Jews and Christians: The Parting of the Ways AD 70 to 135*, ed. James D. G. Dunn, WUNT 66 (Tübingen: Mohr Siebeck, 1992), 177–211.

42 See the editors' introduction to Bieringer, Pollefyt, and Vandecasteele-Vanneuville, *Anti-Judaism and the Fourth Gospel*, 5–17, on the levels of author, text, and interpreter, quotation from 8.

43 See the editors' introduction to Bieringer, Pollefyt, and Vandecasteele-Vanneuville, *Anti-Judaism and the Fourth Gospel*, 30–33.

44 James D. G. Dunn, *Jesus Remembered* (Grand Rapids: Eerdmans, 2003), 255–325, quotation from 283–84; see also James D. G. Dunn, "The Embarrassment of History: Reflections of the Problem of 'Anti-Judaism' in the Fourth Gospel," in Bieringer, Pollefyt, and Vandecasteele-Vanneuville, *Anti-Judaism and the Fourth Gospel*, esp. 59–60; Lieu discusses this in her "Anti-Judaism in the Fourth Gospel" in the same volume, 131–33.

45 Adele Reinhartz, "'Jews' and Jews in the Fourth Gospel," in Bieringer, Pollefyt, and Vandecasteele-Vanneuville, *Anti-Judaism and the Fourth Gospel*, 354.

46 The editors' introduction to Bieringer, Pollefyt, and Vandecasteele-Vanneuville, *Anti-Judaism and the Fourth Gospel*, 44.

47 For further detail about John's gospel, see Burridge, *Imitating Jesus*, 312–22.

48 For how this developed through the first centuries, especially after the Christianization of the Roman Empire from Constantine onward, see the following chapter by Guy G. Stroumsa.

49 Levine, "Anti-Judaism and the Gospel of Matthew," 19.

50 See further Burridge, *Imitating Jesus*, 347–409, esp. 388–405.

3 OPEN RELIGION AND ITS ENEMIES

1 For a major attempt at understanding the contemporary political role of traditional religions from a comparative viewpoint, see Michael Cook, *Ancient Religions, Modern Politics: The Islamic Case in Comparative Perspective* (Princeton, N.J.: Princeton University Press, 2014).

2 Henri Bergson, *Les deux sources de la morale et de la religion* (Paris: Universitaires de France, 1932).

3 Karl Popper, *The Open Society and Its Enemies* (London: Routledge, 1945).

4 See in particular Jan Assmann, *The Price of Monotheism*, trans. Robert Savage (Stanford, Calif.: Stanford University Press, 2010), originally published as *Die Mosaische Unterscheidung oder der Preis des Monotheismus* (Munich: Carl Hanser, 2003). See further Jan Assmann, *Violence et monothéisme* (Paris: Bayard, 2009). In a protracted polemic since the publication of his *Moses the Egyptian: The Memory of Egypt in Western Monotheism* (Cambridge, Mass.: Harvard University Press, 1997) when the accusation of anti-Semitism was scandalously hurled at him, Assmann has now clarified his views in *Exodus: Die Revolution der Alten Welt* (Munich: Beck, 2015). As is well known, the French philosopher Simone Weil expressed radically negative views of the biblical God. See Guy G. Stroumsa, *Religions abrahamiques: histoires croisées* (Geneva: Labor et Fides, 2017), chap. 13 ("Tentations du christianismes: Henri Bergson, Simone Weil, Emmanuel Levinas").

5 See the challenging views of Jan Bremmer, "Religious Violence and Its Roots: A View from Antiquity," *Asdiwal* 6 (2011): 71–79.

6 Guy G. Stroumsa, "Le radicalisme religieux du christianisme ancien," in *Retours aux Ecritures*, ed. A. Le Boulluec and E. Patlagean, Bibliothèque de l'Ecole Pratique des Hautes Etudes (Leuven: Peeters, 1993), 347–74. Slightly revised in translation, "Early Christianity as Radical Religion: Context and Implications," *Israel Oriental Studies* 14 (1994): 173–93.

7 See for instance E. P. Sanders, ed., *Jewish and Christian Self-Definition*, vol. 1, *The Shaping of Christianity in the Second and Third Centuries* (London: SCM Press, 1980).

8 See Guy G. Stroumsa, *Barbarian Philosophy: The Religious Revolution of Early Christianity* (Tübingen: Mohr Siebeck, 1999), chap. 8 ("From Anti-Judaism to Antisemitism in Early Christianity"). For later developments, see P. Stefani, *L'antigiudaismo: Storia di un'idea* (Rome: Laterza, 2004).

9 Robert L. Wilken, *John Chrysostom and the Jews: Rhetoric and Reality in the Late Fourth Century* (Berkeley: University of California Press, 1983).

10 On Christian self-definition, see Sanders, *Jewish and Christian Self-Definition*.

11 See Stroumsa, *Religions abrahamiques*, chap. 13 ("Tentations du christianismes").

12 J. Gager, *Kingdom and Community: The Social World of Early Christianity* (Englewood Cliffs, N.J.: Prentice Hall, 1975). In his analysis, Gager refers to the *cargo cults* in twentieth-century Polynesia. The term *cognitive dissonance* seems to have been coined by Leon Festinger; see Leon Festinger, Henry Riecken, and Stanley Schachter, *When Prophecy Fails: A Social and Psychological Study of a Modern Group That Predicted the Destruction of the World* (Minneapolis: University of Minnesota Press, 1956). For the application of the term on early Christianity, see Alan F. Segal, *Rebecca's Children: Judaism and Christianity in the Roman World* (Cambridge, Mass.: Harvard University Press, 1986), 99–105, nn. 191–92. Segal has developed

his ideas on Paul's conversion in his *Paul the Convert: The Apostolate and Apostasy of Saul the Pharisee* (New Haven, Conn.: Yale University Press, 1990).

13   Bibliographical references in H. Kippenberg, "Apokalyptik, Messianismus, Chiliasmus," in *Handbuch religionswissentschaftlicher Grundbegriffe*, vol. 2 (Stuttgart: Kohlhammer, 1990), 9–26, esp. 12.

14   See Guy G. Stroumsa, *Savoir et salut* (Paris: Le Cerf, 1992), esp. chap. 7; and Guy G. Stroumsa, "Moses' Riddles: Esoteric Trends in Patristic Hermeneutics," in *Interpretation in Religion*, ed. Sh. Biedermann and B. A. Scharfstein (Leiden: Brill, 1992).

15   Gerd Theissen, *Sociology of Early Palestinian Christianity*, trans. John Bowden (Philadelphia: Fortress, 1978), 105.

16   Sigmund Freud, *Das Unbehagen in der Kultur* (Vienna: Internationaler Psychoanalitischer, 1930), 243. For a summary treatment of Freud's views on religion in general, and of Christianity in particular, see Martin S. Bergmann, *In the Shadow of Moloch* (New York: Columbia University Press, 1992), 219–43, esp. 241–43.

17   See, for instance, Arnaldo Momigliano, "Roman Religion," in *Encyclopedia of Religion*, repr. in *Religions of Antiquity*, ed. R. M. Seltzer (New York: Macmillan, 1989), 230–33; cf. Albrecht Dihle's claim, "Ein Motiv der Intoleranz freilich fehlte dieser Gesellschaft vollkommen, nämlich der Absolutheitsanspruch irgendeiner Religion oder Weltanschauung." *Die griechische und lateinische Literatur der Kaiserzeit* (Munich: Beck, 1989), 26.

18   Paul Veyne, *Les grecs ont-ils cru en leurs dieux?* (Paris: Le Seuil, 1983), trans. as *Did the Greeks Believe in Their Gods?* (Chicago: University of Chicago Press, 1988).

19   See Arnaldo Momigliano, "Empieta ed eresia nel mondo antico," in *Sesto contributo alla storia degli studi classici e del mondo antico*, vol. 2 (Rome: Edizioni di storia e letteratura, 1980), 437–58. See also idem, "Freedom of Speech and Religious Tolerance in the Ancient World," in *Anthropology and the Greeks*, ed. S. C. Humphreys (London: Routledge, 1978), 179–93.

20   This concept is discussed by Wilhelm Halbfass, *India and Europe: An Essay in Understanding* (Albany: SUNY Press, 1988), 403–18 and notes.

21   See R. Hammerton-Kelly, *Sacred Violence: Paul's Hermeneutic of the Cross* (Minneapolis: Fortress, 1991), who applies it to Paul Girard's ideas.

22   See Peter Brown, "The Saint as Exemplar in Late Antiquity," *Representations* 2 (1983): 1–25.

23   For a bibliography and a definition of fanaticism, see Hildegard Cancik-Lindemaier, "Fanatismus," in *Handbuch religionswissenschaftliche Grundbegriffe*, vol. 1 (Stuttgart: Kohlhammer, 1988), 414–20.

24   One may point out that Jewish scholars often seem to have problems with the Sermon on the Mount. In front of this sublime ethics, rabbinic ideas might appear somewhat pale. For Solomon Zeitlin, the weakness of Jesus' love commands lies precisely in their utopian character, since it is only in

a utopian world that a utopian ethics can be applied. See his "Prolegomenon," *The Jewish Sources of the Sermon on the Mount*, by Gerald Friedlander (New York: Ktav, 1969), xxv.

25 On religious memory, see Guy G. Stroumsa, "Religious Memory, between Orality and Writing," *Memory Studies* 9 (2016): 332–40.

4 RADICAL ENCOUNTERS

1 Jonathan Sacks, "Rabbi Jonathan Sacks on What It Takes to End Violence in God's Name," interview by Lauren Markoe, *HuffPost*, November 8, 2015, www.huffingtonpost.com/entry/rabbi-jonathan-sacks-not-in-gods -name_us_5632697ae4b0c66bae5b9a10.

2 Eliza Griswold, *The Tenth Parallel: Dispatches from the Fault Line between Christianity and Islam* (New York: Farrar, Straus & Giroux, 2010).

5 EMPATHY AS POLICY IN THE AGE OF HATRED

1 See, for instance, Amineh Hoti, "An Unfair Image: Dear Mr. Trump, Please Read This Book by a Fellow-Christian on 'A Sacred Land,'" *HuffPost*, January 14, 2018, www.huffing-tonpost.com/entry/an-unfair-image-dear-mr-trump-please -read-this-book_us_5a5c2c83e4b01ccdd48b5ddc.

2 Helena Merriman, "Why Are 10,000 Migrant Children Missing in Europe?" *BBC News*, October 12, 2016, sec. Europe, www.bbc.com/ news/world-europe-37617234.

3 UNESCO, *UNESCO World Report: Investing in Cultural Diversity and Intercultural Dialogue* (Paris: UNESCO, 2009), http://unesdoc.unesco. org/images/0018/001852/185202e.pdf.

4 David Howe, *Empathy: What It Is and Why It Matters* (London: Palgrave Macmillan, 2012).

5 Institute for Economics and Peace, *Global Terrorism Index 2015: Executive Summary* (Sydney: IEP, 2015).

6 Dr. Shabbir Akhtar wrote: "The next time there are gas chambers in Europe, there is no doubt concerning who'll be inside them." Shabbir Akhtar, "Whose Light? Whose Darkness?" *Guardian*, February 27, 1989. See also idem, *Be Careful with Muhammad! The Salman Rushdie Affair* (London: Bellew, 1989). Dr. Kalim Siddiqui is reported to have referred to "Hitler-style gas chambers for Muslims"; see Daniel Pipes, *Militant Islam Reaches America* (New York: W.W. Norton, 2003), 23. One character in Hanif Kureishi's novel *The Buddha of Suburbia* says, "the whites finally turned on the blacks and Asians and tried to force us into gas chambers." Hanif Kureishi, *The Buddha of Suburbia* (New York, Penguin, 1991), 56.

7 See Elizabeth Schumacher, "Shake-Up for Germany's Right-Wing AfD over Anti-Semitism Row," *DW*, July 5, 2016, www.dw.com/en/shake-up -for-germanys-right-wing-afd-over-anti-semitism-row/a-19379702;

Akbar S. Ahmed, *Journey into Europe: Islam, Immigration, and Identity* (Washington, D.C.: Brookings Institution Press, 2018).

8 Jonathan Sacks, *Not in God's Name: Confronting Religious Violence* (London: Hodder & Stoughton, 2015), 8.

9 Amineh Hoti, "Negative Coverage of Muslims Led to Trump's Rise," *HuffPost*, November 30, 2016, www.huffingtonpost.com/entry/decades-of-negative -coverage-on-muslims-has-led-to_us_583f9f7ce4b04587de5de758.

10 Maximilian Popp, "Europe's Deadly Borders: An Inside Look at EU's Shameful Immigration Policy," *Spiegel Online*, September 11, 2014, www.spiegel.de/international/europe/europe-tightens-borders-and-fails -to-protect-people-a-989502.html.

11 Popp, "Europe's Deadly Borders."

12 Jan Culik, "Prague Springs to Intolerance," *Politico*, August 21, 2015. See also Ahmed, *Journey into Europe*.

13 Selma Muhič Dizdarevič, "Islamophobia in Czech Republic," in *European Islamophobia Report*, ed. Enes Bayrakli and Farid Hafes (Ankara: SETA, 2015): 129, www.islamophobiaeurope.com/reports/2015/en/ EIR_2015.pdf.

14 UNESCO, *UNESCO World Report*, 910.

15 E.g., Howe, *Empathy*, 18, 204.

16 Howe, *Empathy*.

17 Daniel Goleman, *Emotional Intelligence: Why It Can Matter More than IQ* (New York: Bantam Books, 1996), 54.

18 Amineh Hoti, "Interfaith at the White House," *Friday Times*, December 25, 2015, www.thefridaytimes.com/tft/interfaith-at-the-white-house/.

19 UNESCO, *UNESCO World Report*, 47.

20 UNESCO, *UNESCO World Report*, 113 (emphasis original).

21 UNESCO, *UNESCO World Report*, 114.

22 UNESCO, *UNESCO World Report*, 119.

23 "It is this society that produced an Ibn Firnas who attempted flight and religious philosophers like Maimonides and Averroes who sought to balance reason and faith. Andalusian society in turn laid the seeds for what would become the European Renaissance, which in turn would lead to the Enlightenment and shape our modern world." Ahmed, *Journey into Europe*, 488.

24 A variety of topics were taught, from the difference between religion and culture to examples of historical conflicts and peaceful coexistence. A number of books and local articles were used to teach, including the following compulsory readings: Howe, *Empathy*; María Rosa Menocal, *The Ornament of the World: How Muslims, Jews and Christians Created a Culture of Tolerance in Medieval Spain* (New York: Little, Brown, 2002); Jonathan Sacks, *The Dignity of Difference: How to Avoid the Clash of Civilizations* (London: Continuum, 2002); Karen Armstrong, *A Letter to Pakistan* (Oxford: Oxford University Press, 2011); Amineh Hoti, *Sorrow and Joy*

among Muslim Women: The Pukhtuns of Northern Pakistan (Cambridge: Cambridge University Press, 2006); Zahid Shahab Ahmed and Michelle Baxter, *Texts and Contexts: Attitudes of Teachers in India and Pakistan* (New Delhi: WISCOMP, 2007); Salim T. S. al-Hassani, ed., *1001 Inventions: The Enduring Legacy of Muslim Civilization* (Washington, D.C.: National Geographic, 2012); Jonathan Lyons, *The House of Wisdom: How the Arabs Transformed Western Civilization* (New York: Bloomsbury, 2010); Ghazi bin Muhammad bin Talal, "A Common Word between Us and You," *A Common Word*, October 13, 2007, www.acommonword.com/category/new-fruits/publications.

25 UNESCO, *UNESCO World Report*, 244 (emphasis added).

26 See, e.g., the edited text of Akbar S. Ahmed's 2004 Miliband Lecture, titled "Islam under Siege: From Clash to Dialogue of Civilizations," delivered at London School of Economics, June 15, 2004, www.lse.ac.uk/website-archive/publicEvents/pdf/20040615AkbarAhmed.pdf; Akbar S. Ahmed, "And Ne'er the Twain Shall Meet?" *NewsLine*, February 2015, www.newslinemagazine.com/; Hassan bin Talal and Alain Elkann, *To Be A Muslim: Islam, Peace and Democracy* (Brighton: Sussex Academic Press, 2004). These were some of the texts studied in class.

27 The subject of this chapter is important and one that has been recognized before in the Muslim world by IRCICA (Research Centre for Islamic History, Art and Culture), which convened a session titled "Coexistence of Different Cultures: Examples from History as Lessons for the Future," held in Bali, Indonesia, on August 29, 2014, at the Sixth Forum of the UN Alliance of Civilizations (UNAOC). The booklet of this title was printed in Istanbul in 2015 by IRCICA and UNAOC. The ideas in this chapter are also based on my work, which I have explored in other lectures and articles, including Amineh A. Hoti, "The Challenges and Practical Outcomes of Interfaith Dialogue in Pakistan and the UK: Anthropological Notes from the Field of a Muslim Woman Leading Dialogue," in *Interculturalism at the Crossroads: Comparative Perspectives on Concepts, Policies and Practices,* ed. F. Mansouri (Paris: UNESCO, 2017), 227–56; and Amineh Ahmed Hoti and Zahid Shahab Ahmed, "Peace Education in Pakistan: A Case Study of the Centre for Dialogue and Action, FC College University," in *Promoting Global Peace and Civic Engagement through Education*, ed. Kshama Pandey, Pratibha Upadhyay, and Amita Jaiswal (Hershey, Penn.: IGI Global, 2016), 323–37.

28 Amineh Hoti, "The Birth of a Messianic Jewish Community in Pakistan," *HuffPost*, December 19, 2016, www.huffingtonpost.com/entry/the-birth-of-a-messianic-jewish-community-in-pakistan_us_58577819e4b0d5f48e165129.

29 UNESCO, *UNESCO World Report*, 257.

30 Ahmed, "And Ne'er the Twain."

31 UNESCO, *UNESCO World Report*, 141.

32 UNESCO, *UNESCO World Report*, 144–45.

33 Akbar S. Ahmed, *Journey into Europe*, film, 2:01:05, posted February 23, 2017, https://youtu.be/gyHsfV6sW70.

34 See Akbar S. Ahmed, "To Prevent More Attacks like Nice, We Must Integrate Muslims, Not Simply Bomb ISIS," *HuffPost*, July 18, 2016, www.huffington post.com/akbar-ahmed/nice-attack-muslims-isis_b_11061076.html.

35 Howe, *Empathy*.

36 Our textbooks, *Teaching Acceptance* (Islamabad: Emel, 2015) and *Accepting Difference* (Islamabad: Emel, 2015), may be used to accompany and elaborate on these policy suggestions; see www.emel.com.pk/product/accepting-difference/.

37 Enes Bayrakli and Farid Hafez, eds., *European Islamophobia Report 2015* (Ankara: SETA, 2016), quotation from back cover of report.

38 Ahmed, *Journey into Europe* (book), 487.

39 Ahmed, *Journey into Europe* (book).

40 Bayrakli and Hafez, *European Islamophobia Report 2015*.

6 DEVOTED ACTORS IN AN AGE OF RAGE

1 Pankaj Mishra, *Age of Anger: A History of the Present* (London: Allen Lane, 2017).

2 Theodore Roosevelt, "First Annual Message," December 3, 1901, www.presidency.ucsb.edu/ws/?pid=29542.

3 Theodore Roosevelt, "Roosevelt Corollary to the Monroe Doctrine: Excerpt from the President's Annual Message to Congress," December 6, 1904, www.theodore-roosevelt.com/images/research/speeches/trmdcorollary.pdf.

4 Erich Fromm, *Escape from Freedom* (New York: Farrar & Rinehart, 1941).

5 Søren Kierkegaard, *The Concept of Anxiety* (New York: Liveright, 2014 [1844]).

6 World Values Survey Association, *World Values Survey*, 2005–2014, http://www.worldvaluessurvey.org/WVSDocumentationWVL.jsp.

7 Honor Mahony, "Orban Wants to Build 'Illiberal State,'" *EUobserver*, July 28, 2014, https://euobserver.com/political/125128.

8 James Kirchick, *The End of Europe* (New Haven, Conn.: Yale University Press, 2017).

9 International Republican Institute, "Visegrad Four Poll Reveals Vulnerabilities to Russian Influence," May 27, 2017, www.iri.org/resource/visegrad-four-poll-reveals-vulnerabilities-russian-influence.

10 World Economic Forum, *Global Gender Gap Report 2016* (Cologny: World Economic Forum, 2016), http://reports.weforum.org/global-gender-gap-report-2016/rankings/.

11 Michael Lipka, "Muslims and Islam: Key Findings in the U.S. and around the World," Pew Research Center, August 9, 2017, http://www

.pewresearch.org/fact-tank/2017/05/26/muslims-and-islam-key
-findings-in-the-u-s-and-around-the-world/.

12 Emile Durkheim, *Les formes élémentaires de la vie religieuse: Le système totémique en Australie* (Paris: F. Alcan, 1912).

13 Ara Norenzayan, *Big Gods: How Religion Transformed Cooperation and Conflict* (Princeton, N.J.: Princeton University Press, 2015).

14 Thomas Hobbes, *Leviathan* (New York: E.P. Dutton, 1901 [1651]).

15 Charles Darwin, *The Descent of Man* (London: John Murray, 1871).

16 Scott Atran, "Religion's Cognitive and Social Landscape: An Evolutionary Perspective," in *Handbook of Cultural Psychology*, ed. S. Kitayama and D. Cohen (New York: Guilford, 2007), 429.

17 Scott Atran, *In Gods We Trust: The Evolutionary Landscape of Religion* (Oxford and New York: Oxford University Press, 2002); Scott Atran and Joseph Henrich, "The Evolution of Religion: How Cognitive By-Products, Adaptive Learning Heuristics, Ritual Displays, and Group Competition Generate Deep Commitments to Prosocial Religions," *Biological Theory* 5, no. 1 (2010): 18–30.

18 Alan Page Fiske and Tage Shakti Rai, *Virtuous Violence: Hurting and Killing to Create, Sustain, End, and Honor Social Relationships* (New York: Cambridge University Press, 2014).

19 Robert Jay Lifton and Eric Markusen, *The Genocidal Mentality: Nazi Holocaust and Nuclear Threat* (London: Macmillan, 1991).

20 *The 9/11 Commission Report* (Washington, D.C.: Government Printing Office, 2004), 169.

21 Neta C. Crawford, "Update on the Human Costs of War for Afghanistan and Pakistan, 2001 to Mid-2016," paper of the Watson Institute, Brown University, Providence, R.I., August 2016, watson.brown.edu/costsofwar/files/cow/imce/papers/2015/War%20in%20Afghanistan%20and%20Pakistan%20UPDATE_FINAL.pdf.

22 Graham Allison, "Why ISIS Fears Israel," *National Interest*, August 8, 2016: "A few months from now, a newly elected president will be thinking about how he—or she—will deal with ISIS . . . A serious review would begin with recognition of a brute fact: a decade and a half beyond the 9/11 attacks and President Bush's declaration of a 'War on Terrorism,' the United States undoubtedly faces more terrorists determined to do harm than when this effort began."

23 Herbert A. Simon, *Models of Bounded Rationality* (Cambridge, Mass.: MIT Press, 1997).

24 Thomas C. Schelling, *The Strategy of Conflict* (Cambridge, Mass.: Harvard University Press, 1960).

25 James D. Fearon, "Rationalist Explanations for War," *International Organization* 49, no. 3 (1995): 379–414.

26 Daniel Kahneman, *Thinking, Fast and Slow* (New York: Farrar, Strauss & Giroux, 2011).

27 Steven Pressfield, *The Warrior Ethos* (Los Angeles: Black Irish Entertainment, 2011). Although the Taliban claim credit for this saying, the sentiment recurs in many situations throughout history.

28 Scott Atran and Jeremy Ginges, "How Words Could End a War," *New York Times*, January 25, 2009, http://www.nytimes.com/2009/01/25/opinion/25atran.html?_r=2&pagewanted=all.

29 Morteza Dehghani et al., "Emerging Sacred Values: The Iranian Nuclear Program," *Judgment and Decision Making* 4, no. 7 (2009): 990–93.

30 Richard E. Nisbett and Dov Cohen, *Culture of Honor: The Psychology of Violence in the South* (Boulder, Colo.: Westview, 1996).

31 Scott Atran and Jeremy Ginges, "Religious and Sacred Imperatives in Human Conflict," *Science* 336 (2012): 855–57.

32 Bruce Hoffman and Gordon H. McCormick, "Terrorism, Signaling, and Suicide Attack," *Studies in Conflict & Terrorism* 27 (2004): 243–81.

33 P. Tetlock, "Thinking the Unthinkable: Sacred Values and Taboo Cognitions," *Trends in Cognitive Science* 7 (2003): 320–24; Jeremy Ginges et al., "Sacred Bounds on Rational Resolution of Violent Political Conflict," *Proceedings of the National Academy of Sciences, USA* 104, no. 18 (2007): 7357–60.

34 William B. Swann Jr. et al., "Identity Fusion: The Interplay of Personal and Social Identities in Extreme Group Behavior," *Journal of Personality and Social Psychology* 96 (2009): 995–1011; Ángel Gómez et al., "On the Nature of Identity Fusion: Insights into the Construct and Validation of a New Measure," *Journal of Personality and Social Psychology* 100 (2011): 918–33.

35 Ivan Arreguín-Toft, "How the Weak Win Wars: A Theory of Asymmetric Conflict," *International Security* 26, no. 1 (2001): 931–28.

36 Darwin, *Descent of Man*, 159–60.

37 Scott Atran, "The Devoted Actor: Unconditional Cooperation and Intractable Conflict across Cultures," supplement, *Current Anthropology* 57, no. S13 (2016): 192–203; Ángel Gómez et al., "The Devoted Actor's Will to Fight and the Spiritual Dimension of Human Conflict," *Nature Human Behaviour* 1 (2017): 673–79.

38 Roy A. Rappaport, "The Sacred in Human Evolution," *Annual Review of Ecology and Systematics* 2 (1971): 23–44; Jonathan Baron and Mark Spranca, "Protected Values," *Organizational Behavior and Human Decision Processes* 70 (1997): 1–16; Jesse Graham and Jonathan Haidt, "Sacred Values and Evil Adversaries: A Moral Foundations Approach," in *The Social Psychology of Morality: Exploring the Causes of Good and Evil*, ed. Mario Mikulincer and Phillip R. Shaver (New York: APA, 2012), 11–31.

39 William B. Swann Jr. et al., "Identity Fusion and Self-Sacrifice: Arousal as Catalyst of Pro-Group Fighting, Dying, and Helping Behavior," *Journal of Personality and Social Psychology* 99 (2010): 824–41; Michael D. Buhrmester et al., "When Terror Hits Home: Identity Fused Americans Who Saw

Boston Bombing Victims as 'Family' Provided Aid," *Self and Identity* 14, no. 3 (2015): 253–70.

40 Sebastian Payne, "Obama: U.S. Misjudged the Rise of the Islamic State, Ability of Iraqi Army," *Washington Post*, September 28, 2014.

41 Scott Atran, Robert Axelrod, and Richard Davis, "Sacred Barriers to Conflict Resolution," *Science* 317 (2007): 1039–40; Morteza Dehghani et al., "Sacred Values and Conflict over Iran's Nuclear Program," *Judgment and Decision Making* 5, no. 7 (2010): 540–46.

42 Hammad Sheikh, Jeremy Ginges, and Scott Atran, "Sacred Values in Intergroup Conflict: Resistance to Social Influence, Temporal Discounting, and Exit Strategies," *Annals of the New York Academy of Sciences* 1299 (2013): 11–24.

43 Jeremy Ginges et al., "Psychology out of the Laboratory: The Challenge of Violent Extremism," *American Psychologist* 66, no. 6 (2011): 507–19.

44 Dominique J.-F. de Quervain et al., "The Neural Basis for Altruistic Punishment," *Science* 305 (2004): 1254–58.

45 On neural signatures see Gregory S. Berns et al., "The Price of Your Soul: Neural Evidence for the Non-Utilitarian Representation of Sacred Values," *Philosophical Transactions of the Royal Society B* 367 (2012): 754–62.

46 Swann et al., "Identity Fusion."

47 Hammad Sheikh, Ángel Gómez, and Scott Atran, "Empirical Evidence for the Devoted Actor Model," supplement, *Current Anthropology* 57, no. S13 (2016): 204–9.

48 Scott Atran, "On the Front Line against ISIS: Who Fights, Who Doesn't, and Why," *Daily Beast*, April 19, 2016, www.thedailybeast .com/articles/2016/04/19/on-the-front-line-against-isis-who-fights -who-doesn-t-and-why.html.

49 Gómez et al., "Devoted Actor's Will to Fight," supplementary information, static-content.springer.com/esm/art%3A10.1038%2Fs41562-017 -0193-3/MediaObjects/41562_2017_193_MOESM1_ESM.pdf, 5.

50 Scott Atran, Hammad Sheikh, and Ángel Gómez, "Devoted Actors Sacrifice for Close Comrades and Sacred Cause," *Proceedings of the National Academy of Sciences, USA* 111, no. 50 (2014), 11702–3.

51 Gómez et al., "Devoted Actor's Will to Fight," 674.

52 Three-way interaction, $F_{[1,808]} = 13.74$, $p < .001$, $\eta^2 p = .02$.

53 S. Stouffer et al., eds., *Studies in Social Psychology in World War II*, 2 vols. (Princeton: Princeton University Press, 1949); Robert Smith, "Why Soldiers Fight. Part I. Leadership, Cohesion and Fighter Spirit," *Quality and Quantity* 18 (1983): 1–32; Charles C. Moskos, "The American Combat Soldier in Vietnam," *Journal of Social Issues* 31, no. 4 (1975): 25–37; Harvey Whitehouse et al., "Brothers in Arms: Libyan Revolutionaries Bond like Family," *Proceedings of the National Academy of Sciences, USA* 111 (2014): 17783–85.

54 Ángel Gómez et al., "Morir y matar por un grupo o unos valores. Estrategias para evitar, reducir y/o erradicar el comportamiento grupal extremista," *Anuario de Psicología Jurídica* 26, no. 1 (2016): 122–29.

55 AhlulBayt News Agency, "ISIS Militant Executes Own Father in Mosul for Insulting Abu Bakr al-Baghdadi," *ABNA*, October 13, 2016, en.abna24 .com/service/middle-east-west-asia/archive/2016/10/13/785201/ story.html.

56 Francis Fukuyama, *The Origins of Political Order* (New York: Farrar, Strauss & Giroux, 2012); Colin Holbrook and Daniel M. T. Fessler, "Sizing Up the Threat: The Envisioned Physical Formidability of Terrorists Tracks Their Leaders' Failures and Successes," *Cognition* 127, no. 1 (2013): 46–56.

57 Gómez et. al., "Devoted Actor's Will to Fight," 674.

58 In the Hebrew Bible/Old Testament, see Gen 22:1-19. In the Qur'an, see Saffat 37:99–109.

59 Fukuyama, *Origins of Political Order*.

60 Holbrook and Fessler, "Sizing Up the Threat."

61 According to Brig. Gen. William Turner, a deputy commander of the U.S.– led coalition offensive against ISIS in Mosul: "ISIS as a whole is a cornered force. . . . They are fierce fighters, there is a core of ISIS fighters that are fighting to death."

62 Gómez et. al., "Devoted Actor's Will to Fight," 674.

63 Pairwise comparisons with Bonferroni Tests p < .001 compared to remaining conditions.

64 Arnold J. Toynbee, *A Study of History* (Oxford: Oxford University Press, 1934).

65 Charles Darwin, *Descent of Man and Selection in Relation to Sex* (New York: D. Appleton, 1872).

66 For an example of such sacrifice, see Chris Buckley, "Liu Xiaobo, Chinese Dissident Who Won Nobel while Jailed, Dies at 61," *New York Times*, July 13, 2017, https://www.nytimes.com/2017/07/13/world/asia/liu -xiaobo-dead.html.

67 Marc Sageman, *Understanding Terror Networks* (Philadelphia: University of Pennsylvania Press, 2004).

68 Diego Gambetta and Steffen Hertog, *Engineers of Jihad* (Princeton, N.J.: Princeton University Press, 2016).

69 Peter Bergen and Michael Lind, "A Matter of Pride: Why We Can't Buy Off Osama Bin Laden," *Democracy* 3 (Winter 2007), https://democracy- journal.org/magazine/3/a-matter-of-pride/.

70 Atran and Ginges, "Religious and Sacred Imperatives in Human Conflict."

71 Jesse J. Norris and Hanna Grol-Prokopczyk, "Estimating the Prevalence of Entrapment in Post–9/11 Terrorism Cases," *Journal of Criminal Law and Criminology* 105, no. 3 (2015): 609–78. The study of 580 terrorism convictions in the United States found that only 9 percent concerned genuine jihadi threats; 55 percent of all convictions involved a facilitating

government undercover agent. In some cases there was no indication that the convicted "terrorist" had prior sympathy for jihadi terrorism or was capable of committing a terror act without extraordinary inducement by the government.

72 Arie Perliger and Daniel Milton, *From Cradle to Grave: The Lifecycle of the Foreign Fighters in Iraq and Syria* (West Point, N.Y.: Combating Terrorism Center, 2016), www.ctc.usma.edu/posts/from-cradle-to-grave-the-lifecycle-of-foreign-fighters-in-iraq-and-syria.

73 Scott Atran and Nafees Hamid, "Paris: The War ISIS Wants," *New York Review of Books*, November 16, 2015, www.nybooks.com/daily/2015/11/16/paris-attacks-isis-strategy-chaos.

74 Graph and background prepared by Nafees Hamid for ARTIS International.

75 Robert M. Bond and Brad J. Bushman, "The Contagious Spread of Violence among US Adolescents through Social Networks," *American Journal of Public Health* 107, no. 2 (2017): 288–94.

76 Scott Atran, *Talking to the Enemy: Violent Extremism, Sacred Values, and What It Means to Be Human* (London: Penguin, 2010).

77 Samuel Huntington, *The Clash of Civilizations and the Remaking of World Order* (New York: Simon & Schuster, 2011).

78 Scott Atran, "On Youth, Violent Extremism, and Promoting Peace," address to the UN Security Council, April 23, 2015, http://blogs.plos.org/neuroanthropology/2015/04/25/scott-atran-on-youth-violent-extremism-and-promoting-peace/.

79 Atran, "On Youth, Violent Extremism, and Promoting Peace"; and idem, "Statement of Scott Atran: Pathways to and from Violent Extremism: The Case for Science-Based Field Research," testimony before the Subcommittee on Emerging Threats & Capabilities, Committee on Armed Services, U.S. Senate, March 9, 2010.

80 George Orwell, "Review of *Mein Kampf* by Adolf Hitler" (1940), in *The Collected Essays, Journalism and Letters of George Orwell*, ed. Sonia Orwell and Ian Angus (New York: Harcourt Brace Jovanovich, 1968), 2.

81 See Scott Atran, "Analysing the Limits of Rational Choice in Political and Cultural Conflict," presentation at the World Economic Forum, Davos, January 19, 2017, https://www.youtube.com/watch?v=SxDS2g4qSO8.

82 Anandi Mani et al., "Poverty Impedes Cognitive Function," *Science* 341 (2013): 976–80.

83 Merrill D. Peterson, *Thomas Jefferson and the New Nation: A Biography* (Oxford: Oxford University Press, 1970), 90.

7 RELIGIOUS FREEDOM AND HUMAN FLOURISHING

1 Some of this essay reworks my material previously published as Robert P. George, "Religious Liberty and the Human Good," *International Journal of Religious Freedom* 5, no. 1 (2012): 35–44, with kind permission of *IJRF*.

2 John Henry Newman, "A Letter Addressed to the Duke of Norfolk on Occasion of Mr. Gladstone's Recent Expostulation," in *Certain Difficulties Felt by Anglicans in Catholic Teaching*, vol. 2 (London: Longmans, Green, 1900), 250.

3 See John Finnis, *Natural Law and Natural Rights*, 2nd ed. (Oxford: Oxford University Press, 2011), chaps. 3–4.

4 Germain Grisez, "The First Principle of Practical Reason: A Commentary on the *Summa Theologiae*, 1–2, Question 94, Article 2," *Natural Law Forum* 10 (1965): 168–96.

5 Grisiz, "First Principle."

6 Finnis, *Natural Law and Natural Rights*, 450–52.

7 Martin Luther King Jr., *Letter from Birmingham Jail* (1963; New York: HarperCollins, 1994).

8 John Rawls, "On the Priority of Right and Ideas of the Good," *Philosophy and Public Affairs* 17, no. 4 (1988): 251–76.

9 There are, of course, many people today who contest my view that the life of a human being is intrinsically and not merely instrumentally valuable. So the position I hold on the matter needs to be defended. For a defense see Patrick Lee and Robert P. George, *Body-Self Dualism in Contemporary Ethics and Politics* (New York: Cambridge University Press, 2008), 160–62. See also John Finnis, Joseph M. Boyle Jr., and Germain Grisez, *Nuclear Deterrence, Morality and Realism* (Oxford: Clarendon, 1987), 304–9.

10 On religion as a basic human good, see Finnis, *Natural Law and Natural Rights*, 89–90.

11 For a deeply informed and sensitive treatment of similarities and differences in the world historical religions, see Augustine DiNoia, *The Diversity of Religions: A Christian Perspective* (Washington, D.C.: Catholic University Press, 1992).

12 See Kevin J. Hasson, *The Right to Be Wrong: Ending the Culture War over Religion in America* (New York: Encounter, 2005).

13 *Dignitatis Humanae*, 23.

14 On natural law and religious freedom in the Jewish tradition, see David Novak, *In Defense of Religious Liberty* (Wilmington, Del.: ISI Books, 2009).

15 John Rawls, *Political Liberalism* (New York: Columbia University Press, 1993), 137.

16 Judith N. Shklar, "The Liberalism of Fear," in *Liberalism and the Moral Life*, ed. Nancy L. Rosenblum (Cambridge, Mass.: Harvard University Press, 1989), 21–38.

17 *Nostra Aetate*, 2–4. This follows the text on the Vatican's website with slight modifications, www.vatican.va/archive/hist_councils/ii_vatican_council/ documents/vat-ii_decl_19651028_nostra-aetate_en.html.

8 COMPASSIONATE REASON

1   Steven Pinker, *The Better Angels of Our Nature* (New York: Viking, 2011). See also Steven Pinker, "The Surprising Decline in Violence," *TED Talks*, March 2007, www.ted.com/talks/steven_pinker_on_the_myth_of_violence.

2   Belden C. Lane, *Ravished by Beauty: The Surprising Legacy of Reformed Spirituality* (New York: Oxford University Press, 2011), 33.

3   Viktor Frankl, *Man's Search for Meaning* (Boston: Beacon Press, 1959); see also Martin Seligman on the deepest of three kinds of happiness, in "The New Era of Positive Psychology," *TED Talks*, February 2004, www.ted .com/talks/martin_seligman_on_the_state_of_psychology.

4   W. A. Spooner, "The Golden Rule," in *Encyclopedia of Religion and Ethics*, ed. James Hastings (New York: Charles Scribner's Sons, 1914), 6:310–12; for some citations, see B. A. Robinson, "The 'Golden Rule' (a.k.a. Ethics of Reciprocity)," Ontario Consultants on Religious Tolerance, last updated December 30, 2016, www.religioustolerance.org/reciproc2.htm.

5   Genesis Rabbah 24.

6   Marc Gopin, *Healing the Heart of Conflict: Eight Crucial Steps to Making Peace with Yourself and with Others*, rev. ed. (North Charleston, S.C.: Create Space, 2016).

7   See, e.g., David DeSteno, "The Kindness Cure," *Atlantic*, July 21, 2015, www.theatlantic.com/health/archive/2015/07/mindfulnes s-meditation-empathy-compassion/398867/; and Paul Condon et al., "Meditation Increases Compassionate Responses to Suffering," *Psychological Sciences* 24, no. 10 (2013): 2125–27, journals.sagepub. com/doi/abs/10.1177/0956797613485603.

8   For his classic study, see George Lakoff and Mark Johnson, *Metaphors We Live By* (Chicago: University of Chicago Press, 1980). For a recent, helpful application to political discourse, see George Lakoff, "The Public's Viewpoint: Regulations Are Protections," *George Lakoff* (blog), January 28, 2017, georgelakoff.com/2017/01/28/the-publics-viewpoint-regulation s-are-protections/.

9   See George Lakoff, interview by Tavis Smiley, *Tavis Smiley*, February 7, 2017, https://www.youtube.com/watch?v=_OC-aS_QyHU.

10   Marc Gopin, *To Make the Earth Whole: The Art of Citizen Diplomacy in an Age of Religious Militancy* (Lanham, Md.: Rowman & Littlefield, 2009).

11   Daniela Lamas, "My New Iron Lung," *New Yorker*, June 26, 2014, www .newyorker.com/tech/elements/my-new-iron-lung.

12   Marc Gopin, "The Religious Ethics of Samuel David Luzzatto" (Ph.D. diss., Brandeis University, 1993). See also Gopin, *To Make the Earth Whole*, on negotiating ethics and compassion in the context of complex situations of war and peacebuilding.

13   Frankl, *Man's Search for Meaning*.

14   See, e.g., Myriam Bechtoldt and Vanessa Schneider, "Predicting Stress from the Ability to Eavesdrop on Feelings: Emotional Intelligence and

Testosterone Jointly Predict Cortisol Reactivity," *Emotion* 16, no. 6 (2016): 815–25: "Thus, the effects of EI are not unequivocally positive. While EI may positively affect the course of social interactions, it also inflicts stress on the emotionally intelligent individuals themselves." See also Nasrin Zamani Fourshani and Mohammad Ali Besharat, "Relation between Emotional Intelligence and Perceived Stress among Female Students," *Procedia-Social and Behavioral Sciences* 30 (2011): 1109–12.

15 Olga M. Klimecki et al., "Functional Neural Plasticity and Associated Changes in Positive Affect after Compassion Training," *Cerebral Cortex* 23, no. 7 (2013): 1552–61; and Olga M. Klimecki, "The Neuroscience of Empathy" (lecture, Empathy and Compassion in Society conference, London, November 2012), https://www.youtube.com/watch?v=GxH-Oiqz-14.

16 See www.jewishvirtuallibrary.org/gemilut-hasadim.

9 THE SUPERORGANISM CONCEPT AND HUMAN GROUPS

1 Margaret Thatcher, interview by Douglas Keay, *Women's Own*, September 23, 1987.

2 Rodney Stark and William Sims Bainbridge, *A Theory of Religion* (New Brunswick, N.J.: Rutgers University Press, 1987).

3 Elliott Sober and David Sloan Wilson, *Unto Others: The Evolution and Psychology of Unselfish Behavior* (Cambridge, Mass.: Harvard University Press, 1998).

4 William P. Provine, *The Origins of Theoretical Population Genetics* (Chicago: University of Chicago Press, 2001).

5 Mark E. Borrello, *Evolutionary Restraints: The Contentious History of Group Selection* (Chicago: University of Chicago Press, 2010).

6 George C. Williams, *Adaptation and Natural Selection: A Critique of Some Current Evolutionary Thought* (Princeton, N.J.: Princeton University Press, 1966).

7 Williams, *Adaptation and Natural Selection*, 90.

8 E.g., John Maynard Smith, "Group Selection and Kin Selection," *Nature* 201 (1964): 1145–46.

9 W. D. Hamilton, "The Genetical Evolution of Social Behavior: I and II," *Journal of Theoretical Biology* 7 (1964): 1–52.

10 John Maynard Smith, *Evolution and the Theory of Games* (Cambridge: Cambridge University Press, 1982).

11 Richard Dawkins, *The Selfish Gene* (Oxford: Oxford University Press, 1976).

12 E.g., David Sloan Wilson, "Altruism in Mendellian Populations Derived from Kin Groups: The Haystack Model Revisited," *Evolution* 41 (1987): 1059–70.

13 Sober and Wilson, *Unto Others*. See also David Sloan Wilson, *Does Altruism Exist? Culture, Genes, and the Welfare of Others* (New Haven, Conn.: Yale University Press, 2015), esp. chap. 3.

14 Jonathan Birch and Samir Okasha, "Kin Selection and Its Critics," *BioScience* 65, no. 1 (2014): 22–32.

15 For more on a "post-resolution" account of MLS theory, please consult David Sloan Wilson and Edward O. Wilson, "Rethinking the Theoretical Foundation of Sociobiology," *Quarterly Review of Biology* 82, no. 4 (2007): 327–48; Wilson, *Does Altruism Exist?*; and David Sloan Wilson, "Reaching a New Plateau for the Acceptance of Multilevel Selection," *Evolution Institute*, September 22, 2017, evolution-institute.org/focus-article/reaching -a-new-plateau-for-the-acceptance-of-multilevel-selection/?source=tvol.

16 Lynn Margulis, *Origin of Eukaryotic Cells* (New Haven, Conn.: Yale University Press, 1970).

17 John Maynard Smith and Eörs Szathmáry, *The Major Transitions in Evolution* (New York: W.H. Freeman, 1995); John Maynard Smith and Eörs Szathmáry, *The Origins of Life: From the Birth of Life to the Origin of Language* (Oxford: Oxford University Press, 1999).

18 Bert Hölldobler and Edward O. Wilson, *The Superorganism: The Beauty, Elegance, and Strangeness of Insect Societies* (New York: W.W. Norton, 2008).

19 Maynard Smith and Szathmáry, *Major Transitions*; and Maynard Smith and Szathmáry, *Origins of Life*.

20 Christopher Boehm, "Egalitarian Behavior and Reverse Dominance Hierarchy," *Current Anthropology* 34, no. 3 (1993): 227–54; idem, *Hierarchy in the Forest* (Cambridge, Mass.: Harvard University Press, 1999); and idem, *Moral Origins: The Evolution of Virtue, Altruism, and Shame* (New York: Basic Books, 2011).

21 Frans de Waal, *The Bonobo and the Atheist: In Search of Humanism among the Primates* (New York: W.W. Norton, 2013).

22 David Sloan Wilson, "Multilevel Selection and Major Transitions," in *Evolution: The Extended Synthesis*, ed. Massimo Pigliucci and Gerd B. Müller (Cambridge, Mass.: MIT Press, 2009), 81–94; and idem, *Does Altruism Exist?*

23 Peter J. Richerson and Robert Boyd, *Not by Genes Alone: How Culture Transformed Human Evolution* (Chicago: University of Chicago Press, 2005); Joseph Henrich, *The Secret of Our Success: How Culture Is Driving Human Evolution, Domesticating Our Species, and Making Us Smarter* (Princeton, N.J.: Princeton University Press, 2015); Robert A. Paul, *Mixed Messages: Cultural and Genetic Inheritance in the Constitution of Human Society* (Chicago: University of Chicago Press, 2015).

24 Peter Turchin, *Ultrasociety: How 10,000 Years of War Made Humans the Greatest Cooperators on Earth* (Storrs, Conn.: Baresta Books, 2015), 75.

25 Peter Turchin, *War and Peace and War: The Rise and Fall of Empires* (Upper Saddle River, N.J.: Pi Press, 2005).

26 C. Athena Aktipis and Randolph M. Nesse, "Evolutionary Foundations for Cancer Biology," *Evolutionary Applications* 6, no. 1 (2013): 144–59.

27 Robert Axelrod, *The Complexity of Cooperation: Agent-Based Models of Competition and Collaboration* (Princeton, N.J.: Princeton University Press, 1997); Maynard Smith, *Evolution and the Theory of Games.*

28 Wilson and Wilson, "Rethinking the Theoretical Foundation of Sociobiology," 345. The original quote from Rabbi Hillel is "What is hateful to you, do not do to your neighbor. That is the whole Torah. The rest is commentary. Go and learn!" (*b. Shabbath* 31a, Babylonian Talmud).

29 N. Tinbergen, "On Aims and Methods of Ethology," *Zeitschrift Für Tierpsychologie* 20 (1963): 410–33.

30 Ernst Mayr, "Cause and Effect in Biology," *Science* 134, no. 3489 (1961): 1501–6.

31 R. S. Brennan, F. Galvez, and A. Whitehead, "Reciprocal Osmotic Challenges Reveal Mechanisms of Divergence in Phenotypic Plasticity in the Killifish *Fundulus heteroclitus*," *Journal of Experimental Biology* 218, no. 8 (2015): 1212–22.

32 Brennan, Galvez, and Whitehead, "Reciprocal Osmotic Challenges."

33 David Sloan Wilson, *Darwin's Cathedral: Evolution, Religion, and the Nature of Society* (Chicago: University of Chicago Press, 2002); David Sloan Wilson et al., "The Nature of Religious Diversity: A Cultural Ecosystem Approach," *Religion, Brain & Behavior* 7, no. 2 (2017): 134–53.

34 Wikipedia, s.v. "desecration," last modified October 24, 2017, 22:27, https://en.wikipedia.org/wiki/Desecration.

35 *Merriam-Webster*, s.v. "sacred," definitions 1a and 2b, https://www.merriam-webster.com/dictionary/sacred.

36 Yasha M. Hartberg and David Sloan Wilson, "Sacred Text as Cultural Genome: An Inheritance Mechanism and Method for Studying Cultural Evolution," *Religion, Brain & Behavior* 7, no. 2 (2017): 178–90.

37 Hartberg and Wilson, "Sacred Text as Cultural Genome."

38 See examples in Hartberg and Wilson, "Sacred Text as Cultural Genome."

39 Bruce Chilton, *Abraham's Curse: The Roots of Violence in Judaism, Christianity, and Islam* (New York: Doubleday, 2008).

40 Turchin, *Ultrasociety.*

41 Pippa Norris and Ronald Inglehart, *Sacred and Secular: Religion and Politics Worldwide* (Cambridge: Cambridge University Press, 2004).

42 Kurt Johnson and David Robert Ord, *The Coming Interspiritual Age* (Vancouver: Namaste, 2013); Kurt Johnson, "Evolution and the Coming Interspiritual Age: A Conversation with Kurt Johnson," by David Sloan Wilson, *This View of Life*, May 20 2015, evolution-institute.org/article/evolution-and-the-coming-interspiritual-age-a-conversation-with-kurt-johnson/; and David Sloan Wilson and Kurt Johnson, "Steering toward the Omega Point: A Roundtable Discussion of Altruism, Evolution, and Spirituality," *This View of Life*, December 10, 2015, evolution-institute.org/article/

steering-toward-the-omega-point-a-roundtable-discussion-of-altruism
-evolution-and-spirituality/.

10 MONOTHEISM, NATIONALISM, VIOLENCE

1 I am grateful to the researchers at the Yale Center for Faith and Culture (Matt Croasmun, Drew Collins, Justin Crisp, Sarah Farmer, Angela Gorrell, and Ryan McAnnally-Linz) for a critical reading of the early draft of this text. Karin Fransen deserves special mention as she functioned as both a critical reader and editor. I have learned much from the discussions at the symposium at King's College London on "Redeeming the Past and Building the Future: Confronting Religious Violence with a Counter Narrative" where this text was originally presented, particularly from Guy G. Stroumsa's response to my presentation. Part of the research for this essay was made possible by McDonald Agape Foundation.

2 My point here is not that the consequences of market-driven globalizing processes have only been negative but that these processes have *also* had undeniable and significant negative consequences. The effects of market-driven globalization have been highly ambivalent. With regard to the three effects of globalization mentioned in the main body of the text, it is true to say that unconscionable disparities in wealth, environmental degradation, and loss of identities are generated simultaneously with unprecedented economic growth, partial environmental improvements, and revitalization of traditions. It is easy to identify other ambivalences of globalization processes: ease of communication combines with loss of privacy; lifesaving and life-enhancing technological innovations combine with the threat of technological self-destruction; and so on.

3 On fascism raising its ugly head in the West in the second decade of the twenty-first century, see Rob Riemen, *To Fight against This Age: On Fascism and Humanism* (New York: W.W. Norton, 2018). See also Timothy Snyder, *On Tyranny: Twenty Lessons from the Twentieth Century* (New York: Tim Duggan, 2017).

4 See Jan Assmann, *Of God and Gods: Egypt, Israel, and the Rise of Monotheism* (Madison: University of Wisconsin Press, 2008), 106–11; see also idem, *The Price of Monotheism*, trans. Robert Savage (Stanford, Calif.: Stanford University Press, 2010). Assmann qualifies his thesis somewhat with regard to biblical monotheism in *Exodus: Die Revolution der Alten Welt* (Munich: Beck, 2015).

5 Scripture translations are the author's own.

6 On the relationship between the one and the whole, between singularity and universality, see Joseph Ratzinger, *Introduction to Christianity*, trans. J. R. Foster (San Francisco: Ignatius Press, 2004), 136, 187–88.

7 On idolatry as error, see Moshe Halbertal and Avishai Margalit, *Idolatry* (Cambridge, Mass.: Harvard University Press, 1992), 108–36.

8 On axial transformations, see Robert N. Bellah and Hans Joas, eds., *The Axial Age and Its Consequences* (Cambridge, Mass.: Belknap Press, 2012). The idea of axiality has entered contemporary discussion through the work of Karl Jaspers. See his *The Origin and Goal of History*, trans. Michael Bullock (London: Routledge & Kegan Paul, 1953), 121.

9 For an argument for these features of monotheisms, as well as other axial religions and philosophies, see Miroslav Volf, *Flourishing: Why We Need Religion in a Globalized World* (New Haven, Conn.: Yale University Press, 2016).

10 At the symposium in London at which these theses were originally presented, Guy G. Stroumsa objected that early Christians, not unlike the Jews, understood themselves as a nation. In his apologetic book *Praeparatio Evangelica*, Eusebius does argue that Christians are a "real people," that they, as Aryeh Kofsky puts it, "constitute a nation with a true past and history" ("Eusebius of Caesarea and the Christian-Jewish Polemic," in *Contra Iudaeos: Ancient and Medieval Polemics between Christians and Jews*, ed. Ora Limor and Guy G. Stroumsa [Tübingen: Mohr Siebeck, 1996], 71). But Eusebius was a court theologian and his interests were political and at odds with the then prevalent self-understanding of Christians. True, the early Christians have been called "a third nation" next to Jews and Gentiles. But both the advocates of Christianity, like Tertullian (*Nat.* 1.8), and its enemies, like Celsus (*Cels.* 5.33), pushed against the claim. The Epistle to Diognetus expresses early Christian nonnational and nonethnic cosmopolitan self-understanding with unmatched precision and eloquence: "Christians cannot be distinguished from the rest of the human race by country or language or customs. They do not live in cities of their own; they do not use a peculiar form of speech; they do not follow an eccentric manner of life. . . . They live in Greek and barbarian cities alike, as each man's lot has been cast, and follow the customs of the country in clothing and food and other matters of daily living." Diogn. 5, trans. Richardson, Christian Classics Ethereal Library, https://www.ccel.org/ccel/richardson/fathers.x.i.ii.html.

11 Jewish monotheism represents a unique and changing blend of particularism and universalism. For an argument for the dominance of the universalist strand in Jewish monotheism and for the conception of Israel in transcendental rather than ethnic terms, see Jacob Neusner, *Children of the Flesh, Children of the Promise: A Rabbi Talks with Paul* (Cleveland, Ohio: Pilgrim, 1995).

12 See Matthias Köckert, *Abraham: Ahnvater—Vorbild—Kultstifter* (Leipzig: Evangelische, 2017), 301–7.

13 See Martin Lings, *Muhammad: His Life Based on the Earliest Sources* (Rochester, Vt.: Inner Traditions, 1983), 45.

14 I follow here the argument of Jan Assmann that monotheism implies that "*the principle of the state is left behind* and an anti-statist *countersociety* set up in which the influence of the principle of statehood is reduced to a bare minimum" (*Price of Monotheism*, 45 [emphasis original]). I reject, however,

his polemic against monotheism's introduction of the category of truth in the sphere of religions.

15 Writing from the standpoint of Christian monotheism and creation of Christian communities, Nicholas Wolterstorff notes: "On the one hand, its [the church's] membership included people from other nations; on the other hand, its membership never included all from any nation. . . . The church included more than Slavs but not all Slavs; the church is not Slavic. The church includes more than Americans but not all Americans; the church is not American. And so forth, for all nations, all peoples. The church is not the church *of* any nation or people. It does not belong to the social identity of any natural people." Wolterstorff, *The Mighty and the Almighty. An Essay in Political Theology* (Cambridge: Cambridge University Press, 2012), 121–22.

16 I use the phrase prompted by a strand of Christianity called, by critics, "the prosperity Gospel" and in analogy to ancient "fertility religions" (in contrast to which the axial religions and philosophies emerged). Whereas in preindustrial societies the wealth of an individual or a tribe rested to a large degree on fertility, in industrial and postindustrial societies, the role of fertility as a source of wealth has progressively diminished. Hence today it is more accurate to say that the major temptation of monotheism with regard to material wealth consists in becoming a "prosperity religion" rather than "fertility religion." See Kate Bowler, *Blessed: A History of the American Prosperity Gospel* (Oxford: Oxford University Press, 2013).

17 Among modern thinkers, Georg W. F. Hegel gave the most compelling articulation of this position. See especially his *Philosophy of Right*, trans. Alan White (Indianapolis: Hackett, 2002); and his *Lectures on the Philosophy of History*, trans. Robert F. Brown and Peter C. Hodgson (Oxford: Oxford University Press, 2011).

18 For an argument that today the nation-state has given way to the market-state, see Philip Bobbitt, *The Shield of Achilles: War, Peace, and the Course of History* (New York: Random House, 2002); and idem, *Terror and Consent: The Wars for the Twenty-First Century* (New York: Random House, 2008).

19 Thomas Hobbes, *Leviathan*, ed. C. B. MacPherson (New York: Penguin, 1968 [1651]), 168, 173.

20 Immanuel Kant, *Toward Perpetual Peace*, in *Immanuel Kant: Practical Philosophy*, trans. and ed. Mary J. Gregor (Cambridge: Cambridge University Press, 1996), 336.

21 Examples of merging of the political functions of religion as a tool in the hands of those who govern (or aspire to govern) and religion as a marker of communal identity are not hard to find. In the conflict between Christians and Muslims in Kosovo (the birthplace of Serbian Orthodox civilization now populated primarily by Muslim Albanians), as well as in the conflicts between Hindus and Muslims in Ayodhya (the birthplace of the god-king Rama and the site of Babri Mosque), religions functioned,

arguably, primarily as legitimacy-granting and aggression-motivating markers of identity.

22 David Martin, *Does Christianity Cause War?* (Oxford: Oxford University Press, 1997), 134.

23 See Miroslav Volf, *Allah: A Christian Response* (San Francisco: HarperCollins, 2011), 227–31.

24 The claim assumes, of course, the continued existence and vibrancy of religions. For an argument that religions are not disappearing and that they will continue to wield social power in the foreseeable future, see Volf, *Flourishing*, 59–67.

25 For the correlation of the articulations and rearticulation of the stance toward violence with respective attitudes to worldly rule in the three monotheistic religions—Judaism, Christianity, and Islam—see the extended comments in Volf, *Flourishing*, 265, n. 68.

26 On the fundamental importance of boundaries and therefore of their maintenance, as well as on the need for the porousness of the boundaries and their dynamic character, see Miroslav Volf, *Exclusion and Embrace: A Theological Exploration of Identity, Otherness, and Reconciliation* (Nashville: Abingdon, 1996), 58–71.

11 COUNTERING RELIGIOUS, MORAL, AND POLITICAL HATE-PREACHING

1 Anton Moortgat and Alexander Scharff, *Ägypten und Vorderasien im Altertum* (Munich: Bruckmann, 1950), 243, author's translation.

2 See Michael Welker, *God the Spirit*, trans. John Hoffmeyer (Philadelphia: Fortress, 1994; repr., Eugene, Oreg.: Wipf & Stock, 2013), 134–47, 228–39.

3 F. Charles Fensham, "Widow, Orphan, and the Poor in Ancient Near Eastern Legal and Wisdom Literature," *Journal of Near Eastern Studies* 21, no. 2 (1962): 129–39; cf. Jan Assmann, *Ma'at: Gerechtigkeit und Unsterblichkeit im Alten Ägypten* (Munich: Beck, 1990), 246–47.

4 Leonard William King, trans., *The Code of Hammurabi* (North Charleston, S.C.: CreateSpace, 2015 [1910]), epilogue.

5 Scripture translations are the author's own.

6 Michael Welker, "The Power of Mercy in Biblical Law," *Journal of Law and Religion* 29, no. 2 (2014): 234. In the following, I refer to some ideas of this text.

7 Alfred North Whitehead, *Process and Reality: An Essay in Cosmology*, corrected edition, ed. David Ray Griffin and Donald W. Sherburne (1929; New York: Free Press, 1978), 105. The context of this statement reads: all living individuals and "all societies require interplay with their environment; and in the case of living societies this interplay takes the form of robbery. The living society may, or may not, be a higher type of organism than the food which it disintegrates. But whether or no it be for the general

good, life is robbery. It is at this point that with life morals become acute. The robber requires justification."

8 Cf. Alisa L. Carse, "Vulnerability, Agency, and Human Flourishing," in *Health and Human Flourishing: Religion, Medicine, and Moral Anthropology*, ed. Carol R. Taylor and Roberto Dell'Oro (Washington, D.C.: Georgetown University Press, 2006), 33–52; Kristine Culp, *Vulnerability and Glory: A Theological Account* (Louisville, Ky.: Westminster John Knox, 2010); and Heike Springhart, *Der verwundbare Mensch: Sterben, Tod und Endlichkeit im Horizont einer realistischen Anthropologie* (Tübingen: Mohr Siebeck, 2016), 203–16.

9 See Exod 6:6; 22:20 (22:21 in many versions); Exod 23:9; Lev 19:34; Deut 5:15; 10:19; 23:7; 26:5-8, which use the Hebrew *ger*, variously translated as "stranger" or "alien."

10 Michael Welker, "Security of Expectations: Reformulating the Theology of Law and Gospel," *Journal of Religion* 66 (1986): 237.

11 Michael Welker, "Gottes Gerechtigkeit," *Neue Zeitschrift für Systematische Theologie und Religionsphilosophie* 56, no. 4 (2014): 412.

12 See Michael Welker, "Romantic Love, Covenantal Love, Kenotic Love," in *The Work of Love: Creation as Kenosis*, ed. John Polkinghorne (Grand Rapids: Eerdmans, 2001), 133–36.

13 See *Duden: Sinn- und sachverwandte Wörter*, ed. Wolfgang Müller (Mannheim: Bibliographisches Institut, 1997), s.v. "hassen," 321.

14 *Heidelberg Catechism: 450th Anniversary Edition* (Grand Rapids: Faith Alive Christian Resources, 2013).

15 Jonathan Sacks, *Not in God's Name: Confronting Religious Violence* (New York: Schocken Books, 2015).

16 Sacks, *Not in God's Name*, 238–51.

17 Sacks, *Not in God's Name*, 238, cf. 239.

18 Cf. Sacks, *Not in God's Name*, 242–43.

19 Sacks, *Not in God's Name*, 246; cf. Henri Atlan, "Founding Violence and Divine Referent," in *Violence and Truth: On the Work of René Girard*, ed. Paul Dumouchel (Stanford, Calif.: Stanford University Press, 1988), 198–208.

20 Sacks, *Not in God's Name*, 248.

21 Sacks, *Not in God's Name*, 250.

22 Cf. also the results of a multiyear international and interdisciplinary research project: Michael Welker, ed., *Quests for Freedom: Biblical—Historical—Contemporary* (Neukirchen-Vluyn: Neukirchener Verlag, 2015).

23 See Niklas Luhmann, "Soziologie der Moral," in *Theorietechnik und Moral*, ed. Niklas Luhmann and Stephan H. Pfürtner (Frankfurt: Suhrkamp, 1978), 43–63; and Michael Welker, "God's Power and Powerlessness: Biblical Theology and the Search for a World Ethos in a Time of Short-Lived

Moral Markets," in *Power, Powerlessness, and the Divine*, ed. Cynthia L. Rigby (Atlanta: Scholars, 1997), 40–43.

24   See *Duden: Sinn- und sachverwandte Wörter*, s.v. "hassen," 321.

12 BETWEEN URGENCY AND UNDERSTANDING

1   Rabbi Lord Jonathan Sacks and Heather Templeton Dill, letter of invitation to a symposium on religion and violence, King's College London, January 2017.

2   Jonathan Sacks, *Not in God's Name: Confronting Religious Violence* (London: Hodder & Stoughton, 2015).

3   See the published work of these projects in Peter Ochs and William Stacy Johnson, eds., *Crisis, Call, and Leadership in the Abrahamic Traditions* (New York: Palgrave Macmillan, 2009); Anver Emon, Mark S. Ellis, and Benjamin Glahn, eds., *Islamic Law and International Human Rights Law: Searching for Common Ground?* (Oxford: Oxford University Press, 2012); and Robin W. Lovin and Joshua Mauldin, eds., *Theology as Interdisciplinary Inquiry: Learning with and from the Natural and Human Sciences* (Grand Rapids: Eerdmans, 2017).

4   Robin W. Lovin, "Epilogue: Common Ground or Clearing Ground?" in Emon, Ellis, and Glahn, *Islamic Law*, 379–80 (emphasis added).

5   Aryeh Cohen, "Hearing the Cry of the Poor," in Ochs and Johnson, *Crisis, Call, and Leadership*, 109.

6   Sacks, *Not in God's Name*, 326.

7   Ochs and Johnson, *Crisis, Call, and Leadership*, 2.

8   Ochs and Johnson, *Crisis, Call, and Leadership*, 3.

9   Mehdi Aminrazavi, "Qur'an and the Image of the 'Other': The Good, the Bad, the Ugly," in Ochs and Johnson, *Crisis, Call, and Leadership*, 47.

10   Maria Massi Dakake, "Human Contention and Divine Argument: Faith and Truth in the Qur'anic Story of Abraham," in Ochs and Johnson, *Crisis, Call, and Leadership*, 191–92.

11   Dakake, "Human Contention," 6.

12   Dakake, "Human Contention," 6.

13   Dakake, "Human Contention," 7 (emphasis original).

14   Dakake, "Human Contention," 8.

15   Dakake, "Human Contention," 8.

16   Emon, Ellis, and Glahn, *Islamic Law*, vii.

17   Lovin, "Epilogue," 381.

18   Lovin, "Epilogue," 382.

19   Robin Lovin et al., "Introduction: Theology as Interdisciplinary Inquiry: The Virtues of Humility and Hope," in Lovin and Mauldin, *Theology as Interdisciplinary Inquiry*, xxx.

20   Lovin et al., "Introduction," xxix.

21 Celia Deane-Drummond, "Looking at Humans through the Lens of Deep History: A Transdisciplinary Approach to Theology and Evolutionary Anthropology," in Lovin and Mauldin, *Theology as Interdisciplinary Inquiry*, 1–22, quotation from 15.

22 Lovin et al., "Introduction," xxxi–xxxiii.

23 Jonathan Sacks, *The Dignity of Difference: How to Avoid the Clash of Civilizations* (London: Continuum, 2002).

24 Deane-Drummond, "Looking at Humans," 14–15; see also Kenneth A. Reynhout, *Interdisciplinary Interpretation: Paul Ricoeur and the Hermeneutics of Theology and Science* (Lanham, Md.: Lexington, 2014), 153 (emphasis original).

25 Deane-Drummond, "Looking at Humans," 15 (emphasis original).

26 Tracy argues that all theology is "public discourse" which "addresses three distinct and related social realities: the wider society, the academy, and the church"; see David Tracy, *The Analogical Imagination: Christian Theology and the Culture of Pluralism* (New York: Crossroad, 1981), 3, 5.

CONCLUDING REFLECTIONS

1 Joseph Heller, *Good as Gold* (New York: Simon and Schuster, 1979), 72.

2 The original form of the quotation is found in Theodore Parker, "Of Justice and the Conscience," in *Ten Sermons of Religion* (Boston: Crosby, Nichols and Company, 1853), 84–85. The version made famous by Martin Luther King Jr. appeared in "Out of the Long Night," *The Gospel Messenger*, February 8, 1958, 14.

3 Matthew Arnold, "To a Friend" (1849), in *The Poems of Matthew Arnold, 1840–1867* (London: Henry Frowde, 1909), line 12.

BIBLIOGRAPHY

AhlulBayt News Agency. "ISIS Militant Executes Own Father in Mosul for Insulting Abu Bakr al-Baghdadi." *ABNA*, October 13, 2016. en.abna24.com/service/middle-east-west-asia/archive/2016/10/13/785201/story.html.

Ahmed, Akbar S. "And Ne'er the Twain Shall Meet?" *Newsline*, February 2015. newslinemagazine.com/magazine/and-neer-the-twain-shall-meet/.

———. "Islam under Siege: From Clash to Dialogue of Civilizations." Miliband Lecture, London School of Economics, June 15, 2004. www.lse.ac.uk/website-archive/publicEvents/pdf/20040615AkbarAhmed.pdf.

———. *Journey into Europe*. Film, 2:01:05. Posted February 23, 2017. https://youtu.be/gyHsfV6sW70.

———. *Journey into Europe: Islam, Immigration, and Identity*. Washington, D.C.: Brookings Institution Press, 2018.

———. "To Prevent More Attacks like Nice, We Must Integrate Muslims, Not Simply Bomb ISIS." *HuffPost*, July 18, 2016. www.huffingtonpost.com/akbar-ahmed/nice-attack-muslims-isis_b_11061076.html.

Ahmed, Zahid Shahab, and Michelle Baxter. *Texts and Contexts: Attitudes of Teachers in India and Pakistan*. New Delhi: WISCOMP, 2007.

Akhtar, Shabbir. *Be Careful with Muhammad! The Salman Rushdie Affair*. London: Bellew, 1989.

———. "Whose Light? Whose Darkness?" *Guardian*, February 27, 1989.

Aktipis, C. Athena, and Randolph M. Nesse. "Evolutionary Foundations for Cancer Biology." *Evolutionary Applications* 6, no. 1 (2013): 144–59. doi:10.1111/eva.12034.

Allison, Graham. "Why ISIS Fears Israel." *National Interest*, August 8, 2016.

Aminrazavi, Mehdi. "Qur'an and the Image of the 'Other': The Good, the Bad, the Ugly." In Ochs and Johnson, *Crisis, Call, and Leadership*, 47–58.

Anscombe, Elizabeth. "Modern Moral Philosophy." *Philosophy* 33, no. 124 (1958): 1–19.

Armstrong, Karen. *A Letter to Pakistan*. New York: Oxford University Press, 2011.

Arreguín-Toft, Ivan. "How the Weak Win Wars: A Theory of Asymmetric Conflict." *International Security* 26, no. 1 (2001): 93–128.

Ashton, John. *The Religion of Paul the Apostle*. New Haven, Conn.: Yale University Press, 2000.

Assmann, Jan. *Exodus: Die Revolution der Alten Welt*. Munich: Beck, 2015.

———. *Ma'at: Gerechtigkeit und Unsterblichkeit im Alten Ägypten*. Munich: Beck, 1990.

———. *Moses the Egyptian: The Memory of Egypt in Western Monotheism*. Cambridge, Mass.: Harvard University Press, 1997.

———. *Of God and Gods: Egypt, Israel, and the Rise of Monotheism*. Madison: University of Wisconsin Press, 2008.

———. *The Price of Monotheism*. Translated by Robert Savage. Stanford, Calif.: Stanford University Press, 2010. Originally published as *Die Mosaische Unterscheidung oder der Preis des Monotheismus*. Munich: Carl Hanser, 2003.

———. *Violence et monothéisme*. Paris: Bayard, 2009.

Atlan, Henri. "Founding Violence and Divine Referent." In *Violence and Truth: On the Work of René Girard*, edited by Paul Dumouchel, 198–208. Stanford, Calif.: Stanford University Press, 1988.

Atran, Scott. "Analysing the Limits of Rational Choice in Political and Cultural Conflict." Presentation at the World Economic Forum, Davos. January 19, 2017. www.youtube.com/watch?v=SxDS2g4qSO8.

———. "The Devoted Actor: Unconditional Cooperation and Intractable Conflict across Cultures." Supplement, *Current Anthropology* 57, no. S13 (2016): 192–203.

———. *In Gods We Trust: The Evolutionary Landscape of Religion*. Oxford and New York: Oxford University Press, 2002.

———. "On the Front Line against ISIS: Who Fights, Who Doesn't, and Why." *Daily Beast*, April 19, 2016. www.thedailybeast.com/articles/ 2016/04/19/on-the-front-line-against-isis-who-fights-who-doesn-t -and-why.html.

———. "On Youth, Violent Extremism, and Promoting Peace." Address to the UN Security Council, April 23, 2015. blogs.plos .org/neuroanthropology/2015/04/25/scott-atran-on-youth-violent -extremism-and-promoting-peace/.

———. "Religion's Cognitive and Social Landscape: An Evolutionary Perspective." In *Handbook of Cultural Psychology*, edited by S. Kitayama and D. Cohen, 417–53. New York: Guilford, 2007.

———. "Statement of Scott Atran: Pathways to and from Violent Extremism: The Case for Science-Based Field Research." Testimony before the Subcommittee on Emerging Threats & Capabilities, Committee on Armed Services, U.S. Senate, March 9, 2010.

———. *Talking to the Enemy: Violent Extremism, Sacred Values, and What It Means to Be Human*. London: Penguin, 2010.

Atran, Scott, Robert Axelrod, and Richard Davis. "Sacred Barriers to Conflict Resolution." *Science* 317 (2007): 1039–40.

Atran, Scott, and Jeremy Ginges. "How Words Could End a War." *New York Times*, January 25, 2009. http://www.nytimes.com/2009/01/25/opinion/25atran.html?_r=2&pagewanted=all.

———. "Religious and Sacred Imperatives in Human Conflict." *Science* 336 (2012): 855–57.

Atran, Scott, and Nafees Hamid. "Paris: The War ISIS Wants." *New York Review of Books*, November 16, 2015. www.nybooks.com/daily/2015/11/16/paris-attacks-isis-strategy-chaos.

Atran, Scott, and Joseph Henrich. "The Evolution of Religion: How Cognitive By-Products, Adaptive Learning Heuristics, Ritual Displays, and Group Competition Generate Deep Commitments to Prosocial Religions." *Biological Theory* 5, no. 1 (2010): 18–30.

Atran, Scott, Hammad Sheikh, and Ángel Gómez. "Devoted Actors Sacrifice for Close Comrades and Sacred Cause." *Proceedings of the National Academy of Sciences, USA* 111, no. 50 (2014): 11702–3.

Axelrod, Robert. *The Complexity of Cooperation: Agent-Based Models of Competition and Collaboration*. Princeton, N.J.: Princeton University Press, 1997.

Barclay, John. *Paul and the Gift*. Grand Rapids: Eerdmans, 2015.

Baron, Jonathan, and Mark Spranca. "Protected Values." *Organizational Behavior and Human Decision Processes* 70 (1997): 1–16.

Bayrakli, Enes, and Farid Hafez, eds. *European Islamophobia Report 2015*. Ankara: SETA, 2016.

Bechtoldt, Myriam, and Vanessa Schneider. "Predicting Stress from the Ability to Eavesdrop on Feelings: Emotional Intelligence and Testosterone Jointly Predict Cortisol Reactivity." *Emotion* 16, no. 6 (2016): 815–25.

Becker, Jürgen. *Paul: Apostle to the Gentiles*. Louisville, Ky.: Westminster John Knox, 1993.

Bellah, Robert N., and Hans Joas, eds. *The Axial Age and Its Consequences*. Cambridge, Mass.: Belknap Press, 2012.

Bellah, Robert N., Richard Madsen, William M. Sullivan, Ann Swidler, and Steven M. Tipton. *Habits of the Heart: Individualism and Commitment in American Life*. London: Hutchinson, 1988.

Berger, Peter L. *The Desecularization of the World: Resurgent Religion and World Politics*. Washington, D.C.: Ethics and Public Policy Center, 2008.

———. *The Sacred Canopy: Elements of a Sociological Theory of Religion*. Garden City, N.Y.: Doubleday, 1967.

Bergen, Peter, and Michael Lind. "A Matter of Pride: Why We Can't Buy Off Osama Bin Laden." *Democracy* 3 (Winter 2007). www.democracy journal.org/article.php?ID=6496.

Bergmann, Martin S. *In the Shadow of Moloch*. New York: Columbia University Press, 1992.

Bergson, Henri. *Les deux sources de la morale et de la religion*. Paris: Universitaires de France, 1932.

Berns, Gregory S., Emily Bell, C. Monica Capra, Michael J. Prietula, Sara Moore, Brittany Anderson, Jeremy Ginges, and Scott Atran. "The Price of Your Soul: Neural Evidence for the Non-Utilitarian Representation of Sacred Values." *Philosophical Transactions of the Royal Society B* 367 (2012): 754–62.

Best, Ernest. *Mark: The Gospel as Story*. Edinburgh: T&T Clark, 1983.

Bieringer, Reimund, Didier Pollefyt, and Frederique Vandecasteele-Vanneuville. *Anti-Judaism and the Fourth Gospel: Papers of the Leuven Colloquium, 2000*. Assen: Royal Van Gorcum, 2001.

Birch, Jonathan, and Samir Okasha. "Kin Selection and Its Critics." *BioScience* 65, no. 1 (2014): 22–32.

Bobbitt, Philip. *The Shield of Achilles: War, Peace, and the Course of History*. New York: Random House, 2002.

———. *Terror and Consent: The Wars for the Twenty-First Century*. New York: Random House, 2008.

Bockmuehl, Markus. *The Epistle to the Philippians*. 4th ed. London: Black, 1997.

Boehm, Christopher. "Egalitarian Behavior and Reverse Dominance Hierarchy." *Current Anthropology* 34, no. 3 (1993): 227–54.

———. *Hierarchy in the Forest*. Cambridge, Mass.: Harvard University Press, 1999.

———. *Moral Origins: The Evolution of Virtue, Altruism, and Shame*. New York: Basic Books, 2011.

Bond, Robert M., and Brad J. Bushman. "The Contagious Spread of Violence among US Adolescents through Social Networks." *American Journal of Public Health* 107, no. 2 (2017): 288–94.

Borrello, Mark E. *Evolutionary Restraints: The Contentious History of Group Selection*. Chicago: University of Chicago Press, 2010.

Bovon, François. *Studies in Early Christianity*. WUNT 161. Tübingen: Mohr Siebeck, 2003.

Bowler, Kate. *Blessed: A History of the American Prosperity Gospel*. Oxford: Oxford University Press, 2013.

Boyarin, Daniel. *A Radical Jew: Paul and the Politics of Identity*. Berkeley: University of California Press, 1994.

Bremmer, Jan. "Religious Violence and Its Roots: A View from Antiquity." *Asdiwal* 6 (2011): 71–79.

Brennan, R. S., F. Galvez, and A. Whitehead. "Reciprocal Osmotic Challenges Reveal Mechanisms of Divergence in Phenotypic Plasticity in the Killifish *Fundulus heteroclitus*." *Journal of Experimental Biology* 218, no. 8 (2015): 1212–22.

Brown, Peter. "The Saint as Exemplar in Late Antiquity." *Representations* 2 (1983): 1–25.

Bruce, F. F. *Paul: Apostle of the Free Spirit*. Exeter: Paternoster, 1977.

Bruner, Jerome. *Actual Minds, Possible Worlds*. Cambridge, Mass.: Harvard University Press, 1986.

Buckley, Chris. "Liu Xiaobo, Chinese Dissident Who Won Nobel while Jailed, Dies at 61." *New York Times*, July 13, 2017. https://www.nytimes.com/2017/07/13/world/asia/liu-xiaobo-dead.html.

Buhrmester, Michael D., William T. Fraser, Jonathan A. Lanman, Harvey Whitehouse, and William B. Swann Jr. "When Terror Hits Home: Identity Fused Americans Who Saw Boston Bombing Victims as 'Family' Provided Aid." *Self and Identity* 14, no. 3 (2015): 253–70.

Burridge, Richard A. "Biographies of Jesus: Joseph Ratzinger and the Gospels." In *Cooperatores Veritatis: Tributes to Pope Emeritus Benedict XVI on His 90th Birthday*, edited by Pierluca Azzaro and Federico Lombardi, 47–88. Vatican City: Libreria Editrice Vaticana, 2017.

———. *Four Gospels, One Jesus? A Symbolic Reading*. Three editions. London: SPCK; Grand Rapids: Eerdmans, 1994, 2005, 2013/2014.

———. "Graeco-Roman Biography and the Gospels' Literary Genre." In *I Vangeli: Storia e Cristologia. La ricerca di Joseph Ratzinger-Benedetto XVI / The Gospels: History and Christology. The Search of Joseph Ratzinger-Benedetto XVI*, edited by Bernardo Estrada, Ermenegildo Manicardi, Armand Puig I Tarrech, and Fondazione Vaticana Joseph Ratzinger-Benedetto XVI, 151–98. Vatican City: Libreria Editrice Vaticana, 2013.

———. *Imitating Jesus: An Inclusive Approach to New Testament Ethics*. Grand Rapids: Eerdmans, 2007.

———. *What Are the Gospels? A Comparison with Graeco-Roman Biography*. SNTSMS 72. First edition, Cambridge: Cambridge University Press, 1992; second revised edition, Grand Rapids: Eerdmans, 2004; thirrd/twenty-fifth anniversary edition, Waco, Tex.: Baylor University Press, 2018.

Campbell, Douglas. *The Quest for Paul's Gospel*. London: T&T Clark, 2005.

Cancik-Lindemaier, Hildegard. "Fanatismus." In *Handbuch religion-swissentschaftlicher Grundbegriffe*, 414–20. Vol 1. Stuttgart: Kohl-hammer, 1988.

Carse, Alisa L. "Vulnerability, Agency, and Human Flourishing." In *Health and Human Flourishing: Religion, Medicine, and Moral Anthropology*, edited by Carol R. Taylor and Roberto Dell'Oro, 33–52. Washington, D.C.: Georgetown University Press, 2006.

Carter, Warren. *Matthew and the Margins: A Sociopolitical and Religious Reading*. Maryknoll, N.Y.: Orbis, 2000.

Chadwick, Owen. *The Secularization of the European Mind in the 19th Century*. Cambridge: Cambridge University Press, 1975.

Chester, S. J. *Conversion at Corinth*. London: T&T Clark, 2003.

Chilton, Bruce. *Abraham's Curse: The Roots of Violence in Judaism, Christianity, and Islam*. New York: Doubleday, 2008.

Cohen, Aryeh. "Hearing the Cry of the Poor." In Ochs and Johnson, *Crisis, Call, and Leadership*, 109–22.

Condon, Paul, David DeSteno, Gaelle Desbordes, and Willa Miller. "Meditation Increases Compassionate Responses to Suffering." *Psychological Sciences* 24, no. 10 (2013): 2125–27. journals.sagepub.com/doi/abs/10.1177/0956797613485603.

Cook, Michael. *Ancient Religions, Modern Politics: The Islamic Case in Comparative Perspective*. Princeton, N.J.: Princeton University Press, 2014.

Corley, Bruce. "Interpreting Paul's Conversion—Then and Now." In *The Road from Damascus: The Impact of Paul's Conversion on His Life, Thought, and Ministry*, edited by Richard N. Longenecker, 1–17. Grand Rapids: Eerdmans, 1997.

Cox, Harvey. *Secular City: Secularization and Urbanization in Theological Perspective*. New York: Macmillan, 1966.

Cranfield, C. E. B. *The Epistle to the Romans*. 2 vols. ICC. Edinburgh: T&T Clark, 1975–1979.

Crawford, Neta C. "Update on the Human Costs of War for Afghanistan and Pakistan, 2001 to Mid-2016." Paper of the Watson Institute, Brown University, Providence, R.I., August 2016. watson.brown.edu/costsofwar/ files/cow/imce/papers/2015/War%20in%20Afghanistan%20 and%20Pakistan%20UPDATE_FINAL.pdf.

Culik, Jan. "Prague Springs to Intolerance." *Politico*, August 21, 2015.

Culp, Kristine. *Vulnerability and Glory: A Theological Account*. Louisville, Ky.: Westminster John Knox, 2010.

Cupitt, Don. *The Sea of Faith*. London: SCM Press, 1994.

Dakake, Maria Massi. "Human Contention and Divine Argument: Faith and Truth in the Qur'anic Story of Abraham." In Ochs and Johnson, *Crisis, Call, and Leadership*, 191–208.

Darwin, Charles. *The Descent of Man.* London: John Murray, 1871; Princeton, N.J.: Princeton University Press, 1981.

Davies, W. D. *Paul and Rabbinic Judaism: Some Rabbinic Elements in Pauline Theology.* 3rd ed. London: SPCK, 1970.

Dawkins, Richard. *The Selfish Gene.* Oxford: Oxford University Press, 1976.

Deane-Drummond, Celia. "Looking at Humans through the Lens of Deep History: A Transdisciplinary Approach to Theology and Evolutionary Anthropology." In Lovin and Mauldin, *Theology as Interdisciplinary Inquiry*, 1–22.

Dehghani, Morteza, Scott Atran, Rumen Iliev, Sonya Sachdeva, Douglas Medin, and Jeremy Ginges. "Sacred Values and Conflict over Iran's Nuclear Program." *Judgment and Decision Making* 5, no. 7 (2010): 540–46.

Dehghani, Morteza, Rumen Iliev, Scott Atran, Jeremy Ginges, and Douglas Medin. "Emerging Sacred Values: The Iranian Nuclear Program." *Judgment and Decision Making* 4, no. 7 (2009): 990–93.

de Quervain, Dominique J.-F., Urs Fischbacher, Valerie Treyer, Melanie Schellhammer, Ulrich Schnyder, Alfred Buck, and Ernst Fehr. "The Neural Basis for Altruistic Punishment." *Science* 305 (2004): 1254–58.

DeSteno, David. "The Kindness Cure." *Atlantic*, July 21, 2015. www.theatlantic.com/health/archive/2015/07/mindfulness-meditation-empathy-compassion/398867/.

Devlin, Patrick. *The Enforcement of Morals.* Oxford: Oxford University Press, 1965.

de Waal, Frans. *The Bonobo and the Atheist: In Search of Humanism among the Primates.* New York: W.W. Norton, 2013.

Dihle, Albrecht. *Die griechische und lateinische Literatur der Kaiserzeit.* Munich: Beck, 1989.

DiNoia, Augustine. *The Diversity of Religions: A Christian Perspective.* Washington, D.C.: Catholic University Press, 1992.

Dizdarevič, Selma Muhič. "Islamophobia in Czech Republic." In *European Islamophobia Report*, edited by Enes Bayrakli and Farid Hafes, 115–30. Ankara: SETA, 2015. www.islamophobiaeurope.com/reports/2015/en/EIR_2015.pdf.

Donaldson, Terence L. *Paul and the Gentiles: Remapping the Apostle's Convictional World.* Minneapolis: Augsburg Fortress, 1997.

Dreher, Rod. *The Benedict Option: A Strategy for Christians in a Post-Christian Nation.* New York: Penguin Random House, 2017.

Dunbar, Robin. *Grooming, Gossip, and the Evolution of Language.* London: Faber & Faber, 1996.

Dunn, James D. G. "The Embarrassment of History: Reflections of the Problem of 'Anti-Judaism' in the Fourth Gospel." In Bieringer, Pollefyt, and Vandecasteele-Vanneuville, *Anti-Judaism and the Fourth Gospel*, 47–67.

―――. *Jesus Remembered*. Grand Rapids: Eerdmans, 2003.

―――. *The New Perspective on Paul*. Grand Rapids: Eerdmans, 2007.

―――. "The Question of Anti-Semitism in the New Testament Writings of the Period." In *Jews and Christians: The Parting of the Ways AD 70 to 135*, edited by James D. G. Dunn, 177–211. WUNT 66. Tübingen: Mohr Siebeck, 1992.

―――. *Romans*. WBC 38 and 38A. Milton Keynes: Word, 1991.

Durant, Will. *The Story of Civilization*. Vol. 1. New York: Simon & Schuster, 1935.

Durkheim, Emile. *Les formes élémentaires de la vie religieuse: Le système totémique en Australie*. Paris: F. Alcan, 1912.

―――. *Suicide*. London: Routledge, 1951.

Emon, Anver, Mark S. Ellis, and Benjamin Glahn, eds. *Islamic Law and International Human Rights Law: Searching for Common Ground?* Oxford: Oxford University Press, 2012.

Engberg-Pedersen, Troels, ed. *Paul beyond the Judaism/Hellenism Divide*. Louisville, Ky.: Westminster John Knox, 2001.

Farmer, William R., ed. *Anti-Judaism and the Gospels*. Harrisburg: Trinity International, 1999.

Fearon, James D. "Rationalist Explanations for War." *International Organization* 49, no. 3 (1995): 379–414.

Fensham, F. Charles. "Widow, Orphan, and the Poor in Ancient Near Eastern Legal and Wisdom Literature." *Journal of Near Eastern Studies* 21, no. 2 (1962): 129–39.

Ferguson, Niall. *Civilization: The West and the Rest*. London: Allen Lane, 2011.

Festinger, Leon, Henry Riecken, and Stanley Schachter. *When Prophecy Fails: A Social and Psychological Study of a Modern Group That Predicted the Destruction of the World*. Minneapolis: University of Minnesota Press, 1956.

Finnis, John. *Natural Law and Natural Rights*. 2nd ed. Oxford: Oxford University Press, 2011.

Finnis, John, Joseph M. Boyle Jr., and Germain Grisez. *Nuclear Deterrence, Morality and Realism*. Oxford: Clarendon, 1987.

Fiske, Alan Page, and Tage Shakti Rai. *Virtuous Violence: Hurting and Killing to Create, Sustain, End, and Honor Social Relationships*. New York: Cambridge University Press, 2014.

Fitzmyer, Joseph A. *Romans: A New Translation with Introduction and Commentary*. AB 33. New York: Doubleday, 1993.

Fourshani, Nasrin Zamani, and Mohammad Ali Besharat. "Relation between Emotional Intelligence and Perceived Stress among Female Students." *Procedia-Social and Behavioral Sciences* 30 (2011): 1109–12.

Frankl, Viktor. *Man's Search for Meaning*. Boston: Beacon Press, 1959.

Franklin, Eric. *Luke: Interpreter of Paul, Critic of Matthew.* JSNTSS 92. Sheffield: Sheffield Academic, 1994.

Freud, Sigmund. *Das Unbehagen in der Kultur.* Vienna: Internationaler Psychoanalitischer, 1930.

Fromm, Erich. *Escape from Freedom.* New York: Farrar & Rinehart, 1941.

Fukuyama, Francis. *The End of History and the Last Man.* London: Free Press, 2006.

————. *The Origins of Political Order.* New York: Farrar, Strauss & Giroux, 2012.

Gager, J. *Kingdom and Community: The Social World of Early Christianity.* Englewood Cliffs, N.J.: Prentice Hall, 1975.

Gambetta, Diego, and Steffen Hertog. *Engineers of Jihad.* Princeton, N.J.: Princeton University Press, 2016.

George, Robert P. "Religious Liberty and the Human Good." *International Journal of Religious Freedom* 5, no. 1 (2012): 35–44.

Ghazi bin Muhammad bin Talal. "A Common Word between Us and You." *A Common Word*, October 13, 2007. www.acommonword.com/category/new-fruits/publications.

Ginges, Jeremy, Scott Atran, Douglas Medin, and Khalil Shikaki. "Sacred Bounds on Rational Resolution of Violent Political Conflict." *Proceedings of the National Academy of Sciences, USA* 104, no. 18 (2007): 7357–60.

Ginges, Jeremy, Scott Atran, Sonya Sachdeva, and Douglas Medin. "Psychology out of the Laboratory: The Challenge of Violent Extremism." *American Psychologist* 66, no. 6 (2011): 507–19.

Glover, Jonathan. *Humanity: A Moral History of the Twentieth Century.* London: Jonathan Cape, 1999.

Goleman, Daniel. *Emotional Intelligence: Why It Can Matter More than IQ.* London: Bloomsbury, 1996; New York: Bantam Books, 1996.

Gómez, Ángel, Matthew L. Brooks, Michael D. Buhrmester, Alexandra Vázquez, Jolanda Jetten, and William B. Swann Jr. "On the Nature of Identity Fusion: Insights into the Construct and Validation of a New Measure." *Journal of Personality and Social Psychology* 100 (2011): 918–33.

Gómez, Ángel, Lucía López-Rodríguez, Hammad Sheikh, Jeremy Ginges, Lydia Wilson, Hoshang Waziri, Alexandra Vázquez, Richard Davis, and Scott Atran. "The Devoted Actor's Will to Fight and the Spiritual Dimension of Human Conflict." *Nature Human Behaviour* 1 (2017): 673–79. doi:10.1038/s41562-017-0193-3.

Gómez, Ángel, Lucía López-Rodríguez, Alexandra Vázquez, Borja Paredes, and Mercedes Martínez. "Morir y matar por un grupo o unos valores. Estrategias para evitar, reducir y/o erradicar el comportamiento grupal extremista." *Anuario de Psicología Jurídica* 26, no. 1 (2016): 122–29.

Gopin, Marc. *Healing the Heart of Conflict: Eight Crucial Steps to Making Peace with Yourself and with Others.* Rev. ed. North Charleston, S.C.: CreateSpace, 2016.

———. "The Religious Ethics of Samuel David Luzzatto." Ph.D. diss., Brandeis University, 1993.

———. *To Make the Earth Whole: The Art of Citizen Diplomacy in an Age of Religious Militancy.* Lanham, Md.: Rowman & Littlefield, 2009.

Gottlieb, Anthony. *The Dream of Enlightenment: The Rise of Modern Philosophy.* London: Allen Lane, 2016.

Gottschall, Jonathan. *The Storytelling Animal: How Stories Make Us Human.* Boston: Mariner, 2013.

Graham, Jesse, and Jonathan Haidt. "Sacred Values and Evil Adversaries: A Moral Foundations Approach." In *The Social Psychology of Morality: Exploring the Causes of Good and Evil,* edited by Mario Mikulincer and Phillip R. Shaver, 11–31. New York: APA, 2012.

Grisez, Germain. "The First Principle of Practical Reason: A Commentary on the *Summa Theologiae,* 1–2, Question 94, Article 2." *Natural Law Forum* 10 (1965): 168-96.

Griswold, Eliza. *The Tenth Parallel: Dispatches from the Fault Line between Christianity and Islam.* New York: Farrar, Strauss & Giroux, 2010.

Guelich, Robert A. *Mark 1–8.26.* WBC 34A. Dallas: Word, 1989.

Gurel, Perin. *The Limits of Westernization: A Cultural History of America in Turkey.* New York: Columbia University Press, 2017.

Halbertal, Moshe, and Avishai Margalit. *Idolatry.* Cambridge, Mass.: Harvard University Press, 1992.

Halbfass, Wilhelm. *India and Europe: An Essay in Understanding.* Albany: SUNY Press, 1988.

Hamilton, W. D. "The Genetical Evolution of Social Behavior: I and II." *Journal of Theoretical Biology* 7 (1964): 1–52.

Hammerton-Kelly, R. *Sacred Violence: Paul's Hermeneutic of the Cross.* Minneapolis: Fortress, 1991.

Hartberg, Yasha M., and David Sloan Wilson. "Sacred Text as Cultural Genome: An Inheritance Mechanism and Method for Studying Cultural Evolution." *Religion, Brain & Behavior* 7, no. 2 (2017): 178–90. doi:10.1080/2153599X.2016.1195766.

Hassan bin Talal, and Alain Elkann. *To Be a Muslim: Islam, Peace, and Democracy.* Brighton: Sussex Academic Press, 2004.

Hassani, Salim T. S. al-, ed. *1001 Inventions: The Enduring Legacy of Muslim Civilization.* Washington, D.C.: National Geographic, 2012.

Hasson, Kevin J. *The Right to Be Wrong: Ending the Culture War over Religion in America.* New York: Encounter, 2005.

Hauerwas, Stanley, and L. Gregory Jones, eds. *Why Narrative? Readings in Narrative Theology.* Grand Rapids: Eerdmans, 1989.

Hawthorne, Gerald F. *Philippians*. WBC 43. Nashville: Nelson, 2004.

Hegel, Georg W. F. *Lectures on the Philosophy of History*. Translated by Robert F. Brown and Peter C. Hodgson. Oxford: Oxford University Press, 2011.

———. *Philosophy of Right*. Translated by Alan White. Indianapolis: Hackett, 2002.

Heidelberg Catechism: 450th Anniversary Edition. Grand Rapids: Faith Alive Christian Resources, 2013.

Hengel, Martin. *The Pre-Christian Paul*. London: SCM Press, 1991.

Hengel, Martin, and Anna Maria Schwemer. *Paul between Damascus and Antioch: The Unknown Years*. London: SCM Press, 1997.

Henrich, Joseph. *The Secret of Our Success: How Culture Is Driving Human Evolution, Domesticating Our Species, and Making Us Smarter*. Princeton, N.J.: Princeton University Press, 2015.

Hobbes, Thomas. *Leviathan*. New York: E. P. Dutton, 1901 (1651). Edited by C. B. MacPherson. New York: Penguin, 1968.

Hoffman, Bruce, and Gordon H. McCormick. "Terrorism, Signaling, and Suicide Attack." *Studies in Conflict & Terrorism* 27 (2004): 243–81.

Holbrook, Colin, and Daniel M. T. Fessler. "Sizing Up the Threat: The Envisioned Physical Formidability of Terrorists Tracks Their Leaders' Failures and Successes." *Cognition* 127, no. 1 (2013): 46–56.

Hölldobler, Bert, and Edward O. Wilson. *The Superorganism: The Beauty, Elegance, and Strangeness of Insect Societies*. New York: W.W. Norton, 2008.

Hooker, Morna D. *The Gospel according to St Mark*. London: Black, 1991.

Horrell, David G. *An Introduction to the Study of Paul*. 2nd ed. London: T&T Clark, 2006.

Hoti, Amineh Ahmed. *Accepting Difference*. Islamabad: Emel, 2015.

———. "The Birth of a Messianic Jewish Community in Pakistan." *HuffPost*, December 19, 2016. www.huffingtonpost.com/entry/the-birth-of-a -messianic-jewish-community-in-pakistan_us_58577819e4b0d5f48e 165129.

———. "The Challenges and Practical Outcomes of Interfaith Dialogue in Pakistan and the UK: Anthropological Notes from the Field of a Muslim Woman Leading Dialogue." In *Interculturalism at the Crossroads: Comparative Perspectives on Concepts, Policies and Practices*, edited by F. Mansouri, 227–56. Paris: UNESCO, 2017.

———. "Interfaith at the White House." *Friday Times*, December 25, 2015. www.thefridaytimes.com/tft/interfaith-at-the-white-house/.

———. "Negative Coverage of Muslims Led to Trump's Rise." *HuffPost*, November 30, 2016. www.huffingtonpost.com/entry/decades-of -negative-coverage-on-muslims-has-led-to_us_583f9f7ce4b04587de5de 758.

———. *Sorrow and Joy among Muslim Women: The Pukhtuns of Northern Pakistan*. Cambridge: Cambridge University Press, 2006.

———. *Teaching Acceptance*. Islamabad: Emel, 2015.

———. "An Unfair Image: Dear Mr. Trump, Please Read This Book by a Fellow-Christian on 'A Sacred Land.'" *Huffpost*, January 14, 2018. www.huffingtonpost.com/entry/an-unfair-image-dear-mr-trump-please-read-this-book_us_5a5c2c83e4b01ccdd48b5ddc.

Hoti, Amineh Ahmed, and Zahid Shabab Ahmed. "Peace Education in Pakistan: A Case Study of the Centre for Dialogue and Action, FC College University." In *Promoting Global Peace and Civic Engagement through Education*, edited by Kshama Pandey, Pratibha Upadhyay, and Amita Jaiswal, 323–37. Hershey, Penn.: IGI Global, 2016.

Howe, David. *Empathy: What It Is and Why It Matters*. London: Palgrave Macmillan, 2012.

Hübner, Hans. *Law in Paul's Thought: A Contribution to the Development of Pauline Theology*. Edinburgh: T&T Clark, 1984.

Huntington, Samuel. *The Clash of Civilizations and the Remaking of World Order*. New York: Simon & Schuster, 2011.

Hurtado, L. W. "Convert, Apostate, or Apostle to the Nations: The 'Conversion' of Paul in Recent Scholarship." *Studies in Religion/Sciences Religieuses* 22 (1993): 273–84.

Ignatieff, Michael. *Blood and Belonging: Journeys into the New Nationalism*. London: Vintage, 1994.

Institute for Economics and Peace. *Global Terrorism Index 2015: Executive Summary*. Sydney: IEP, 2015.

International Republican Institute. "Visegrad Four Poll Reveals Vulnerabilities to Russian Influence." May 27, 2017. www.iri.org/resource/visegrad-four-poll-reveals-vulnerabilities-russian-influence.

Jaspers, Karl. *The Origin and Goal of History*. Translated by Michael Bullock. London: Routledge & Kegan Paul, 1953.

Johnson, Dominic. *God Is Watching You: How the Fear of God Makes Us Human*. Oxford: Oxford University Press, 2016.

Johnson, Kurt. "Evolution and the Coming Interspiritual Age: A Conversation with Kurt Johnson." By David Sloan Wilson. *This View of Life*, May 20, 2015. evolution-institute.org/article/evolution-and-the-coming-interspiritual-age-a-conversation-with-kurt-johnson/.

Johnson, Kurt, and David Robert Ord. *The Coming Interspiritual Age*. Vancouver: Namaste, 2013.

Kahneman, Daniel. *Thinking, Fast and Slow*. New York: Farrar, Strauss & Giroux, 2011.

Kant, Immanuel. *Toward Perpetual Peace*. In *Immanuel Kant: Practical Philosophy*, translated and edited by Mary J. Gregor, 311–52. Cambridge: Cambridge University Press, 1996.

Katz, Steven T. "Issues in the Separation of Judaism and Christianity after 70 C.E.: A Reconsideration." *JBL* 103, no. 1 (1984): 43–76.

Kaufmann, Eric. *Shall the Religious Inherit the Earth? Demography and Politics in the Twenty-First Century.* London: Profile Books, 2010.

Kee, Howard C. *Community of the New Age: Studies in Mark's Gospel.* London: SCM Press, 1977.

Keener, Craig S. *The Gospel of John: A Commentary.* 2 vols. Peabody, Mass.: Hendrickson, 2003.

Kelley, Dean M. *Why Conservative Churches Are Growing: A Study in Sociology of Religion.* New York: Harper & Row, 1972.

Kierkegaard, Søren. *The Concept of Anxiety.* New York: Liveright, 2014 (1844).

King, Leonard William, trans. *The Code of Hammurabi.* North Charleston, S.C.: CreateSpace, 2015 (1910).

King, Martin Luther, Jr. *Letter from Birmingham Jail.* 1963. New York: HarperCollins, 1994.

Kippenberg, H. "Apokalyptik, Messianismus, Chiliasmus." In *Handbuch religionswissentschaftlicher Grundbegriffe*, 9–26. Vol. 2. Stuttgart: Kohlhammer, 1990.

Kirchick, James. *The End of Europe.* New Haven, Conn.: Yale University Press, 2017.

Kissinger, Henry. *World Order.* London: Allen Lane, 2014.

Klimecki, Olga M. "The Neuroscience of Empathy." Lecture at the Empathy and Compassion in Society conference, London, November 2012. https://www.youtube.com/watch?v=GxH-Oiqz-14.

Klimecki, Olga M., Tania Singer, Susanne Leiberg, and Clauss Lamm. "Functional Neural Plasticity and Associated Changes in Positive Affect after Compassion Training." *Cerebral Cortex* 23, no. 7 (2013): 1552–61.

Köckert, Matthias. *Abraham: Ahnvater—Vorbild—Kultstifter.* Leipzig: Evangelische, 2017.

Kofsky, Aryeh. "Eusebius of Caesarea and the Christian-Jewish Polemic." In *Contra Iudaeos: Ancient and Medieval Polemics between Christians and Jews*, edited by Ora Limor and Guy G. Stroumsa, 59–83. Tübingen: Mohr Siebeck, 1996.

Kureishi, Hanif. *The Buddha of Suburbia.* New York: Penguin, 1991.

Lakoff, George. Interview by Tavis Smiley. *Tavis Smiley*, February 7, 2017. www.pbs.org/wnet/tavissmiley/interviews/professor-cognitive-science-george-lakoff/.

———. "The Public's Viewpoint: Regulations are Protections." *George Lakoff* (blog), January 28, 2017. georgelakoff.com/2017/01/28/the-publics-viewpoint-regulations-are-protections/.

Lakoff, George, and Mark Johnson. *Metaphors We Live By.* Chicago: University of Chicago Press, 1980.

Lamas, Daniela. "My New Iron Lung." *New Yorker*, June 26, 2014. www.
    newyorker.com/tech/elements/my-new-iron-lung.

Lane, Belden C. *Ravished by Beauty: The Surprising Legacy of Reformed
    Spirituality.* New York: Oxford University Press, 2011.

Lapide, Pinchas, and Peter Stuhlmacher. *Paul: Rabbi and Apostle.* Minne-
    apolis: Augsburg, 1984.

Lee, Patrick, and Robert P. George. *Body-Self Dualism in Contemporary
    Ethics and Politics.* New York: Cambridge University Press, 2008.

Levine, Amy-Jill. "Anti-Judaism and the Gospel of Matthew." With responses
    from Philip L. Shuler and Warren Carter. In Farmer, *Anti-Judaism and
    the Gospels*, 9–62.

Liebman, Charles. "Orthodoxy in Modern Jewish Life." In *Dimensions
    of Orthodox Judaism*, edited by Reuven Bulka, 33–105. New York:
    Ktav, 1983.

Lieu, Judith M. "Anti-Judaism in the Fourth Gospel: Explanation and
    Hermeneutics." In Bieringer, Pollefyt, and Vandecasteele-Vanneuville,
    Anti-Judaism and the Fourth Gospel, 126–43.

Lifton, Robert Jay, and Eric Markusen. *The Genocidal Mentality: Nazi Holo-
    caust and Nuclear Threat.* London: Macmillan, 1991.

Lings, Martin. *Muhammad: His Life Based on the Earliest Sources.* Rochester,
    Vt.: Inner Traditions, 1983.

Lipka, Michael. "Muslims and Islam: Key Findings in the U.S. and
    around the World." Pew Research Center, August 9, 2017. http://
    www.pewresearch.org/fact-tank/2017/05/26/muslims-and-islam
    -key-findings-in-the-u-s-and-around-the-world/.

Loader, William. *Jesus' Attitude towards the Law: A Study of the Gospels.*
    Grand Rapids: Eerdmans, 2002.

Lovin, Robin W. "Epilogue: Common Ground or Clearing Ground?" In
    Emon, Ellis, and Glahn, *Islamic Law*, 379–86.

Lovin, Robin W., Peter Danchin, Agustín Fuentes, Friederike Nüssel, and
    Stephen Pope. "Introduction: Theology as Interdisciplinary Inquiry:
    The Virtues of Humility and Hope." In Lovin and Mauldin, *Theology
    as Interdisciplinary Inquiry*, viii–xxxiii.

Lovin, Robin W., and Joshua Mauldin, eds. *Theology as Interdisciplinary
    Inquiry: Learning with and from the Natural and Human Sciences.*
    Grand Rapids: Eerdmans, 2017.

Lüdemann, Gerd. *Paul, Apostle to the Gentiles: Studies in Chronology.*
    London: SCM Press, 1984.

Luhmann, Niklas. "Soziologie der Moral." In *Theorietechnik und Moral*,
    edited by Niklas Luhmann and Stephan H. Pfürtner, 8–116. Frankfurt:
    Suhrkamp, 1978.

Luz, Ulrich. "Anti-Judaism in the Gospel of Matthew as a Historical and Theological Problem: An Outline." In *Studies in Matthew*, 243–61. Grand Rapids: Eerdmans, 2005.

Lyons, Jonathan. *The House of Wisdom: How the Arabs Transformed Western Civilization*. New York: Bloomsbury, 2010.

MacIntyre, Alasdair. *After Virtue: A Study in Moral Theory*. London: Duckworth, 1981.

———. *A Short History of Ethics*. London: Routledge & Kegan Paul, 1967.

Mahony, Honor. "Orban Wants to Build 'Illiberal State.'" *EUobserver*, July 28, 2014. https://euobserver.com/political/125128.

Malik, Kenan. *From Fatwa to Jihad: The Rushdie Affair and Its Consequences*. London: Atlantic Books, 2010.

Mani, Anandi, Sendhil Mullainathan, Eldar Shafir, and Jiaying Zhao. "Poverty Impedes Cognitive Function." *Science* 341 (2013): 976–80.

Marguerat, Daniel. *The First Christian Historian: Writing the "Acts of the Apostles."* SNTSMS 121. Cambridge: Cambridge University Press, 2002.

Margulis, Lynn. *Origin of Eukaryotic Cells*. New Haven, Conn.: Yale University Press, 1970.

Marshall, I. Howard. "'Israel' and the Story of Salvation: One Theme in Two Parts." In Moessner, *Jesus and the Heritage of Israel*, 340–58.

Martin, David. *Does Christianity Cause War?* Oxford: Oxford University Press, 1997.

Maynard Smith, John. *Evolution and the Theory of Games*. Cambridge: Cambridge University Press, 1982.

———. "Group Selection and Kin Selection." *Nature* 201 (1964): 1145–46.

Maynard Smith, John, and Eörs Szathmáry. *The Major Transitions in Evolution*. New York: W.H. Freeman, 1995.

———. *The Origins of Life: From the Birth of Life to the Origin of Language*. Oxford: Oxford University Press, 1999.

Mayr, Ernst. "Cause and Effect in Biology." *Science* 134, no. 3489 (1961): 1501–6.

McAdams, Dan P. *The Stories We Live By: Personal Myths and the Making of the Self*. New York: Guilford, 1997.

McKnight, Scot. "A Loyal Critic: Matthew's Polemic with Judaism in Theological Perspective." In *Anti-Semitism and Early Christianity: Issues of Polemic and Faith*, edited by Craig A. Evans and Donald A. Hagner, 55–79. Minneapolis: Augsburg Fortress, 1993.

Menocal, María Rosa. *The Ornament of the World: How Muslims, Jews and Christians Created a Culture of Tolerance in Medieval Spain*. New York: Little, Brown, 2002.

Merriman, Helena. "Why Are 10,000 Migrant Children Missing in Europe?" *BBC News*, October 12, 2016. http://www.bbc.com/news/world-europe-37617234.

Micklethwait, John, and Adrian Wooldridge. *God Is Back: How the Global Revival of Faith Is Changing the World*. New York: Penguin, 2010.

Mishra, Pankaj. *Age of Anger: A History of the Present*. London: Allen Lane, 2017.

Moessner, David P., ed. *Jesus and the Heritage of Israel: Luke's Narrative Claim upon Israel's Legacy*. Harrisburg: Trinity International, 1999.

Momigliano, Arnaldo. "Empieta ed eresia nel mondo antico." In *Sesto contributo alla storia degli studi classici e del mondo antico*, 437–58. Vol. 2. Rome: Edizioni di storia e letteratura, 1980.

———. "Freedom of Speech and Religious Tolerance in the Ancient World." In *Anthropology and the Greeks*, edited by S. C. Humphreys, 179–93. London: Routledge, 1978.

———. "Roman Religion." In *Encyclopedia of Religion*. Reprinted in *Religions of Antiquity*, edited by R. M. Seltzer, 230–33. New York: MacMillan, 1989.

Moortgat, Anton, and Alexander Scharff. *Ägypten und Vorderasien im Altertum*. Munich: Bruckmann, 1950.

Moskos, Charles C. "The American Combat Soldier in Vietnam." *Journal of Social Issues* 31, no. 4 (1975): 25–37.

Motyer, Stephen. "The Fourth Gospel and the Salvation of Israel: An Appeal for a New Start." In Bieringer, Pollefyt, and Vandecasteele-Vanneuville, *Anti-Judaism and the Fourth Gospel*, 92–110.

Murphy-O'Connor, Jerome. *Paul: A Critical Life*. Oxford: Clarendon, 1996.

———. *Paul: His Story*. Oxford: Oxford University Press, 2004.

Myers, Ched. *Binding the Strong Man: A Political Reading of Mark's Story of Jesus*. Maryknoll, N.Y.: Orbis, 1988.

Neusner, Jacob. *Children of the Flesh, Children of the Promise: A Rabbi Talks with Paul*. Cleveland, Ohio: Pilgrim, 1995.

The 9/11 Commission Report. Washington, D.C.: Government Printing Office, 2004.

Nisbett, Richard E., and Dov Cohen. *Culture of Honor: The Psychology of Violence in the South*. Boulder, Colo.: Westview, 1996.

Norenzayan, Ara. *Big Gods: How Religion Transformed Cooperation and Conflict*. Princeton, N.J.: Princeton University Press, 2015.

Norris, Jesse J., and Hanna Grol-Prokopczyk. "Estimating the Prevalence of Entrapment in Post–9/11 Terrorism Cases." *Journal of Criminal Law and Criminology* 105, no. 3 (2015): 609–78.

Norris, Pippa, and Ronald Inglehart. *Sacred and Secular: Religion and Politics Worldwide*. Cambridge: Cambridge University Press, 2004.

Novak, David. *In Defense of Religious Liberty*. Wilmington, Del.: ISI Books, 2009.

O'Brien, Peter T. *Commentary on Philippians*. NIGTC. Grand Rapids: Eerdmans, 1991.

Ochs, Peter, and William Stacy Johnson, eds. *Crisis, Call, and Leadership in the Abrahamic Traditions*. New York: Palgrave Macmillan, 2009.

Okasha, Samir. *Evolution and the Levels of Selection*. Oxford: Oxford University Press, 2006.

Orwell, George. "Review of *Mein Kampf* by Adolf Hitler" (1940). In *The Collected Essays, Journalism and Letters of George Orwell*, edited by Sonia Orwell and Ian Angus, 12–14. New York: Harcourt Brace Jovanovich, 1968.

Paul, Robert A. *Mixed Messages: Cultural and Genetic Inheritance in the Constitution of Human Society*. Chicago: University of Chicago Press, 2015.

Payne, Sebastian. "Obama: U.S. Misjudged the Rise of the Islamic State, Ability of Iraqi Army." *Washington Post*, September 28, 2014.

Perliger, Arie, and Daniel Milton. *From Cradle to Grave: The Lifecycle of the Foreign Fighters in Iraq and Syria*. West Point, N.Y.: Combating Terrorism Center, 2016. www.ctc.usma.edu/posts/from-cradle-to-grave-the-lifecycle-of-foreign-fighters-in-iraq-and-syria.

Peterson, Merrill D. *Thomas Jefferson and the New Nation: A Biography*. Oxford: Oxford University Press, 1970.

Pinker, Steven. *The Better Angels of Our Nature*. New York: Viking, 2011.

———. "The Surprising Decline in Violence." *TED Talks*, March 2007. www.ted.com/talks/steven_pinker_on_the_myth_of_violence.

Pipes, Daniel. *Militant Islam Reaches America*. New York: W.W. Norton, 2003.

Pokorný, Petr. "Das Markusevangelium: Literarische und theologische Einleitung mit Forschungsbericht." *ANRW*, 2nd ser., 25, no. 3 (1985): 1969–2035.

Popp, Maximilian. "Europe's Deadly Borders: An Inside Look at EU's Shameful Immigration Policy." *Spiegel Online*, September 11, 2014. www.spiegel.de/international/europe/europe-tightens-borders-and-fails-to-protect-people-a-989502.html.

Popper, Karl. *The Open Society and Its Enemies*. London: Routledge, 1945.

Pressfield, Steven. *The Warrior Ethos*. Los Angeles: Black Irish Entertainment, 2011.

Provine, William B. *The Origins of Theoretical Population Genetics*. Chicago: University of Chicago Press, 2001.

Rappaport, Roy A. "The Sacred in Human Evolution." *Annual Review of Ecology and Systematics* 2 (1971): 23–44.

Ratzinger, Joseph. *Introduction to Christianity*. Translated by J. R. Foster. San Francisco: Ignatius Press, 2004.

Ravens, David. *Luke and the Restoration of Israel*. JSNTSup 119. Sheffield: Sheffield Academic, 1995.

Rawls, John. "On the Priority of Right and Ideas of the Good." *Philosophy and Public Affairs* 17, no. 4 (1988): 251–76.

———. *Political Liberalism*. New York: Columbia University Press, 1993.

Reinhartz, Adele. "'Jews' and Jews in the Fourth Gospel." In Bieringer, Pollefyt, and Vandecasteele-Vanneuville, *Anti-Judaism and the Fourth Gospel*, 341–56.

Rese, M. "The Jews in Luke–Acts: Some Second Thoughts." In *The Unity of Luke–Acts*, edited by J. Verheyden, 185–201. BETL 142. Leuven: Peeters, 1999.

Research Centre for Islamic History, Art and Culture [IRCICA]. *Coexistence of Different Cultures: Examples from History as Lessons for the Future*. Istanbul: IRCICA and UNAOC, 2015.

Reuters. "Religious Conflict in Global Rise—Report." *Telegraph* (London), January 14, 2014. https://www.telegraph.co.uk/news/worldnews/middleeast/10572342/Religious-conflict-in-global-rise-report.html.

Reynhout, Kenneth A. *Interdisciplinary Interpretation: Paul Ricoeur and the Hermeneutics of Theology and Science*. Lanham, Md.: Lexington, 2014.

Richerson, Peter J., and Robert Boyd. *Not by Genes Alone: How Culture Transformed Human Evolution*. Chicago: University of Chicago Press, 2005.

Ridley, Matt. *The Origins of Virtue*. London: Viking, 1996.

Riemen, Rob. *To Fight against This Age: On Fascism and Humanism*. New York: W.W. Norton, 2018.

Riesner, Rainer. *Paul's Early Period: Chronology, Mission Strategy, Theology*. Grand Rapids: Eerdmans, 1998.

Robinson, B. A. "The 'Golden Rule' (a.k.a. Ethics of Reciprocity)." Ontario Consultants on Religious Tolerance. Last updated December 30, 2016. www.religioustolerance.org/reciproc2.htm.

Roosevelt, Theodore. "First Annual Message." December 3, 1901. www.presidency.ucsb.edu/ws/?pid=29542.

———. "Roosevelt Corollary to the Monroe Doctrine: Excerpt from the President's Annual Message to Congress." December 6, 1904. www.theodore-roosevelt.com/images/research/speeches/trmdcorollary.pdf.

Roskam, H. N. *The Purpose of the Gospel of Mark in Its Historical and Social Context*. NovTSup 114. Leiden: Brill, 2004.

Russell, Bertrand. *History of Western Philosophy*. London: Allen & Unwin, 1962.

Sacks, Jonathan. "Cultural Climate Change: The Role of Religion in a Secularised West." Lecture presented to the Chautauqua Institution, Lake Chautauqua, N.Y., July 21, 2017. www.youtube.com/watch?v=2GC_xLuKl5Q&t=169s.

———. *The Dignity of Difference: How to Avoid the Clash of Civilizations*. London: Continuum, 2002.

———. "Faith in the Future: The Promise and Perils of Religion in the 21st Century." *Rabbisacks.org*, November 30, 2016. rabbisacks.org/faith-future-promise-perils-religion/.

———. *The Great Partnership*. London: Hodder & Stoughton, 2012.

———. *Not in God's Name: Confronting Religious Violence*. London: Hodder & Stoughton; New York: Schocken Books, 2015.

———. *The Politics of Hope*. London: Vintage, 2000.

———. "Rabbi Jonathan Sacks on What It Takes to End Violence in God's Name." Interview by Lauren Markoe. *HuffPost*, November 8, 2015. www.huffingtonpost.com/entry/rabbi-jonathan-sacks-not-in-gods -name_us_5632697ae4b0c66bae5b9a10.

Sageman, Marc. *Understanding Terror Networks*. Philadelphia: University of Pennsylvania Press, 2004.

Saldarini, Anthony J. *Matthew's Christian-Jewish Community*. Chicago: University of Chicago Press, 1994.

Sanders, E. P. *The Historical Figure of Jesus*. London: Penguin, 1993.

———. *Jesus and Judaism*. London: SCM Press, 1985.

———, ed. *Jewish and Christian Self-Definition*. Vol. 1, *The Shaping of Christianity in the Second and Third Centuries*. London: SCM Press, 1980.

———. *Jewish Law from Jesus to the Mishnah*. London: SCM Press, 1990.

———. *Judaism: Practice and Belief 63 BCE–66 CE*. London: SCM Press, 1992.

———. *Paul*. Oxford: Oxford University Press, 1991.

———. *Paul, the Law, and the Jewish People*. Philadelphia: Fortress, 1983.

———. *Paul and Palestinian Judaism*. London: SCM Press, 1977.

Sandmel, Samuel. *Anti-Semitism in the New Testament?* Philadelphia: Fortress, 1978.

Schelling, Thomas C. *The Strategy of Conflict*. Cambridge, Mass.: Harvard University Press, 1960.

Schmidt, Daryl D. "Anti-Judaism and the Gospel of Luke." With responses from David L. Balch and Allan J. McNichol. In Farmer, *Anti-Judaism and the Gospels*, 63–119.

Schumacher, Elizabeth. "Shake-Up for Germany's Right-Wing AfD over Anti-Semitism Row." *DW*, July 5, 2016. www.dw.com/en/shake-up -for-germanys-right-wing-afd-over-anti-semitism-row/a-19379702.

Segal, Alan F. *Paul the Convert: The Apostolate and Apostasy of Saul the Pharisee*. New Haven, Conn.: Yale University Press, 1990.

———. *Rebecca's Children: Judaism and Christianity in the Roman World*. Cambridge, Mass.: Harvard University Press, 1986.

Seligman, Martin. "The New Era of Positive Psychology." *TED Talks*, February 2004. www.ted.com/talks/martin_seligman_on_the_state _of_psychology.

Sheikh, Hammad, Jeremy Ginges, and Scott Atran. "Sacred Values in Intergroup Conflict: Resistance to Social Influence, Temporal Discounting, and Exit Strategies." *Annals of the New York Academy of Sciences* 1299 (2013): 11–24.

Sheikh, Hammad, Ángel Gómez, and Scott Atran. "Empirical Evidence for the Devoted Actor Model." Supplement, *Current Anthropology* 57, no. S13 (2016): 204–9.

Shklar, Judith N. "The Liberalism of Fear." In *Liberalism and the Moral Life*, edited by Nancy L. Rosenblum, 21–38. Cambridge, Mass.: Harvard University Press, 1989.

Simon, Herbert A. *Models of Bounded Rationality.* Cambridge, Mass.: MIT Press, 1997.

Smith, Robert. "Why Soldiers Fight. Part I. Leadership, Cohesion and Fighter Spirit." *Quality and Quantity* 18 (1983): 1–32.

Snyder, Timothy. *On Tyranny: Twenty Lessons from the Twentieth Century.* New York: Tim Duggan, 2017.

Sober, Elliott, and David Sloan Wilson. *Unto Others: The Evolution and Psychology of Unselfish Behavior.* Cambridge, Mass.: Harvard University Press, 1998.

Spooner, W. A. "The Golden Rule." In *Encyclopedia of Religion and Ethics*, edited by James Hastings, 6:310–12. New York: Charles Scribner's Sons, 1914.

Springhart, Heike. *Der verwundbare Mensch: Sterben, Tod und Endlichkeit im Horizont einer realistischen Anthropologie.* Tübingen: Mohr Siebeck, 2016.

Stanton, G. N. *A Gospel for a New People: Studies in Matthew.* Edinburgh: T&T Clark, 1992.

Stark, Rodney, and William Sims Bainbridge. *A Theory of Religion.* New Brunswick, N.J.: Rutgers University Press, 1987.

Stefani, P. *L'antigiudaismo: Storia di un'idea.* Rome: Laterza, 2004.

Stendahl, Krister. "Call Rather Than Conversion." In Krister Stendahl, *Paul among Jews and Gentiles*, 7–23. London: SCM Press, 1977.

Stevens, Leon G. *One Nation under God: A Factual History of America's Religious Heritage.* New York: Morgan James Faith, 2013.

Storr, Will. *Selfie: How We Became So Self-Obsessed and What It's Doing to Us.* London: Picador, 2017.

Stroumsa, Guy G. *Barbarian Philosophy: The Religious Revolution of Early Christianity.* Tübingen: Mohr Siebeck, 1999.

———. "Le radicalisme religieux du christianisme ancien." In *Retours aux Ecritures*, edited by A. Le Boulluec and E. Patlagean, 347–74. Bibliothèque de l'Ecole Pratique des Hautes Etudes. Leuven: Peeters, 1993. Slightly revised in translation as "Early Christianity as Radical Religion: Context and Implications." *Israel Oriental Studies* 14 (1994): 173–93.

———. "Moses' Riddles: Esoteric Trends in Patristic Hermeneutics." In *Interpretation in Religion*, edited by Sh. Biedermann and B. A. Scharfstein, 336–41. Leiden: Brill, 1992.

————. *Religions abrahamiques: histoires croisées*. Geneva: Labor et Fides, 2017.

————. "Religious Memory, between Orality and Writing." *Memory Studies* 9 (2016): 332–40.

————. *Savoir et salut*. Paris: Le Cerf, 1992.

Swann, William B., Jr., Ángel Gómez, Carmen Huici, J. Francisco Morales, and J. Gregory Hixon. "Identity Fusion and Self-Sacrifice: Arousal as Catalyst of Pro-Group Fighting, Dying, and Helping Behavior." *Journal of Personality and Social Psychology* 99 (2010): 824–41.

Swann, William B., Jr., Ángel Gómez, D. Conor Seyle, J. Francisco Morales, and Carmen Huici. "Identity Fusion: The Interplay of Personal and Social Identities in Extreme Group Behavior." *Journal of Personality and Social Psychology* 96 (2009): 995–1011.

Tannehill, Robert C. "The Story of Israel within the Lukan Narrative." In Moessner, *Jesus and the Heritage of Israel*, 325–39.

Templeton, John. *Possibilities for Over One-Hundred Fold More Spiritual Information*. Philadelphia: Templeton Foundation Press, 2001.

Tetlock, P. "Thinking the Unthinkable: Sacred Values and Taboo Cognitions." *Trends in Cognitive Science* 7 (2003): 320–24.

Thatcher, Margaret. Interview by Douglas Keay. *Women's Own*, September 23, 1987.

Theissen, Gerd. *Sociology of Early Palestinian Christianity*. Translated by John Bowden. Philadelphia: Fortress, 1978.

Tiede, David L. "'Fighting against God': Luke's Interpretation of Jewish Rejection of the Messiah Jesus." In *Anti-Semitism and Early Christianity: Issues of Polemic and Faith*, edited by Craig A. Evans and Donald A. Hagner, 102–12. Minneapolis: Augsburg Fortress, 1993.

Tilling, Chris. *Beyond Old and New Perspectives on Paul: Reflections on the Work of Douglas Campbell*. Eugene, Oreg.: Cascade, 2014.

Tinbergen, N. "On Aims and Methods of Ethology." *Zeitschrift für Tierpsychologie* 20 (1963): 410–33.

Tocqueville, Alexis de. *Democracy in America*. Abridged and with an introduction by Thomas Bender. New York: Modern Library, 1981.

Toulmin, Stephen. *Cosmopolis: The Hidden Agenda of Modernity*. Chicago: University of Chicago Press, 1990.

Toynbee, Arnold J. *A Study of History*. Oxford: Oxford University Press, 1934.

Tracy, David. *The Analogical Imagination: Christian Theology and the Culture of Pluralism*. New York: Crossroad, 1981.

Turchin, Peter. *Ultrasociety: How 10,000 Years of War Made Humans the Greatest Cooperators on Earth*. Storrs, Conn.: Baresta Books, 2015.

————. *War and Peace and War: The Rise and Fall of Empires*. Upper Saddle River, N.J.: Pi Press, 2005.

UNESCO. *UNESCO World Report: Investing in Cultural Diversity and Intercultural Dialogue.* Paris: UNESCO, 2009. http://unesdoc.unesco.org/images/0018/001852/185202e.pdf.

van der Horst, Pieter W. "The *Birkat ha-minim* in Recent Research." *ExpTim* 105, no. 12 (1994): 363–68.

Veyne, Paul. *Les grecs ont-ils cru en leurs dieux?* Paris: Le Seuil, 1983. Translated as *Did the Greeks Believe in Their Gods?* Chicago: University of Chicago Press, 1988.

Volf, Miroslav. *Allah: A Christian Response.* San Francisco: HarperCollins, 2011.

———. *Exclusion and Embrace: A Theological Exploration of Identity, Otherness, and Reconciliation.* Nashville: Abingdon, 1996.

———. *Flourishing: Why We Need Religion in a Globalized World.* New Haven, Conn.: Yale University Press, 2016.

von Wahlde, Urban C. "'You Are of Your Father the Devil' in Its Context: Stereotyped Apocalyptic Polemic in John 8:38-47." In Bieringer, Pollefyt, and Vandecasteele-Vanneuville, *Anti-Judaism and the Fourth Gospel,* 418–44.

Vorster, Willem S. "Literary Reflections on Mark 13:5-37: A Narrated Speech of Jesus." *Neotestamentica* 21 (1987): 91–112. Reprinted in *The Interpretation of Mark,* edited by William Telford, 269–88. London: SPCK, 1985.

Walzer, Michael. *The Paradox of Liberation: Secular Revolutions and Religious Counterrevolutions.* New Haven, Conn.: Yale University Press, 2016.

Watson, Francis. *Paul, Judaism and the Gentiles: A Sociological Approach.* SNTSMS 56. Cambridge: Cambridge University Press, 1986.

———. *Paul, Judaism, and the Gentiles: Beyond the New Perspective.* 2nd ed. Grand Rapids: Eerdmans, 2007.

Weber, Max. *The Protestant Ethic and the Spirit of Capitalism.* New York: Charles Scribner's Sons, 1958.

Welker, Michael. "God's Power and Powerlessness: Biblical Theology and the Search for a World Ethos in a Time of Short-Lived Moral Markets." In *Power, Powerlessness, and the Divine,* edited by Cynthia L. Rigby, 39–55. Atlanta: Scholars, 1997.

———. *God the Spirit.* Translated by John Hoffmeyer. Philadelphia: Fortress, 1994. Reprint: Eugene, Oreg.: Wipf & Stock, 2013.

———. "Gottes Gerechtigkeit." *Neue Zeitschrift für Systematische Theologie und Religionsphilosophie* 56, no. 4 (2014): 409–21.

———. "The Power of Mercy in Biblical Law." *Journal of Law and Religion* 29, no. 2 (2014): 225–35.

———, ed. *Quests for Freedom: Biblical—Historical—Contemporary.* Neukirchen-Vluyn: Neukirchener Verlag, 2015.

———. "Romantic Love, Covenantal Love, Kenotic Love." In *The Work of Love: Creation as Kenosis*, edited by John Polkinghorne, 127–36. Grand Rapids: Eerdmans, 2001.

———. "Security of Expectations: Reformulating the Theology of Law and Gospel." *Journal of Religion* 66 (1986): 237–60.

Westerholm, Stephen. *Perspectives Old and New on Paul*. Grand Rapids: Eerdmans, 2004.

Whitehead, Alfred North. *Process and Reality: An Essay in Cosmology*. 1929. Corrected ed. Edited by David Ray Griffin and Donald W. Sherburne. New York: Free Press, 1978.

Whitehouse, Harvey, Brian McQuinn, Michael Buhrmester, and William B. Swann Jr. "Brothers in Arms: Libyan Revolutionaries Bond like Family." *Proceedings of the National Academy of Sciences, USA* 111 (2014): 17783–85.

Wilken, Robert L. *John Chrysostom and the Jews: Rhetoric and Reality in the Late Fourth Century*. Berkeley: University of California Press, 1983.

Williams, George C. *Adaptation and Natural Selection: A Critique of Some Current Evolutionary Thought*. Princeton, N.J.: Princeton University Press, 1966.

Williams, Raymond. *Keywords*. London: Flamingo, 1981.

Wilson, Brian. *Religion in Secular Society*. London: Watts, 1966.

Wilson, David Sloan. "Altruism in Mendellian Populations Derived from Kin Groups: The Haystack Model Revisited." *Evolution* 41 (1987): 1059–70.

———. *Darwin's Cathedral: Evolution, Religion, and the Nature of Society*. Chicago: University of Chicago Press, 2002.

———. *Does Altruism Exist? Culture, Genes, and the Welfare of Others*. New Haven, Conn.: Yale University Press, 2015.

———. "Multilevel Selection and Major Transitions." In *Evolution: The Extended Synthesis*, edited by Massimo Pigliucci and Gerd B. Müller, 81–94. Cambridge, Mass.: MIT Press, 2009.

———. "Reaching a New Plateau for the Acceptance of Multilevel Selection." *Evolution Institute*, September 22, 2017. evolution-institute .org/focus-article/reaching-a-new-plateau-for-the-acceptance-of-multi level-selection/?source=tvol.

Wilson, David Sloan, Yasha Hartberg, Ian MacDonald, Jonathan A. Lanman, and Harvey Whitehouse. "The Nature of Religious Diversity: A Cultural Ecosystem Approach." *Religion, Brain & Behavior* 7, no. 2 (2017): 134–53. doi:10.1080/2153599X.2015.1132243.

Wilson, David Sloan, and Kurt Johnson. "Steering toward the Omega Point: A Roundtable Discussion of Altruism, Evolution, and Spirituality." *This View of Life*, December 10, 2015. evolution-institute.org/article/steering -toward-the-omega-point-a-roundtable-discussion-of-altruism-evolution -and-spirituality/.

Wilson, David Sloan, and Edward O. Wilson. "Rethinking the Theoretical Foundation of Sociobiology." *Quarterly Review of Biology* 82, no. 4 (2007): 327–48.

Witherington, Ben, III. *The Gospel of Mark: A Socio-Rhetorical Commentary.* Grand Rapids: Eerdmans, 2001.

———. *The Paul Quest: The Renewed Search for the Jew of Tarsus.* Downers Grove, Ill.: InterVarsity, 1998.

Wolter, Michael. "Israel's Future and the Delay of the Parousia, according to Luke." In Moessner, *Jesus and the Heritage of Israel*, 307–24.

Wolterstorff, Nicholas. *The Mighty and the Almighty. An Essay in Political Theology.* Cambridge: Cambridge University Press, 2012.

World Economic Forum. *Global Gender Gap Report 2016.* Cologny: World Economic Forum, 2016. http://reports.weforum.org/global-gender-gap-report-2016/.

World Values Survey Association. *World Values Survey.* 2005–2014. http://www.worldvaluessurvey.org/WVSDocumentationWVL.jsp.

Wright, N. T. *Paul: Fresh Perspectives.* London: SPCK, 2005.

Wright, Robert. *The Moral Animal: Evolutionary Psychology and Everyday Life.* New York: Vintage, 1995.

Yarbro Collins, Adela. *The Beginning of the Gospel: Probings of Mark in Context.* Minneapolis: Augsburg Fortress, 1992.

Yee, G. A. *Jewish Feasts and the Gospel of John.* Wilmington, Del.: Glazier, 1989.

Yinger, Kent L. *The New Perspective on Paul: An Introduction.* Eugene, Oreg.: Cascade, 2010.

Zeitlin, Solomon. Prolegomenon to *The Jewish Sources of the Sermon on the Mount*, by Gerald Friedlander, xi–xxxv. New York: Ktav, 1969.

References in **bold** indicate a major treatment of the topic.

Abraham, 12, 34, 39, 42–44, 45, 50, 54, 120, 143–44, 189–90, 210
Abrahamic faiths, 5, 14, 20, 31, 32, **34**, 78, 98, 101, 206–7, **208–11**, 215, 217, 220
Acts of the Apostles, 6, 43, **47–48**, 53, 88
Afghanistan, 24, 33, 82, 84
Africa, 7, 8, 40, **77–81**, 83, **85–91**, 105, 113, 115
altruism, 4, 11, **28–29**, 32, 33, 35, 117, 160–61, **168–70**, 174, 208
al-Qaeda, 24, 90, 104, 109, 114, 115, 123, 126, 127
America: *see* United States of America

amygdala, 24, 149, 151, 152, 154, 155, 157
anti-Semitism, 4, 6, 7, 41, 42, 43, 44, **50–58**, 61, 66, 67, 94, 96, 100, 101–2
Arab Spring, 7, 24, 80, 89, 211
Assmann, Jan, 61, 187

Bible, x, 22, **39–58**, 61–62, 88, 179–80, 192, 208, 221; *see also* Hebrew Bible/Old Testament; New Testament; scripture(s)
Bosnia, 11, 24, 97, 102, 163

common ground, 14, 90, 94, 207, 211–13
Central African Republic (CAR), 8, **86–88**, 90
Christianity/Christians, 3, 6, 7, 8, 13, 14, 23, 27, 30–31, 32, 34, 41–42, 43, 44, 45, 46, 48,

51–52, 60, 61, **62–67**, 68, 69, 70–72, 78, 79, 80, **81–86**, 87, 88, 89, 97, 120, 142–44, 145, 153, 156, 168, 179, 186, 187, 188, 192, 195, 197, **207–11**

church, 6, 7, 11–12, 20, 22, 23, 40, 42, 46, 49, 50, 51, 52, 53, 57, 58, 59, 60, 65, 68, 77, 79, 94, 141, 142–44, 179–80

Clash of Civilizations, 9, 98, 127

climate change, 4, 77, 79, 80, **88–91**, 219

compassion, 10, 13, 95, 102, 127, 147, 148, **149**, 151–52, 153–55, 156, 157, 158, 159, 160–61, 162, 165, 196, 199

compassionate reason, 10–11, 147, 153, 154, 155, 157–58

conscience, 44, 59, 134, 144

conflict resolution, 10, 102, 160, 163, 220

consequentialism, 10, **150–52**

cultural evolution, 5, 11, 28, 149, 152, 158, 170, 173, 178, 180–81, 214

cultural genome, 11–12, **178–80**

Daesh: *see* Islamic State

Darwin, Charles, 11, 28, 108, 112, 123, 168–69, 171, 178, 181

democracy, 21, 22–23, 24, 25, 80, 84, 106–7, 109, 112, 115, 116, 118, 122, 135, 152, 159

deontology, 10, 115, 150–52, 153–54

dialogue, 8, 14, 90, 93, 94–95, 96, **97–99**, 206, 208–9, 210–11, 212–13, 214, **215–17**

dignity of difference, 96, 102

dualism, 5, **31–33**, 34, 35, 64, 198

education, 2, 4–5, 8, 9, 12, 13–14, 15, 20, 78, 84, 89, 91, 96, **97–98**, 101, 102, 123, 147, 152, 153, 155–56, 157, 160, 163, 199, 200, 202, 203–4, **205–17**, **221–22**

empathy, 4, 8, 9, 10, 11, **93–102**, 137, 148, 150, 160–61, 162, 164, 165, 217

"end of history" thesis, 5, 21, **24**

Enlightenment, the, 5, 10, 25, 26–27, 28, 30, 61, 149–50, 152–53, 158, 159

Esau, 2, 32, 39, 41, 42, 44, 58

eschatology, 47, 62, 72

ethnicity, 57, 67, 68, 70, 73, 78, 79, 89, 98, 188–89, 192

exclusive nationalism, 12, 185, **186–88**, 193

exclusivism, 12–13, 63, 65, 70, 72, 185, 186–87, 191, 193

freedom, 5, 13–14, 22, 24, 29, 34, 69, 84, 103, 105, 109, 129, 155–56, 188, 189, 192, **195–96**, 198, 202, 203, 204

freedom of religion, 5, 9–10, 12–13, 60, **133–46**, 189, 192, 213

Freud, Sigmund, 26, 27, 69–70, 71, 78

Galatians (Letter to the), 42, **43–44**, 46, 144

Genesis (Book of), 2, **32–33**, 35, 39, 41, 42, 50, 56, 57, 58, 189

genocide, 102, 163; victims of, 94

Global South, 4, 7, 78, **79–80**, 81, 85, **88–90**

Golden Rule, 10, **154–55**, 188

group conflict, 113, 173, 175

hate/hatred, 5, 8, 13, 14, 32, 33, 61, 65, 66, 67, 69, 94, 98, **101–2**, 149, 152, 154, 155, 158, 159, 162, 186, 191, **200–202**, 203, 204, 221–22

healing conflict, 102, **156–57**, 161, 162

Hebrew Bible/Old Testament, 61–62, 71, 144, 198, 202, 208, 210, 221; *see also* Bible; scripture(s); Torah

Heidelberg Catechism, 13, 201

heretics, 52, 65, 66

Holocaust, the, 6, 27, 41, 53, 57, 94, 161, 163, 202, 222

honesty, 14, 144, 168, 206, 211, 213, 217, 219–20

hope, 9, 11, 14, 15, 108, 126, 148, 157, 196, 206, **213–15**, 217, **220–22**

hospitality, 14, 206, **208–10**, 211, 215, 217

human goods, 9–10, **137–39**, 140, 141, 145

human rights, 9, 10, 94, 97, 98–99, 109, **133–35**, 136, **137–40**, 142, 146, 150–51, 206, 207, 211, 212, 216–17

humility, 14, 157, 206, **213–14**, 215, 217

identity, 3, 5, 6, 7, 8, 9, 12, 19, 20, 21, **26–27**, **28–29**, 30, 31, 33, 34–35, 42, 43, 45–46, 49, 52, 56, 57, 60, 63–64, 65, 66,

67–69, 73, 78, **79–80**, 81, 84, 86, 90, 100, 107, 108, 112, 127, 156, 185, 191, 198, 199, 213; identity fusion, 113, **115–16**, 118

individuals/individualism, 5, 9–10, 11, 21, 22–23, 26, 27, 28, 30, 67–68, 73, 109, 111, 112, 114, 115, 123, 129, 134, 135, 153, 167, 168, 169, 170, 174, 190, 199, 200, 202, 203

immigration/immigrants, 23, 93, 95, 100, 106, 107; *see also* refugees

inclusive nationalism, 12, 13, 185, 186, 193

injustice, 31, 138, 145, 191

interiorization, 68, 69

interspirituality, 12, 181

intolerance, 7, 60, 61, 62–63, 65–66, 68, **69–71**, 72, 102

Iran, 24, 25, 31, 77, 112

Isaac, 2, 32, 39, 41, 42, 43, 58, 189, 190, 210

Ishmael, 2, 32, 39, 41, 42, 43, 58

ISIS: *see* Islamic State

Islam/Muslims, 3, 7, 8, 14, 23, 24, 25, 31, 32, 34, 60, 79, 80, 81, 82, 83, 84, 85, 86, 87, 88, 89, 91, 94, 96, 97, 98, 99, 100–101, 102, 104, 106, 117, 119, 120, 142, 143–44, 154, 164, 181, 187, 188, 206, 207, 208–9, 211, 212, 216, 220

Islamic State, 5, 8–9, 90, 104, 109, 110, 112, **113–18**, **120–22**, 123–24, 125, 126, 127

Islamophobia, 4, 8, 94, 96, 100, 101, 102

Israel (biblical), 7, 32, 45–46, 47, 50–51, 52, 53, 60, 61, 62, 63, 64, 66, 198, 202, 222

Israel (modern state of), 23, 30, 112

Jacob, 2, 32, 39, 41, 42, 44, 58

Jesus, 12, 34, 40, 41–42, 44, 45, 47, 48–49, 50, 51, 52–54, 56, 57, 64, 67, 68, 69, 71, 81, 142, 143, 189, 190

John (Gospel of), 6, **53–56**, 57, 66, 180

Judaism/Jews (ancient and modern), 3, 6, 7, 13, 14, 23, 30, 31, 32, 34, 40, 41, 42, 43, 44, 45, **46–48**, 49–50, 51, 52, 53, **54–56**, 57, 58, 60, **61–65**, 66–67, 68, 72, 79, 80, 94, 96, 97, 99, 120, 142, 144, 145, 153, 154, 161, 162, 164–65, 174, 187, 188, 189, 195, 197, 207, 208, 209, 210, 211, 220, 221

justice, 3, 13, 14, 102, 134, 135, 144, 146, 159, 191, **195–97**, 198, **199–200**, 201, 204, 207, 214, 220

Kant, Immanuel, 10, 12, 25, 27, 147–48, 150, 152, 153, 155, 161, 191

King, Martin Luther, Jr., 135, 137–38, 139, 220, 222

King's College London, **2–3**, 15, 40, 222; International Centre for the Study of Radicalisation (ICSR), 124

labeling, 89, 94, 99, 101, 108–9, 117, 170, 171

law codes in antiquity, 80, 196

Locke, John, 22, 155

love, 6, 7, 13, 14, 33, 41, 44, 46, 52, 56, 57, 58, 60, 65, **69–71**, 102, 127, 143, 148, 151, 154, 180, 186, 189, 193, 195, 197, 198, 199, **200–201**, 202, 203, 204, 209, 211

Luke (Gospel of), 6, 50, **52–53**

major evolutionary transitions, 11, **171–74**

Mark (Gospel of), **48–50**, 189

Matthew (Gospel of), 6, **50–52**, 53, 55, 57

memory, 11, 64, 66, 73, 91, 95, 162, 164, 172, 199, 221

mercy, 5, 13–14, 45, 46, 144, 195–96, **197–200**, 201, 204

metanarrative, 20–21, 25, 220; *see also* narrative

monotheism, 5, 7, 12–13, 20, 31, 32, 35, 61, 62, 70, 119–20, 139, 185, **187–93**, 202, 220; political monotheism, 191

moral sense theory, 10, 32, 147, **150–54**

Moses, 34, 43, 45, 47, 50, 51, 54, 144, 222

Muhammad, 81, 82, 84, 91, 188, 189

multilevel selection (MLS), 11–12, 169, 170–71, **172–74**, 181–82

narrative, x, 5, **19–35**, 40, 41, 42, 43, 53, 56, 59, 95, 111, 181, 200, 204, 213, 216

nation-state, 5, 22, 27, 103, 104, 105, 106, 155, 190

nationalism, 5, 8, 12, 13, 77, 107, 151, 185, 186, 187, 193, 219

Nazis/Nazism, 55, 57, 94, 105, 151, 164

neuroscience, 5, **147–49**, 162

New Testament, **39–58**, 69, 71, 72, 197, 208, 210

Nigeria, xx, 7, 8, 78, 79, 82, 83, 84, 85, 86, 89

Palestine/Palestinians, xix, 62, 64, 112

Paul, 6, 39, **41–46**, 47, 48, 53, 57, 67, 70, 71, 187, 200

Philippians (Letter to the), 6, 44, 45

political religion, 12, 13, 185, 188, 190, 192, 193

Popper, Karl, 60

prosperity religion, 12, 190, 191

Qur'an, x, 80, 81, 85, 134, 208, 209, 210; *see also* scripture(s)

race, 5, 12, 27, 30, 78, 89, 148, 186; *see also* ethnicity

radical religion, 61–67

refugees, xix, 8, 81, 93–96, 97, 100, 156; *see also* immigration/ immigrants

religious freedom/liberty, xviii, 5, 9, 10, 60, **133–46**, 213

revolution, xxv, 22, 46, 69, 105, 109, 112, 198

Romans (Letter to the), 6, 42, 44, 46

Russia, xvii, 24, 25, 27, 103, 104, 105, 107, 186

sacred values, 8, 108, **112–20**

scripture(s), 32–33 **39–58**, 64, 71, 78, 90, 139, 142, 197, 208–11, 213; *see also* Bible; Hebrew Bible/Old Testament; New Testament; Qur'an

secularization, ix, xv, 5, 21, 22, 23, 30, 35

Serbia, xxiii, 186

sharia, 80, 115, 116

sibling/sibling rivalry, 2, 3, 5, 6, 7, 28, **32–35**, 39, 40, 42, 48, 50, 52, 56, 78

society, xxi, xxii, 10, 11, 13, 14, 20, 21, 22, 23, 26, 28, 29, 30, 64, 66, 73, 98, 99, 100, 101, 102, 104, 107, 110, 129, 150, 152, 153, 155, 158, 162, 163, 165, 167, 173, 174, 191, 198, 200

spiritual strength, 112, 114, 122

supersessionism, 4, 6, 39, 41, 42, 49, **50–58**

superorganism, 5, 11, 12, 167, 172, 175, 177, 181

Syria, xix, 5, 33, 77, 80, 94, 125, 126, 127, 156

tenth parallel, xx, 4, 8, 81, 83, 84

Tikkun Olam, 102

Torah, x, 41, 47, 49, 55, 57, 64, 202, 210; *see also* Hebrew Bible/Old Testament

transnational terrorism, xvi, 8, 111, 112, 122, 126

United Kingdom, 78, 96, 97, 99

United States of America, 8, 9, 22, 23, 24, 25, 29, 33, 35, 57, 84,

89, 93, 94, 98, 104, 120–21, 145, 178, 179, 186, 205, 216
universalism, 65, 70, 71, 98, 187
Utopia, 64, 69, 71, 72, 221

Vatican II (Second Vatican Council), 10, 141, 142
violence, x, xiv, xvi, 2, 4, 5, 7, 8, 10, 11, 12, 13, 14, 15, 19, 21, 26, 27, 30, 31, 32, 33, 39, 41, 47, 58, 60, 61, 66, 67, 71, 72, 73, 78, 79, **81–91**, 99, 100, 103, 104, 109, 111, 112, 114, 121, 123, 148, 149, 150, 151, 152, **156–59**, 162, 168, 174, 177, 178, 180, 181, 182, 185, 187, 191, 192, 200, 201, 202, 203, 204, 205, 206, 208, 213, 215, 216, 217, 219, 220, 221

Westernization, 5, 21, 25